The Caliphate at War

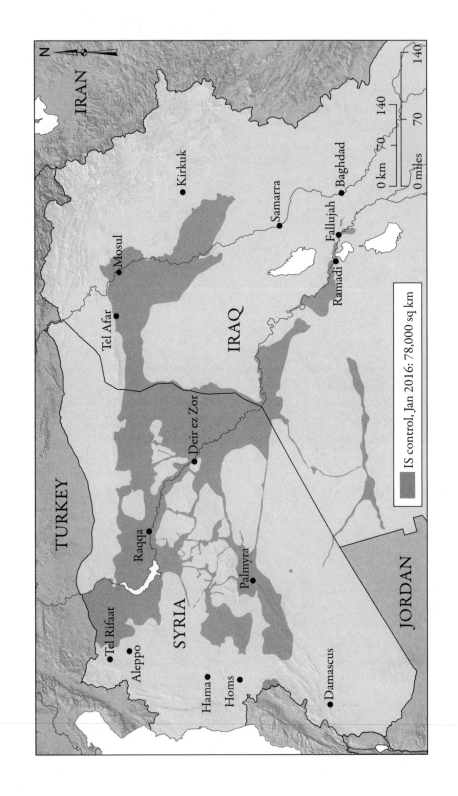

IS control, Jan 2016: 78,000 sq km

The Caliphate at War

Operational Realities and
Innovations of the Islamic State

AHMED S. HASHIM

OXFORD
UNIVERSITY PRESS

OXFORD
UNIVERSITY PRESS

Oxford University Press is a department of the University of Oxford.
It furthers the University's objective of excellence in research, scholarship,
and education by publishing worldwide. Oxford is a registered trade mark of
Oxford University Press in the UK and certain other countries.

Published in the United States of America by Oxford University Press
198 Madison Avenue, New York, NY 10016, United States of America.

CIP data is on file at the Library of Congress

ISBN 978-0-19-066848-8

1 3 5 7 9 8 6 4 2

Printed by Sheridan Books, Inc., United States of America

To my beloved sister Munah Hashim
1966–2017

Contents

Acknowledgments

Acknowledgments cannot be overlooked in a work of this nature, particularly in light of the fact that I undertook it at lightning speed and under tremendous pressure due to other commitments. My publisher and friend at Hurst and Company, Michael Dwyer, deserves many thanks for the encouragement he gave me to undertake this work and for putting up with my perennial efforts to make it "better." Kathleen Weaver of Oxford University Press substantially improved the manuscript in its early drafts and taught me how to be a better and more accurate writer. I also wish to extend my profound gratitude to Alexandra Dauler, Martha Ramsey, and Gwen Colvin at Oxford for working closely with me to bring the project to fruition.

I would like to thank Harshita Kohli for wading through pages of this enterprise as it unfolded over the course of one and a half years. It could not have been done without her "brutal" editorial skills. A number of my students wrote master's dissertations that proved helpful or aided in the collection of data: Jesse Caemmerer, Mathilde Lang, and Henrik Paulsson. Jesse Caemmerer was particularly helpful in reading through the manuscript and making sense of it. At the Rajaratnam School of International Studies at Nanyang Technological University, which has been my home for the past six years, I would like to thank the following individuals in senior management: Ambassador Ong Ken Yong, Joseph Liow, Ralf Emmers, Tan See Seng, Barry Desker, and Eddie Lim, for encouraging me to do my own research despite a heavy institutional workload. I would like to thank my family members at home for their kind understanding and patience as I got absorbed in the research and writing of this book.

Finally, many thanks go out to the reviewers who took the time to provide extensive critical comments and suggestions: Ali Allawi, David Kilcullen, and Michael Ryan. Without the help of all the people I have acknowledged above, this manuscript would not have been transformed into a readable book. Any errors are mine alone.

The Caliphate at War

I

Understanding the "Islamic State"

Hadha wa'd Allah: This Is the Promise of Allah!

On June 29, 2014, or the first day of Ramadan (1435), Abu Mohammad al-Adnani, a senior Syrian member and official spokesman of the notorious organization the Islamic State of Iraq and Syria (ISIS), triumphantly proclaimed the return of the caliphate in an audio address, "Hadha wa'd Allah." The Islamic State of Iraq and Syria, said al-Adnani, was no more. "Iraq" and "Syria" would be dropped from the title, and the entity was to be known as the Islamic State (IS), or the Caliphate. The leader of all Muslims was now the "Caliph Ibrahim." This new "caliph" was Abu Bakr al-Baghdadi, the emir (commander) of the now defunct ISIS, which had risen like a phoenix from the ashes after near defeat in Iraq in 2009. Born Ibrahim Awaad Ibrahim Ali Mohammad al-Badri al-Samarrai in the city of Samarra, north of Baghdad, in July 1971, he had had a tumultuous life before his ascension to his exalted status of "caliph." Going forward, all other jihadist groups had no reason to exist anymore, said al-Adnani, and all Muslims were called upon to pledge allegiance (bayaa) to the Caliph Ibrahim. Adnani had reason to crow. The Islamic State had managed to win a string of remarkable victories and capture considerable territory in the preceding months against a variety of lackluster enemies.

The world had not yet absorbed this momentous declaration when barely a week later, on the morning of July 4, 2014, a seemingly mild-mannered, bearded, and innocuous middle-aged Iraqi man mounted the pulpit of the famous Nur Zengi Great Mosque in the Iraqi city of Mosul. The elusive Caliph Ibrahim was going to give the Friday khutba (sermon), in which he "reluctantly" accepted the "heavy burden" of taking on the role of caliph. One could almost hear him sighing as he uttered the next few sentences, which were an almost verbatim repetition of the words of the first caliph, Abu Bakr al-Siddiq, who succeeded the Prophet Mohammad as ruler of the Islamic state after the latter's death on June 8, 632 AD: "I have been appointed to rule over you, though I am not the best among you.... If you see that I do right, help me, and if you see that I do wrong, set me right. And obey me so long as I obey God touching you. If I disobey Him, no obedience is owed me from you."[1] Caliph Ibrahim called upon Muslims to undertake hijra (emigration) to the Caliphate. For sympathizers, supporters, adherents, and those flocking to the ranks of ISIS (now IS), the proclamation of the Caliphate needed no explanation. They believed that it was God's will that an Islamic system of governance return after an absence of eight decades, when the caliphate had been extinguished by the emerging secular Turkish state in 1924.[2] Opponents within the wider Islamist constellation—not only mainstream, but even radical—reacted with derision, dismay, and contempt. They railed that conditions were not propitious, IS had not yet fully conquered the territory it claimed, and it had yet to establish effective rule over Muslims. Moreover, was this organization, which had left a trail of blood and destruction in its wake in Syria and Iraq, the right one to proclaim the return of the caliphate? The event captured the attention of the wider world. It had to: the Islamic world was in turmoil, and the larger world was not insulated from what was transpiring in Iraq and Syria, where IS was ensconced. Peoples and governments were fascinated, worried, repelled, and bewildered. They wanted explanations.

What Is the Islamic State?

The purpose of this book is to explain IS from its origins to mid-2017. There are an ever-increasing number of books on IS. So why write yet another one? The partial answer is that not all of the books in this saturated market are the same. There is no space here for a "literature review" of the myriad books in order to assess their strengths and weaknesses in depth. There have been some excellent book reviews to date of the good, the bad, and the hastily written.[3] It suffices to say that each book has its own approach, its strengths and weaknesses. A number do add significantly to our knowledge of this entity; others simply do not. I have found *ISIS: Inside the Army of Terror* by Michael Weiss and Hassan Hassan and *ISIS: The State of Terror* by Jessica Stern and J. M. Berger particularly useful as sources.[4] Two of the best books, Joby Warrick's *Black Flags: The Rise of ISIS* and Will McCants's *The ISIS Apocalypse: The History, Strategy, and Doomsday Vision of the Islamic State,* have been favorably reviewed. Ben

Fishman, the reviewer, succinctly points out that Warrick delivers his narrative by addressing the roles of the central characters, most notably Abu Musab al-Zarqawi, the original founder of IS. McCants on the other hand relies on textual analysis of the primary and secondary sources to understand the history of the group.[5] Brian Fishman has written an outstanding book, on which I relied heavily for the chapter on the organization and structure of IS and its predecessors: *The Master Plan: IS, Al-Qaeda, and the Jihadi Strategy for Victory*. It is one of the best analyses of the evolution of IS and its predecessors as organizations.

The approach of this book is to look at the roles key personalities play in the fortunes of IS, to examine in detail the primary texts and speeches in order to understand the ideological evolution of this entity from its inception at the beginning of the twenty-first century to mid-2017, and to assess the structural factors in Syria and Iraq, as well as the regional and international politics, that contributed to its emergence. I have decided to give a general account, including a historical overview that helps to understand the context, rather than focus on one particular aspect of IS. While this might mean losing granularity on certain aspects (e.g., the enormous role of foreign fighters or IS's use of the media, both of which have already been explored in depth), what I hope to accomplish here is a *tour d'horizon* of IS from its origins in 2003 to the time of this writing, the end of July 2017.

For this book, the "story" of IS "ends" in mid-2017, though on the ground the monumental fight between it and its foes will continue for an unspecified period of time. The probable demise of the Caliphate in 2017 will not be the end of the IS story; the entity will seek to regenerate itself and carry on the fight in some form or other. To be sure, IS will continue to be a nettlesome problem well into 2017 and beyond, but the book assesses IS's strengths and weaknesses in each area—ideology, organization, state building, and nation formation—and concludes that the prospects for IS's ability to "remain" and "expand" were tenuous at best. The ferocious battles of October 2016–July 2017, waged by an unwieldy anti-IS coalition to recapture Mosul and the surrounding areas, served to highlight profound structural limitations of the IS enterprise. It had become all too clear that IS had bitten off more than it could chew: it made too many enemies because of its ideological rigidities; it had insufficient resources and manpower for the tasks of organizing effectively, fighting, and building a state; and it alienated those it ruled. To be sure, the fighting to dislodge IS from northern Iraq and Syria proved to be a hard slog as

2016 drew to a close. The defining battle for Mosul began in October 2016 and was still ongoing when this manuscript went to press in late July 2017. (For a description of the battle for Mosul see chapter 5.) Throughout this defensive urban battle, the Islamic State proved to be resilient and capable of devastating surprise assaults against the various enemies that were besieging it on all sides.

This book will look at IS "holistically," examining all of its pertinent institutions, structures, belief systems, and actions as part of a system, a system that its opponents need to understand fully in order to dismantle it. *The primary goal of this book is to explain and understand IS. More specifically, this book is about the ideology, organization, war-fighting, and state-building enterprises of IS.* What is IS? From where did it emerge? What does it want? And how does it function? How does it fight and what was the secret to its initial military successes—and why did it continue to show resilience in the face of increasing adversity in 2016? How did it go about building its so-called state and Islamic nation and why does it behave in such a brutal and genocidal manner? Despite the severe pressures under which it came in late 2016 and 2017, is there a chance that it could survive and thrive? These are deeper issues that go beyond a mere focus on the current affairs aspect of the problem. In order to implement its goal of a religiously based state, IS had to organize and then establish a system of management. It also had to set up a military capability in order to fight, or "wage war," because it faced opposition to its mission. Finally, because its goal was to set up a state, it had to govern, administer its territories, and control people. How has it fared in this multilevel enterprise?

The secondary goal of this book is to address the historical, the contingent, the structural, and the personality-driven factors that promoted the emergence of IS. While the primary goal of this study is to understand what IS is, it is also important to understand how it came about. I argue that the history and political evolution of Iraq have played an important factor in creating conditions that promoted the emergence of IS. The importance of structural factors should not allow one to ignore the role of personalities who, through their actions, visions, and policies, are not free of fault.

Conceptual Framework and Plan of the Book

This book will address the origins and emergence of IS in Iraq between 2003 and mid-2017. The remainder of this chapter lays out the sections of the book conceptually. Chapter 2 gives a brief analysis of the trajectory of Iraqi history. The bulk of the book, chapters 3–6, applies the theories discussed in chapter 2 to the realities on the ground. These chapters are focused on analyzing and unraveling the origins of IS, its ideology and worldview, its organization and structure, its way of warfare, and finally its efforts to set up a state. The intent here is not to develop a new theory or theories; rather it is to use a mixture of existing theories from strategic studies, comparative politics, and organization theory to understand the IS phenomenon, specifically what are its ideology and goals, how it arose and organized itself, how it fights, and how it seeks to build an *Islamic* state and nation.

The Islamic State has goals, or *ends*, that it wishes to implement in the real world as per its ideology.[6] To achieve its wide-ranging ambitions, IS needs organization, and "organization happens when people work together to accomplish some desired end state or goal."[7] An organization is both a structure and a process; both require coordinated effort by a number of people.[8] Violent nonstate actors, such as IS, have to proceed along three distinct but related organizational processes to achieve their goals: building an organization, developing a way of war to fight the enemy, and building an administration and bureaucracy to control people and build a state.

Though IS is not unique as an example of a violent nonstate actor, I argue that IS has innovated in the fields of ideology, organization, warfighting, and strategies of state-formation. "Innovation" means adopting new ideas, methods, and technologies that the particular entity did not have before. It does not mean that these innovations did not exist before or had not been undertaken by others. I am addressing innovation in a variety of areas and not just military. In terms of ideology, IS created a caliphate, while its competitor al-Qaeda waffled and tiptoed around the idea. In terms of organization, IS created a centralized entity at the top and allowed a more decentralized structure to exist in the provinces. In terms of warfighting, IS created a more robust and resilient entity able to conduct terrorism, guerrilla warfare, and semimobile warfare. However, innovation should not be equated with ultimate success. Innovations can fail because they are not capable of being sustained by the particular organization or because the "other side" finds a way to defeat these innovations.

The Role of History

Chapter 2 is a historical and political introduction that acts as a foundational framework for understanding contemporary events in Iraq. How

Iraq evolved from the past to the present is very relevant to the discussion of IS. While I address distant history briefly in chapter 2, the focus, naturally, is on the recent past: the Baathist regime, the American interlude (2003–2011), and the post-American interlude from 2011 to late 2016. Iraq's recent history did not *cause* the rise of IS; rather, it has provided the fertile ground within which IS emerged and thrived.

Ideology and Goals

In the academic literature, there has been considerable debate concerning the relevance of ideology for an insurgent or rebel group. An ideology is a set of beliefs or ideas that are elaborate, coherent, and integrated and that its adherents put forward to justify the raison d'être of their group, organization, or community. More specifically, ideologies are useful for those who articulate them to explain why they are seeking certain goals (e.g., political power), to justify their exercise of power and the policies or actions they take, to explain and judge historical events, to identify friends and enemies, and to define the connections between the political and the nonpolitical spheres of human activities.[9] Some might argue that most rebel groups are motivated by a quest for material rewards, greed, or even merely a sense of adventure, instead of ideology. Undeniably, IS's ranks include their share of sociopaths, adventurers, people who are "bored," and people who have joined so as to obtain weapons for protection and a salary of sorts. Some have joined IS because of its view that the current conflict in Syria heralds the apocalyptic end of days. In Syria and Iraq, some have joined it because they have lost everything and are seeking revenge. However, to focus on the material, revenge, and apocalyptic aspects is to trivialize the role of ideas and ideology, which also help inform the quest for identity consolidation among many who join the entity. Ideology is central to understanding IS. It does not reflect the entirety of Islam, but, contrary to what some observers claim, it certainly emerged out of a particular and idiosyncratic reading of Islamic theology and political philosophy. Even so, not everyone involved with the movement is fully cognizant of the ideology or its relevance. The Islamic State's ideology is totalistic and uncompromising and sees the world in black and white; it is dangerous and revolutionary.

Chapter 3 addresses this ideology and the goals of IS. Though the chapter focuses on the ideology of ISIS and IS (as well as that of its predecessors) from 2003 onward, it needs to be understood that IS was in violent ideological contestation with the United States' vision for Iraq. This contest was what brought the group into Iraq in the first place. The Islamic State was also in contestation with the ideological visions of three distinct feuding communities: the Sunnis who were involved in the political process, as opposed to the fighting (the weakest group); the Shias; and the Kurds. The Islamic State was in contestation with a wide range of Iraqi insurgent groups, including some who were kindred militant Islamist groups, as well as with the organization it had paid homage to and then split from in acrimony in 2013: al-Qaeda. This multilevel ideological contestation within Iraq has contributed enormously to IS's inability to establish ideological hegemony either within Iraq (or Syria) or within the Sunni community that it claims it is protecting.

Building an Organization

A group of ideologically like-minded people will get nowhere unless they work together first in the basic task of setting up an organization. All organizations engage in this process: peaceful ones, economic ones, and ones engaged in "contentious politics," which might involve violence. All organizations need leadership, management, and administration. An organization's identity, existence, and cohesion need to be maintained against the opposition of competitors and enemies. An organization also needs to be maintained so as to avoid an unraveling from within due to corruption, inefficiency, and desertion. Since IS is not merely a clandestine terrorist organization hiding in the shadows but an entity that seeks to fight myriad enemies, to take and consolidate control over territory and people, and to provide services, it needs to build a substantial organization and infrastructure. While these sets of activities are in line with its goals and vision, the formulation and implementation poses a dilemma: the more it moves out of the clandestinity in which it was born and into the open, the greater the opportunity for bureaucratic problems and administrative failures and for divergences between the center and the peripheries, over which control has not been fully consolidated. Just as important is the fact that the bigger a terrorist organization gets as it transitions from being a terrorist organization to a guerrilla entity and then to a state-making entity, the more opportunities arise for its enemy or enemies to target it more effectively.[10]

Chapter 4 addresses how a group of militants came together first under Abu Musab al-Zarqawi, the notorious Jordanian terrorist who can justifiably be seen as the original founder of IS, and how his successors subsequently set up the organization and structure of the entity that ultimately became IS.

Organizing to Fight: The Islamic State Way of Warfare

The Islamic State is a violent nonstate actor whose adherents believe that violence is the only way to achieve their goals. As a weaker entity facing vastly more powerful state actors—even if they can be inept—with greater resources, IS has had to devise new ways to deal with the imbalance of power. The theoretical literature on the topic of how the weak fight the strong, and specifically on insurgency and guerrilla warfare, is too vast to summarize here.[11] The Islamic State has been no different in seeking the best way to face off its enemies. While it was technically weaker than its state and quasi-state opponents—Syria, Iraq, and the Kurds—on the ground in 2014, it proved more adept at fighting during that period and into 2015 because of its military innovations, which have now been checked to some extent by its opponents' better preparations and even innovations. So what did IS do to build a resilient military capability that is still in the fight, even though it is inexorably being eroded?

Chapter 5 is an analysis of IS's way of warfare as it evolved over time and in combat against its opponents. It is not simply a traditional insurgent group, nor is it a purely terrorist entity. It has also sought to create semiconventional forces to fight its enemies and to hold territory in accordance with its imperative of creating an Islamic state. Jack Keane, the American four-star general who advised the U.S. Army commanders on the U.S. Surge to defeat the jihadists in 2009, said of the current IS: "this organization has grown into a military organization that is no longer conducting terrorist activities exclusively but is conducting conventional operations. They are attacking Iraqi military positions with company and battalion-size formations."[12] He was absolutely right, but in his focus on the conventionalization of IS's military capabilities, he downplayed the continued relevance of the use of terror as a key instrument in IS's repertoire. In this context, *IS is an example of a nonstate hybrid warfare organization.*[13] The first key characteristic of such an entity is the creation of capabilities in all three spectrums of warfare. Nonstate actors that combine terrorism, the guerrilla tactics of hit-and-run ambushes and raids, and semiconventional warfare can maximize their strengths and minimize vulnerabilities against a variety of enemies.[14] A second key characteristic of a hybrid warfare entity such as IS is the flexibility to move up and down the spectrum of violence from terrorism to insurgency to conventional warfare, depending on circumstances, environment, terrain, and the nature of the enemy it is facing.

The traditional terrorist and insurgent methods of nonstate actors are familiar; however, the notion of them developing conventional capabilities strikes most people as odd. In the past, many guerrilla movements have sought to move from the spectrum of terrorism—which was regarded as a temporary measure that should be used judiciously, as both Mao Zedong and Ernesto "Che" Guevara advised—to guerrilla warfare and then ultimately to the creation of "mobile" (i.e., conventional) capabilities for the eventual takeover of the state.

In more recent decades, nonstate actors, like Hezbollah and the Liberation Tigers of Tamil Eelam (commonly known as the LTTE or Tamil Tigers), created a set of niche capabilities along the spectrum of violence from terrorism through guerrilla warfare to specialized conventional capabilities. The conventional capabilities of these "hybrid" nonstate actors do not fully emulate those of states, but the nonstate actor conventional forces have strong similarities to "regular" military forces because they wear recognizable uniforms, have a more or less regular table of organization and equipment, and conduct conventional military operations, such as movement to make contact with enemy forces, assault on enemy positions, and defense of fortified positions. The Islamic State has followed this trajectory of building parallel military capabilities. It captured scores of weapons from its enemies. The greatest windfall came in the summer of 2014, when several Iraqi divisions collapsed, leaving a sizeable and impressive set of weapons systems and Russian and American vehicles in the hands of the group. From 2015 onward IS was forced to fall back on its traditional repertoire of guerrilla warfare and terrorism, as Western air raids and the improvement in the ground capabilities of the Iraqi forces and the Kurdish paramilitary, the Peshmerga, took a heavy toll on IS's conventional capabilities.[15] In this context, IS dispersed and reduced the size of its maneuver forces and reverted to the use of small units to conduct lightning raids and terrorist attacks. Moreover, as the bloody nine-month urban battle for Mosul—October 2016 to June 2017—has shown, IS fighters proved formidable in defense in built-up areas. They showed tremendous skill and determination and inflicted severe casualties on the advancing Iraqi forces. This was a far cry from the early days of the insurgency between 2003 and 2011, when most insurgent groups, including the predecessors of IS, showed little aptitude for or skill in urban warfare.

Organizing to Build

The Islamic State's ideology and actions reflect its interest in creating a state. The Islamic State does not exist merely to maintain itself or to fight its opponents. It has taken on the mission of building a state and "creating an Islamic nation." It organized itself to control populations and territory in order to re-create and sustain the caliphate. In the case of an entity like IS, ideology provides the justification for what it does and the framework for its state-formation and nation-building enterprises.

Chapter 6 explores IS's state-formation and -building enterprise in both Syria and Iraq. State-formation should not be confused with nation-building, even if the two often go together. State-formation is the creation of institutions and infrastructure associated with the state. It means administration, or the establishment of formal rules and regulations for exercising control over people, territory, and the use of instruments of coercion.

In recent times international nation- or state-building has come to mean intervention by foreign powers to rebuild fragile or failing states that are trying to recover from profound domestic turmoil.[16] However, in this book "nation-building" is defined as a project—pursued by those seeking power or already holding it—of creating a common "history," culture, and identity among the people whom they control. It is the conscious construction and shaping of a national identity by the power-holders. It is an approach that uses ideology, even war against an enemy, education, and indoctrination to create this national identity.[17] A particularly insidious aspect of the strategies of state-formation and nation-building is a process that can be referred to as cultural or "pathological" "homogenization," defined as a sustained effort to wipe out all vestiges of the historical past that are in conflict with the building party's ideological views, to eradicate or expel groups of people or individuals who are portrayed as the enemy, and to install a system of total control over the people within the entity that the building group governs.[18]

State-formation and nation-building are often very violent enterprises and have been so throughout the world since time immemorial.[19] These processes involve the destruction or takeover of opposing structures and institutions. Furthermore, nation-building entails the killing not only of enemies but also of supporters who have lost favor or position and of opposition that has been qualified as the enemy. There is a vast literature on state-formation and nation-building.[20] While most of the classical models of them focused on the twin processes in Western states, there has been greater application of theories to the Global South in recent years. However, very little analysis has focused on state-formation and nation-building enterprises by nonstate actors. The classical models of the origins of states focus on interaction between rulers and a range of domestic actors. Most models of state origins include only domestic actors, omitting international participation. However, in many cases the involvement of outside actors in neighbors' state-formation processes has been influential in shaping the trajectory of state-formation. Similarly, in the case of *nonstate actors* in the Global South, the classical models must be adjusted. Violent nonstate actors like IS operate in a multiactor environment, in particular one that involves *outside actors*. Intrastate war can attract international interest. Sometimes, this international involvement is in favor of the incumbent and threatened government. Other times it is in favor of the nonstate actor. In the case of IS, the international pressures have been uniformly hostile. Regional and international pressures have thwarted IS's efforts to engage in state-formation and nation-building.

Another structural factor distinguishes state-formation by a *nonstate actor* in the Global South: these efforts often occur in the context of the fragility of the existing state. Governments earn the contempt of their populations (or segments thereof) due to lack of services or discriminatory politics and thus lose credibility. The extent and span of their control then attenuates.[21] A nonstate actor challenges the fragile state and offers an alternative ideology as a basis for legitimacy. State fragility in Iraq and Syria—which has been worsened by imprudent policies imposed by those in power in Baghdad and Damascus, the state's loss of the instruments of coercion or their atrophy, and the actions of myriad competing groups—has opened the way for groups like IS to come up with an alternative. The Islamic State has sought to establish a state and nation in parts of Iraq and Syria. What are the contours, characteristics, strengths, and weaknesses of such a "nation-state?"

Insurgents, particularly those on a state-formation trajectory, need two kinds of resources. First, there are the fungible inputs, such as weapons, fighters, and cash. Attracting recruits is one of the most obvious needs for any organization.[22] Behind the combatants are a host of operations that support the front lines and sustain the organization. Insurgency is a costly activity. Extortion of resources from civilians, particularly from businesses and other commercial enterprises, and the selling of drugs, diamonds, and oil yield a high cash return with minimal investment on the insurgents' part. Second, insurgents need the support of the population, since insurgency is more than a military contest. While armed confrontation is the most visible face of insurgency against the state, insurgents have a complex relationship with the civilians who come under their control. Some insurgents provide civilians with a wide range of services; others rely primarily on coercion and rule through fear and terror.[23] Insurgents seeking to challenge the government and set up a "counter-state" use three tools with which to govern: ideology or "soft power," coercion and surveillance, and the provision of security and social services. If one uses these indicators to measure IS's success, it is clear that by the end of 2016, despite early achievements, IS was facing opposition from within its supposed "flock" and its capacity for effective coercion of people under its thumb had loosened, due to loss of personnel and territory and increasingly straitened finances. It ceased to provide security and effective services long before the Iraqi and Kurdish counteroffensives of 2016. Like states, insurgents face the challenge of sustaining themselves, often while simultaneously conducting a war.[24] They need to generate quasi-voluntary compliance. In quasi-voluntary compliance, the civilians acquiesce, but the authority maintains the ability to sanction noncompliance. For insurgents, compliance furthers legitimacy and facilitates military effectiveness and resource extraction.[25] It was clear by late 2015 that civilian compliance with IS was no longer as voluntary as it had been in the earlier halcyon days of IS's victories. Indeed, given IS's focus on its existential struggle against enemies who were closing in on it in 2017, governance gave ground to fighting. By mid-2017, when this book was completed, governance was the last thing IS was concerned about. The fact that it was not only fighting for survival but had lost most of its territory and population in Iraq meant that it had precious little to govern.

Methodology and Limitations of the Book

I must address the limitations of the study. First, this is not a policy book, as it offers no extensive recommendations. I have not specifically offered a counterterrorist or counterinsurgency "basket of measures," though I hope the book will nevertheless be useful for policy-makers.[26] Second, the crisis I address is ongoing and subject to the emergence of new information on a daily basis, which must be vetted.[27]

Third, Iraq is not easy to study.[28] It was well-nigh impossible to do so under Saddam Hussein, and researchers and academics avoided the country. As for the present, it is too dangerous to go in alone without the sponsorship of a group, or even of the Iraqi state. This in itself creates biases and problems in field research. Sponsorship by the Iraqi state gives you only one side of the story. The Islamic State does not encourage outsiders researching it, and we have a paucity of information on it, even in comparison with that on its competitor, al-Qaeda, as a study from the West Point–based Combating Terrorism Center highlights. Daniel Milton, points out in a piece in this study: "one of the challenges in doing this type of analysis [i.e., addressing IS's activities] is the lack of primary source information on the IS."[29] Similarly, going into IS territory under the sponsorship of IS is not an option for most, and the few who have done so, such as the German journalist Jürgen Todenhöfer, were shown what IS personnel wanted them to see.[30]

Fourth, largely for reasons of space, I do not focus on the Syrian civil war. I only discuss Syria in the context of IS activities in Syria and the clash with then al-Qaeda affiliate Jabhat al-Nusra. The Islamic State is primarily an Iraqi creation, and the Syrian imbroglio has been covered in detail elsewhere, especially by Charles Lister in his enormously detailed book *The Syrian Jihad*. The Iraqi crisis needs its own full story, and this book is meant to be that story.

ISIS, ISIL, IS, Daesh: A Note on Terminology

What to call this organization has been a controversial matter and has been tied to one's ideological and policy stance toward it.[31] There are a number of names for this organization. I begin by referring to the Abu Musab al-Zarqawi Network, which existed between 2000 and 2003. This network consisted of a small group of Levantine—Jordanian, Palestinian, Syrian, and Lebanese—Islamists, a number of whom had known each other "back home" or had come to know each other in Afghanistan. Many of them gravitated toward the Jordanian jihadist Abu Musab al-Zarqawi and moved with him to Iraq. The organization that began its operations in Iraq in 2003 under Abu Musab al-Zarqawi was called Jamiat al-Tawhid wa al-Jihad (the Group of Monotheism and Jihad). When it joined al-Qaeda in 2004, it came to be called Tanzim Qaedat al-Jihad fi Bilad al-Rafidain (Organization of the Jihad Base in the Land of the Two Rivers), simplified in English to al-Qaeda in Iraq (AQI).

When the conflict with the other Iraqi insurgent groups started, AQI gathered like-minded insurgent groups and began to refer to itself as

Majlis Shura al-mujahidin fi al-Iraq (the Mujahidin Shura Council; MSC) in 2006. A short while later, the MSC's leader at the time, Abu Omar al-Baghdadi, established al-dawla al-islamiyya fi al-Iraq (the Islamic State of Iraq; ISI). The most commonly used name, Dawlat al-Islam fi al-Iraq wa Bilad al-Sham (the Islamic State of Iraq and Syria; ISIS), came into use in mid-2013 after its leader, Abu Bakr al-Baghdadi, began interfering in Syria. The U.S. government's preferred name and acronym for ISIS is the Islamic State of Iraq and the Levant (ISIL). Most notably, upon the declaration of a new caliphate in June 2014, the group officially changed its name to the Islamic State (IS), or the Caliphate. These are the names it has continued to call itself through late 2016 and into 2017.

Given the controversial nature of declaring a singular, true representative of Muslims worldwide, the name "Islamic State" has proven problematic for a number of people. The group is also known as "Daesh," the Arabic acronym that is equivalent to the English acronym ISIS: Dawlat al-Islam fi al-Iraq wa Bilad al-Sham. Supporters of the group view the name "Daesh" as derogatory because they know its use by the outside world is intended to question the legitimacy of the entity and because the word itself is strikingly close to the Arabic word for "to crush" or "to trample upon." In this book, I follow the names the organization has adopted in accordance with chronology. I refer to it as the Islamic State (IS) in chapter 2, which deals with context. In subsequent chapters I follow the organization's own nomenclature at each stage of the story.

"The Unlucky Country"

A HISTORICAL AND POLITICAL SURVEY OF IRAQ

Ancient Mesopotamia and the Invention of Terror

One cannot fully understand the entity that calls itself the Islamic State without addressing the historical, political, and cultural milieu of Iraq itself. Iraq, or Mesopotamia as the Greeks called it, has a rich, ancient history.[1] Sedentary civilization probably first emerged there. Situated at the crossroads of invasion routes, Iraq has been the scene of armies marching back and forth over its lands and either lording over it or looting its people.

Iraq, or Mesopotamia, is known as the cradle of civilization, but terror was most likely invented there as well. Terror has come back full circle in contemporary times to devastate the country.[2] Iraq had its moments of glory and fear under the Assyrians, whose army, system of totalitarian rule, and infliction of terror as state policy was the scourge of the Middle East between 2500 and 605 BC. It is ironic that IS, based in a region in northern Iraq that was the center of the Assyrian Empire, has set out to destroy the priceless artifacts of a system of rule and terror with which they could readily sympathize. The political scientist Jonathan Fine points out, in his excellent survey of political and religious terrorism throughout the ages, that among the ancients in the Western world and its immediate environs, it was not the Greeks, Jews, or Romans "who first sought to name the use of violence to instill fear in a political context. It was the Assyrians who first coined expressions for the use of political and military means to instill fear and terror in one's enemies."[3] Assyria was an expansionist power that used its military as an instrument of terror to expel or kill people from lands its rulers coveted and to expand its territories. This was best reflected in the astounding statement by one of its more successful rulers, Sargon II, who said: "Ashur, father of the gods, empowered me to depopulate and repopulate, to make broad the boundary of the land of Assyria."[4] No doubt, IS's leadership could relate to this kind of policy, even as they gleefully destroyed the artifacts of a pre-Islamic civilization that they perceived to be *jahili* (non-Islamic; ignorant). In the end, Assyria, which lived by the sword, died by the sword. Subsequently, while other civilizations developed in Mesopotamia, the territory ultimately came under the Iranian Sassanian Empire, which lasted until the Arab Muslim invaders destroyed it and claimed Mesopotamia and Iran for Islam.

The Sunni–Shia Schism

Iraq was the primary scene of the great schism in Islam between Sunnism and Shiism. The death of the Prophet Mohammad in 632 AD raised the question of who would succeed him to lead the Islamic state.[5] The Muslim state, which he had founded, was thrown into a quandary, since the Prophet had left no male heir who could be designated the head of the umma and no institutionalized method for the transfer of power.[6] The elders of the community convened a meeting to deal with the acute problem they faced.

A quarrel broke out between two groups, the Medinese Ansar (Helpers) on the one hand and the Meccan Muhajirun (Emigrants) on the other. The Ansar, who had welcomed Mohammad and his band of persecuted followers fleeing pagan oppression in Mecca, their home city-state, and had contributed to Mohammad's ultimate success, argued that the successor should be one of them. The Muhajirun argued that since it was they who had been the Prophet's original companions (indeed, many were blood relatives of his from the Hashim clan of the tribe of Qureish in Mecca) leadership should devolve upon one of them. The impasse was broken when Omar Ibn al-Khattab, an influential Meccan (and subsequent ruler), pledged allegiance to the aged Abu Bakr, a respected companion and father-in-law to the deceased Prophet. Other notables quickly followed suit, and Abu Bakr was elected successor or *khalifa* (caliph), supposedly through the consensus (*ijma*) of the community.

Abu Bakr was an innocuous choice from a weak tribe, but his elevation to the caliphate was controversial. Another group of Muslims came to the fore and advanced a different and ultimately revolutionary claim. This small group argued vehemently that the Prophet had, in fact, long before his death, designated his successor: his cousin and son-in-law Ali Ibn

Abu Talib, at a place called Ghadir-ul-Khum, where Mohammad had allegedly said: "He for whom I was master, should henceforth have Ali as his
master."[7] Ali's claim to the succession, argued his supporters, the Shiat Ali
(partisans of Ali, or Shias) was cemented by the fact that he was a member
of the Prophet's household and was above reproach in his behavior. He
had also rendered the Prophet invaluable service as diplomat, soldier,
and confidant.[8]

The claim on behalf of Ali was vigorously opposed by the elders who
had elected Abu Bakr and subsequently by the vast majority of Muslims,
who argued that the Prophet had not designated Ali or anybody else to
succeed him. The principle of electing a successor from among the qualified elders of the community was a long-standing one. Those who adhered
to the majoritarian concept of the succession came to be known as *ahl al
Sunna wa al-jamaa* (People of Custom and Community, or Sunnis). The
fundamental political difference between Sunnis and Shias is that the
Sunnis stand for the right of the Muslim community to choose the successor in political leadership from among members of the Qureish tribe and
the Shias stand for the preemptive right of a member from the Prophet's
family to it. Initially, the rift was merely a political one over who should
succeed the Prophet Mohammad as ruler of the new Islamic polity. Only
much later, in the eleventh century, did the differences between these two
groups take on theological and political tones, as each community developed a distinct set of religious dogmas and theories about the governance
of an Islamic polity.

Ali became caliph in 656 AD, following the murder of the corrupt and
nepotistic third caliph, Osman, by mutinous Egyptian soldiers. In the eyes
of supporters, Ali's tenure as caliph was characterized by an attempt to
establish the rule of justice and piety to an Islamic polity that had strayed
from its original purity. However, because of the revolutionary nature of
his caliphate, Ali trod on the ambitions of many groups, and his rule was
marred by instability and revolts. He was assassinated at a mosque in Kufa
in southern Iraq in 661 by a member of a disgruntled group of Muslims
known as Kharjites, from the verb *kharaja*—to go out of (Islam)—who vio-
lently opposed his tendency to compromise with his enemies.[9]

Ali's son Hasan became caliph but had to contend with the ambitions of
Muawiyya, the powerful governor of Syria, who aspired to leadership of the
Islamic state. With bribes, cajolery, and threats, the weak Hasan, who had
no power base of his own, was forced to cede the caliphate to the Syrian
governor. Hasan elicited a "promise" from Muawiyya that the caliphate

would revert to him in the event of Muawiyya's death. Hasan died in 670 in mysterious circumstances.[10] Muawiyya founded the Ummayyad dynasty, centered in Damascus, but he had become caliph solely based on his military power and adroit political machinations and not because of any religious credentials or political rectitude.

The final act of infamy against the Prophet's family was yet to come. This was the murder of Hussein, Ali's younger son, with members of his family at Karbala on the tenth day (Ashura) of the holy month of Muharram in 680 by the forces of Yazid, Muawiyya's profligate son, who had "inherited" the caliphate upon his father's death, thus establishing the principle of monarchy in Islamic political practice. Shias viewed Yazid as a worse ruler than his father. Over time Shiism grew into a distinct and separate branch of Islam. There are many Shia sects, of which Twelver Shiism is the largest. It holds sway in Iran, Iraq, and Lebanon. Twelver Shiism is based on the belief that twelve male descendants of the Prophet Mohammad, starting with his cousin Ali Ibn Abu Talib and terminating with Mohammad al-Mahdi, who went into occultation (hiding), are imams, or divinely inspired legitimate political and religious leaders from the Prophet's family who were cheated of their right to rule by the Sunnis. In Twelver Shias' belief, Mohammad bin Hasan al-Askari al-Mahdi will return before the Day of Judgment to rid the world of evil and deliver justice.

The Ummayyad dynasty was brought down in 750 by a rebellion led by the Abbasids, descendants of the Prophet, who established their empire in Baghdad. The Abbasid Empire witnessed the flowering of Islamic civilization. However, like many empires before and after it, the Abbasids were not immune from blunders and misrule. Over the course of the centuries the dynasty fought wars that weakened its ranks. The Abbasids succumbed to imperial overextension and were afflicted by dissolute and profligate rulers who became captive to the dictates and whims of their military commanders and viziers (chief ministers). By the time the Mongols erupted onto the scene, the Abbasid Empire was already in terminal decline.[11] The Mongol invaders brought down the weakened Abbasid Empire in 1258 when they laid siege to and then stormed Baghdad, engaging in a campaign of death and destruction.

The Mongols were supposedly aided in their deed by the alleged machinations of the caliph's chief vizier, a Shia named Muayad al-Din Mohammad Ibn al-Alqami. To be sure, Ibn al-Alqami had been disgruntled that the caliph had not properly rewarded him and his family for their service to the empire. The story that has come down over the ages is that al-Alqami secretly negotiated with the Mongols to hand the empire over to them. Of course, the Mongols destroyed the empire and killed the caliph. The story of al-Alqami's alleged treachery resonates with Sunni audiences. Many Sunnis, particularly militant Islamists, often refer to the Shias as "awlad ibn al-Alqami," or the sons of Ibn al-Alqami.

The calumnies against the Shias and minoritarian sects within Islam actually began before the fall of Baghdad, when Ali Ibn al-Hasan Ibn Hibat Allah Ibn Abd Allah, known as Ibn Asakir al-Dimashqi, condemned what he referred to as the external and internal enemies of Islam: the Crusaders and "heretical" Shias, respectively.[12] A century after al-Dimashqi, the prominent jurist and theologian Taqi al-Din Ahmed Ibn Taymiyya (1263–1228) also believed that external forces, the Mongols, and internal dissidents, the heretical sects, threatened Islam. Ibn Taymiyya began a vituperative assault against the weakest and most despised heretical sects who were living within the umma and whose status as part of the faith was somewhat ambiguous: the Nusayris (today's Alawis) and the Druze.[13]

Much of Ibn Taymiyya's ire was reserved for the mainstream Shias (mainly Twelver Shias), presumably because they were a greater danger. He referred to them as the Rafidis (Rejectionists) because of their refusal to accept the legitimacy of the first three caliphs, or successors to the Prophet Mohammad:

> The Rafidis [al-Rafida] come next, for they ally themselves with whoever fights the Sunnis. They allied with the Mongols and with the Christians. Indeed, there was in the coastal areas [of the Fertile Crescent] a truce between the Rafidis and the Franks. The Rafidis would ship to Cyprus [a Crusader bastion during the Crusades] Muslim horses [!] and armor, as well as captive soldiers of the sultan and other fighters and young warriors. When the Muslims defeat the Mongols, they mourn and are saddened, but when the Mongols defeat the Muslims, they celebrate and rejoice. They are the ones who advised the Mongols to kill the [last Abbasid] caliph and massacre the people of Baghdad. Indeed, it was the Rafidi vizier of Baghdad Ibn al-Alqami who, through deception and trickery, conspired against the Muslims and corresponded with the Mongols to incite them to conquer Iraq and instructed people not to fight them.[14]

Several centuries later, Sunni extremists in Iraq regularly accused the Shias of being a heretical sect that threatened Islam and acted as a fifth column (*tabur khamis*) for the "Zionist-Crusader" invaders and occupiers, the extremists' colorful term for the U.S. presence in Iraq.

Ottoman Mesopotamia and Rivalry with Iran

The history of modern Mesopotamia begins with the Ottoman invasion and absorption of this land in the early sixteenth century.[15] Mesopotamia became a bone of strategic and religious contention during the major intra-Islamic clash between the Sunni Ottoman Empire, the seat of the caliphate, and the Shia Safavid Empire of Iran. The most momentous event in Shia political history was the establishment of Twelver Shiism as the official religion of Iran in 1501 by Shah Ismail Safavi, an Iranian Turkmen. Almost two centuries before this event, a holy man named Safi al-Din (1252–1334), who claimed descent from Ali, established a Sunni order in Azerbaijan, in northwestern Iran. The order adopted the Shia denomination, and at the turn of the sixteenth century, headed by Sheikh Ismail Safavi, it set about conquering Sunni Iran in the name of Shiism. Sheikh Ismail founded the Safavid dynasty and established the capital of his new Iran in Tabriz.

Shah Ismail's indefatigable proselytism, practiced so close to the powerful Ottoman Empire, brought him into conflict with that formidable bastion of Sunni orthodoxy. The Safavids and their successor dynasty, the Qajars, stood as unrelenting foes of Ottoman claims to legitimacy over the umma. The struggle between the Ottomans and Iran found its expression in violent polemics and propaganda against one another and, often, in war. Historian Ann Lambton pointed out that polemicists in the Ottoman camp believed that it was better to kill Shias than "Franks," the generic term for Christians.[16] Furthermore, the Ottomans viewed the Shias in Iraq as a potential Iranian "fifth column."[17]

The main arena of conflict between the two sides was Mesopotamia, which was the birthplace of Shiism. It was there that the founding events of Shiism took place: it was at Kufa that Ali was murdered. It was at Karbala that the forces of the Ummayyad caliphate massacred his son Hussein and his followers.[18] Finally, it was in Samarra in central Iraq where the Twelfth Imam went into occultation, or "disappearance," in 874.[19] Shia religious and political dogma was elaborated over the centuries in Baghdad, in Hilla, and then in the holy cities of Najaf, Karbala, and Samarra. The success of the Ottomans in establishing control of that territory and securing dominion over the Shia centers of learning in Najaf, Kazimiyah, and

Karbala was an everlasting source of regret for the rulers of Iran.[20] Recurrent wars between the Ottomans and Iranians until 1818 reinforced the religious ties between the ruling Ottoman Turks and Sunni Arabs in Iraq, while highlighting the Sunni–Shia divide.

Ottoman power over Mesopotamia waxed and waned over the course of the centuries. When Istanbul first came into control of the territory, in 1536, it established centralized direct control over it with a substantial military presence.[21] Intertribal war, and war between the tribes and the Ottoman government, consumed considerable resources and weakened the Ottoman military forces in Mesopotamia. Moreover, as Istanbul became distracted by threats and wars on its western European flank, its control over Mesopotamia loosened. The territory fell under the sway of local rulers with their own militia forces. In 1704, a Mameluke leader, Hasan Pasha, became governor of Baghdad and steadily increased his power, which he passed onto his son, Ahmed Pasha. The historian Albert Hourani describes the Mamelukes as soldier-administrators trained as lifelong servants of the Ottoman state. Between 1704 and 1831, the Mamelukes ruled Mesopotamia, and though they were officially under the sultan's thumb, Istanbul wielded very little actual control over them.[22] The Mamelukes recognized the sultan's sovereignty and obtained formal confirmation of the governorship from him, but they managed to retain considerable autonomy.[23] Istanbul demanded little from the Mamelukes, and they, correspondingly, provided little. Ottoman Janissary troops continued to be stationed in Baghdad, but the Mamelukes kept them under strict control. The Mamelukes funded their own local military forces and managed to keep centrifugal forces within Mesopotamia—usually obstreperous and warring nomadic Arab tribes—in check and maintained the Ottoman frontier against the Iranian enemy to the east.

In 1831 Istanbul decided to reassert direct control over the territory for strategic reasons. The Mamelukes' rule over the province was inept, and as a result the territory was in a state of semianarchy and increasingly subject to depredations at the hands of marauding nomadic Arab tribes. The Mamelukes had maintained a policy of live and let live vis-à-vis the nomadic tribes so long as they did not threaten the few towns in the territory. Moreover, the Mamelukes had begun to exhibit an increasing measure of independence that irritated the sultan in Istanbul.[24] The sultan appointed a governor, Ali Rida, to break the power of the Mamelukes and bring Mesopotamia under central control, which he speedily did.

In the early nineteenth century, when Istanbul regained direct control of the territory, Ottoman Mesopotamia was a sleepy backwater composed of three provinces (vilayets)—Mosul in the north, Baghdad in the center, and Basra in the south—that had little interaction with each other.[25] The population was around 3,650,000 and largely tribal and rural.[26] The sultan generally only sent the incompetent and the lazy to lord over Mesopotamia. As a result, "Iraqis" were not attuned to the dramatic debates in Istanbul over constitutional government, reform, and nationalism. The Sunni Arabs of Iraq, as a community, were hardly politically aware at all. Only a few were educated, and only a few had any sense of a nascent Arab nationalism. Nobody knew what the Kurds—Sunnis, like the ruling Turks, but vastly different in terms of ethnicity, culture, and levels of development—were up to in their mountain fastness or what they wanted. They rebelled a lot, even as they readily provided their ostensible masters with auxiliaries of superb fighting quality to quash "rebellious infidels" or "heretical" Muslim minorities within the empire.

The southern province, Basra, was the Ottoman "Achilles heel" in Mesopotamia. It was the least developed and most insecure part of a backward colony. It had virtually no infrastructure. The writ of the Ottoman government hardly extended into Basra, whose rural areas were plagued by intertribal raids and rampant brigandage. The state's lack of capacity to control Basra allowed the reactionary and austere Sunni Wahhabi sect, which was empowered by the Saud family with its large tribal army, to invade this remote region in 1802. Basra was home to a small but growing Shia population and the holy cities of the Shia sect. The Wahhabis abhorred the "heretical" Shias, and their ideologically motivated tribal army thoroughly sacked Karbala, the holy of holies for the Shias. A Frenchman, J. B. Rousseau, who visited the city shortly thereafter, described the despoliation of Karbala by the Wahhabis in lurid detail in his *Description du Pachalik du Baghdad Suivie d'une Notice Historique sur les Wahabis* (Paris, 1809):

> That day came at last…12,000 Wahhabis suddenly attacked the mosque of Imam Husayn; after seizing more spoils than they had ever seized after their greatest victories, they put everything to fire and sword.…The elderly, women, and children—everybody died by the barbarians' sword. Besides, it is said that whenever they saw a pregnant woman, they disemboweled her and left the fetus on the mother's bleeding corpse. Their cruelty could not be satisfied, they did not cease their murders and blood flowed like water. As a result

of the bloody catastrophe, more than 4,000 people perished. The Wahhabis carried off their plunder on the backs of 4,000 camels. After the plunder and murders they destroyed the Imam's shrine and converted it into a trench of abomination and blood. They inflicted the greatest damage on the minarets and the domes, believing those structures were made of gold bricks.[27]

During the course of the nineteenth century, this region began to undergo an accelerating process of "Shiazation" as the sect began to attract Bedouin Arab tribes, for reasons that have been fully addressed elsewhere; put briefly, many of the Bedouin tribal sheikhs in the south saw in Shiism a useful tool as an ideology of resistance to Ottoman attempts to centralize power in southern Iraq. Furthermore, Shia clerics, flush with money from religious donations from Shias as far away as Iran and India, were able to engage in missionary activities to convert the Bedouin Arabs, whether nomadic or sedentarized.[28] As for the Shia holy towns, they and their clerics maintained a studied "aloofness towards all official institutions such as the army, government, schools and administration."[29] Mystified and baffled, the Ottoman government sent numerous officials to the south to seek explanations of this phenomenon, which was dangerous on multiple levels. It was one thing to have Shia clerics ensconced within the holy cities of Najaf and Karbala, cut off from their immediate social and cultural hinterland and carefully watched concerning links, real or otherwise, with Iran; it was another thing for the population of Basra vilayet to convert to Shiism, a process that by the beginning of the twentieth century ensured that Mesopotamia's total population reflected a slight Shia majority.[30] It was not far-fetched for Istanbul to think that this heterodox population could then act as a "fifth column" for neighboring Iran or any other power with sinister designs over the territory.[31]

As the nineteenth century progressed, the Ottoman Empire found itself in the throes of political and socioeconomic upheaval. This turmoil was brought on by recurring wars with European powers, in which the empire did not fare well, and by rising intellectual ferment due to the advance of secular political ideas. The decay and rising discontent prompted major reformist moves at the turn of the nineteenth century. Istanbul was forced to undertake administrative, bureaucratic, educational, and military reforms within the empire in order to stop and reverse the litany of successive defeats at the hands of Western powers. Reform also meant bringing the peripheral regions of the empire under greater centralized control.

In the middle of the nineteenth century the Ottomans began a belated modernization and development of Iraq.[32] This Ottoman reform and centralization strategy in Iraq began first as a military endeavor. In 1848 the government in Istanbul created the Sixth Army Corps, to be stationed in Iraq. This corps needed manpower, which had to be educated and capable of being trained in modern warfare. Education reforms resulted in the formation of a secular education system whose purpose was also to staff the administration and bureaucracy with locals. Sunni Arabs took advantage of the emergence of secular education institutions, which ultimately broke the Sunni ulemas' monopoly of education. Centralization required that the state break the power of Iraq's powerful tribes, which it did by various means, ranging from bribery to dividing and conquering, assassinations of recalcitrant sheikhs, and military campaigns.[33] Though some of Iraq's Bedouin Arabs, such as the Shammar Jarba, resisted Ottoman efforts to conquer them for almost a century, the military confrontations ultimately ended with the Ottoman state triumphant.[34] The Bedouins loved raiding and waxing lyrical in poetry about warring. However, the reality was that they did not understand modern warfare and their political and socioeconomic structures were not capable of waging and sustaining warfare on an extensive scale for any length of time.[35] The most successful measure against the nomadic tribes was the implementation of land reforms, which forced them to settle and to cultivate land. Sedentarization added to the government coffers through taxation of the agricultural surplus, enabled the military to conscript Arabs into the army, and allowed the government to keep close watch on the hitherto peripatetic tribes.[36]

Reforms in Mesopotamia consisted of defensive modernization to ensure that this fragile, soft underbelly of the empire did not slip out of Istanbul's grasp. The region faced many threats: the machinations of centrifugal tribal forces, the ambitions of the Shia rulers of Iran, and the encroaching British, whose preeminence in the Persian Gulf was now alarming the Ottomans. Turks and European Ottoman officials were loath to serve in Mesopotamia: it was underdeveloped, far away, cursed with a torrid climate, and poorly served by communications.[37] To ensure the modernization, development, and security of Mesopotamia, the Turks ensured that the territory's Sunni Arabs, with whom they were linked by religion and to whom they extended what educational and political opportunities there were in the province, would emerge as the dominant group. Sunni Arabs attended the military academy in Turkey and served in many parts of the Ottoman Empire.[38] Ottoman state-formation in Iraq from the nineteenth century onward, which allowed the Sunnis to emerge as the dominant community, had a decisive impact on the subsequent political history of the country.[39] The British, who wrested the territory from the Ottomans after World War I, further consolidated Sunni power. The Sunnis retained that dominance until 2003, when the Americans knocked them off their perch.[40]

The British Empire and the Emergence of Iraq

Before World War I broke out, Istanbul found itself facing a vastly more powerful enemy than Iran: the British Empire, which was already ensconced in the Persian Gulf as the major naval power and as the patron of various Arab sheikhdoms on the Arabian Peninsula. Istanbul felt that the British were deliberately undermining Ottoman sovereignty over Mesopotamia.[41] Indeed, Britain had been casting covetous eyes on Mesopotamia for geopolitical and economic reasons.[42] The Ottoman vilayets of Mesopotamia abutted Britain's important economic interests in the semiautonomous Iranian province of Arabistan, or Muhammerah. The Arab sheikh who ruled the province thought the British would protect him because they had discovered oil on his territory. The oil in Arabistan offered the Royal Navy, which was transitioning from coal to oil, a ready, British-controlled supply of the precious commodity. The British knew that there were rich oil deposits in Ottoman Mesopotamia as well.[43] British control of emerging Middle Eastern oil resources would reduce the need to import this increasingly strategic commodity from the United States or Mexico.

Geopolitics intruded. The Ottoman Empire was too close a friend of Imperial (Wilhelmine) Germany, increasingly a strategic rival of Britain as the world entered the twentieth century. Before the war, London and its officials looked askance at German attempts to extend the Berlin-to-Baghdad railroad to Basra on the Persian Gulf.[44] Having the Germans in the Gulf and thus closer to India, the crown jewel of the British Empire, was something that London viewed with trepidation.[45] The early twentieth century witnessed the beginnings of political turmoil in colonized territories. The specter of a mobilized political Islam also worried London. The Ottoman Empire was slowly crumbling due to the rise of nationalism and ethnic sentiments among the empire's various peoples. How might Istanbul counteract that steady decline? London believed that Istanbul could resort to rousing Pan-Islamic sentiments to shore itself up, particularly in times of troubles. The British Empire contained a significant population of

Muslims in the Indian subcontinent. The incontrovertible fact was, to quote directly the remarkable words of Paul Knight, "in 1900, the British Empire was the most populous Muslim state in the world."[46] Britain feared that if it and the Ottomans were to come to blows, Istanbul might seek to mobilize global Muslim opinion against the British Empire, particularly in India, which contained a significant percentage of that Muslim population. As early as 1908, a British official noted: "I think...that this Pan-Islamic movement is one of our greatest dangers in the future, and is indeed far more of a menace than the 'Yellow Peril.'"[47] As world war loomed and tensions mounted between two rival European alliance systems, with Britain on one side and the Ottomans on the other, the former began to think of preparing for action in the upper reaches of the Persian Gulf in order to preempt the Turks' entering the waterway.

As soon as the Ottoman Empire entered World War I on Germany's side, Britain invaded Mesopotamia. Britain's initial foray into the territory was muddled. It was not clear what the political goals were: capture a part of the extreme south and consolidate control or march upcountry as the opportunity provided?[48] After a bitter campaign, brilliantly analyzed by the historian Charles Townshend in his book *When God Made Hell,* the British eventually seized Mesopotamia. When the British military commander, Lieutenant-General Stanley Maude, entered Baghdad on March 11, 1917, he issued a proclamation that was penned by Mark Sykes, a British Army officer and diplomat whose racism toward the inhabitants of the "Near East," as it was then known, was ecumenical. He hated Arabs, Jews, Kurds, and Turks in equal measure:

> To the people of Baghdad Vilayet:
>
> In the name of my King, and in the name of the peoples over whom he rules, I address you as follows:
>
> Our military operations have as their objective the defeat of the enemy, and the driving of him from these territories. In order to complete this task, I am charged with absolute and supreme control of all regions in which British troops operate; *but our armies do not come into your cities and lands as conquerors or enemies, but as liberators.* Since the days of Halaka [i.e., Hulegu, the Mongol despoiler of Iraq] your city and your lands have been subject to the tyranny of strangers, your palaces have fallen into ruins, your gardens have sunk into desolation, and your forefathers and yourselves have

groaned in bondage. Your sons have been carried off to wars not of your own seeking, your wealth has been stripped from you by unjust men and squandered in distant places. Since the days of Midhat [Pasha, the Ottoman reformer], the Turks have talked of reform, yet do not the ruins and wastes of today testify the vanity of these promises. It is the wish not only of my King and his peoples, but it is also the wish of the great nations with whom he is in alliance, that you should prosper even as in the past, when your lands were fertile, when your ancestors gave to the world literature, science and art, and when Baghdad was one of the wonders of the world.[49]

Former U.S. president George W. Bush replicated this narrative more than eighty years later to justify his 2003 invasion of Iraq. However, the closest equivalent of General Maude's stentorian declamation was the one issued by the American general Tommy Franks, the commander of U.S. forces invading Iraq. In his speech, delivered with less florid oratory and a more direct American style, General Franks "assured" the Iraqis that U.S. troops were not coming in as occupiers but as liberators.

Following World War I, the disposition of the territory absorbed the attention of the British. Britain could not make a decision independently of regional and international ramifications, particularly as the British and their ally, the French, had engaged in a bit of imperial skulduggery during the course of World War I. In an effort to garner the support of the Muslim inhabitants of the Ottoman Empire, mainly Arabs in the Fertile Crescent, the Arabian Peninsula, and Mesopotamia, the Allied Powers had promised the inhabitants of the disintegrating Ottoman Empire that they would help them achieve freedom and independence after the war was over.

In reality, Turkey proper, which included much of the landmass of Anatolia and the remaining enclave in Europe, was to be split up among the victorious powers and various ethnic minorities, leaving a small rump Turkish state deep in Anatolia. Meanwhile, Britain and France intended to carve up the Arab territories of the Ottoman Empire between themselves. In May 1916, representatives of Britain, led by Sir Mark Sykes, and of France, led by Georges Picot, signed a secret agreement—the infamous Sykes-Picot Agreement—to that effect. Neither Britain nor France expected their partner in crime, tsarist Russia, to succumb to revolution in 1917. The Bolsheviks, who eventually seized power, gleefully revealed the sordid document to the world in November 1917, much to the delight of the Turks, who were pleased with the exposure of Western perfidy; the dismay of the Arabs, who had believed in the empty promises of Britain; and the profound embarrassment of Britain and France.[50]

Notwithstanding the preference of some British officials, it became clear that direct colonial control would not be feasible after World War I, when calls for self-determination of subject peoples were making headway. The victorious powers did not expect these principles to apply to the inhabitants of their own colonies. The victorious allies found a clever solution by coming up with the concept of mandates within the newly established League of Nations, an institution set up to bring order to the messy postwar world. A certain category of territories, the Class A mandates, were to come under the benevolent supervision of the victorious powers, which would gently instruct the "natives" in the intricacies of self-rule and help them build the institutions of government. This was a face-saving solution for the British presence in Mesopotamia, where officials were squabbling over the future disposition of the territory. However, as far as anyone in Iraq could tell, the British mandate over the territory was a mask for old-fashioned colonial control. The Iraqi perception bred not gratitude for liberation from the Turks but violent opposition to the British.

The British did not anticipate the Iraqi Revolt of 1920, which occupies a key position in Iraqi historical consciousness.[51] It began, oddly enough, in a small, peripheral town in northwestern Mesopotamia called Tel Afar. In 1920, Tel Afar's townspeople rose up and killed the British political officer and the crews of two armored cars.[52] The revolt petered out, but it did set the stage for a more widespread insurgency in the Euphrates valley. The inhabitants of Mesopotamia rose up in response to these factors: the intrusion of a foreign Christian power—Britain—into their affairs; its decision to stay in this newly conquered territory; and its refusal to countenance any meaningful self-governance for the population.[53]

The Iraqi insurrection of 1920 was the largest and most serious that British imperial power faced in the twentieth century. When it erupted in June 1920, the British had only 7,200 white troops and 53,000 Indian troops, for a total of 60,000, of which 26,000 were noncombatants.[54] In his monumental history of the early twentieth-century war over the disposition of Iraq, *Enemy on the Euphrates*, historian Ian Rutledge writes that the insurrection "came perilously close to inflicting a shattering defeat upon the British Empire."[55] Easy initial victories gave the insurgency momentum.

Four distinct groups coalesced to support the campaign to get rid of the unwelcome British: the Shia religious community, the urban masses led by notables and intellectuals, expatriates who had formerly been Ottoman officers and officials, and the tribes.[56] There were efforts in the direction of Sunni-Shia cooperation in the fight against the British. The insurrection, however, never attained any ideological cohesion (or organizational efficiency; see below). It was neither a primitive prenationalist anticolonial uprising similar to those that took place in many areas of the world during the nineteenth century in reaction to colonial powers nor a modern national war of independence.[57] The rebels knew what they did not want: the British ruling them. They did not have a positive national agenda stating what they wanted, although this was not for lack of trying. Hanna Batatu, one of the giants of Iraq scholarship, argued the revolt was not "truly nationalist either in its temper or its hopes" but was instead essentially a tribal affair "animated by a multitude of local passions and interests."[58] This is true only up to a point. Iraqi tribal sheikhs, particularly in the Sunni heartland, were no longer ignorant "savages" unaware of the rising tide of nationalism and the turmoil both within their country and further afield in Syria and Istanbul. Nonetheless, the prospect of a united Muslim front against them deeply worried the British.[59] Like many incumbent powerholders or invaders faced with local resistance, the sheer reluctance by the British to concede the legitimacy of the resistance, or make some effort in understanding its roots, led them to maintain the fiction that it was sponsored by malign outside forces.[60]

Ultimately, the insurrection failed, though it gave the British a run for their money. The various elements involved had very different political goals from one another. Iraqi historian Ghassan Attiyah wrote that a major weakness of the tribes was their lack of a command-and-control system to organize a nationwide rebellion. Nor did they have a coherent plan for defeating the British.[61] This lack of coordination meant that some areas of the country rose months after others had done so.[62] The British were able to concentrate their scarce resources where they were needed most. The British also recognized and took advantage of the insurgents' lack of shared interests and organizational incoherence.[63]

The revolt constrained Britain's ability to rule without cooperation from the locals and forced them to create an Iraqi monarchy. The person they put on the throne was Faisal, a patrician Arab from what is now Saudi Arabia: a foreign prince in search of a kingdom. He was the son of the Sharif Hussein, leader of the Arab Revolt against the Ottomans in which the British officer T. E. Lawrence achieved everlasting immortality due to the exploits he exquisitely described in his memoir *The Pillars of Wisdom*. The enthronement of Faisal was a farcical act of desperation on the part of a broke imperial power that hoped to avoid a Levantine tussle with its French wartime ally—the same ally that had driven Faisal from Damascus by force of arms in June 1920.[64]

The pillars of British control over Iraq were the monarchy, the Sunni elite, and the Iraqi army that the British set up, trained, equipped, and commanded. The monarchy was not always as reliable and pliant as Faisal, and his successors sought to demonstrate their legitimacy among the Iraqis by annoying the British. The British relied on the Sunni Arab elite that the Ottomans had built up over decades, including those who had switched sides and allied with the British. The British preferred the Sunni Arab community to the Shia Arabs and the Kurds.[65] Succumbing to Ottoman and Sunni Arab biases against the Shias, the British regarded the Shias as backward, in thrall to their obscurantist clerical establishment and suspiciously close to Shia Iran. British-Shia clashes in 1919, which had led to the death of a British official, served to sour the British against the Shias. The Kurds were too far removed from the centers of power and were a non-Arab minority in a largely Arab country. Kurdish rebellions deepened British suspicions of this community.[66] The British reempowered the tribes in order to have them as an alternative power center to the obstreperous urban nationalists and the monarchy, which chafed under British indirect rule. Nonetheless, the British were not too trusting of the tribes, as their potential for nationwide revolt against the centralizing power of the nascent state was ever present, a sentiment reinforced by the tribes' behavior during the 1920 insurrection.

The British built an Iraqi army that was intended to transform individuals into citizens by training, instilling discipline and civic virtues, and to function as an internal security force to thwart centrifugal forces.[67] To ensure ultimate control over Iraq, and indeed, other colonial and quasi-colonial possessions in the aftermath of the costly World War I, Britain used air power in support of the local internal security forces or constabularies to enforce its rule over its possessions. The new Royal Air Force argued that air control would be effective because it cost less than maintaining huge numbers of ground forces and because air power terrified obstreperous tribes due to its novelty.[68] At the Cairo Conference of March 1921, Winston Churchill, then secretary of state for the colonies, asserted that due to the cost of maintaining a garrison in Iraq, Britain had a choice between abandoning Iraq or adopting the Royal Air Force's doctrine of air control.[69] On October 22, 1922, the Air Ministry took control of Mesopotamia. Colonial administrators stated that the purpose of air power was "to assist [Faisal's] government in the task of bringing order and sta-bility [to Iraq]."[70] History has a remarkable habit of repeating itself: cur-rently, the international community has focused its efforts on trying to control or dismantle IS largely through the use of air power, avoiding a large ground footprint.

Despite gaining a greater measure of independence from the British as time went by, Iraq remained a puppet of the world's most powerful empire, a fact that elicited an expression of smug satisfaction in the 1950s by a British ambassador, Sir John Troutbeck: "When all was said and done we had delivered Iraq from Turkish rule and given her her independence [!], provided a long succession of honest and able administrators for the coun-try, built the railway system and handed it over practically free of charge, and created the oil industry upon which the financing of further develop-ment depended."[71] Troutbeck, of course, could not have poured scorn on Britain's supposedly civilizing mission in that country. The British them-selves may have provided a "long succession of able and honest adminis-trators," but this mattered little if the Iraqis they put in power were venal and corrupt to the core or ruled in a discriminatory manner. Yet Troutbeck was not so obtuse that he did not realize that something was "rotten in Iraq." He worried that the situation in Iraq was politically and socially unstable. The rich, he noted, paid practically no taxes, the majority of peasants were landless, and the cost of living was very high. He also remarked, omi-nously, that "the split between the Sunnis and Shias seemed to be getting wider rather than otherwise."[72] Indeed, a year later, Troutbeck noted the seemingly unassailable position of the Sunni political elite: "it is the Sunni minority that still holds the big jobs whether in government, administra-tion, or army."[73]

The Shias were not entirely powerless. In the period 1921–1922, they occupied 17.7 percent of government positions; this was hardly represen-tative of their proportion of the total population. However, the 1940s and 1950s were times of profound socioeconomic change for the Shias. Rapid urbanization, exposure to secular education, and the absorption of mod-ern political ideas led to the decline in the power and influence of the Shia theological schools in forming the values and shaping the political mind-set of the Shia community.[74] By the period 1947–1958, Shia politicians occupied 34.7 percent of government positions. This was still well below their percentage of the population. Yet, in the words of Iraqi sociologist Faleh Jabar, the Shias were everywhere. They occupied positions in the government, the bureaucracy, and the various political parties. They were to be found among the landed class, the peasantry, the working class, and so on. However, they were largely absent from the upper ranks of government and the army.[75] That was precisely the point: they were everywhere but in the highest corridors of real power.

Britain as an imperial power in Iraq was hindered by its own structure. It was too wedded to a narrowly based ruling elite and it could not implement reform without threatening the entrenched elite and thus its own strategic position. Despite all its claims about the modernization of Iraq and the development of infrastructure, Britain's position was also structurally weak due to its reliance on personalities, often unscrupulous, rather than on building long-lasting institutions; the Americans faced the same problem in Iraq, and in Afghanistan, much later.

Republican Iraq and the Rise of the Baathist State

Britain continued to dictate the tenor of political life until the monarchy's bloody overthrow in 1958 and replacement by a socialist republic under the (initially) hugely popular General Abdel Karim Qassem.[76] He was overthrown in 1962 by members of a conspiratorial pan-Arab nationalist party that called for a "renaissance" of the Arab world, a united Arab state, and implementation of socialist principles: the Baath Party, which was then largely dominated by Shia adherents.[77] Brutal, poorly organized, and lacking any popular support, this regime did not last long. The army, heavily dominated by Sunni Arab officers from the very conservative Sunni Muslim Dulaim tribe (many of whose officers were either open or closet members of the Iraqi branch of the Muslim Brotherhood), overthrew it, and a succession of unstable republics followed. Then, in 1968, a revitalized and better prepared Baath Party took over power for the second time in less than a decade.

This time the Baath Party—now dominated by civilians who came from the small Sunni towns of Tikrit and Samarra north of Baghdad—was much better organized and prepared to maintain power.[78] Led by ruthless men, among whom was one small-time conspirator with a big chip on his shoulder, Saddam Hussein al-Tikriti, the party got rid of enemies, real or imagined, swiftly. The Baath maintained power until 2003, when Saddam Hussein, who had risen through the ranks to become the regime's leader, mainly through the simple expedient of killing his rivals, was overthrown by the U.S. invasion.[79]

Between 1968 and 1975, the Baathists devoted much of their efforts to consolidating power against a variety of opponents, including the Shias.

They reduced Shias' religious, commercial, and socioeconomic power by instituting a state capitalist system and creating a new middle class dependent on the state for its livelihood. The regime also had to deal with a threat from the Iranian-supported, autonomy-seeking Kurds, against whom they fought and won a savage civil war between 1970 and 1975, when the Kurds were abandoned by the machinations of the international community and the shah of Iran. The Baathists' early, radical foreign policy found them embroiled in a variety of entangling conflicts with other states in the region.[80]

After 1975, as a result of a massive increase in oil revenue, Iraq focused on development and modernization in line with its Baathist ideology.[81] Saddam Hussein, second in command officially until 1978, moved into position as president after killing his opponents and set up a terrifying totalitarian political system. He was convinced that it was his destiny to reawaken the Arab world and make Iraq the spearhead of the Arab renaissance. As he told an admiring French Gaullist analyst in the 1980s: "I embarked on my political career with the conviction that I had to shoulder an extraordinary responsibility."[82] In foreign policy, he began to take a moderate stance regionally, following Egypt's defection from Arab ranks after its peace treaty with Israel, thus opening the path for Iraq to become the Arab "big brother." By the late 1970s Iraq was on the way to becoming the Arab "superpower."[83]

However, events within and outside Iraq threatened the Baathist regime's stability even before Saddam Hussein had seized full power.[84] From the beginning, relations between the Baathist regime and Islamists of all stripes had been poor. The regime initially focused its attention on Sunni Islamist politics, which had manifested itself among conservative Sunni circles in rural areas and small cities in Anbar province and among politically powerful tribes like al-Dulaim. The regime executed Sunni clerics for good measure; indeed, the first cleric it executed was Sunni. The Shia community was the greater problem. Relations between the Baath regime and the Shia community were tense from the beginning.[85] Regime officials heaped humiliation after humiliation on the Shia clerical establishment and instituted strictures against ostentatious religious displays.[86] Moreover, resentment grew in segments of the Shia community over the enormous number of casualties that Shia infantrymen and Shia members of the commando units (*maghawir*) suffered in the war against Kurdish secessionism in the early 1970s.[87]

In February 1977, serious Shia disturbances marred the Marad al-Ras religious procession from Najaf to Karbala during the Ashura ceremonies commemorating the martyrdom of the Prophet's grandson Hussein. A scuffle took place between security forces and pilgrims when the security forces tried to interfere with the procession.[88] Outraged Shias went on the rampage, denouncing the Baath government and demanding its overthrow. The government restored order only after regular troops were dispatched to the trouble spots. It arrested hundreds of people, but "only eight" were executed after being tried in special courts.

The demonstrations represented a serious challenge to the government. The 1977 disturbances, which the Baath with profound symbolism referred to as *al-taharuk al-raji* (the "reactionary movement"), threatened to split the party along sectarian lines. Some Shia members of the Baath Party even sided with the rioters. A head-on attack on the Shia demonstrators would have been risky and could easily have been interpreted as an attack on Shia Islam. Such an attack could split the party, create an unbridgeable gulf between the Baathist regime and the Shias, and result in making an enemy of a community that constituted more than 50 percent of the country's population.[89]

This was a clash between religious and secular worldviews. Saddam Hussein decided to launch a head-on assault on political Islam—but *not Islam as a religion and certainly not Shiism* per se—to defend secularism and to fight a dangerous competing ideology based on seemingly alien principles. The regime's decision to defend secularism became salient in light of the emergence of revolutionary Shia political parties dedicated to removing secularism from Iraq and overthrowing the Baath Party.[90] Saddam Hussein delved into the factors behind the reemergence of religious sentiment. In late 1977, he wrote a series of policy lectures on the relationship between Islam and politics. He dissociated himself from atheism but grimly warned against any attempts to mix politics and religion: "our party is with faith [al-iman], but it is not a religious party, nor should it be one."[91] Sharia was seen as "ancient jurisprudence" unsuitable for contemporary times.[92] The Baathists were neither apologetic nor afraid of confrontation. In March 1978, the regime further alienated the Shia ulema by bringing under its control all charitable donations made to the Shia clerical establishment. From now on, the government would have a hand in the collection, allocation, and expenditure of revenues to the Shia clerical establishment.

The Islamic Iranian Revolution in 1979 against a secular nationalist ruler in Iran, Mohammad Reza Shah, had an impact on an Iraq that was already facing domestic religious disturbances. In the words of one senior Baathist official, Shibli al-Aysami: "initially we were happy to see the downfall of the Shah."[93] Indeed, the Baathists had little love for the shah, whom they regarded as an American "puppet." However, in light of the revolutionary drama that was taking place in Iran from the time of the downfall of the monarchy to the outbreak of war with Iraq, officials in Baghdad began to show concern and regret over the shah's departure. The shah had been "reasonable" and secular. He had no reason to interfere in Iraq's domestic politics on the basis of ideological compulsion. Ayatollah Khomeini, the dour leader of the revolution in Iran, declared that his revolutionary Islamic ideology was ecumenical and *directed at the entire Muslim world*. This was a problem for the neighboring Arab countries that suppressed their own Islamists. There was little evidence of the Sunni–Shia sectarian hatred then; indeed, the Muslim Brotherhood, particularly in Egypt, and the *secular* Palestinian movements were among the most enthusiastic supporters of the Iranian revolution.

Following Ayatollah Khomeini's rise to power in Iran, growing numbers of Iraqis began to frequent mosques in both Sunni and Shia areas.[94] The Baathist regime thought it had decisively stamped out Sunni Islamism, whether mainstream or radical, particularly in the city of Mosul, where the Iraqi branch of the Muslim Brotherhood was strong. However, with the Iranian Revolution, attention turned to the dangers posed by political Shiism. Iran was not merely content with the "demonstration effect" of its revolution.[95] It began encouraging Islamist opposition to Arab regimes. Iran supported Shia Islamists in Iraq, such as the militant Shia al-Dawa al-Islamiya Party, whose members began launching hit-and-run attacks in various places around the country, according to Musallam al-Hadi, the president of the Revolutionary Court.[96] Two months later, in June 1980, Fadel al-Barrak, the feared public security director, claimed that under "interrogation" (torture), apprehended al-Dawa members had revealed that they had received arms training in Iran as well as in an unnamed Arab country, presumably Syria, with whom Iraq had poor relations.[97]

The Baathist government worried about the steady emergence of a senior cleric, Ayatollah Mohammad Baqr al-Sadr, an accomplished theologian and philosopher, as a leader of some stature in Iraq following the Iranian Revolution. It did not escape people's attention that Baqr al-Sadr, whose intellectual output was superior to that of Ayatollah Khomeini, could conceivably have been the "Khomeini of Iraq." However, al-Sadr's political acumen was not as sharp as that of his Iranian counterpart. He did not shy away from confrontation with a regime that was made of sterner stuff than the Pahlavi monarchy in Iran.[98] In June 1979, the government arrested him. The response to his incarceration was violent demonstrations in Najaf, Karbala, and the Shia slum of Medinat al-Thawra in Baghdad.[99] Showing its mettle the Baath regime executed him and his activist sister, Amina al-Sadr (aka Bint al-Huda), on April 11, 1980.[100]

Saddam Hussein reportedly confided to Egyptian president Hosni Mubarak that Iraq feared revolutionary Iran more than Israel. Israel was generally perceived as a traditional enemy of the Arab nation because of its seizure of Arab lands and awesome military power, but revolutionary Iran represented an ideological threat to Baathism—as a secular ideology— and to the country's territorial integrity.[101] Baghdad claimed that the "Persians" were using Islam as an ideology to mask their desire to "fulfill the old Persian ambitions in the Arab land and the Arabian Gulf region": to expand and take over Arab lands.[102] To make matters worse, Ayatollah Khomeini referred to Saddam Hussein as a "treacherous parasite" and urged the Iraqi army to overthrow him.[103] Baghdad decided that the revolutionary and subversive virus from Iran and Iran's age-old "expansionist" behavior could be firmly dealt with by a short and decisive military assault, which Saddam Hussein launched on September 22, 1980. Iraq was confident that the revolutionary turmoil had sufficiently devastated the huge military that monarchical Iran had built up before the revolution; this was an assessment shared by outside observers.[104] Iran's precarious military situation would give Iraq an advantage, despite the fact that Iraq itself was in the midst of a major arms modernization and expansion program.[105] The military campaign was supposed to be short; it was designed to humiliate the main source of inspiration for Iraqi Shia revolutionaries and to nip growing Sunni religiosity in the bud.[106] A successful foray would allow Iraq to regain marginal territories it claimed along the border and full control over the Shatt al-Arab waterway. It would also show the region that Iraq was now the most powerful Arab state and the protector of the Arab world against the hated "Persians."[107]

The war turned into a clash of the "inept" versus the "incompetent." Iraqi ineptitude and Iranian incompetence ensured that the war lasted eight years, from 1980 to 1988.[108] Iraq's advance into Iran was slow, unsteady, and disjointed. The Iraqi offensive into Iran did not damage a thoroughly roused revolutionary state to the extent that would have forced it to sue for peace on Iraqi terms. Instead, it fought back. Initially, its counteroffensives to kick the Iraqis out were uncoordinated and enormously wasteful of manpower and materiel. The Iranians learned, however, and in a series of brilliant and painstakingly planned offensives in 1982 they ejected the

Iraqis from occupied Iranian territories and pursued them into Iraqi territory. It looked as if Ayatollah Khomeini's unforgiving goal to overthrow the Baathist regime was about to become a reality. However, it became painfully apparent that Iran's capacity to pursue and sustain offensives into Iraq could not be maintained in the face of formidable Iraqi defenses and revitalized morale.[109] By 1983, due to the repeated failures of the Iranians to break through Iraqi defenses, Saddam Hussein began to breathe more easily. With his army reequipped and with Iran friendless in the world, he wagered that he could fend off Iranian offensives while expressing regret that the two greatest enemies of the Arab world, the "Zionist" entity and the "Persians," had been able to take advantage of Arab weakness and disunity to attack Arab forces in the center in Lebanon (the Israelis invaded Lebanon in the summer of 1982 to strike at the Palestine Liberation Organization) and on the "eastern flank" (Iraq) of the Arab world.[110] By the end of 1983, the Iraqi government and its senior command had also come to the conclusion that the country was in for the long haul of a "comprehensive" war that required the total mobilization of society and all its resources.[111]

Given the material and human costs of a total war effort, Saddam Hussein had to continuously justify his reasons for the war; here is an example from an extensive interview he gave to the Kuwaiti newspaper *al-Anba*:

> The Persians were planning to occupy Iraq and then threaten the Arabs with destruction, and after removing Iraq from the scene and without resorting to military force, compel the Gulf Arabs to feel alien and be swamped by a Persian flood and consequently immigrate [*sic*] from their countries and leave their homes....
>
> We are not only defending Iraq, but we are defending an Arab base called Iraq that is part of the Arab nation and the Arab homeland....Our unflinching and unwavering will draws its strength from our knowledge that we are defending not only Iraq, but the entire Arab nation.[112]

This was one of many expressions of strident Iraqi and Arab nationalism, which was reflected in propaganda, films, and television and, most dramatically, in the conscious decision to officially refer to the war as Saddam's Qadisiyya, after the battle in which the Arab Muslim army defeated a large Iranian Sassanian army in 638 AD.[113] This battle and the one that followed it, Nihavand, resulted in the destruction of the Sassanian Empire and ultimately the Islamization of Iraq and then Iran.[114]

During the early years of the war, Baghdad made strenuous efforts to portray it as a conflict between a progressive and modern Iraq versus a fanatical and backward Iran. Baghdad argued that if Iraq were to succumb, it would surrender to reactionary political ideas.[115] Referring to Khomeini as an "arrogant ignoramus" in an interview with the German magazine *Der Spiegel*, Saddam Hussein blasted the Iranian leader for mixing religion and politics: "We do not rule in the name of religion; it is our belief that is not in the interest of the Arab Nation to do so. The world would succumb to chaos and anarchy when the people of this world allow themselves to be governed by clerics and religious types. We believe that to govern in the name of or through religion causes more problems than it solves."[116] As the war dragged on, for many Iraqis, strident secular nationalism did not seem enough. Many resented the idea that they might die in order to "defend the Arab world." Iraq's defeat in the battles of 1982 "meant for many in Iraq that something was also very wrong with the ruling party and its ideology, and very right with Khomeini's Islamism."[117] Just as in 1977, Saddam Hussein felt the need to shore up the morale of the party and stop the slow but steady glide toward Islamism among the population. He convened the Eighth Regional Iraqi Baath Party Congress in June 1982. The most important theme of the congress was the religious phenomenon, and the party deplored the rise of ultrareligiosity (*al-tadayyun*) among the Iraqi youth and the Shias in particular, ascribing it to the defeat of the pan-Arab movements.[118] Saddam Hussein tried to "nationalize" Islam. In a thinly veiled nationalist screed directed at the Iranians titled *The Arabs Are the Leading Role in the Message of Islam*, he wrote:

> God, the Almighty, sent down the Quran in which he included His Message to humanity—He has sent down an Arabic Quran, revealed in the Arabic tongue, to his Gracious Prophet Mohammad who was illiterate. We may well consider why did the Almighty choose to make the illiteracy of his gracious Prophet a token of belief? Why indeed did He choose to make the Quran an Arabic book....But before all that, [we] may well wonder why had all the Prophets, in the first place, brought their respective messages to, and why had they been chosen from, the people of this worthy land, the Arab homeland?[119]

The years 1986–1987 were terrible ones for Iraq.[120] It confronted an uncompromising Iran in a seemingly endless war.[121] In 1987, Saddam Hussein returned again to what had rapidly become one of his favorite topics, the rise of politicized religion, in a pamphlet titled *Religious Political Movements and Those Disguised with Religion*:

> From the outset we should say that the Arabs are a religious nation, charged with the task of conveying to the peoples of the world the religious message or messages of religion, especially that of Islam. This task is ancient and not modern, divine and not human.... It is perpetual and not transient. This link is clearly illustrated in the fact that God Almighty made the Arab world an exclusive place of all heavenly messages, prophets and messengers. It is also illustrated in the fact that the Holy Quran, the last of all holy books, has given the Arabs the leading role in disseminating the teaching of Islam to other peoples through their...activities or Jihad (Holy Struggle) or through offering a shining and effective model to the people around them.[122]

A year later in 1988, Saddam Hussein revealed his real thinking about Iraq's complex ethno-sectarian makeup, which he implicitly viewed as a weakness: "Ideally we would have liked Iraq to be one nation, one religion, one creed."[123] This sentiment speaks volumes about his political views and belief that a homogenous nation—presumably Sunni Arab—would have had fewer points of domestic vulnerability for outsiders to exploit. He reluctantly conceded: "[but] in reality there is more than one nation, more than one religion.... Given a *wholesome environment*, this plurality can enrich the country's psyche and outlook."[124] Clearly though, the environment had not been "wholesome" when the war started because the Iranian Revolution had some unfortunate resonance within Iraq; while the course of the sanguinary war had highlighted societal weaknesses and ethno-sectarian tendencies within Iraqi society.

The war ended in August 1988, with a revitalized Iraqi army launching several successful offensives against the Iranians that pushed them back across the border into Iran.[125] Iran had run out of seasoned personnel and materiel with which to fight back in 1988. Revolutionary zeal was not enough, and even that had frayed by 1988, after years of frightful losses with little to show for it. Iran sued for peace, albeit reluctantly. Saddam Hussein was convinced that he had won the war. If so, it was purchased at great cost, which ultimately exposed the fragility and brittleness of the Iraqi state.[126] Iraq emerged from the war bankrupt, exhausted, and in desperate need of recovery.[127] The only thing Saddam Hussein had going for him was his enormous and "battle-tested" military establishment, which could just about claim victory because it had fought the Iranians to a standstill in 1988. This army gave him cachet in the region and allowed him to throw his weight around.[128] He could have reduced the size of the military establishment and focused on development. He did not do so because of the perceived Iranian threat and because it was that army that allowed him to swagger into the Middle East between 1988 and 1990 and to claim that Iraq was the deterrent against perceived Israeli machinations.[129] In his colorful words: "We want this big army so that no one can come and tweak our mustaches or pull our beards, and so that we can cut off the hand that tries to do this."[130] Moreover, the end of the Cold War, which witnessed the collapse of the Soviet Union as a balancer vis-à-vis the other superpower, the United States, was bound to expose the Middle East to what the Iraqi leader perceived as the "bullying tendencies" of U.S. foreign policy. Not only would Washington, D.C., continue its anti-Arab stance in the implementation of its foreign policy, it would also seek to dominate the most important resource: oil. Given the fact that the socialist world had collapsed along all dimensions and no longer had a role in the region, it would no longer be ready to thwart the American design; consequently "these two phenomena [U.S. 'covetousness' for Middle Eastern oil and Soviet collapse] will have serious implications for our region... *looting* will increase during that period."[131]

Clearly worried by the evolution of the post–Cold War international structure, stymied by the persistent reluctance of the outside world to give him the respect he felt he deserved, and impatient to kick-start Iraq's development and modernization after an eight-year hiatus, Saddam Hussein took yet another reckless decision: he decided to do his own looting. To the south lay oil-rich Kuwait, a country that had lent Iraq billions of dollars to fight the Iranian revolutionary menace. It was now demanding its money back. Kuwait irritated Saddam Hussein and millions of other Iraqis because of its perceived arrogance and stridency: had Kuwait not once been a part of the Ottoman Empire and thus of Iraq? Kuwait was the world's "biggest bank," and "recovering" it would be the salvation of Iraq's growing post-war political and socioeconomic woes. In August 1990, Saddam Hussein committed the biggest and ultimately most ruinous move of his political career: he invaded Kuwait and claimed it as part of Iraq.[132]

An international coalition of countries led by the United States and several Western and regional powers ejected the Iraqi occupation forces from Kuwait in March 1991 and inflicted a decisive defeat on the fourth largest army in the world. In February 1991, President George H. W. Bush called on the Iraqis to "take matters into their own hands" as the devastated Iraqi military retreated in disorder from Kuwait.

The Inexorable Decline of the Baathist State

The portrait of Saddam Hussein as an omnipotent ruler was shattered by the defeat of 1991. Many Iraqis, particularly in the Sunni areas, expressed profound bitterness and felt that Saddam Hussein had blundered into a trap laid for him by the U.S.-led coalition. In other parts of the country, such as the Shia south and the Kurdish north, communities took the opportunity to rise up in massive insurrections.

The revolt in the south began when infantry and armored units streamed back into Basra from the front, bringing with them harrowing tales of defeat at the hands of a superior foe and mismanagement of the war by their own government. A number of military units defected in the towns of Abu al-Khasib and Zubeir and linked up there with disorganized Shia rebels, including Islamists and deserters from the army. On March 3, 1991, the Shia population rebelled en masse. The rebellion was largely spontaneous, with civilians and clerics joining disgruntled soldiers. The rebels attacked government buildings and killed scores of officials, security personnel, and Baath Party cadre.

The rebellion took the government by total surprise, but Saddam Hussein did not sit idly by. Retribution by the thoroughly frightened regime was swift. The government reorganized what remained of its forces, particularly the loyal and better trained units: the Republican Guards divisions. The Guards used human shields, making women and children walk in front of them and tying people to their armored vehicles. They fired indiscriminately into residential areas with artillery and tanks. Units then went district by district arresting any young men they found. Some were killed in mass executions held at public squares, while others were carted off to Baghdad.

Local clergy were rounded up and arrested or killed as well. In Najaf, rebels had used the Tomb of Imam Ali, one of the sites holiest to Shias, as their headquarters. The tomb was shelled by Iraqi forces and heavily damaged; almost all of those captured inside were killed. The government forces made liberal use of artillery and helicopter gunships against towns where the rebels were holed up. By March 29, 1991, it was all over. The rebels had been able to seize most of the major cities in the south and frighten the regime, which was also facing Kurdish Peshmerga rebels in the north. In the end, however, Saddam was able to hold onto power with his superior military force.[133] The Shia insurrection struck at the legitimacy of the regime even more than the Kurdish insurrection in the north, which ultimately allowed the Kurds to develop a thriving autonomous region after years of internecine conflict. Noteworthy were the expressions of fear on the part of the Sunni community (also expressed by those who made up the Shia middle class) as a result of the Shia revolt; "they [the rebels in the south] are crazy," said a Baghdadi intellectual to a Western journalist.[134]

The Baath Party suffered loss of prestige and morale during the rebellion in the Shia south.[135] Officials were not prepared for the troubles; many were killed by the rebels or panicked and fled. Baghdad established a commission of four high-ranking government officials that was tasked with evaluating the conduct of party cadres during the crisis. The government removed hundreds of them whom it regarded as incompetent and arrested scores who were accused of dereliction of duty, especially in the middle Euphrates region, which was the uprising's center of gravity. The regime felt that it was better to rely on the old vanguard and elitist party organization rather than have the party weakened by the presence of self-seeking and opportunistic individuals. In Saddam Hussein's words: "Let those who wish to leave the Ba'th party do so, so that the Ba'th continue as a bright lantern to our people and glorious nation."[136]

After 1991 the Baath regime, in contrast with its courtship of the Shias during the war with Iran and its strident insistence on the "Arabism" of the Iraqi Shias, became a party of Sunni identity. With that, Shia Arabs became "Persian" and enemies in an ethnic, rather than just religious, conflict that stretched back centuries. The Shias became sullen and withdrew into themselves. After 1991, Shia Baathist functionaries began their schizophrenic life of pretending to be loyal to a regime they now unequivocally detested, while turning a blind eye to the growth of Shia religiosity in secret, or even became more religious themselves. Apparently, this was the case even in Baghdad, in the sprawling slum known as Medinat al-Thawra or Saddam City (later renamed Sadr City).[137]

Paranoia had always been part and parcel of the Baathist mentality; after 1991 it became more institutionalized and was responsible for making enemies of most of the population of Iraq.[138] Baathist coercion throughout the 1990s was systematic and frequent. These were the acts of a frightened and declining system. Through the mid- and late 1990s Shias, and specifically the clergy, were targeted for assassination. While Saddam Hussein singled out specific Shia leaders, he dispatched political enemies of all other sects and ethnicities just as readily. Sunnis suffered because their proximity to the regime's instruments of power made them a potentially untrustworthy element vis-à-vis the regime itself, while Shias and Kurds suffered because of their allegedly "foreign" nature and "treasonous" behavior toward the nation. As religious sentiment took hold of the Sunni community over the course of the 1990s, the old calumnies against the Shias resurfaced. Even before the U.S. invasion and the onset of Sunni–Shia violence, Salafi preachers began to engage in anti-Shia diatribes. In the last Friday prayers before the U.S. assault on Iraq, a preacher in Baghdad stated: "If we do not resist the invaders, the Rafida will kill anyone called Omar."[139]

Fanar Haddad, a British academic of Iraqi origin and a leading expert on modern Iraq, argued that it was the state historiography of the intifada, as the uprising in the south was called, that essentially invented modern Iraqi sectarianism, as before it, "the terms Shia and Sunni were seldom used in Iraqi official discourse."[140] After the intifada, Iraq was a country of two halves—the *muhafadhat al-ghawgha'a* (the provinces of the mobs) and the *muhafadhat al-baydha* (the white provinces, the pure, i.e., Sunni, provinces). This anti-Shiism led the Shias to embrace their own identity and history and the belief that as the majority they represented Iraq. This view stood in stark contrast with that of the Sunnis, who individually and collectively believe that they are the founders of the modern Iraqi nation. In 2005, the Iranian-American journalist Borzou Daragahi of the *Los Angeles Times* quoted Adnan al-Dulaimi, head of the Sunni Awqaf: "There are some voices who say that Sunni Arabs are a minority. We want to prove to them that we are not a minority. We are the sons of the country. We are responsible for the history of Iraq."[141] Sectarianism had never been far below the surface in Iraq since the country's emergence in the 1920s, with various rulers trying to submerge or transcend it, but it became a significant factor in defining people's identities in the 1990s and early 2000s. For this, both Iraqis and foreigners are to blame.

Sectarianism was not the only issue facing Iraq after 1991. The Iraqi state began a slow but inexorable path toward decline. By the end of the twentieth century, the Baath had succeeded in ruining the Iraqi economy, atomizing Iraqi society, and erasing most forms of civil society. The public sector had been a major source of income in the early 1990s. From 1958 to 1977, the number of salaried state employees rose from 20,000 to

500,000, without taking into consideration the 230,000 in the armed forces.[142] An estimated 850,000 Iraqis were on the state payroll in 1991 as civilian employees, military and security personnel, and pensioners. Forty percent of Iraqi households were dependent on state paychecks.[143] The public sector shrank significantly in the 1990s, leaving many Iraqis grasping at straws.

Many Iraqis turned to the informal sector for employment. This shadow economy included activities such as street vending, begging, prostitution, and extensive sale of family goods. In 2000 this informal economy constituted approximately 30 percent of gross domestic product, and the informal labor force constituted just under 70 percent of the total labor force, or 30 percent of the total population. The decline of the secular middle class, hitherto the most supportive pro-Baathist social strata, was dramatic. Hyperinflation wiped out the value of their salaries, leaving them to survive on scanty government pensions that covered less than a third of their needs.[144] Postwar conditions reduced the living standards of the poor to subsistence levels. Real incomes in August 1991 were somewhere between 5 and 7 percent of what they had been a year earlier in terms of purchasing power.[145] The privileged few had access to hard currency, unlike the vast majority of people, and led a good life.[146] The sanctions regime imposed by the UN Security Council in response to the invasion of Kuwait devastated Iraq and embittered its people.[147] As a result of the sanctions, the regime was deprived of its vast oil revenues. The GNP declined to less than a quarter of 1982 levels. Per capita income dwindled from $4,219 in 1979 to $485 in 1993. The state lost much of its capacity to materially reward the bedrock of the system, the state-employed middle class, and its ability to sustain social safety nets and welfare services for the lower social classes. Estimates of inflation in 1994 were at 24,000 percent.[148]

The government sought to lessen the burdens on its shoulders by actively encouraging privatization of small industries, the service sector, much of the agricultural sector, and construction companies. As state capacity waned in the 1990s, due to the effects of the Iran-Iraq and Kuwait wars and sanctions, the regime ceded state powers to supportive societal structures, such as co-opted tribes and religious authorities. During the early years of Saddam Hussein's rule, the regime encouraged measures that marginalized the tribes. The Baath had viewed the tribes as an obstacle to development and modernization and worked to undermine the tribal sheikhs' authority and influence over rural society. Saddam Hussein's relationship with the tribes fundamentally changed after the 1991 uprisings, during which he lost control at one point of all but one province. In the wake of this massive breakdown of the Baath Party's security apparatus, he incorporated a new version of tribalism into the party's political ideology.[149] He assiduously engaged the tribes and provided substantial economic benefits to those who supported him.[150]

In 1993, when Iraq was feeling the full brunt of the international embargo and social collapse, Saddam Hussein announced the opening of his "Faith Campaign" *(al-hamla al-imaniyya)*. He had actually turned to using religion very much earlier on. He had sought a synthesis between Arabism/Iraqism and Islam during the Iran-Iraq War and had expanded on it during the war over Kuwait.[151] With the Kuwait War, however, a number of subtle nuances arose. Iraqis blamed the Arabs for what happened to their country, and they could not forget the Arab military efforts—however ineffectual—against them.[152] Arabism, a subject to which Saddam Hussein had warmed in the brief interlude between the end of the war with Iran in 1988 and the beginning of the Kuwait crisis in August 1990, was no longer de rigueur. There was now a focus on Iraqi Arabism and Islam, a ploy to maintain Sunni Arab and Shia Arab unity despite the rise of sectarian sentiments. People sought solace in the mosques as their world collapsed around them. An Iraqi engineering student in Tikrit told the journalist Hugh Pope: "We have more Islam now. There are many more mosques. We want it that way"; a cleric in Baghdad explained the reason: "People are coming to the mosque more and more. . . . When people lose hope, when they have been bombed, of course they turn to religion."[153] On the eve of the second war with the United States, religious sentiment overshadowed the secularism that once defined Iraq. Through speeches, symbols, slogans, and actions, the Baathist regime had turned to Islam for legitimacy, playing down Arab nationalism and secularism. When the United States invaded Iraq in 2003, it found a society that was more religious and more sectarian than it had been since the 1950s.[154]

As the new millennium began, Saddam Hussein defied predictions that his days were numbered and that he would be overthrown.[155] Indeed, by 2002 the regime seemed to be doing better politically and economically. Observers who visited the country on the eve of the invasion and occupation seemed to indicate that Saddam Hussein's regime was slowly but surely "squirming" its way out of the sanctions regime. Iraq's steady rehabilitation under Saddam Hussein worried the United States.[156] Nonetheless, this was a weak authoritarian system that tried to face the American juggernaut bearing down on it in the aftermath of al-Qaeda's attack on the United States on September 11, 2001. This attack, by a group based out of Afghanistan, which did not include a single Iraqi among its nineteen-man assault team, was used by a belligerent, neoconservative administration in Washington D.C. to justify an invasion of Iraq.

The American Interlude

Fill full the mouth of famine, and bid the sickness cease.
—RUDYARD KIPLING, *"the white man's burden"*

To put it simply, "the good war is any conflict that leads to an outcome that a particular society" or state "finds desirable."[157] The Iraq war was not a "good war." When the George W. Bush administration launched its adventure in Iraq, "Operation Iraqi Freedom," its cheerleaders, the ideological group of intellectuals and government officials known as neoconservatives, declared it was more than revenge for the terrorist attacks of 9/11. Getting rid of Saddam Hussein and his suspected, though nonexistent, weapons of mass destruction were good things. Furthermore, the entire "noble" enterprise was supposedly part of a plan to remake the Middle East and set it on the path to democracy, beginning with Iraq first. (The goals for more distant Afghanistan—the sanctuary of al-Qaeda and Osama bin Laden—were not as ambitious.)[158]

Advocates for the war created the narrative that Iraq was still a secular and modern nation yearning to throw off the yoke of a sanguinary and outdated authoritarian system. Naturally, of course, a selfless United States would do it for them. This neoconservative construct came into contact with a country that was embittered by a decade of sanctions, more radicalized, and bereft of a civil society and middle class that would constitute the backbone of a more democratic entity. The underlying premise of the Bush administration was that promoting democracy in Iraq would have the domino effect of promoting democracy around the region, but this did not happen. The region's elites kept an uneasy quiet as they were loath to cross a vengeful United States. Arab nationalists and Islamists were the most vocal opponents of the U.S. enterprise, but their protestations had little impact except to highlight the impotence of the Arabs, rulers and subjects alike, reminding one of the Arab proverb "The dogs bark but the caravan carries on."

There was not much doubt about the outcome of a conventional war between the United States and its Coalition partners on the one hand and Iraq on the other. Iraq's military forces in 2003 were not the huge forces of 1991 that were manned by veterans, albeit war-weary, of the Iran-Iraq War. In Desert Storm they were outclassed by forces that they could not compete with technologically, in terms of training, or in the conduct of combined arms and joint warfare. The gap in 2003 was even wider. Western sanctions and constant military pressure had devastated the Iraqi military between 1991 and 2003. It was focused on maintaining internal security and terrorizing its own people and had not conducted a major field training exercise for conventional war since 1994. Most of the military could not be trusted, as the bulk of the personnel consisted of poorly trained conscripts with low morale and even lower commitment to defending the regime.

The conventional military part of Operation Iraqi Freedom lasted for three weeks between mid-March 2003 and the first week of April 2003. It was what came after the successful conclusion of the military campaign—reflected in Bush's now unfortunate "Mission Accomplished" speech aboard USS *Abraham Lincoln*—that came as a shock and unpleasant surprise: an insurgency. It was also *who* came along with the U.S. military and *what* they did that proved to be the undoing of the American enterprise. The military made mistakes, which it corrected. The Bush administration civilians went in with an ideological vision that ultimately proved to contrast drastically with reality on the ground. The story has been told many times and only needs to be briefly recounted here, in order to set the stage for the violent response by many Iraqis after 2003.

The American invasion and occupation led to a series of unintended consequences in Iraq, with which the United States continues to struggle to this day. These consequences include an orgy of looting and violence, an insurgency by the now dispossessed Sunni Arab minority, who refused to take their dispossession lightly, and mobilization by the Shia Arab majority, most of whom refused to take on the position of puppets assigned to them by the American neoconservatives, who brought with them into Iraq a number of well-groomed "future leaders" of Iraq, including the recently departed cherubic Ahmed Chalabi, a peripatetic Iraqi exile, banker, and businessman turned politician.

Though America ostensibly entered Iraq in 2003 with the mission of bringing democracy, it had already clearly stated that it was not going to bear the lion's share of the burden of reconstructing post-Saddam Iraq; it was not truly interested in international state- or nation-building.[159] The Iraqis would have to do it on their own, albeit with guidance and support from the Americans. The effort did not get off to a good start. As the Baathist state was dismantled, all forms of governance, law, and order disappeared in the weeks following the assault on Iraq by the international U.S.-led Coalition. Starting in mid-April 2003, a violent spree of looting and destruction erupted throughout the country as Iraqis vented their pent-up frustrations, fears, and anger. The initial governing body set up by the United States to run Iraq, pending the restoration of law and order and governance, the Office of Reconstruction and Humanitarian Assistance, proved ineffective from the outset.[160]

On May 16, 2003, the Bush administration set up the Coalition Provisional Authority under the authority of Ambassador L. Paul Bremer. "Jerry" Bremer would issue two critical orders that would ignite the insurgency. The first order was the call for the "De-Baathification of Iraqi Society." Although the intent was to remove senior Baath Party leadership from playing any role in the future Iraq, it also disenfranchised tens of thousands of people.[161] Many of these people had had no choice but to remain Baath Party members under Saddam's reign if they wanted to keep their jobs and earn a livelihood. This, however, did not mean that they were fervent believers in his ideology. In fact, most were heartily sick of it, while others who maintained a show of being Baathist were also becoming closet Islamists. Bremer's second order, the dissolution of all Iraqi security ministries, the Iraqi army, and intelligence services, put into the street individuals who became insurgents.[162]

3

"Why They Fight"

IDEOLOGY AND GOALS

THE INSURGENCY OF 2003 was not preordained. The American occupation of Iraq generated plenty of ideological opposition within Iraq among the Baathists who had been overthrown, Iraqi nationalists, and Islamists of all stripes.[1] The conflict environment was complicated because there were many groups who were fighting the Americans and their Iraqi allies and who eventually fought one another as well. Iraq (and now Syria) became an arena for ideological contestation and deadly combat between these groups because of competing visions, goals, and different ideas about operational methods. None of these groups managed to achieve ideological hegemony over the others and establish control over the insurgency. However, from 2013 onward ISIS sought precisely to attain ideological control over a revitalized Sunni insurgency in Iraq. Then, flush with victory over Iraqi forces, it confidently proclaimed the Caliphate in mid-2014 in the territories it had seized. Its successes brought about a wide-ranging and disparate coalition of local and international actors against it.

Preinsurgency

The ideological impetus and goals of the various insurgent groups fighting against the Americans has been explored in depth.[2] What took place immediately following Saddam Hussein's overthrow was not an insurgency but violence engendered by the collapse of the state and hostility toward the American presence. Violence erupted during encounters between jittery U.S. troops and suspicious townspeople in places like Fallujah, where the conservative residents got into an altercation with the 82nd Airborne troops at the end of April 2003 that resulted in a number of civilian deaths that infuriated the townspeople.[3] In Baghdad, there was a turn from the looting and pillage that occurred right after the Americans entered the city to a slow but steady descent into localized armed confrontations between groups of Iraqis and U.S. troops during the stifling summer months of 2003.

Iraqis viewed the "muscular" and "threatening" behavior of American troops toward civilians as unnecessarily antagonizing.[4] Notwithstanding statements by U.S. officials that the Iraqis would welcome the Americans with open arms, initial attitudes ranged from "thank you for ridding us of Saddam Hussein, now please get out" to intense hatred, among Sunnis for "what the Americans" had "done to them" by kicking them out of power, and among Shias for the U.S. "betrayal in 1991" of failing to support their anti-Saddam rebellion. Many Iraqi Arabs, both Sunni and Shia, argued that the United States came into Iraq to foment chaos, thereby justifying its presence and keeping Iraq weak for Israel's benefit.[5] Many in the wider Arab world—and it did not matter whether you were an Islamist or an Arab nationalist or even a Sunni or Shia—subscribed to this uncharitable view of the U.S.-led war on Iraq. Only the Kurds were uniformly happy, because the United States had gotten rid of their enemy, Saddam Hussein, and because having unequivocally allied themselves with the United States, they expected substantial political gains in post-Baathist Iraq.

There were shows of unity between Sunni and Shia Arabs in the immediate weeks following the fall of Baghdad to American forces.[6] A senior Shia cleric, Ayatollah Mohammad Baqir al-Hakim, who had returned from exile only to be murdered shortly thereafter, made it clear that the Shias were not going to accede to the American presence when he said: "Foreign troops must leave Iraq at the earliest possible time. The Iraqi people will resist by all available means, including armed struggle, if these foreign forces turn into occupiers."[7] However, the call for intercommunal unity was to split apart shortly thereafter because of a fatal disconnect between the two communities: the Sunnis wanted the Americans out and to *return to power*, while the Shias wanted the Americans out and *to take power* in accordance with their demographic and their new-found political weight.

The Americans were subjected to a string of attacks throughout the occupied country by a wide variety of troublemakers. During the early months following the capture of Baghdad, it would have been a stretch to call these random attacks an insurgency. When it became clear that outraged former military personnel were perpetrating many of the attacks, the Bush administration's response was one of dismissal. Larry Diamond, an American academic who served in Iraq as an advisor, testified to the reluctance of American officials to consider the residual power of the

Sunni community. He wrote: "There are no negotiations with the Sunnis right now, and no dialogue, and that means the U.S. is pressing ahead with a system that will result in a great deal of polarization and disenfranchisement."[8] The attitude among the Bush-appointed American civilian officials ensconced in the Republican Palace in the "Green Zone" of Baghdad was that the Sunnis could be safely ignored; after all, the Americans had the goodwill of the Kurds and the Shias for overthrowing their nemesis, Saddam Hussein. These two communities constituted the majority of the population. The capacity of the Sunnis for creating mayhem was initially discounted, even in the face of growing violence by elements of this community in the summer of 2003. By late fall 2003 the United States was finally faced with an insurgency.

Insurgency

The Iraqi insurgency consisted of five distinct groups. Four of these groups were composed largely of the following: Iraqis from the former regime, nationalists, tribal elements, and various local Islamist fighters. While the ideological variety and number of insurgent groups in Iraq was not unique, it has been rare in history for an insurgency to be fractured into so many groups that fought one another as much as they did the common enemy, the United States, and alleged collaborators. The level of factionalism and rivalry within the Sunni insurgency constituted a major structural flaw; nonetheless, it still managed to fight the United States to a standstill by 2006. However, it was this level of factionalism and ideological rivalries within the disparate strands of the insurgency that allowed the United States to turn the tide against the insurgents in 2007. I won't examine these four groups in detail, but it is important to distinguish them from the fifth group. It consisted of Iraqis and foreign fighters who joined the extremist, transnational Islamist group Jamiat al-Tawhid wa al-Jihad, led by the Jordanian Ahmed Fadhil al-Nazal-al-Khalayleh, also known as Abu Musab al-Zarqawi, or simply Zarqawi.[9] This is the group that evolved much later into IS, or the "Caliphate" of Abu Bakr al-Baghdadi.

The Iraqi Army as Insurgents

We must look to the officers and soldiers of the Iraqi army and security forces for the beginnings of organized violence. Senior Iraqi officers were involved from the outset. They were the first to articulate concrete grievances vis-à-vis the Americans. They were angry at the loss of jobs, incomes, and pensions. They also viewed the abolition of the Iraqi army as an affront. They had the training and the weapons to turn their anger into violence. In May 2003, a large number of military personnel began demonstrating publicly. The demonstrators included Shia officers, whose discontent was echoed by, among others, Voice of the Mujahidin Radio, which was affiliated with the Supreme Council for the Islamic Revolution in Iraq, an Iranian-supported Shia political movement with its own militia force, which had bitterly opposed the deposed regime. On May 26, 2003, Major-General Sahib al-Musawi addressed officers who were demonstrating in front of the headquarters, in the Republican Palace, of the U.S.-led Coalition: "We demand the formation of a government as soon as possible, the restoration of security, rehabilitation of public institutions, and disbursement of the salaries of all military personnel. If our demands are not met, next Monday will mark the start of estrangement between the Iraqi army and people on the one hand and the occupiers on the other."[10] Iraqi military personnel wanted jobs and basic services and threatened to turn to violent if their demands were not met.[11] The militancy of army officers was most evident in cities and towns such as Fallujah, Tikrit, Tel Afar, and Mosul, where they constituted important socioeconomic and political strata because of the prestige associated with their profession and the fact that they stemmed from very influential Sunni tribes.

The town of Fallujah had been "troublesome" for the Americans from the very beginning of the occupation.[12] The resistance to the United States there was initially fomented by army officers, noncommissioned officers, and enlisted personnel whose world was turned upside down when the Americans occupied Iraq and entered their town.[13] Their task of resistance was made much easier for them by the fact that the clerics in the mosques were able to mobilize the overwhelming majority of the townspeople to oppose the Americans.[14] This resistance took on an Islamist hue, which was reinforced when the extremist Islamists—the Salafi-jihadists—joined the fray in the city and the surrounding rural areas. Considerable friction eventually emerged between the local Fallujan military and tribal fighters on the one hand and the Salafi-jihadists—whether local or foreign—on the other. The agenda of the native fighters was local, regional, and national, while that of the jihadists was transnational and religious, as was reflected starkly in the strident comment of one foreign fighter, "Abu Usamah" from Tunisia, who told a journalist, "We are here for one of two things—victory or martyrdom, and both are great. The most important thing is our religion, not Fallujah and not the occupation.... We are not here because we want to liberate Iraq, we are here to fight the infidels and make victorious the name of Islam."[15] The gap in ideological views turned from tension into violence later on.[16]

The largely Turkmen city of Tel Afar in northwestern Iraq, eighty miles from the border with Syria, was a particularly interesting case. It has been widely assumed, erroneously, that Tel Afar was a Shia city in a Sunni sea. It is not; most of the Turkmen there were Sunnis, and 25 percent of the population were Shia Turkmen; indeed, they were relatively recent converts to Twelver Shiism from Bektashi Sufism. The years of the Baath regime were times of plenty for the Sunni Turkmen who joined the army and the security services and served in them throughout the country as salaried employees of the state. Those who became teachers, municipal employees, and policemen stayed home and served their communities. They lived in relatively affluent neighborhoods, such as Hai al-Dhubbat (the Officers' Neighborhood) or Hai al-Muallimin (the Teachers' Neighborhood). The Turkmen made good officers and dominated the logistics and supply and military intelligence branches for reasons that are not easy to fathom.[17] The collapse of the regime meant the collapse of their privileges and positions. Other sources of employment—agriculture, trucking, and petty commerce—were either saturated or dominated by the Shammar Arab tribe living in the vicinity of Tel Afar or by the Shia Turkmen; both groups had largely been excluded from being salaried employees of the state. Not surprising, many of the Sunni Turkmen entered the insurgency out of anger and humiliation as well as in a quest to earn a "living." For the most part, they participated in the nationalist or mainstream Islamist insurgency. However, over the course of time many migrated to the most radical Islamist element of the insurgency, whose adherents were known as Salafists and who called for a return to "true Islam." A significant number joined the Salafi-jihadists, a subgroup within Salafism, whose followers eventually created IS.[18]

The large northern city of Mosul was the home to thousands of senior party members and over one thousand senior former Iraqi army officers with the rank of brigadier-general and above. At the University of Mosul, there were 120 university professors with ranks in the Baath Party. There were also 937 schoolteachers who were members of the Baath Party. The issue of what was to become of them proved nettlesome. This prompted General David Petraeus, commander of the 101st Air Assault Division, then based in Mosul, to ask Ahmed Chalabi, who had been groomed by Bush administration officials to take over in Iraq because they had deluded themselves that he was popular in his country, this question: "Do you throw 900 teachers out of work and tell them they can never work in their field again, and then not expect them to turn against you…? I am not saying that all these people by any means should be kept, but if you are going to tell people that they're never going to work again, you might as well throw them in jail." Chalabi's response was allegedly "At least they can eat there."[19] When Mosul was under the control of General Petraeus's 101st Air Assault Division, the city seemed to be firmly on the way to stability and security. However, once the division left, Mosul quickly descended into chaos, and many areas of the city came under the control of organized criminal gangs, Islamist groups, and insurgents from within the ranks of the former Iraqi military.[20]

The bitter complaints of army officers who were thrown out of their professions are encapsulated in the words of Ismael Mohammad, a former intelligence officer: "We were on top of the system. We had dreams. Now we are the losers. We lost our positions, our status, the security of our families, stability. Curse the Americans. Curse them."[21] Another officer focused on the loss of livelihood. "How can we live?" asked Colonel Abdul Karim Ahmed; "We do not have savings for even one day."[22] Many Iraqi officers found the American attitude toward them to be unjustified and unfair and thus felt that it justified their attacks on U.S. forces. As Major-General Saad Jibouri complained: "we didn't do anything wrong. We've been left with nothing. Mosul didn't put up a fight. We expected the Americans to deal with us fairly. Now we are just out on the streets. There are thousands of us, we are running out of money and we are unhappy. That's why there are attacks."[23] The invasion and occupation of Iraq had also become a threat to Iraqi military personnel's view of history, of their identity, and of their place in Iraqi society. Al-Basrah.Net was a website dedicated to disseminating the views of the nationalist and secular elements of the insurgency. On April 26, 2008, it posted a statement by the "League of Iraqi National Security Agencies, Officers and Associates"— which was loosely affiliated with the Baath Party and whose stronghold was Mosul—in which the group pointed to yet another enemy alongside the usual suspects: Iran. It claimed that Iran was trying to control Iraq with the help of the United States and Israel.[24]

On February 19, 2008, a jihadist website posted an interview with Staff Lieutenant-General "Abu Sayf," spokesman for the General Command of Armed Forces in Iraq, an insurgent group made up of former army officers and other ranks. "Abu Sayf" stated:

it [the army] was founded in 1921 to be a fundamental element of the modern Iraqi state. It is the army of all Iraqis from all different ethnic groups. The Command represents the continuity of the Iraqi Army's command.... Our leadership believes that the Iraqi Army is a national army, which is not guided by a sect or party; its main mission, at this stage, is the liberation of the homeland from the oppressive US occupation. Our command is legitimate and started its jihad immediately after the occupation; it consists of the best and most competent commanders of the army who have a large military and nationalistic background.[25]

He said that any negotiations or truce that did not take into account the insurgency's terms would be a "waste of time."[26] These terms included the unconditional withdrawal of American troops, a national government elected by the Iraqi people, and American occupiers paying damages to Iraq and the Iraqis for their material losses.[27] As the insurgency evolved, Iraqi army officers and other ranks acted as instructors or advisors to insurgent groups, formed their own combat units, and joined the various insurgent organizations en masse as commanders.[28]

The Baath Party and Its Affiliates

The Baathist Party suffered the most trauma following the American invasion and occupation, as it went from being a ruling party to one that was banned by the Americans and thus thrust into resistance. Saddam Hussein's efforts to become head of the Baathist-based resistance was stymied by his being forced into ignominious hiding in the face of an intensive manhunt by American forces and then by his imprisonment under tight security following his capture in December 2003. Nonetheless, this did not prevent him from expressing his views about the American occupation and the obligation of the Iraqis to resist it, right up until the time of his execution in December 2006.[29]

The Baath Party, after it was ejected from power and bereft of direction from its leader, Saddam Hussein, split into two wings, one led by Mohammad Yunus al-Ahmed and one led by Izzat Ibrahim al-Duri, who was allegedly killed in Tikrit in April 2015. The latter wing was much more active and potent in the Baathist strand of the insurgency. Al-Duri hewed to typical Baathist nationalist views of the world concerning the occupation of Iraq. He and the remnants of the Baathist leadership believed that the misfortune that had befallen Iraq was a vast conspiracy by traditional and more contemporary enemies—Iran, Israel, and the United States—of Iraq and the Arab states to loot Iraq's wealth and subjugate it and the Arab world politically and economically: "The ideology and goal of the neoconservatives' Zionist scheme is to colonize Iraq and convert it into a launching pad from which they would exert complete control over the region's oil and countries and provinces.... But Iraqi national resistance groups have destroyed the fundamentals of their plan, which is to successfully occupy Iraq. Thus it is impossible to achieve their second objective, which is to take full control of all oil-producing countries in the region. And thus it is impossible for them to achieve their third objective, which is to colonize the world."[30] The Baathists sought to highlight their importance within the insurgency. They created the narrative that the Baath Party had been responsible for preparing the Iraqis for insurgency against the Americans. The Baath Party had allegedly provided the means to fight a protracted war of liberation without relying on outside support.[31] In addition, "the patriotic, nationalist, Islamic culture of the people of Iraq, which [the] Baath helped created [sic] during their 35 years of rule, prepared the people of Iraq to embrace and support the resistance and to sacrifice for victory regardless of the cost."[32] As a result of the Baath Party's supposed prewar preparations, the insurgency found a supportive demographic environment in which to operate, and this environment was supposedly the "lifeblood" that provided the insurgents with the key to victory.[33] For the Baathists, the Iraqi resistance confirmed that what prevailed in warfare were primarily factors such as morale and will and not tanks and aircraft. The strong desire of the Iraqi people for freedom and independence from foreign occupation would be the "decisive factor" in the war in Iraq.[34]

In 2007, al-Jazeera TV interviewed "Dr. Abu Mohammad" of the Baath Party, who characterized the resistance to the occupation as "nationalist, pan-Arab and Islamic resistance," demonstrating the party's growing reference to religion as a source of resistance as much as nationalism.[35] The Baath Party also cooperated with other groups who were not ideological soulmates but shared the common goal of expelling the foreign presence. "Abu Mohammad" denied any relationship whatsoever with al-Qaeda, "whose doctrine, vision and strategy differ from those of the Baath and the remaining national resistance factions."[36] The situation on the ground, however, was vastly more complicated than that offered by "Abu Mohammad."

By the time of his interview, many Baathist officials and former army and security officials of the Saddam Hussein regime had already thrown in their lot with the Islamists. To be sure, a greater number did so later, between 2011 and 2014, as is discussed in the following chapter; however, the number of former regime personnel who joined the jihadists during the first insurgency was significant. Their reasons varied. Some were already closet Islamists but had hid it well during the dying years of Saddam Hussein's regime. The fact that the regime itself had initiated "re-Islamization" of the country did not mean that these Islamists were safe from the regime's wrath. Once it fell from power in 2003, they were free to express their views and their resistance to the American presence in religious terms. Others joined the jihadists because they felt that they were more motivated, better prepared, and less hypocritical than the other groups.

Another group that was linked to the Baath was Jaysh al-Rijal al-Tariqa al-Naqshabandiya. Dr. Salah al-Din al-Ayubi, the official spokesman of the al-Naqshabandi Order, articulated his organization's ideology, which seemed to be a mishmash of Baathist, Arab nationalist, and Islamist motifs. It was remarkable for its articulation of the distinctly non-Islamic but very Baathist view that the Arabs occupied a leading role in Islam: "we understand and believe that the Arabs are the essence and spirit of Islam. They are the first bearers of the banner, and they disseminated Islam throughout the world.... [T]he other matter is that the Arabs have precedence in Islam due to the fact that the Koran was revealed to their Prophet and in their language."[37] Al-Ayubi added that Jaysh al-Rijal al-Tariqa al-Naqshabandiya coordinated and cooperated with most of the "Islamic and national jihad factions, which have national agendas and do not have external connections or other objectives they want to achieve on the Iraqi territory."[38] Jaysh al-Rijal al-Tariqa al-Naqshabandiya was a thinly disguised organization made up of former regime elements. Its original website was established in January 2007, was initially armyrtn.com, and then became alnakshabandia-army.com. The website contained documents describing the group and its ideology. The website described Jaysh al-Rijal al-Tariqa al-Naqshabandiya as a faith-based military order with affiliation to the Sufi Naqshabandi Order at its core and traced its evolution from a loose conglomeration of cells into an organized and disciplined structure.[39]

Baathist and similar insurgents sought to fuse nationalist and Islamic motifs as part of their resistance ideology and portrayed the resistance as a national one, popular with all Iraqis irrespective of ethnicity, sect, or religion. A nationalist group that was aligned with the Baath was the Supreme Command for Jihad and Liberation. Its spokesman, Dr. Kanaan Amin, declared that his group was set up in September 2007 and consisted of twenty-two jihadist factions that were both Iraqi nationalist and Islamist. These groups included in their ranks all segments of the "great Iraqi nation such as Arabs, Kurds, Turkmen, Christians, and Muslims, including Sunni and Shia."[40] Indeed, in order to win over the Shias to the resistance against occupation, the nationalist insurgents and those affiliated with the Baath fighters tried to promote the idea that Arab Shiism was not at all similar to Persian Shiism. The latter sect was viewed as a front for Persian nationalism and attempts by Iran to achieve a dominant position within Islam. This was the same argument that Saddam Hussein repeatedly made during the Iran-Iraq War, as was reflected, for example, in a wartime pamphlet called *The Khomeini Religion*: "there is a religion in Iran, but it is definitely not Islam....The Iranian conception of Shi'ism is totally different from the Arab mentality."[41] The Shias viewed the insurgents in Iraq as tainted by the Sunni Arab chauvinism of the nationalist and Baathist groups and by the largely anti-Shia sectarianism of the Sunni Islamist fighters. Both strands of the insurgency were exclusivist in their own peculiar ways that could hardly have appealed to the Shias. One largely denied their identity as Arabs and sought to lord it over them again when they "returned to power." The other denied their identity as Muslims and sought to exterminate them. Unsurprisingly, the Shias were ambivalent about and reluctant to join what the Sunni Arabs generally billed as a nationalist resistance (*muqawama*).

Iraqi Sunni Islamists

Sunni Arab Islamist groups, whether they turned to insurgency or sought to play a role in politics, were quite implacable in their opposition to the American invasion and occupation. Their hostility to the American presence was aided and abetted by the Sunni clerical establishment, which was almost uniformly hostile to the American presence. Sheikh Ahmed Abdul Ghafour al-Samarrai, a preacher at the Umm al-Maariq Mosque in Baghdad, viewed the United States with immense suspicion because he believed that the American occupiers had plans to tear Iraq "apart and destroy its unity" by fomenting conflict between sects, ethnic groups, tribes, the military, and civilians.[42] Another cleric, Sheikh Mahmud al-Mashhadani of the State Council for the Sunnis, was exultant that Islam had come to the fore as the major political force for the mobilization of the Sunnis for a wide range of goals, including resistance to occupation. The "national secular movement" had proven to be a failure, he pointed out, and "now the young want the Islamists. Now you have no choice."[43] While there had been some secret proselytization during the time of the regime, following its downfall the Sunni clerics lost no time in seeking to mobilize the devastated community along religious lines to oppose the U.S. presence in Iraq.[44]

Mosul's younger clerical establishment had become unequivocally in favor of radical change in the 1990s and 2000s. Sheikh Ibrahim Abu Namaa was one of those who were able to speak more freely after Saddam Hussein's downfall. His argument was that the objective of the Americans in invading Iraq had been "to destroy the cultural values of Islam. They brought with them nationalism, democracy, liberalism, communism, Christianity and all their materialistic idols so that the Muslims turn their backs on the injunctions of God."[45] The Iraqis were suffering, he argued, because they had forgotten the principles of Islam, principles that would have allowed them to withstand the "injustices" of the occupiers. In 2004, however, in an effort to present a political framework for the expression of Sunni political demands, clerics from the Muslim Brotherhood, the Sufis, and the Salafists formed a 180-man shura council to represent Sunni interests.[46]

It is small wonder, then, that for many Sunnis it was Islam that acted as a motivating force for the insurgency in 2003. At the end of December 2003, a British journalist interviewed some insurgents in remote Rutba. The capture of Saddam Hussein that month by the U.S.-led Coalition forces did not move these Rutba insurgents, one of whom, "Mohammad," declared: "it's all lies that the resistance is led by Ba'athists. The resistance is Islamic, we are ordered by God, we have no relation to that party."[47] "Mohammad" was a former officer in the Iraqi army, as were apparently many of the men with him in Rutba. Their inspiration was Osama bin Laden, though the group claimed that they had no contact with him or al-Qaeda. However, he added that al-Qaeda was an Islamic group from which they had learned much, specifically from Osama bin Laden, whom he described as being "our sheikh also."[48] The admiration for al-Qaeda did not, however, last very long for a significant number of the Iraqi insurgent groups, because by 2006 they had fallen out with al-Qaeda's Iraqi affiliate.

For the Sunni Islamist insurgents, the American presence, as well as the governing body they had installed, was illegitimate. In the words of Sheikh Mahdi Ahmed al-Sumaidi, "neither the occupation forces nor the government they installed is acceptable. The legitimate power is the resistance.... America's brutality has caused many to understand that Islam is the answer to our problems. The only solution is Islamic government."[49] An insurgent from Fallujah, "Ahmad," recounted to the Lebanese newspaper the *Daily Star* how an insurgent cell was established in Fallujah to fight the U.S. presence: "When the Americans came in, there was a negative reaction, but it did not translate immediately into resistance, more a period of watching and waiting. I think the Americans sensed our mood and they quickly began arresting people."[50] The inspiration for resistance came from the mosques. The clerics made oblique references to jihad and resistance in their sermons, messages understood by those listening. In the words of "Ahmad," "the clerics called for resistance and jihad against the Americans. They told us not to mix with them or help... because the arrests and shootings... proved they were not here to help us. We responded because we love our religion and we love our clerics."[51] Clerical power within the Sunni community had grown because during the course of the 1990s most Iraqis had found succor in religion to ease the pains of their deteriorating material conditions and felt freer to practice their religions following the implementation of Saddam Hussein's self-serving Faith Campaign. The vacuum in political power and hostility to the American presence further deepened the role of the Sunni clerical establishment in politics.[52]

However, this did not mean that all "mainstream" Iraqi Islamists necessarily wanted an Islamic state. "Abu Ammar," an insurgent leader in Fallujah, a city that also contained many extremist Islamist groups, was representative of the perceptions of mainstream Islamist insurgents when he declared:

> I am an Iraqi citizen, but above all a Muslim. I received a certain upbringing and I studied fine arts. My family belongs to the Al-Dulaim tribe.... What human being can stand to watch his country, his house destroyed by people who respect nothing? These people have no motivation except material interests. We want an Islamic regime... this government will not be composed of religious figures. Only men of science will be allowed to hold these positions. However the government must take its inspiration from religion and establish its laws according to the principles of the Sharia.[53]

The Mujahidin Army was another Islamist group whose spokesman, Sheikh Abdel Rahman al-Qaysi, had a great deal to say about organization and relations between insurgent groups, the Shias, and the United States. The views about the Shias are particularly noteworthy. The Shias "are a large segment of the Iraqi people, who have lived for a long time in this country."[54] However, it was the leading Shia personalities, parties, and militias, he went on to add, who had "paved the way for and enabled the army of the US occupation in Iraq."[55] They thus had succeeded in turning themselves "into a pillar" for the occupation. The Shias had predecessors who had done the same, such as Ibn al-Alqami. Those who had turned themselves into pillars for the Jews and the Crusaders would be treated "like we treat the occupier and [we will] consider them part of the occupation army."[56] He was careful to add that his organization did not attack those who had nothing to do with the occupiers and their collaborators. When asked by the interviewer whether the organization killed Shias simply because they were Shias, the spokesman responded: "We do not kill them because they are Shiis, but because they are fighters and obedient tools in the hands of the occupation."[57] Naturally, these subtle distinctions make no difference to a Shia who is killed, or to his or her survivors seeking revenge. However, Qaysi claimed that they were being killed because they were collaborators, not because they were Shias, which was a very different stance from that of the extremist organization that became IS, which killed them precisely because they were Shias.

The Islamic Resistance Movement, Hamas-Iraq, which split from the more radical 1920 Revolutionary Brigades, espoused a mix of nationalist and more mainstream Islamist beliefs—close in many ways to the Muslim Brotherhood, the mass Islamist political movement with many branches throughout the Arab world—in an attempt to expand its reach within the Sunni population in Iraq and among the Arab populations of the Sunni world. In May 2007, Hamas-Iraq issued its political program, a mix of Sunni and Arab nationalist motifs. The group accused Iran of seeking to ignite sectarianism within Iraq and later implicated Iran in the bombing of the al-Askari shrine in Samarra.[58] One of Hamas-Iraq's leaders, Ahmed Said al-Hamid, a senior member of its political bureau, affirmed the adoption of the "moderate, centrist ideology" of the Muslim Brotherhood, confirming widespread speculation about the group's mainstream Muslim Brotherhood roots.[59] Another group, called the Front of Iraq, outlined its political program in a jihadist website, 'Ana al-Muslim.net, in which it laid out its ideology and goals, which again espoused a mix of nationalist and Islamist motifs:

> we are committed to the cause of Islam and to defending it against every mischievous aggressor. Iraq is a great nation; God granted it blessings and goodness, made it a meeting point of the earliest

civilizations...a storehouse of humanity's loftiest experiences and discoveries. Tolerant Islam then came and purged it of paganism and infidelity....

There is no such thing as Shiites or Sunnis...we Muslims abide both by the Koran and Sunnah, as instructed to do by our tolerant religion.[60]

The various groups classified as "mainstream" Islamist had certain characteristics that set them apart from the more militant and radical Islamists—the Salafists—who are discussed below. First, many of these mainstream Islamist groups claimed that they were not sectarian. Their ire against the Shias had nothing to do with whether they had deviated from Islam but rather with their collaboration with Iraq's enemies after the invasion. The Shias of Iraq had "gone over to the other side" by collaborating with the occupation and, worst of all, with Iraq's "historic" enemy, Iran. Second, these "mainstream" Islamists were not averse to spouting pronounced Arab nationalist motifs, which were quite common to the more secular or nationalist insurgent groups. Many of these motifs were directed against what was seen as a hostile triumvirate of Israel/Zionists, the West, and Iran, also taking into consideration the fight against the so-called collaborators from within the ranks of the umma. Third, the socioeconomic background of the Sunni Islamist groups was not much different from that of the groups who could be classified as more nationalist and less religiously motivated. Members of the Sunni Islamists included the Iraqi branch of the Muslim Brotherhood, who came out of "hiding," or exile, and appeared in Mosul. This group included well-known clerics and many former regime officials and officers who had kept their religious orientation under wraps, Saddam Hussein's "Return to Faith" campaign notwithstanding.

The Iraqi Salafists

In order to understand Salafist political mobilization in Iraq, we must first understand Salafism as an ideology.[61] Salafism is a very diverse theological movement.[62] The term "Salafism" refers to the theological movement whose adherents strive to emulate Mohammad close companions, known as the "righteous predecessors" of Islam (*salaf*). This historical community—the original *salaf*—had the opportunity to experience religious revelations directly from the Prophet and to hear what he said and to observe his actions and behavior. Salafism believes that the Muslim community must return to the practices of these "pious ancestors," *al salaf al-salihin*—meaning the first three generations of Muslims, beginning with the Prophet Mohammad and his Companions (the Sahaba) and incorporating the two next generations. These *salaf* were able to understand and practice Islam in its purest form, and thus without innovations (*bida'*) that were later added to the religion. In other words, they lived and experienced Islam in its purest and most pristine form.[63] Salafism posits that the perfect Islamic society emerges out of the strict observance of two sources: the Quran and the Prophetic Tradition (the Sunna, the actions and deeds of the Prophet Mohammad, and, strictly verified, the Hadith, the sayings of Mohammad). The sacred texts are unchanging and unchangeable and must be applied in their entirety. The result will be a society controlled by and functioning according to the sacred texts. The state the Salafists seek will base its legal system, governing bodies, and foreign policy on the sacred texts alone. They reject any system of laws not based on the texts and any political ideology created by man to rule over man: particularly democracy, which is seen as *shirk*, or idolatry.

Salafism as an exclusivist ideology that insists upon a division between true Muslims and those who have deviated from "true Islam," defined by the Salafists as adherence to the practices of the original Salaf. The belief in the oneness of God, Allah, is a fundamental principle embraced by all Muslims, but for the Salafists it is *the* defining basis of Islam. This principle, known as *tawhid*, denotes monotheism or faith in a single deity and the only Being deserving of worship and obedience. The principle of *tawhid* means that God is the only one who can regulate human life (defined by Salafists as "God's sovereignty on earth"); consequently for Salafists the only legal system for regulating human affairs is the one believed to emanate from God: sharia. Linked to this system of law is the ultimate Salafi goal of a unified umma (the Muslim community) governed in strict accordance with sharia. This goal is often expressed as the Salafi quest toward the establishment of a politico-religious and territorial unit known as the caliphate.[64]

While many Islamic scholars, ancient, modern, and contemporary, have shaped the ideological tenets of Salafism, one individual is key to the foundation of Salafi thought and practices: the medieval scholar Taqi al-Din Ahmed Ibn Taymiyya, to whom I alluded in chapter 2. He lived in a period of turmoil for Islam, when Muslims were engaged in fighting off the Christian Seventh Crusade on their western flank and constantly subject to violent incursions by the Mongols on their eastern flank.[65] In the midst of this troublesome environment, Taymiyya referred to the era of *al-salaf al-salahin* as the model to follow in order to counter the various challenges faced by Islam. However, contrary to popular perception, while Ibn Taymiyya wrote about the necessity for a government to implement the Divine Law, he never developed a theory of the caliphal state, as did other giants of Islamic philosophy, such as Abu al-Hasan Ali Ibn Mohammad Ibn Habib al-Mawardi (972–1058 AD).

The modern Salafists aspire to re-create the idyllic state of *al-salaf al-salahin*, which in fact only exists in their fevered imagination, since in reality the original era of the pious ancestors was one of turmoil and bloodshed. To be sure there were plenty of pious and virtuous people, but the period was equally characterized by the presence of the impious, the venal, and the corrupt who were seeking power and advancement of their material well-being. Indeed, Salafism is a utopian movement because it seeks to (re)establish the perfect society, which can only be done, in their view, by going back to a supposedly perfect society that existed in the past. This makes it different from most nontheological utopias, whose authors invariably posit an idyllic society that has never existed before. Indeed, the word combines two Greek neologisms, *outopia*, "no-place," and *eutopia*, "good place." The active emphasis on restoring the original forms of Islamic tradition makes contemporary Salafism a revivalist movement that is truly revolutionary in its methods and approaches and is thoroughly a creature of the twentieth and twenty-first centuries in its use of the organizational and technological artifacts of these centuries.

Within Salafism, one can identify a violent strand, the jihadi subset, which has given rise to the moniker Salafi-jihadism. Within the vast Salafi constellation, Salafi-jihadists strongly advocate for the use of force as a means to promote their ideology. Before delving into what it means to be a Salafi-jihadist, we need to first understand the historically contentious term "jihad." The sources of Islamic guidance and action, the Quran, the Prophetic Tradition, and Islamic jurisprudence have never offered a single accepted definition of jihad. Herein lies the problem. The word "jihad" means "to struggle" or "to strive" or "to exert effort" (toward a particular goal). In its primary spiritual connotation, it means the struggle of the soul to overcome temptations and obstacles standing in the way of a virtuous life and nearness to God. "Jihad" has meant physical fighting for the sake of Islam as well, and over the centuries numerous jurists have written extensively about the conditions under which it is lawful to fight and what is permissible to do in warfare. In this context, Islam differentiates between just and unjust wars; the notion of jihad being "holy war" is erroneous.

However, in contemporary times, because of the prominence of the Salafi-jihadists, jihad has been popularly associated more with the physical struggle to promote and extend Islam, to defend Islam and its peoples from foreign invaders, and to eliminate oppression and tyranny imposed on Muslims by their rulers. For the Salafi-jihadists, jihad is about fighting and not about anything else, as other Muslims have "convinced" themselves. Indeed, jihad as war is a central pillar of their ideology.

The Salafi-jihadists use the Quran and the Prophetic Tradition as blueprints for revolutionary action. Ibn Taymiyya's recipe for dealing with infidel threats to Muslims as well as the failure of Muslim rulers to rule according to God's Law has been adopted wholeheartedly by the Salafi-jihadists. Among Taymiyya's numerous writings, *Governance According to God's Law in Reforming Both the Ruler and His Flock* is dedicated to the exaltation of "jihad fi-sabil Allah" by placing it at the level of the core principles of Islam: "The command to participate in jihad and the mention of its merits occur innumerable times in the Quran and the Sunnah. Therefore, it is the best voluntary act that man can perform. All scholars agree that it is better than the *hajj* [greater pilgrimage] and the *'Umrah* [lesser pilgrimage], than voluntary *Salaah* [prayer] and voluntary fasting, as the Qur'an and the Sunnah indicate. The Prophet...has said: 'The head of the affair is Islam, its central pillar is the Salaah and the summit is the Jihad.'"[66]

Though the Salafi-jihadists would like to go on the offensive and extend the territories of the umma, for now revolutionary violence, defined as defensive jihad, is first an all-consuming struggle against the foreign despoilers of Islamic lands who have achieved undue influence in and control over the umma. Second, jihad is also defensive revolutionary action against the Muslim rulers of Islamic lands whose sins are manifold. One of Taymiyya's important contributions to the Salafi-jihadi doctrine is his legitimizing of rebellion against rulers who have deviated from sharia or have not applied it in its entirety. In this context, he justified rebellion against the Mongol rulers, who adopted Islam but, in his view, should be deemed apostates, since they deviated from the true faith. This justification for the use of violence against "apostate" Muslim rulers is an important precedent for a highly controversial practice known as "takfir." "Takfir" refers to the process by which a Muslim is excommunicated from Islam and deemed an infidel or unbeliever (*kaffir*). Although not all Salafis embrace this practice, many Salafi-jihadists have used it to justify their attacks against contemporary Muslim regimes and, in extreme circumstances, to legitimize the use of force against Muslim civilian targets.

The best-known transnational Salafi-jihadist group, but by no means the only one, is, of course, al-Qaeda, which for the time being has been eclipsed by the dominance of IS under the helm of its caliph, Abu Bakr al-Baghdadi. When the large number of largely Arab foreign fighters entered Afghanistan to fight the Soviet occupation of that country alongside the Afghan mujahidin ("holy warriors"), their needs were initially met by a unit called Maktab al-Khidamat, the Office of Services, which was set up and led by a Palestinian revolutionary known as Abdullah Azzam, who exhorted Muslims to emigrate to the land of jihad to fight the Soviet infidels. As it increased in size and prestige, the unit was renamed al-Qaeda al-sulbah, the Solid Base. When Abdullah Azzam died in mysterious circumstances in 1989, the Saudi Osama bin Laden emerged as the unit's leader until his death in 2011 at the hands of U.S. special operation forces. It was bin Laden who presided over al-Qaeda's emergence as a deadly transnational terrorist organization dedicated to fighting Western, and specifically American, influence and presence in the Muslim world.[67]

Salafism made an appearance in Iraq even during the regime of Saddam Hussein, which was clearly alarmed by the emergence of this strain of Islamism in Iraq. For the regime, any revival of Islam was going to be under the regime's helm and not under the auspices of what was perceived as a virulent and regime-threatening form of Islamism. There was a wave of arrests and executions of such people in the waning days of his regime. Those who avoided execution came out of prison in an amnesty program in 2002. They had become hardened militants who had organized in prison. A large number of Salafi-jihadist individuals and groups were present within the insurgent landscape.[68] Iraqi Salafist "emirs," or commanders, controlled Fallujah in 2004. Imams Abdullah al-Janabi and Jaafar al-Obeidi were the spiritual imams of the mujahidin in Fallujah. Al-Janabi was believed to be the leader of the most extremist jihadist faction and to be linked to foreign jihadists.

Salafi-jihadist rule over Fallujah was characterized by paranoia about spies and infiltrators. The atrocities the jihadists committed while holding sway over Fallujah were a foretaste of things to come: beheadings of dozens of people, including Iraqi Shia truckers from the south, an event that caught the attention of Baghdad. The people of Fallujah, who are tribal and conservative, grew increasingly frightened by the Salafi-jihadists' rapid descent into violent radicalism—or takfirism, which refers to the willful excommunication of Muslims that permits the spilling of their blood. The jihadists put up "decrees" of Allah on the walls of the city that included an invitation to denounce strangers, prohibitions against drinking alcohol, and injunctions to women to wear the abaya.[69]

There were a number of Iraqi Salafi-jihadist insurgent organizations. Ansar al-Sunna was particularly close in ideological sentiment to the foreign group that came into Iraq to fight in the anti-American jihad. In March 2005, Ansar al-Sunna published its creed on a jihadist website, declaring:

> We renounce and disbelieve in any giver of Laws except Him. . . .
>
> We believe that democracy is a call to disbelief that seeks to deify mere humans and worship them. It has no connection with true Islamic Shura in any way. We disagree with those Muslims who advocate democracy. . . . We believe that the existing man-made regimes in the Muslim countries, and what is called a constitution are an idolatrous practice.[70]

Ansar al-Sunna reaffirmed its radical position in 2007, at a time when many insurgent groups were thinking about participation in the political process or were turning on the al-Qaeda subsidiary in a bloody internecine war among the insurgents.

One of the most influential and powerful Iraqi Salafist groups was the Islamic Army of Iraq (IAI). Ultimately it emerged as one of the most powerful insurgent groups and one of the staunchest opponents of the foreign Salafists who had come from outside Iraq. The IAI adopted a mixture of nationalist and religious motifs, a strategy that allowed it to attract former regime army and security officers into its ranks, although it strenuously denied links with Baathists and their ideology. However, some of its views were not that different from those of the Baathists, given the prevalence of former regime officers and personnel within its ranks. On December 28, 2006, a jihadist website posted a twenty-one-minute audio message issued by the emir of the IAI, "Concerning the Safavid-Iranian Scheme." It provided an overview of its ideological thinking and was racist and offensive in the extreme, particularly toward Jews and Iranians. The statement began with invective directed at the "Safavids," that is, the Iranians. The IAI leader accused them of having a history of hatred for Islam and of either directly attacking Iraq or infiltrating it to cause problems. The U.S. occupation, he stressed, had provided the "Safavids" with a majoropportunity to advance their long-standing nefarious twin goals of destroying Iraq and undermining Islam, a position that made them allies of the "Zionist-Crusader" occupiers of Iraq:

> It is neither new nor unheard of for the Safavids to attack the Land of al-Rashid, or to become the stepping stone of betrayal and the axe of barbarism that attempts to smash the skull of all Muslims in general and the Arabs in particular, namely Iraq.
>
> [The] history of the Safavids is filled with hatred against Islam and its people. The world has not yet forgotten the criminal minister, Ibn al-Alqami, or al-Tusi (the founder of Shi'a theology).... Iran was the one who enticed, helped, and supported the occupation of Iraq.... From the beginning of the occupation, Iran began its Safavid Magi assassination campaign against the Sunnis, especially the imams of the mosques, the clerics, and the patrons of the house of God, the worshippers, the scholars, and the college professors, as well as the doctors, the engineers, the pilots, the tribal notables, and the merchants....
>
> Most of those in authority in Iraq today are Iranians or are holders of the Iranian citizenship.... There is no doubt that the Safavid-Iranian project in Iraq is the worst and most hideous.
>
> Today, Iran is racing against time to spread its control over the political and military decisions in the region's nations just as it is blatantly doing in Iraq and Lebanon, and to a lesser extent in the Gulf nations...and their criminal plans targeting Syria are not secret. At which point will Iran know that its masters and allies, the Americans and the Jews, will not benefit it, that...warring against more than a billion Sunnis was a grave mistake.[71]

A few months later, Dr. Ibrahim al-Shammari, one of the IAI's spokesmen, reiterated IAI's position on the political situation in Iraq in the program "Without Borders" on Al-Jazeera TV: Iraq was suffering from an "Iranian occupation," which was more dangerous than the American one because the American occupation was "the disease and the Iranian occupation was the symptom, but the symptom has now become more dangerous than the disease."[72] The United States did not claim that Iraq is part of it; rather it came to serve its interests reflected "in the imperialist project" of the Bush administration and its top leaders.[73] Iran, however, was more dangerous because it was irredentist and considered Iraq to be a part of it.

Its policy in Iraq had been one of "uprooting those opposing it," which meant primarily the Sunnis and Arabs.[74] Iran, said Shammari, helped create forty Iranian-backed sectarian militias that were involved in sectarian violence against the Sunnis. While Iran might be more dangerous than the United States, there was full agreement and coordination between the U.S. and Iranian projects in Iraq.[75]

Shammari also wished to show how responsible and careful the IAI was: while the resistance "targets all enemies of the Iraqi people and all those who occupy Iraq," including the (Shia) militias, "targeting any innocent person in Iraq is absolutely not one of our aims."[76] He added that every Iraqi who was not involved in any collaboration with the occupiers was an "innocent citizen," whether that Iraqi was Muslim or non-Muslim. He referred specifically to the Christians, whom, he said, constituted 3 percent of the population, adding: "we do not target these people."[77] Shammari was displeased by the fact that the Shias were not part of the resistance against the Americans. Instead, he claimed that he had "evidence from the highest Shiite authorities" showing that they believed that the U.S. occupation "was considered an excellent and blessed action."[78] The clerics had not issued a single fatwa urging the Shias to carry arms against the U.S. forces.[79]

A year later in an interview with the magazine *al-Bayan*, Shammari discussed at length the IAI's views of the main U.S. objectives in invading and occupying Iraq and the state of relations between the Sunni resistance and the other Iraqi communities, and he refuted claims that the Baathists were playing a significant role in the insurgency. He asserted that the United States had two primary objectives in Iraq. The first was to ensure the fragmentation of Iraq as a favor to Israel and was part of "the opening stages of a game which aims at turning the region into a mosaic consisting of weak countries dominated by Israel."[80] This narrative was not new; it was adopted by the Islamists from Arab nationalist and left-wing sources and thinkers. The second U.S. objective was to loot Iraq's oil wealth and use it as part of a "project of building the new empire [that] will dominate the world."[81] This diatribe against Israel and neocolonialism was strikingly concordant with those of many of the nationalist Sunni Arab positions.

The views of IAI on the Shias and the Kurds are also interesting. No vile sectarian or ethnic invective was directed against them, as would have been expected. Instead, there seemed to be sadness, coupled with annoyance and resignation, concerning the stances of the two groups:

As for the Shiites, they have fallen between two fires; the fire of the
religious authorities, who heralded the occupation, and issued religious verdicts that call for cooperation with the occupation and
made its fighting unlawful, and the fire of the sectarian militias
which were trained in Iran and are loyal to it.... As for the Kurds,
they see in the occupation a blessing and call it liberation. Thus the
task of resisting the occupation has fallen on the shoulders of the
Sunnis alone... in spite of all that, we were not drawn into an ethnic
war with the Kurds or a sectarian war with the Shiite [sic]. That is
because we are keen that the enemy does not take advantage of
such wars.[82]

It is noteworthy that Shammari directed most of his invective at the
"Safavids," or "Iranian Shiism," and its "nefarious" political agenda, rather
than at Shiism as a sect per se. His pronouncements were appealing to
many Iraqi nationalists who were enamored neither with the Baath Party,
because it was such a manifest failure, nor with the hardline Islamists,
because of their extremism.

Transnational Salafi-Jihadists

The Iraqi Salafi-jihadists were not the only Salafist strain fighting in Iraq.
A group of foreign Salafi-jihadist fighters appeared in Iraq in mid-2003
and eventually grew to dominate the insurgency. This group, which went
through many confusing name changes, was the predecessor of IS. The
ideology that IS has embraced is usually labeled Salafi-jihadi; there is
no need to repeat here the fundamental premises of Salafi-jihadism discussed above.

The American occupation of Iraq prompted militant Islamists to offer
theories about why such an event took place and what it meant for the
umma. Yusuf al-Ayiri, a Saudi militant and cofounder of al-Qaeda in the
Arabian Peninsula, wrote a short tract before his death at the hands of
Saudi authorities. It was titled "The Future of Iraq and the Peninsula after
the Fall of Baghdad: Religious, Military, Political and Economic Prospects"
and was published within a larger study put out by an al-Qaeda entity
known as the Center for Islamic Studies and Research. Al-Ayiri wrote that
he was delighted that the invasion had led to the "collapse of the Arab
Baath" because it constituted the prelude to the "downfall of the nationalist, atheistic slogans that have invaded the Islamic nation.[83] It did not

matter that the collapse of the Baath Party came at the hands of "infidels," only that the end result would be its replacement by the "Islamic banner," which had been a source of resistance throughout history. The collapse of the Baathist regime was a godsend and an opportunity for the "Islamic banner to be raised on its ruins."[84] God, not the Americans, had denied the Baathists victory during the war because such a victory would have led to the dissemination and popularity of Baathist doctrine among Muslims.[85]

It would have been hard for Muslims to reject a party that had achieved such a great victory. Even more so, said Ayiri, because the party had begun to assimilate and adopt Islamic beliefs. Its message had changed from purely Baathist slogans to Baathist-Islamic ones, which presumably were sufficiently powerful to seduce many people. If the Baath had been victorious, this would have caused a huge fracture within the Islamic nation, he argued. A Baathist military victory would certainly have been less dangerous than the "Crusader" invasion. However, the Baath constituted a danger that threatened the beliefs of the umma, and it would have been difficult for the umma to wage war against it. What, asked Ayiri, were the true motivations for the "Zionist-Crusader" war being waged in Iraq? The invaders' motivations were to promote Christianity, "delink" Muslims from their faith, and enhance the security of Israel.

For al-Qaeda's leadership, battered by the American war against it in Afghanistan, Iraq was a heaven-sent opportunity to seek revenge. It was, however, more than that. Iraq came to be seen as the most important battleground in thwarting the "Zionist-Crusader" assault on Islam.[86] In 2002, on the eve of the assault on Iraq, al-Qaeda's then deputy leader, Ayman al-Zawahiri, elaborated at some length on what he believed was behind the coming U.S. move against Iraq.[87] For Zawahiri, the American campaign against Iraq in 2003 was designed to destroy any effective military force in the proximity of Israel. Its second aim was to consolidate the supremacy of Israel with weapons of mass destruction in the region without any rival. This, he added, was to "ensure that subjugation of the Arabic Islamic countries is completely to the wishes and greed of Israel."[88] Its third aim was to split the Arab world into smaller states that were incapable of protecting themselves.[89] He concluded by exhorting Muslims to fight in Iraq because the "Iraqi arena today is the most serious arena of jihad in this age. The nation must support the heroic mujahidin in Iraq who are fighting on the frontline for the sake of Islam's honor and might."[90] Al-Qaeda Central (AQC) could only rant and rave about the perceived iniquities of the American invasion and occupation of Iraq or write voluminous strategic studies on the topic, advising how Muslims must thwart this assault on Iraq.

It took an individual and his group, one on the margins of al-Qaeda but within the Salafi-jihadi constellation, to make his mark on the situation on the ground in Iraq: this was the Jordanian Ahmed Fadhil al-Nazal al-Khalayleh (1966–2006), or, as he is better known, Abu Musab al-Zarqawi, an unlikely candidate to be the first Pol Pot of the Salafi-jihadist world. I will henceforth refer to him simply as Zarqawi to avoid confusion over nomenclature.

Zarqawi: The Mastermind

The Islamic State, or the Caliphate, has occupied the attention of the international community for the past five years because of its military exploits, its efforts to build a state and "Islamic nation," and its genocidal brutality and terrorism. Its achievements in the arena of social media have also been noteworthy, as has its nihilistic destruction of the pre-Islamic heritage of Syria and Iraq, on account of their being *jahili* (non-Islamic or "ignorant"). To be sure, addressing IS as a structure—that is, as an organization, military group, and state-forming and nation-building entity—is absolutely critical to understanding it. However, what is often lost in the ever-multiplying quantity of analyses—some of it excellent and some of it less so—is an understanding or analysis of the key personalities involved in the forming, building, and sustaining of IS from its foundations to the present (mid-2017). Furthermore, whenever personalities are addressed, the focus, and rightly so, is on IS's current leader, Abu Bakr al-Baghdadi, the so-called Caliph Ibrahim. He is, after all, the man most responsible for IS's trajectory and actions since 2010. However, he is not the first leader of IS nor will he be, probably, the last. The purpose of this section is to rectify this lacuna by providing an analysis of the life, ideology, and exploits of IS's original mastermind, Zarqawi.[91]

The Trajectory of a "Born-Again" Muslim

The Islamic State has its origins in an obscure militant group that emerged out of the peripatetic activities of Zarqawi. Born on October 20, 1966, in the industrial city of Zarqa, he was a member of the Khalayleh clan of the Bedouin Bani Hasan tribe, one of the largest tribes in Jordan.[92] He was not a Palestinian, contrary to early U.S. government and some academic accounts. He dropped out of school in eleventh grade and worked as a low-level employee in the al-Zarqa municipality. Some reports have him entering the army in 1984 to do his national service, which is possible, given that the country had conscription until 1992. It is not clear, however, whether the professional Jordanian Armed Forces, which had stringent requirements, would have accepted Zarqawi as a conscript. After his supposed stint in the military, he seems to have led a dissolute life. He was arrested in 1987 for assault—invariably described as "sexual"—on a cousin, but his incarceration did not last long. A neighbor described Zarqawi before his turn to religion as follows: "He was so far away from religion. He went out with a gang that liked to drink. We even called him the Green Man because he had so many tattoos. He was drunk once and he had a fight with his cousin. He had a knife in his hand and he cut his cousin. After that he quit drinking, and he started praying."[93] The stories about his early, "sinful" youth may have been magnified in order to highlight his later supposedly new-found sense of religion. However, Zarqawi's trajectory from dissolute and indifferent youth to a jihadist with a purpose in life was not uncommon and was followed by many, including thousands, who joined IS in later years.

Following his release, Zarqawi began attending a local mosque in his hometown, allegedly on the advice of his mother. In an old interview that was released in early December 2006, after his death, he said that his turn to religion occurred in the late 1980s at the al-Hussein Bin Ali Mosque in al-Zarqa.[94] He added that his adherence to Islam was in the form of a general religious awakening and was not influenced by any one particular individual. The fundraising visit to Jordan by Afghan mujahidin commander Abdul Rasul Sayyaf, whose stories of the glorious and epic struggle of the outgunned mujahidin against the Soviets, apparently had an impact on the Jordanian neophyte.[95] The ideological exhortations of leading Salafi thinkers already on the ground in Afghanistan also influenced Zarqawi, as he himself put it: "During the time I spent with the brothers in the mosque, with the grace of God I attended group prayers. The brothers used to discuss the news of the jihad in Afghanistan. We used to receive audiocassettes recorded by Shaykh Abdallah Azzam, may he rest in peace. He had a great influence on my decision to engage in jihad. We also received issues of *al-Jihad* magazine and some video materials about combat operations. I decided to migrate...and I was only 23 years old."[96] As Zarqawi's awareness of current affairs developed in the late 1980s, he decided to travel to Afghanistan in December 1989 with a group of "Levantine" enthusiasts to participate in the jihad or "holy war" that the Afghan mujahidin had been waging for years against the Soviet occupiers of their country. Foreign fighters from far and wide, but especially from the Arab world, had flooded into Afghanistan in significant numbers to fight the "godless" Communist invasion of a Muslim land. The exploits of the mujahidin had reached the wider Muslim world, including Jordan, not through the Internet or social media, neither of which existed then, but as a result of the words, writings, and exhortations of Arab fighters.

Hudhayfah Azzam, the son of the famed Jordanian thinker and jihadist Abdullah Azzam, the man most responsible for bringing foreign fighters into Afghanistan to fight the Soviet occupation, met the group at the Peshawar airport. Hudhayfah's impression of Zarqawi appeared in an article in the *Atlantic* several years ago. In reference to Zarqawi's first stay in Afghanistan, Hudhayfah said: "He was an ordinary guy, an ordinary fighter, and didn't really distinguish himself."[97] Zarqawi arrived too late to participate in the anti-Soviet jihad. The long and costly Soviet effort to shore up a Marxist regime in Kabul had ended when the Soviet leadership told their Afghan allies that they were on their own and proceeded to withdraw their "limited" contingent of combat and support forces from Afghanistan between May 1988 and February 1989. Any fighting that was taking place when Zarqawi arrived was between the surprisingly resilient Marxist regime and its foes, the mujahidin, or among the various mujahidin insurgent organizations as they competed for dominance with one another. Zarqawi did fight at the battles of Khost and Gardez against the Communist regime that was on its last legs, and in April 1992 he witnessed the liberation of the capital, Kabul, by the Afghan mujahidin.

Zarqawi ended up in Peshawar, a logistics center for the Afghan mujahidin and the foreign fighters who helped them, including the thousands of "Arab Afghans." Zarqawi met the Palestinian-Jordanian intellectual Abu Mohammad al-Maqdisi (aka Isam Tahir al-Barqawi), a towering figure in Salafi-jihadist circles, at the Peshawar home of one of the leading Arab Afghans, Abu al-Walid al-Ansari, who was often confused with Abu al-Walid al-Masri (aka Mustafa Hamid). The date of the meeting is not certain, but most analysts think it was in 1990.[98] Zarqawi found work as a correspondent at *al-Bunyan al-Marsous* (The Solid Edifice), a jihadist magazine published in Arabic and Urdu in the Hayatabad neighborhood of Peshawar. Zarqawi eventually made his way into Afghanistan and allegedly received military training at Abdullah Azzam's Sada camp, run by the Maktab al-Khidamat (Office of Services).

After a brief sojourn in Pakistan and Afghanistan, Zarqawi returned to Jordan and looked up Maqdisi. According to Maqdisi, Zarqawi "expressed enthusiasm in support of tawhid and propagating the faith."[99] They started cooperating with one another and built up a group of like-minded jihadists to oppose the Jordanian state. Maqdisi and Zarqawi ran afoul of the authorities because of their extremism and alleged plots in conjunction with other radicals to embarrass the Jordanian monarchy by targeting neighboring Israel and committing other acts of violence within Jordan itself. The government arrested them, put them on trial, found them guilty, and imprisoned them separately, initially in various maximum-security prisons throughout the country.

Eventually, Maqdisi and Zarqawi found themselves incarcerated together in a notorious and remote prison.[100] Maqdisi was, without doubt, the leading luminary in this prison, which contained political prisoners of the Islamist persuasion. Not surprising, the "brothers" chose Maqdisi as the emir (leader) among them. Maqdisi stated that he held the position for a year and gave it up in order to focus on intellectual pursuits, such as writing and propagating "true" Islam among the "brothers," whose enthusiasm could not hide the fact that they were ideological neophytes when it came to "true" Islam. Maqdisi has written that he convinced the "brothers" to appoint Zarqawi as the leader of the prisoners and as the one individual to represent them vis-à-vis the prison administration. Maqdisi claimed that he stood solidly behind Zarqawi as emir "in the face of the enemy" and of those among the prisoners who disputed his appointment to leadership.[101] Maqdisi waxed lyrical about their relationship once Zarqawi had become leader: "I spared no effort to give him help and advice, since he asked me to do that before he succeeded me as amir [emir]. He also stood by my side in propagating the faith. He was compliant and enthusiastic about everything I wrote in support of tawhid and renunciation of polytheism. We were in agreement concerning the foundations of the Islamic jurisprudence....He admired my writings and supported them. He urged every young man whom he knew in jail and elsewhere to photocopy, read, and circulate them."[102] Others might convincingly argue that Maqdisi reluctantly conceded leadership to Zarqawi because of Zarqawi's ability to "understand" and more easily reach out to those who were uninitiated in Islamic ideology and related more readily to the more "down to earth" Zarqawi than the intellectual Maqdisi. Many of the incarcerated young men were either petty criminals or Islamist radicals whose level of literacy and education made them incapable of readily understanding the scholar.[103]

Released in a major amnesty program in 1999, Zarqawi returned to Afghanistan, where he eventually ran an Islamist training camp for jihadist militants from the Levant—Syria, Lebanon, Jordan, and the Palestinian territories. Maqdisi later claimed that he was unhappy about Zarqawi's decision to leave, along with a small group. He believed they were not focused or prepared. It seems that a gap began to open between Maqdisi the mentor and his protégé Zarqawi. Maqdisi claimed that he was extremely worried by the Jordanian jihadists' lack of strategy and organization when they left for Afghanistan, a lacuna that plagued them in that war-torn country.

Maqdisi's worry concerning the amateurishness and sloppiness of the Jordanian Salafists, such as Zarqawi, whom he saw as a ringleader in the migration of young Jordanians to Afghanistan, was upstaged by a growing ideological gulf between the two men that ended in mutual recriminations between 2004 and 2006. It was during his second stay in Afghanistan that Zarqawi eventually came under the influence of Abu Abdullah al-Muhajir (aka Mohammad Ibrahim al-Saghir).[104] A recent article referred to this man as the "obscure theologian" who has had the most ideological impact on the emergence of IS and by implication its predecessors, going back to the founding father, Zarqawi himself.[105] Getting hold of the writings or audio statements of Abu Abdullah al-Muhajir has been difficult, as has been establishing his current whereabouts. Rumors of his demise at the end of 2016 were much overblown and must have come as a surprise to him; apparently his pseudonym was confused with that of another jihadist who was a fighter, not an intellectual, and was killed in Syria. Abu Abdullah al-Muhajir the scholar is presumed to be either back in Egyptian custody or in Afghanistan. He is among the most extreme of the extremists in the Salafi-jihadist constellation, but even then, he has attained some stature, even though he is a long-winded intellectual, like his fellow Egyptian Zawahiri, the current leader of al-Qaeda. Zawahiri, however, has been quite cognizant of the fact that indiscriminate violence against Muslims, the "flock" whose "hearts and minds" the jihadists are seeking to win over, has backfired against them very badly in many places.

Similarly, Maqdisi was no moderate, but as I will show, he did put limits on aspects of the jihadists' operational methods, such as takfir, the excommunication of an individual Muslim or a whole community of them, thus legally allowing the spilling of their blood. The other operational method that began to cause controversy was suicide bombings, which many leading Salafi-jihadist thinkers came to believe were being overused and conducted in an indiscriminate manner. To put it briefly, Abu Abdullah al-Muhajir was not one for limitations on either method, and this suited Zarqawi admirably in his bloody war in Iraq. Indeed, Abu Abdullah al-Muhajir provided the intellectual justification for Zarqawi's own reign of mayhem in Iraq between 2003 and 2006.[106]

As America's confrontation with the regime of Saddam Hussein loomed in the period between 2001 and 2003, Zarqawi saw an opportunity to take a concrete stance against both of them in an emerging battlefield. He and his small network of jihadists made their way to northern Iraq, though not without difficulties, where they eventually set up the organization called Jamiat al-Tawhid wa al-Jihad, which ultimately evolved into IS, after several other intermediate names.

"Zarqawism" as a Salafi-Jihadi Ideology

Zarqawi was neither a political philosopher nor an articulate or polished scholar, unlike some of the key jihadists whom he admired or followed and then in the end fell out with. Moreover, given his lack of education, he could never have been an armchair scholar content merely with understanding the world and its ills. He wanted to take action to eradicate what he saw as the ills afflicting the umma. In this context, he did write several speeches and letters and gave a number of long and rambling interviews between 1994 and 2006, when the Americans killed him.[107]

Zarqawi saw the world in terms of a struggle between "good" and "evil." Naturally, Zarqawi and his followers—part of the vast jihadist constellation who referred to themselves as mujahidin—were on the side of good facing a vast pantheon of enemies who represented evil. In this existential struggle between Islam and its enemies, there is no gray, just black and white. Muslims who collaborate with the enemy *are* the enemy, and those who do not actively partake in the jihad against the enemy might as well be in the ranks of the enemy. If this binary division of the world affects families, so be it. In 2005, Zarqawi highlighted his belief in this grim and unforgiving approach and admitted that he knew that he and his supporters would be soundly condemned for excesses. He was unapologetic about it, justifying his stance by saying that Islam was facing the most dangerous set of enemies ever. In its latest manifestation, he argued, this fight between good and evil had started in Iraq with the American invasion of that country in 2003 and would terminate in Dabiq, a small village in Syria, in a cosmic apocalyptic end-of-days battle. But that was to come later; the more pressing issue was the war on the ground against a number of formidable and devious enemies and the perceived indifference of the vast majority of Muslims in the world. Who were these enemies and who were the indifferent Muslims?

Foremost in the lineup of enemies were what Zarqawi and most other Islamists referred to as the "Crusaders," or the West, at the head of which was its most powerful entity, the United States, the culprit behind the attack on Iraq. One of Zarqawi's first utterances concerning the situation in Iraq was an audio message in early April 2004 that was noteworthy for being his first list detailing the enemies of Islam and for threatening a series of attacks on the Americans in Iraq. It was primarily a polemical ideological diatribe against America's supposedly nefarious role in global politics and "history" of colonialism and "rampant capitalism." Sounding like a disgruntled and indignant Marxist of the 1960s, "America," said Zarqawi, "came with its fleets and mad dogs and settled in our homeland with its men and weaponry." America had many reasons for coming over to despoil Muslim lands, he continued.

First, America wanted to acquire the "resources and treasures" of Iraq, which was a rich land. These "resources and treasures" had "attracted the attention of bloodsuckers, the rich capitalists, whose lust for wealth has driven them to commit every dirty and mean act." Second, America had come to Iraq to change the people's culture and principles and "to spread its obscenity and vice and establish its decadent and ribald culture in the name of freedom and democracy." America wanted to change the political, religious, and cultural map of the region in accordance with its own interests and values. Third, Iraq had to be attacked, because according to the "Talmudic prophesies"—Zarqawi did not identify what these alleged prophesies were—which the rulers in Washington and London were following, Iraq "is the land of evil, whore city, and first enemy of the Israelites." These "prophesies" called for "killing Iraqis, raping their women, smashing the heads of their children and pouring death on their heads." Naturally, Zarqawi was quick to point out that this was what America and her allies were doing in Iraq.

Proceeding further with his anti-Western and anti-Semitic calumnies, fourth, argued Zarqawi, America invaded and occupied Iraq in order to "guarantee security for its Israeli protégé and eliminate any threat against it." Finally, Zarqawi believed that America had come to the Middle East to dismember the big Arab states and transform them into petty and mutually feuding "statelets." This situation would be to the benefit of Israel, which Zarqawi and other Islamists—whether radical or mainstream in many cases—believed had always been actively seeking to bring about the dissolution of the Arab states. Zarqawi claimed that Israel's political founding father and first prime minister, David Ben-Gurion, said "we are living in a Sunni region" and Israel had to cooperate with and promote the power of ethnic and sectarian communities to serve Israeli interests. Not surprising, according to Zarqawi, the "Israeli octopus has penetrated the country [Iraq] politically and economically through its intelligence men." It is not clear whether Ben-Gurion actually said what Zarqawi ascribed to him; however, when it was faced with the solid wall of unremitting Arab hostility to its existence and policies in the 1950s and 1960s, Israel did develop a strategy known as the periphery strategy, which was designed to seek friendship with peoples and states among the non-Arab states within the region or in the vicinity of the Middle East.

Scurrilous anti-Semitic and anti-Israel outpourings were common among the jihadists and the nationalist and Baathist elements of the insurgency. There were some subtle and nuanced differences in the views of nationalists and Baathist insurgents on the one hand and the Islamists on the other. For the Islamists, like Zarqawi, America's presence and actions in the Middle East in unfailing support of Israel were intended to hinder the unity of the umma, the Islamic world. For nationalists and Baathists in Iraq and, indeed, for nationalists in the wider Arab world, the American presence in the Middle East and specifically its occupation of Iraq was designed to thwart Arab nationalism, hinder Arab unity and cooperation, and fragment the Arab world into ministates. All of this was done for the benefit of Israel and the securing of American interests in the region and the wider Islamic world.

The second set of enemies of Islam was more problematic as far as Zarqawi was concerned; whereas the "Crusaders" and "Zionists," often abbreviated to the "Zionist-Crusader entity," represented the most formidable material enemy because of its global reach and financial and technological powers, the greatest and most insidious enemy of Islam lay intrinsically *within* the umma: the Shias, who had allegedly forsaken Islam and now followed another religion with strange dogmas and beliefs. That was the first strike against them in the minds of extremists like Zarqawi. The second strike against them was their history of acting as a "Trojan horse" whom the enemies of Islam, such as the Mongols long ago and America and Israel in the present, used as a tool with which to undermine Islam. The Shias, said Zarqawi, were the bigger threat because their history had unfailingly been one of betrayal of Islam; they had been, in his colorful and hateful words, "a thorn in the throat for the people of Islam and a dagger in their back. They are the fault that brings the bridge down and the bridge on which the enemies of the nation cross." Zarqawi's aversion to the Shias was not an uncommon sentiment among Salafi-jihadists, but differences eventually emerged between him and many others, including former mentors, concerning his violent actions against the Shias.

Zarqawi's statement of April 2004 was not the first verbal assault on the Shias and certainly not the most vitriolic. His venomous views of the Shias had already been apparent in a well-known letter he wrote to Osama bin Laden in February 2004 in which he more or less declared the Shias to be the primary enemy of Islam. The Rafida—the derogatory name for the Shias among many Sunnis because of their rejection of three of the four Rightly Guided Caliphs—"have declared a covert war on the people of Islam," in Iraq in conjunction with the American invaders. The Shias acted as the eyes and ears of the "Crusaders." Furthermore, since their empowerment they had taken over the Iraqi army, police, and security forces to advance their political agenda of consolidating power over the state and proceeding to "liquidate the Sunnis under the pretext that they are saboteurs, Ba'th remnants, and terrorists who seek to sow corruption on earth." Zarqawi's verbal histrionics against the Shias ended with one of the most often quoted statements made against them by a Salafist militant: "It [the Shia sect] is the biggest obstacle, the lurking serpent, the cunning and vicious scorpion, the waylaying enemy, and the deadly poison." As I will show, this depiction of the Shias as the enemy was translated with deadly effectiveness into a strategy of murderous violence against them.

Once Zarqawi had started on the Shias there was no stopping him. On May 18, 2005, a jihadist, "Abu Mohammad al-Kuthayri," posted to the Ana al-Muslim forum several links to an audiotape by Zarqawi titled "The Descendants of Ibn al-Alqami Are Back." Ibn al-Alqami, one may recall, was the Shia minister whom many Sunnis view as the traitor who surrendered Baghdad to the Mongols in 1258, leading to the downfall of the Abbasid caliphate. On this audiotape Zarqawi expressed his concern over the "Crusader"-aided rise of the Shia to power in Iraq. Indeed, whenever there was "any given war against Islam, [the Shias] were in the lead." Zarqawi goes back in history and argues that what Sheikh al-Islam [Ibn Taymiyya] said about the Shias is applicable today. In Zarqawi's words: "they were known for their loyalty to the Jews, Christians and polytheists....The rejectionists [Shias] have blessed the acts of the grandsons of pigs and monkeys [Jews and Christians] and helped them seize mosques, spread profanity, and humiliate Muslims in the Land of the Two Rivers [Iraq]." The purpose of Shiism as a religion and the goals of the Shia community, Zarqawi went on, were to destroy Islam by sowing sedition and discord within Islam and to help outsiders consummate the process of destruction that had been started from *within*. Ever since its emergence, he argued, Shiism had been an offensive tool and ideology designed to destroy Islam.

The third set of enemies of Islam against whom Zarqawi railed were the (Sunni) Muslims, specifically in Iraq, and the Muslims in general for their political immaturity and inability to rise to meet the challenges they were facing. Of course, the Muslim community was not an enemy of the mujahidin, the fighters who were defending Islam against its enemies. However, because of its "slumber," indifference, and poorly developed political awareness and level of mobilization, a state of affairs that has been the topic of vigorous discussion among jihadists, it might as well have been an ally of Islam's enemies. The enemies of Islam were able to engage in their evildoing, argued Zarqawi, because the leaders and scholars of the Muslim peoples had either been absent or had forsaken their religion for cheap material gains in this world, while the vast bulk of the people were either in "deep sleep" or blind to the dangers that Islam was facing.

From the moment he set foot in Iraq until his death in 2006, Zarqawi never stopped exhorting the Sunnis to battle the Shias. However, only a minority of "Muslims" have "awoken" to the "reality" that the Shias insult the Prophet Mohammad and His Companions, have "deviated" from Islam, and have a long history of betraying Islam to its enemies, such as the "Crusaders," Jews, Sassanians (the Iranian dynasty whose official religion was Zoroastrianism, which Islam supplanted), and Safavids (the Iranian dynasty that introduced Shiism as Iran's official religion). Zarqawi was frustrated by what he saw as the Sunnis' inability to understand and act against the dire threat facing them. The Sunnis were often totally oblivious of the treachery and deceptive nature of the Shias.

It was not surprising, then, according to Zarqawi, that resistance to the enemies of Islam had devolved upon the ranks of a small group of courageous individuals, the mujahidin, who were well aware that the odds were stacked against them because they were facing the "strongest and most advanced army in modern times." Zarqawi argued that although the mujahidin lacked the material resources their enemies enjoyed, they benefited from adherence to their religious mission. Furthermore, given the "huge disparity in numbers and armaments between them and the enemy," they had looked for ways to "amend this deficiency," and God had permitted them to use any methods necessary to fight and kill their enemies even if it meant that Muslims were killed in the process. It is clear here that Zarqawi was making a pitch for the "legitimacy" of suicide bombing ("martyrdom" operations), given the extensive debates among jihadist circles concerning the permissibility of and limitations on that specific tactic.

Despite all of the obstacles that faced the "righteous" mujahidin, Zarqawi believed that God was on the side of the mujahidin because He had granted them victories in the past against their enemies. Now, in Iraq it was time to up the ante and move forward. The future "work plan" that Zarqawi proceeded to elaborate was diabolical. He classed the enemies of Islam in Iraq into four categories: the Kurds were at the bottom of the list to be targeted for attack; their turn would come later. The Americans were easy prey because they were all over the country and their presence was hated. The "puppet" Iraqi state, particularly its security services, was an important target. The soldiers, police, and agents "are the eyes of the occupiers the ears with which they hear, and the hand with which they strike."

The center of gravity, though, was the fourth enemy, the Shia community. It is clear from Zarqawi's assessment of the Shias in his missive to bin Laden that he planned to foment sectarian war. He made the profound claim that "these people [the Shias] are the key to change" in Iraq. He told bin Laden that "targeting them and striking them in their religious, political, and military depth would provoke them and make them come out against the Sunnis, bare their fangs and bring out the internal hatred in their hearts." The Shias would then retaliate against the Sunnis, forcing the Sunnis to awaken from their "slumber" and to defend themselves. The logic was impeccable and diabolic: the Shias were the enemy, if they were provoked they would fight back, and when they fought back they would attack the Sunnis indiscriminately. The retaliation by the Shias would force the Sunnis to awaken from their "slumber" and solicit the help of the mujahidin to defend themselves.

By mid-2004, Jamiat al-Tawhid wa al-Jihad came out of the shadows and into the limelight. By then everyone in Iraq knew about this organization's bloody trail in Iraq, particularly after it undertook several shocking attacks that resulted in the deaths of hundreds of civilians and important figures (see chapter 5). Its goals were now also well known, and these were (1) to force a withdrawal of coalition forces from Iraq and to thwart what

Zarqawi and other Salafi-jihadists referred to as the "Zionist-Crusader" conspiracy in the umma; (2) to topple the Iraqi interim government; (3) to assassinate collaborators with the occupation regime; (4) to attack the Shia population and their clerics; and (5) to establish an Islamic state in which sharia would reign supreme—and ultimately to work toward the establishment of a caliphate.

In October 2004, Jamiat al-Tawhid wa al-Jihad claimed another surprise, but this one was different. Zarqawi officially pledged allegiance to Osama bin Laden's al-Qaeda network, adding a new organization to those supporting al-Qaeda.[108] The new organization, officially called Tanzim Qaedat al-Jihad fi Bilad al-Rafidain (Organization of the Base of Jihad in the Land of the Two Rivers) but more popularly known as al-Qaeda fi Bilad al-Rafidain, or al-Qaeda in Iraq (AQI), provided al-Qaeda with a ready-made base from which to strike the United States and garnered Zarqawi the prestige of being part of a brand name. This would draw recruits to his organization, and foreign fighters who would now know that they were fighting under the banner of the famous Osama bin Laden. For al-Qaeda, allying with Zarqawi was, on the face of it, a good thing. His organization had an established presence in Iraq and, it was presumed, good intelligence capabilities and situational awareness.[109] Finally, it had money, which meant that AQC would not have to fund it. Indeed, at one point AQC asked Zarqawi and AQI for money.

A few months after formally joining al-Qaeda, Zarqawi's organization issued its creed and methodology, in which it reiterated the mandate of jihad and the battling of infidels and the apostate Shias as declared by the Legal Council of the group on Al-Ansar.net, a jihadi website. Zarqawi did not see any reason to tone down his vituperative and venomous views of the Shias after becoming an affiliate of al-Qaeda. Al-Qaeda in Iraq expressed its determination to promote and defend *tawhid*—monotheism—and eliminate polytheism. Anyone who did not believe in the essential unity/oneness of God was an infidel and subject to takfir and death. The Prophet Mohammad was God's messenger for the entire human race. Al-Qaeda in Iraq viewed secularism—*ilmaniyya*—and all other isms, like nationalism, tribalism, communism, and Baathism, as "blatant violations of Islam." Jihad was the duty of all Muslims if the infidels attacked Muslims and their territories. Waging jihad against the enemies of Islam was next in importance to the profession of the *shahada*—faith. Al-Qaeda in Iraq argued that all Muslims—excluding the Shias, of course—constituted one nation. There was no differentiation between Arabs and non-Arabs: piety was what counted.[110] According to Abu Maysara al-Iraqi, then the chief spokesman of AQI, the goals were clear-cut and explicit:

- Removal of the "aggressor from Iraq"
- Affirmation of *tawhid*, or monotheism, among Muslims, and elimination of polytheism (Shiism)
- Waging of jihad to liberate Muslim territories from "infidels and apostates"
- Fighting the *taghut*—or tyrants—ruling Muslim lands
- "Establishing a wise caliphate" in which sharia would rule supreme as it did during the time of the Prophet Mohammad[111]

While the Bush administration deliberately injected sectarianism into the Iraqi body politic by apportioning positions and resources according to sect and ethnicity, the Salafi-jihadists bear the bulk of the blame for plunging the country into the nightmare of sectarian violence. Even the Sunnis in general cannot escape censure, due to their disdain for and fear of the Shias. Sunnis openly expressed derisive comments about the Shias to Western journalists, as in this representative comment by a Sunni in Baghdad: "Honestly, I prefer Saddam to the situation as it is now. There was security when he was here.... [The Shias] cannot rule Iraq properly. They cannot take charge of Iraqis in the same manner as the Sunnis. The Shi'a are backward. They are barbarian savages. They do not know the true religion; theirs is twisted, it is not the true religion of Muhammad."[112] Even though the vast majority of Sunni Arabs never shared Zarqawi's murderous intentions toward the Shias, their denigration and fear of that community had grown steadily over the years since the uprising in the south in 1991. Sunnis expressed their disdain more openly after the Shias' rise to power following the downfall of Saddam Hussein's regime.

The Shias reciprocated with contempt and indifference toward the insurgency. A number of Shias initially participated in it, especially in Diyala province, where a legendary Shia leader, Abbas al-Karbalai, who was killed by Salafists, led one of the insurgent units. The Shias turned away en masse when they saw the insurgency's true colors: a restorationist Baathist or Sunni extremist enterprise rather than a nationalist uprising against a foreign presence. The Shias knew that their time to partake in the spoils of power long denied them had come. Why spoil that opportunity to join what was manifestly a sectarian insurgency designed to restore Sunni privileges rather than a national insurgency out to get rid of the occupier? More reflective of their views were statements like that of

Sheikh Ahmed al-Saidi, a clerical scholar at the Hawza, the senior Shia clerical authorities in Najaf: "we represent power because the Shiites are the majority. We want a government that includes the Shiites."[113] By mid-2004, Shias' political power at the center in Baghdad, expressed in terms of dominating the political scene via their parties or militias, was no longer in doubt. The Shias, the numerical majority, were no longer the political minority.

Even though the insurgency was not a nationalist one, because it was limited largely to the Sunni community, it was nationwide. It was clear by 2006 that things were not going well in Iraq for the United States. The U.S. military was struggling in the war against the insurgents, who, despite their disunity, seemed to be ensconced in every nook and cranny of the Sunni Arab–majority areas and were able to inflict violence in Shia and mixed sectarian areas as well. While sectarian cleansing had already started, what propelled it further was the crowning achievement of Zarqawi's terrorist campaign: the bombing of the al-Askari Mosque in Samarra, which contains the tombs of two imams of the Shia faith, in February 2006. Shia fury was unleashed, and a full civil war was on, with ethnic cleansing and mass killings by both sides.

The Bush administration was facing a no-win situation in Iraq and had to call upon outside expertise in order to find a way out of the morass. Ultimately, they were saved by two distinct but separate factors. First, upon advice that they received from serving military officers, retired officers, and civilian strategists, the administration implemented an effective counterinsurgency strategy and dispatched more troops to Iraq in an approach known as the Surge.[114] Second, the violence between Sunni and Shia, which Zarqawi's group had instigated and had led to a virtual civil war, resulted in the dissipation of the Sunni insurgency's efforts to fight the Americans as it diverted its energies to defending the Sunni community from attacks by Shia death squads and ultimately to fighting the jihadists of Zarqawi's organization. Even before the upsurge in Sunni–Shia violence, many people—from the leadership of al-Qaeda to that of the Iraqi insurgency—had begun to question Zarqawi's strategy and methods. After the outbreak of the full-scale civil war, which the Sunnis lost to the Shia, the insurgency, in effect, fractured.

The Onset of the Rift between Zarqawi and al-Qaeda

Zarqawi's tactic of inflicting mass civilian casualties, particularly against the Shias—earning him the sobriquet "sheikh of the slaughterers"—aroused grave concern among many jihadists, not because of any liking for the Shias but because they viewed the tactic as a threat to the jihadist enterprise. Zarqawi's obsession with committing spectacular acts of savagery against the Shias began to worry leading Salafist thinkers outside the conflict zone and AQC's senior leadership, who were soon reminded of the self-destructive path of the Algerian Salafists in their bloody war with the Algerian state in the 1990s.

By 2004, Maqdisi, Zarqawi's erstwhile mentor, had already begun to show concern over Zarqawi's excesses in Iraq:

> Beware of complacency on what we used to be strict about regarding the protected status of Muslim blood, money, and honor, even if they were mutineers or wantons: shedding protected blood is one of the predictors of doomsday. We have studied and taught in the chapters of creed that allowing the bloodshed of Muslims is a grave danger, and that making the mistake of letting a thousand infidels go free is better than shedding a few drops of the blood of one Muslim.... I say this and stress it while I hear and follow the huge chaos happening today in Iraq, by which they want to distort jihad and its bright image through blowing up cars, placing explosives on public roads, and shelling streets, markets, and other Muslim public places with mortar and similar shells. The clean hands of mujahidin should be protected from being tarnished with the blood of the protected people.[115]

In July 2005, differences in opinion concerning the jihad in Iraq erupted between Maqdisi and Zarqawi. Maqdisi started by trying to defuse in advance any potential negative fallout from his critique by stating that Zarqawi was in "dire need for advice," particularly following the loss of his dear friend, spiritual advisor, and operational commander Abu Anas al-Shami (aka Omar Yusuf Jumaa) in September 2004 in a U.S. missile strike near Abu Ghraib.[116] In Maqdisi's "Message of Support and Advice," published on his website, Minbar al-Tawhid wa al-Jihad, he advised Zarqawi to stop targeting civilians, churches, and Shias. Maqdisi told Zarqawi that he must not confuse his days of "leading" a prison group with the heavy responsibilities associated with leading an armed organization. The requirements for setting up "armed organized action" were stringent, and amateurishness led to operational mistakes and either the capture or killing of operatives. Maqdisi also told Zarqawi that he must listen to the opinions of the ulema, particularly as they related to the use of suicide or "martyrdom" operations.

The ulemas' strictures against indiscriminate and widespread use of suicide operations must be adhered to by all jihadist organizations.[117]

Zarqawi responded shortly thereafter on July 12, 2005, that the advice was unfair and firmly reiterated his views.[118] He claimed to have been pained that criticism was directed at him from a "man who is considered to be a supporter of our path."[119] The Shias were rejectionists and apostates, and Zarqawi stipulated that fighting them was more important than fighting non-Muslims. In response to Maqdisi's admonitions, Zarqawi blamed the Shias for the vicious sectarian conflict, stating mendaciously that it was not his group that had initiated fighting with them. Rather, it was the Shias who had started attacking the Sunni community, killing the innocents, destroying homes, and taking over Sunni mosques.[120] Zarqawi pushed back against Maqdisi on the controversial matter of suicide ("martyrdom") operations, which Zarqawi's organization had used liberally in Iraq to kill thousands of people. Maqdisi had expressed unease concerning their extensive use and had intimated that Zarqawi's position had initially been one of disapproval of such an operational method. Zarqawi stated that Maqdisi had misrepresented him. Yes, at one point Zarqawi's position toward "martyrdom" operations had been similar to that of the scholar. However, Zarqawi recounted, after his own return to Afghanistan for the second time, his views on the permissibility of "martyrdom" operations had changed, because:

> there I met Sheikh Abu Abdullah al-Muhaajir and we discussed the matter of martyrdom. He considered it permissible, and I read an excellent paper by him on the subject and I listened to some of his tapes as well....Not only did I see that they [martyrdom operations] are permitted but I was convinced that they are desirable. I proceeded then to arrange for Sheikh al-Muhaajir to give a 10-days [sic] workshop in Hirat [sic] Camp to explain the legality of these operations to the brothers there—this had a very positive impact on the brothers.[121]

Even AQC voiced concern over Zarqawi's tactics in Iraq, particularly in relation to the targeting of innocent civilians and the pathological obsession with the Shia enemy. Simply put, for AQC Zarqawi's strategy of causing mayhem to prevent the Americans from consolidating their occupation of Iraq was excellent; however, his strategy of fomenting a civil war among Iraqis of different sects was bad and a potentially fatal distraction from the jihad against the Americans.

The second in command of AQC, Zawahiri, sent a letter to Zarqawi on July 9, 2005, that was intercepted by U.S. forces. In the letter, Zawahiri expressed total agreement with the goals of the jihadist military efforts in Iraq but added that AQC had grave reservations with Zarqawi's modus operandi. The jihadists could not win unless they won the hearts and minds of the Muslim (Sunni) masses and ulema. More locals—Iraqis— needed to be the face of AQI. The Taliban in Afghanistan had lacked popular support; hence they had succumbed. Zawahiri agreed with Zarqawi that the Shias could not be trusted but did not feel that it was necessary to slaughter them. He believed that it was alienating Muslims at large and distracting jihadists from fighting the Americans. The conflict with the Shias, he believed, could wait. He also believed that Zarqawi's public displays of brutality, such as beheading hostages, were ineffective and bad public relations.

In September 2006, three months after the Americans killed Zarqawi, the Iraqi government released a letter that had been written by one Attiya abd al-Rahman (better known as Attiyatullah al-Libi, killed in a U.S. drone strike in 2011), a senior al-Qaeda operative, offering advice to Zarqawi, that had been intercepted on the way to him. The letter began by praising Zarqawi and his "campaign" in Iraq but also sought to persuade Zarqawi to "remedy shortcomings and guard against flaws and errors."[122] Attiya wrote that because Zarqawi was a public figure and had attracted global attention, what he and his group did and how they did it would have a wide impact. Patience was important, said Attiya, because this was a protracted war, that is, it would take a long time and witness victories and setbacks. The enemy the mujahidin were fighting "is resilient," and victory for the mujahidin would come only with the "triumph of principles and values" against this enemy.[123] Attiya argued that in war policy and the goals that flowed from policy dominate military action; this fact, he pointedly remarked, was known to all nations whether Muslim or "infidel." Sounding almost Clausewitzian in his approach, Attiya emphasized that "military action is a servant to policy."[124] Attiya warned Zarqawi not to become too confident by small and incremental successes in the jihad against the enemy, as such ephemeral successes led to overconfidence and mistakes.

Furthermore, he warned him to be "watchful of your mistakes, however small, for if mistakes pile up upon you, they will destroy you."[125] Attiya advised Zarqawi not to repeat the mistakes of the jihadists in Algeria in the 1990s who had massacred thousands of people for no logical reason. They managed to alienate the vast majority of the Algerian people and allowed the government to recover from its own mistakes and successfully turn the tide against the jihadists. The jihadists in Algeria, stated Attiya, succeeded in destroying themselves with their own hands because of their irrationality and their delusions, ignoring the needs of the people and alienating them with their severity and bloodthirstiness. It was not surprising, then, that "their enemy did not defeat them, but rather they defeated themselves, were consumed and fell."[126] The "tragedy" of the mujahidin in Algeria, whose defeat came largely as a result of their own mistakes and hubris, was an event that jihadist writers and thinkers could not help but compare with the collapse of the first jihadist effort in Iraq because of Zarqawi's mistakes. Attiya may have been the first to point out the similarities between the two efforts at opposite ends of the Middle East, but he was certainly not the last. Indeed, the excesses of Zarqawi's successors, particularly Abu Bakr al-Baghdadi's IS, would once again force jihadists to point to the unwelcome example of the failed Algerian jihad.

Attiya ended his letter by telling Zarqawi to adhere to the following guidelines: (1) do not make any major decisions without consulting with al-Qaeda leadership, for example, announcing a comprehensive war against the Shia "turncoats" or "expanding the arena of the war" to neighboring countries (presumably a reference to Zarqawi's bloody operation in Amman, the Jordanian capital), and (2) consult with members of the Sunni community, such as the religious scholars and the tribes, even if they are "religiously unorthodox at times, or even hypocritical."[127] Attiya warned Zarqawi against the killing of religious scholars and tribal sheikhs, who were respected within the Sunni community, encouraging him to (3) embrace the people and win their hearts; this would add to the mujahidin's ranks and aid in their fight against the enemy.

From the Mujahidin Shura Council to the Islamic State of Iraq

It is not clear what impact AQC's expression of concern had, but in January 2006 AQI created an umbrella organization called the Mujahidin Shura Council (MSC) in an attempt to unify Sunni insurgents in Iraq.[128] A jihadist website, Hanein.net, posted a statement attributed to the media spokesman for AQI in which he claimed that the MSC consisted of key combatant groups that had joined with AQI to manage better "the battle of confrontation" with the occupiers and their "stooges," and to ensure that they, "hold fast, all together, by the rope which Allah stretches out for you and be not divided among yourselves."[129] The statement concluded by urging all groups to unite under the banner of MSC in this crucial phase of the battle. The MSC also claimed some groups as part of this new organization, much to their chagrin.

It is also possible that Zarqawi was preparing to declare an Islamic state in 2006. If he was leaning that way, he did not live to implement such a plan. After months of painstaking intelligence work in collaboration with the Jordanians, Zarqawi was traced to a house in the nondescript village of Hibhib in the northern part of Diyala province. An aerial strike by the U.S. military killed him on June 7, 2006. A top AQI operative, Abu Hamza al-Muhajir (aka Abu Ayub al-Masri; not to be confused with Abu Abdullah al-Muhajir, mentioned earlier) was promoted to the positions of new emir of AQI in Iraq and chief coordinator for all the groups within the umbrella MSC. On June 13, 2006, Abu Hamza al-Muhajir issued a statement in which he vowed to follow in the footsteps of his predecessor, Zarqawi, and to maintain allegiance to bin Laden. Given the unease with which the senior al-Qaeda leadership was beginning to view Zarqawi's modus operandi in Iraq, this was going to be a difficult promise to keep. Abu Hamza al-Muhajir was no different from Zarqawi in his ideological rigidity, particularly vis-à-vis the Shia community: "To the grandchildren of al-Alqami we say: Oh, you polytheists, who insulted the honor of the best of the Messengers, cursed the venerated companions, and devoted yourselves to serve the Crusaders. We shall implement on you the verdict of Abu Bakr al-Siddiq in his fight with the apostates, and we shall continue what our Shaykh Abu Mus'ab, may God have mercy on him, has started with you. We shall fight you until the word of monotheism is supreme and the word of your idols becomes worthless."[130] He then addressed himself to bin Laden and told him that AQI was waiting "for your directives" and that the organization's members "are at your disposal. The good news is that the morale of your soldiers is very high. They are proud to be serving under your banner."[131] This was hyperbole; the efforts to recruit Iraqi Sunni nationalists and secular groups continued to be undermined by the violent tactics it used against civilians in its zeal to implement its vision of Islam. The tepid reaction of Sunni groups to the emergence of the MSC and the scramble of a number of them to point out that they had not been consulted about its formation or alleged inclusion in this umbrella group dismayed the post-Zarqawi top leadership of AQI .

They decided to up the ante dramatically. On October 15, 2006, the Media Council of the MSC issued an eight-minute statement declaring the founding of the Islamic State of Iraq (ISI) under the leadership of Abu Omar al-Baghdadi (aka Hamid Dawud al-Zawi, a former policeman from Haditha who had been cashiered from his position during the time of the regime of Saddam Hussein for radical tendencies). Abu Hamza al-Muhajir, who was relegated to a position subordinate to the new emir, euphorically declared that the mujahidin had "reached the end of a stage of jihad and the start of a new one, in which we lay the first cornerstone of the Islamic Caliphate project and revive the glory of religion."[132] The condition of the Sunnis "has become the same as the condition of the orphans on the table of wicked people."[133] Thus it had become necessary to establish an Islamic state to protect the Muslim religion and its people. The statement quoted Ibn Taymiyya's view that governing the people's affairs "is one of the greatest of duties and that religion and life cannot thrive without this duty. People cannot serve their interests unless they get together for they need each other, and when they get together they should select a leader."[134] Establishing an Islamic state was based on the example of the Prophet's migration from Mecca to Medina, where he established the state of Islam. Abu Hamza al-Muhajir reinforced the point that the organization had established control over many areas, "which have an area equal to the size of the first state of Medina."[135] The conditions for an Islamic state were propitious, argued Abu Hamza al-Muhajir, because according to him and the other leadership of the new state, the enemies of the nascent Islamic state had no control over the areas in Iraq in which the said state had been set up. Indeed, he crowed, ISI had more viability than the so-called Palestinian state under the Palestine Liberation Organization, whose legitimacy and sovereignty Israel undermined every day and at every opportunity.

Abu Hamza al-Muhajir insisted that the mujahidin had implemented sharia—governance and administration in accordance with God's law—at the demand and persistence of the Sunnis themselves. This new state would decisively "confront any attempt to infringe on Sunnis with the strongest, hardest, and most harmful unlimited response."[136] Abu Hamza al-Muhajir promised that ISI would march on Baghdad, which was "the land of the Khilafah" (Caliphate) and had been "built by our forefathers and will not be taken from us but over our remains and skulls. We shall reinstate the flag of monotheism, the flag of the state of Islam, in it anew."[137] Finally, he called upon "all of Iraq's mujahidin, clergymen, chieftains, and Sunnis to pledge allegiance to the amir [emir] of believers," the "virtuous" Sheikh Abu Omar al-Baghdadi, to obey him in "good and bad times" and to work hard to strengthen the Islamic state and to be prepared to sacrifice themselves and their possessions for its sake.

Shortly after the proclamation of ISI, the leadership launched a media campaign to promote the new entity. Combining coverage in mainstream media and on jihadist websites, this campaign conferred to the brand-new, self-styled state the trappings of sovereignty, ministries (including a Ministry of Fisheries, as if that were a prime concern for an organization under increasing military pressure), a legal system, and security forces. In May 2007 Othman Abd al-Rahman, head of the new state's Sharia Council, declared that the most important tasks and duties of ISI were to spread monotheism on earth and cleanse it of polytheism; to repulse the "aggressors"; to govern according to the laws of God; to provide for the martyrs, for prisoners' families, and for those in need; and to support the fighters. The intent was to show that the entity was moving beyond representing a revolutionary ideology to becoming a full-fledged state.[138]

The Islamic State of Iraq proved to be a catastrophic failure ideologically. Few were seduced by its pretenses of being a state; even the wife of Abu Omar al-Baghdadi allegedly took her husband to task for bringing the family out into the desert. The declaration of a state caused massive confusion within the jihadist constellation. To be sure, the declaration was met with joyous celebrations by some jihadists who saw it as the logical step toward the revival of the long-hoped-for caliphate. However, this did not prevent more serious thinkers from wondering what was the nature of this entity: was it an *imara*, or emirate, that is, a state within an Islamic empire or state, which did not as yet exist? Or did its leadership seriously believe that this was a state, *dawla*, that is, the stepping-stone toward a caliphate? If so, who authorized them to declare a state? Who was this mysterious and largely unseen emir Abu Omar al-Baghdadi? What were his qualifications and who "elected" him? Furthermore, what was the relationship of this state to AQC and to the leader of the Taliban, Mullah Omar?

Another matter that concerned many jihadists, particularly within the AQC leadership, was Abu Hamza al-Muhajir's alleged obsession with millenarian and apocalyptic thinking. One of ISI's first senior defectors, Suleiman al-Oteibi (killed by a U.S. drone strike in early 2008 in Paktika province on Pakistan's border with Afghanistan), the senior judge on ISI's Sharia Council, was removed from his position for transgressions that ISI never fully clarified. It is possible that he had expressed reservations about ISI's trajectory. In any event, he wrote a letter to AQC in which he claimed (falsely) that there was no Abu Omar al-Baghdadi; he was just a fictitious figure. Al-Oteibi remarked on significant organizational weaknesses and failures (true) of ISI: for example, subordinate leadership's unwillingness to convey bad news to the top leadership and rerunning old footage of jihadist attacks as if they were fresh ones.[139] He also claimed that Abu Hamza al-Muhajir was obsessed with apocalyptic and millenarian thinking and had declared the establishment of ISI in anticipation of the apocalypse, which he claimed would occur a year later. While the quest to revive the Islamic state and apocalyptic thinking were not mutually exclusive, in that one can hold beliefs about the desirability of both simultaneously, mainstream Islamic thinking, even within jihadist circles, had tended to eschew thinking about the end of days. For AQC it was distasteful and a diversion from the material conflict on the ground between Islam and its "real" and deadly foes.[140]

The sparring between ISI and other jihadists over the matter of the proclamation of an Islamic state and the peculiar adherence of some of its leaders to apocalyptic thinking paled in comparison with the massive ideological and other (material) rifts between it and the rest of the Iraqi insurgency. This external pressure on the entity, which took advantage of its internal problems, along with the maturation of U.S. counterinsurgency techniques and increasing political savvy to mobilize groups against ISI, proved to be the final nail in the coffin of the first Islamic state experiment of 2006–2010. For Iraqi Islamist insurgent groups, the proclamation of ISI by the jihadists was the final straw. This was not because they theoretically or ideologically opposed the concept of a state. Rather, and here they pointed more to the material and concrete problems of ISI, it was not a propitious time to be declaring a state when the focus should be fighting off the enemy and expanding and consolidating control over people and territory. Moreover, who had granted foreign fighters the legitimacy to dictate the political goals of the jihad against the enemy? Indeed, even the Iraqi Islamists were quite nationalistic, in the sense that they believed that they should be at the helm of the insurgency and that it should focus on restoring Iraqi sovereignty and independence. Higher ideological goals should wait.

The Insurgency Rifts

The now wide-open rift between ISI on the one hand and the local Iraqi insurgents on the other can only be understood within the context of the

structural vulnerabilities and inherent weaknesses of a movement composed of myriad groups. The insurgency was fractured and suffered from
rampant incoherence in terms of ideologies, end goals, strategies, operational methods, and tactics from day one. The relations between the five
different strands of the insurgency were complex and often characterized
by profound differences over ideology, objectives, modus operandi, and
policy toward the mainstream Sunni political parties and, of course, the
U.S.-led Coalition and the Shia-dominated governments since 2004.
There were two distinct splits within the insurgency. The first pitted the
mainstream insurgents against the transnational Salafists. The second
and concurrent split occurred between the tribes and the transnational
Salafists.

The Rift between the Iraqi Insurgents
and the Islamic State of Iraq

Cracks were already evident even in 2004 in Fallujah, where the local
Iraqi insurgents, despite the show of unity against the Americans, had
differences with AQI under Zarqawi over turf, resources, and application
of Islamic codes. The local groups and Zarqawi's organization initially
tried to ignore these cracks or smooth things over in the interest of unity
and coordination in the fight against the Americans. However, as 2004
turned into 2005 it became readily apparent that the gulf between the
Iraqi groups and Zarqawi's organization concerning ideology, modus operandi, and goals was too wide to close. More insurgents began openly
expressing their concerns about his modus operandi in early 2005. An
insurgent leader, "Abu Thub" (Father of the Wolf), was extensively interviewed by a British journalist in October 2005. He was not fond of the
Americans, saying: "When the infidel conquers your home, it's like seeing
your women raped in front of your eyes and like your religion being
insulted every day."[141] At the same time, he expressed a willingness to ally
with these very enemies against AQI. For him, AQI was practicing a false
form of Islam because in their extreme view "anyone who doesn't follow
the Koran literally is a Kaffir—apostate—and should be killed. This is
wrong."[142] It was wrong, too, of AQI to call for the establishment of a caliphate. For this Iraqi operational commander, it was a question of being
pragmatic and flexible. He argued that since "the resistance now is made
up of nationalist and religious elements," by calling for a caliphate "you
will alienate not only the resistance but the support we get from Syria and

the Gulf countries."[143] He concluded that AQI's assault on the Shias was a strategic disaster, because the attacks on the Shias and their religious institutions had succeeded in turning that community into an enemy of the insurgency. The attacks on the Shias had also diverted the attention of the insurgency away from the American enemy.[144]

By the time AQI had transformed itself into ISI, a wide gap between the Iraqi insurgents, of all stripes, and AQI was already in full bloom. Major Sunni insurgent groups had already begun cutting their ties to AQI.[145] The rupture between AQI and the Iraqi insurgent groups emerged as a result of conflict over turf and resources, the targeting of civilians, and AQI's efforts to impose its strict values. Despite AQI having a large number of Iraqis within its ranks, its dominance—as a foreign entity—within the ranks of the insurgency rankled among the Iraqi insurgents. Finally, the transformation from AQI to ISI, in other words the declaration of an Islamic state, confirmed among the more nationalist-minded insurgents that this was a foreign entity with its own agenda beyond and above the welfare of Iraq. For the Islamists, the declaration of the Islamic state was premature. Vehement expression of opposition to ISI, whether verbal or violent, by most of the Iraqi groups was not long in coming.

The General Command of the Iraqi Armed Forces, a small Baathist group composed largely of former officers, had initially adopted an attitude of live and let live with the AQI jihadist fighters and even cooperated and exchanged expertise and resources, but it split with AQI in September 2006 after AQI assassinated two of its members in Anbar province. "Abu Marwan," a spokesman for the General Command of the Iraqi Armed Forces, detailed the factors behind the split: "al-Qaeda killed two of our best members, the general Mohammad and General Sa'ab, in Ramadi, so we took revenge and now we fight al-Qaeda."[146] The violence between the two groups intensified after the announcement of ISI. The struggle between the Baath and its affiliates versus ISI grew more venomous in November 2006. Fierce firefights broke out between the Baathist al-Awda (The Return) and ISI in the western regions of Anbar province, where ISI gunmen distributed flyers threatening to execute anyone from the al-Awad tribe, whose menfolk constituted the mainstay of al-Awda. The Islamic State of Iraq killed several more insurgent commanders who were high-ranking officers from the former Iraqi army.[147]

The common ideological foundations of the local Salafists and the foreign Salafi-jihadists of ISI did not prevent conflicts from erupting.

A 1920 Revolution Brigades member with the nom de guerre "Haj Mohammad Abu Bakr" acknowledged to an Arab journalist that at one point the two groups had had a common goal of resisting and expelling the occupation but added that at present "we have some disagreements with al-Qaeda [AQI], especially about targeting civilians, places of worship, state civilian institutions and services."[148] Mahmud al-Zubeidi, the spokesman for the 1920 Revolution Brigades, said that the 1920 Revolutionary Brigades did not target innocent civilians and focused its efforts on fighting the occupier and its collaborators.[149] When asked by the journalist whether the brigades agreed with AQI on operations against the U.S.-led Coalition but disagreed with it on the killing of innocent civilians, Zubeidi answered: "Yes, exactly."[150]

The establishment of ISI by Zarqawi's successors widened the ideological rift. An Iraqi insurgent commander, Jihad al-Ansari, founder of the Ali Ibn Abi Talib Brigade and the al-Marsad Brigade, posted a letter on a popular jihadist website addressed to the ISI in general and to the purported leader of the ISI, Abu Omar al-Baghdadi, in December 2006. Titled "The Solid Structure," the statement questioned ISI's call for allegiance and the appointment of Abu Omar al-Baghdadi as leader without consultation. It was not received well by the ISI-affiliated groups. In March 2007 al-Ansari followed with "After the Solid Structure," in which he criticized the ISI for ignoring his call for clarifications and instead launching into a tirade. He accused AQI of taking the unilateral and harmful step of setting up the ISI without consultation with other groups:

> Four months have passed since you one-sidedly started the project of your state, thereby dispensing with everyone around you. We say frankly that matters have deteriorated in the interim in a way that we never wanted to happen. This step of yours, which you have attempted to secure by every means, has caused innumerable negative results that have harmed the jihadists as a class and hurt the reputation of jihad and mujahidin. One of the most serious and prominent repercussions of your one-sided step has been that many of your groups and organization members, desiring to confirm your authority over Muslims in Iraq, have presumed to attack one and all and have continued to incite [hostility] against anyone who abstains from swearing allegiance to you.... We say all this, knowing that the organization didn't use[d] to be the way it is today. However, your headstrong effort to gather individual mujahidin to your banner,

thinking that this would strengthen the power of your organization and facilitate the independent proclamation of your state, is precisely what has made your organization adopt horizontal expansion (quantity) at the expense of vertical expansion (quality). This has had the dangerous effect of summoning every ignorant and unprincipled individual to join your "state."

If, as you maintain, the majority of people have sworn allegiance to your emirate, why are disagreement with you and dissent constantly increasing? Don't you see that the gap, despite the many people around you, is widening and growing, the more effort you make to insist on your project?[151]

The rejection of ISI's goals and modus operandi was widespread. In a panel discussion on al-Arabiya TV, in April 2007, Zubeidi, the official spokesman for the 1920 Revolution Brigade, stated that there were differences between his group and ISI. They had launched attacks on the 1920 Revolution Brigades. Having stated that "they [AQI/ISI] are our brothers and they beset the enemy grievously" and that both sides agreed that they must work to "kick the aggressor and those collaborating with it out of the country," Zubeidi added that the 1920 Revolution Brigades was "against them regarding the killing of civilians, bombings, indiscriminate attacks, and attacks on the mujahidin groups in the country."[152]

The most outspoken foe of ISI was the influential Salafist insurgent organization the IAI, which issued a litany of complaints against ISI. On April 5, 2007, a jihadist website posted a statement by IAI'S leader, "Abu Azzam," in which he accused ISI of murdering thirty of its combatants and commanders. It warned ISI to soften its stance toward the other jihadist groups and appealed to bin Laden to take legal and moral responsibility for an organization that the IAI leaders believed was running amuck. In a swipe at the type of men in Zarqawi's network, IAI stated that it relied on the "authority of the men of learning, wisdom, experience, and precedence."[153] The Islamic Army of Iraq contrasted itself with Zarqawi's organization, which it believed had veered away from true Islam in its murderous actions and its disdain for the community leaders. The Islamic Army of Iraq pointedly criticized the practice of takfir and insisted that it did not accept declaring that someone had become an infidel without proof or evidence. Even if an action was proven to be one of unbelief, not "everyone who commits an act that renders [him or her] infidel has actually committed infidelity."[154] The Islamic Army of Iraq stressed that it had chosen to be patient and cautious in the face of ISI's provocations and mistakes, preferring instead to advise and persuade others to mend their ways.[155] However, the transgressions of AQI and its successor, ISI, such as the indiscriminate killing of Muslims, particularly "soft" targets like civilians and clergy, and the seizure of people's property, had become too great to ignore.[156] Abu Omar al-Baghdadi, in IAI's view, had offended against the entire umma and against the Salafi movement and its scholars by "pronouncing amazing judgments and rulings" that baffled and disturbed everyone in the resistance.[157]

"Abu Azzam" statement contained three distinct appeals: (1) to the religious scholars to issue rulings that would put the jihad project back on the right track. They must not stay silent in the face of ISI's transgressions. "God," says the statement, "has put them under obligation to clarify the truth"; (2) to bin Laden: "Let him vindicate his religion and honor and take legal and organizational responsibility for the al-Qaida organization.... It is not enough to disown actions; the course must be corrected"; (3) to "everyone affiliated with al-Qaida.... Let them examine their souls and fear God."[158]

Almost a year after his first verbal assault on ISI, the leader of IAI delivered another onslaught in which he expressed anger at ISI's excessiveness, which, he said,

> has caused great damage to jihad and the people due to the wrong policies it carried out.... The jihadist arenas in the occupied countries like Iraq are fertile ground for excessiveness for many reasons, including the absence of any united Muslim group; rather there are many groups, parties and blocs; the spread of ignorance in the religion and jihad issues in particular; and the almost nonexistent impact of the scholars and imams on the conduct of jihad.
>
> The disagreement between us and the Shiites is one of creed, and at the social level, we support any social accord that is in the interest of religion and the country through expelling the occupation and remedying the injustice inflicted on the people.... We call on the *Arab* Shiites and the entire people to reject the occupation in all its shapes and forms and not to go along with the ambitions of the Safavids. Iraq is an *Arab* and Islamic country and we cannot ignore this fact by any means.[159]

"Abu Azzam" stated that IAI had cooperated with AQI and then initially with ISI when insurgent armed action was targeting the U.S. forces.

However, when ISI deviated from the legitimate path, the Iraqi organizations (IAI and the other big insurgent groups) distanced themselves from it and were now bitterly fighting it in all areas of Iraq.[160] "Abu Azzam" stated that some of the Iraqi insurgent leaders had met with Zarqawi at the beginning and suggested that they form a unified organization headed by an Iraqi. However, Zarqawi, according to "Abu Azzam," went off on his own and formed an organization in which he distributed key roles to his closest followers.

A former senior member of IAI by the name of Abu Azzam al-Tamimi, hit the nail on the head when he suggested that one of the key reasons for the falling out between the Iraqi insurgent groups on the one hand and ISI on the other was the Iraqi insurgent groups growing dislike of foreigners being in charge of the insurgency.[161] He was voicing the opinion of many Iraqi insurgent leaders when he said: "no non-Iraqi has the right to lead a group in Iraq. The leaders of the major factions objected to Abu Musab or other non-Iraqis leading groups in Iraq. Any non-Iraqi coming to Iraq for jihad should operate under the supervision of Iraqis."[162] To reinforce this view, Abu Azzam al-Tamimi pointed to the war in Afghanistan as an example, saying that the foreign Arab fighters in Afghanistan operated under the supervision and command of the Afghan mujahidin. Even the head of the foreign fighters' contingent, Osama bin Laden, was a "guest" and operated under the command of Mullah Omar, the emir of the Taliban state, with which al-Qaeda became allied. Bin Laden was not allowed to operate independently without the knowledge or permission of the Afghan mujahidin. Finally, when Abu Azzam al-Tamimi was asked whether ISI was a terrorist organization, his answer was unequivocal:

> Yes, it is. Most of al-Qa'ida's victims in Iraq are civilian and innocent citizens.... Al-Qa'ida was worse than the [Shia] militias because it was killing soldiers, officers, policemen, doctors, engineers, and contractors. Many Sunnis were displaced by al-Qa'ida from al-Anbar, Abu Ghurayb, and Salah al-Din. If the US forces leave Iraq under the current circumstances, a disaster will befall the country and the entire region will probably fall under Iranian influence....
>
> We held dialogues with key leaders in al-Qa'ida last year.... [W]e discussed many issues, like killing, and tried to encourage the leading Iraqi figures in al-Qa'ida to hold the reins of power in their hands, since evil comes from non-Iraqi Arabs in the country.... [M]any Iraqis in al-Qa'ida are also evil.

A spokesman for the Hamas-Iraq insurgent group Ahmed Salah al-Din declared in an interview that the Political Council of the Iraqi Resistance, made up of several groups, accused ISI of being more concerned with a transnational agenda and goals rather than with liberating Iraq from occupation, saying "we do not consider Al-Qa'ida as a resistance organization as it has a special agenda which goes beyond Iraq," and that this fact had been clear to the Iraqi groups since the time when Zarqawi pledged allegiance to Osama bin Laden.[163]

In an interview with a Western journalist, a member of Ansar al-Sunna known as "Zubeidy" declared that al-Qaeda had brought "benefits and problems" for the Iraqi resistance. Certainly, al-Qaeda attacked the "occupiers," but its presence had generated more problems than benefits. Resistance was not just about killing Americans without any aims or goals:

> Our people have come to hate Al-Qa'ida, which gives the impression to the outside world that the resistance in Iraq are terrorists. Suicide bombing is not the best way to fight because it kills innocent civilians. We are against indiscriminate killing—fighting should be concentrated only on the enemy. They believe that all the Shia are kuffar [unbelievers]—and most of the Sunnis as well.
>
> An alliance with the Shia is no longer easy: A great gap has opened up between Sunni and Shia under the occupation and Al-Qa'ida has contributed to that—as have the US and Iran. Most of Al-Qa'ida's members are Iraqis but its leaders are mostly foreigners. The Americans magnify their role, even though they are responsible for a minority of resistance operations—remember that the Americans brought Al-Qa'ida to Iraq.[164]

Brigadier-General "Abu Basir" of the Islamic Front for the Iraqi Resistance viewed ISI with considerable bitterness. He blamed it for being behind much of the fractiousness of the insurgency. He accused ISI of the widespread killing of Muslims without due process. Conflating ISI and its supposed mother organization, al-Qaeda, he asked why al-Qaeda did not engage in mass indiscriminate killing in Afghanistan but was doing so in Iraq? Why, he pressed, was there so much lack of clarity within al-Qaeda's methodology? His biggest concerns centered on the declaration of the Islamic state in Iraq and on the prevalence of foreigners at the helm of the insurgency. First, ISI was a sham because it came into being without consensus and an emir about whom nothing was known headed it. Second, foreigners should take a "back seat" to the Iraqis in the leadership of the jihad because they knew the land and its people and invariably had military training.[165]

The Islamic Army of Iraq took a firm stance against the declaration of ISI by its leaders. Barely two weeks after the emergence of ISI, the leadership of IAI denounced the move. They argued that the move had no political or ideological sanctions, as it met none of the required conditions for the declaration of a state: safe and consolidated territory, economic resources, known boundaries (where exactly was this state?), and people. This stage of the conflict had to focus on jihad (fighting), and specifically, because all the mujahidin were fighting a guerrilla type of war, which required hit and run and constant movement, they could not spare scarce resources for establishing a state that the powerful enemy forces could take out.[166] The Islamic Army of Iraq focused not only on what it saw as the erroneous declaration of an Islamic state but also on the negative behavior and actions of its leaders and personnel. On December 9, 2007, the al-Boraq Media Establishment posted to its website a statement by and questions posed to an IAI spokesman, Dr. Ali al-Nuaimi, concerning the deterioration in relations between ISI and the mainstream Iraqi factions.[167] The Islamic State of Iraq, he said, was now unwelcome because it killed people indiscriminately. He pointed out that the bad behavior of ISI commanders and personnel were not aberrations but policy: "When the behavior and mistakes of the soldiers are repeated by the leaders without punishment, it means that the leaders agree with it. Silence over such conduct means that they are satisfied."[168] The fact that IAI, one of the most important insurgent organizations and a jihadist one to boot, took an anti-ISI stance infuriated the leaders of ISI, and the verbal sparring, as well as the fighting between the two, constituted the most damaging fracture within the jihadist constellation of the insurgency.

The IAI adamantly refused to acknowledge the so-called Islamic State of Iraq, referring throughout to AQI rather than ISI. Nuaimi rejected the organization's claim to be a state: "the Al-Qa'ida Organization is neither a person nor a state in legal terms. They have to be called by their real name."[169] The statement accused the so-called ISI of killing innocent people with chlorine gas, implying that this was an immoral method. Nuaimi denounced ISI for killing IAI leaders and clerics because they had expressed a willingness to negotiate with the Americans over their exit from Iraq. He expressed disdain for the ISI's tactics of imposing Taliban-type mores and codes of conduct on the local populace in Sunni areas.

This depth of distaste for ISI was expressed by a number of IAI commanders. Abu Mohammad al-Salmani, a commander in the IAI, stated: "al-Qaeda has killed more Iraqi Sunnis in Anbar province during the past month than the soldiers of the American occupation have killed within three months. People are tired of the torture. We cannot keep silent anymore."[170] Other insurgent groups also criticized ISI's tactics of "mindless" killings of both innocent Sunnis and Shias: "We do not want to kill the Sunni people nor displace the innocent Shia, and what the al-Qaeda organization is doing is contradictory to Islam," said "Abu Marwan," a commander of the Mujahidin Army in Baqubah, the capital of Diyala province.[171]

An individual named Abu Osama al-Iraqi wrote bin Laden to urge him to cut his ties to ISI because of its deviant behavior under Zarqawi. He told bin Laden that al-Qaeda had made a mistake in selecting Zarqawi as leader of the al-Qaeda subsidiary organization in Iraq. He suggested that an Iraqi should lead it, rather than foreigners such as Zarqawi and his successor, Abu Hamza al-Muhajir. He finally presented bin Laden with the following choices:

> Dear Sheikh, we ask God to convey our words to you and that he not hide them from you and some of those around you, so that you can make the appropriate decision. Either you dissolve [AQI's] oath of allegiance [to you], and we will be your sons, able to cope with leading the war and the jihad here, or you remain silent—and don't expect us to take it well.... The keys to the lock of strife are in your hands, so either lock or unlock it.[172]

The Islamic State of Iraq also found itself besieged on another flank: the Sunni Arab tribes, with whom tensions had been brewing for some time.

The Islamic State of Iraq's Rift with the Iraqi Tribes

The Sunni Arab inhabitants of the rural areas did initially provide the jihadists with resources and support, including to the extent of marrying off some of their daughters to jihadist fighters. However, the situation did not remain rosy for long. The opposition of the tribes people to ISI was brought about by differences over ideology and modus operandi and struggles over the division of economic resources.[173] The rift with the tribes was serious because it attenuated ISI's control over rural areas, reducing the territories it controlled, and opened ISI to attack because the tribes provided information to the U.S.-led Coalition forces about ISI's personnel, military activities, and logistical infrastructure in rural areas following the fissure.

The presence of armed and arrogant men, often from other areas or even foreigners, who used their power to demand things and to get what they wanted by brandishing weaponry generated resentment. The imposition of their strict interpretation of Islam was anathema to the customs of the tribes: closing down markets during prayer times, imposition of the veil upon women, prohibition of satellite TV and mobile phones, closing down of tea and coffee shops, and muscling in on the lucrative import-export businesses of the sheikhs were sources of conflict. The tribes began to express considerable disgust with and concern over Zarqawi's targeting of the civilian population, including both Sunni and Shia. The tribal Sahwa (Awakening) against the Salafi-jihadists can be dated from the time when the albu-Mahal tribe—who live in the remote western extremity of Anbar province close to the Syrian border and have traditionally been involved in the lucrative cross-border smuggling trade, which they slyly have termed the "import-export" business—took the lead in instigating a tribal uprising against AQI in 2005 after it started to muscle in on their "import-export" business and to try to implement its conception of a virtuous and vice-free society. The trigger for the revolt was AQI's beheading of a police officer from the tribe.[174]

Further to the east and in the heart of Anbar province, prominent Sunni tribal sheikhs began to express their hostility to AQI more openly. Sheikh Osama al-Jadaan, who was later assassinated by ISI, expressed frustration with the extremists' modus operandi, saying: "we realized that these foreign terrorists were hiding behind the veil of the noble Iraqi resistance. They claim to be striking at the US occupation, but the reality is they are killing innocent Iraqis in the markets, in mosques, in churches, and in our schools."[175] Other tribal leaders joined in the chorus of complaints. Sheikh Haqi Ismail al-Fahdawi of the albu-Fahd complained that his tribe had gone through a most "difficult period" as it had lost "many dear sons."[176] He also expressed deep concern that some of the young men within the tribes had been seduced by ISI's message and joined the organization. Another tribal notable, Hussein Zubeir, expressed a similar sentiment when he complained about the seduction of his tribe by ISI's extremists: "if it was not for the coyotes among us, no one would have been killed, kidnapped, or bombed. You know who among you [who] brought the Yemeni with the suicide vest."[177]

Clashes between jihadist and tribal fighters became more frequent. When the clashes began, the tribes simply could not comprehend, let alone deal with, much of AQI's modus operandi. In small unit firefights, the better armed and trained jihadists outperformed them, although some of the tribes Saddam Hussein had favored had been well equipped with small and light arms. Other techniques used by AQI and then ISI proved unfathomable, particularly the suicide bombing operations. A suicide bombing in Ramadi in early January 2006—when Zarqawi was still alive— proved essentially to be the final straw. The suicide bombing killed over seventy Sunni recruits in the Iraqi police force. They were from local tribes and had been persuaded to join the security forces by the sheikhs of their respective tribes. The sheikhs' rationale was twofold. First, it would provide income for restless young men, and second, the Sunni community preferred having Sunni security personnel policing their areas rather than units dominated by the hated and vengeful Shias.

A series of further attacks and clashes occurred during 2006 that forced the tribes to respond. In August 2006, after Zarqawi's death, Anbar's tribes took the significant step of forming the Anbar Salvation Council under the leadership of Sheikh Sattar Buzaigh al-Rishawi, who expressed the tribes' frustrations and anger at the rising carnage in various statements.[178] He called upon the tribes to "awaken" and rise up against the jihadists. The Anbar Salvation Council was the clearest indication of the mobilization of the tribes against the extremists and following the adoption of the model by Sunni tribes in other provinces, constituted the core of what came to be called the "Awakening Councils." Based in the provincial capital of Ramadi, the Anbar Salvation Council was made up of twenty-five tribes who had gone sour on AQI.[179] The Anbar Salvation Council worked with the U.S. military and Iraqi Security Forces. Zarqawi's response to the tribes' growing opposition was to gun down several prominent Sunni clerics and sheikhs, setting the stage for a fight to the death.[180]

The tribal Sahwa learned how to counter the jihadist propaganda, and many of its leading luminaries took to the airwaves to justify their stance and highlight the Awakening movement's progress in combating the jihadists. In April 2007, Sheikh Ali Hatim Suleiman al-Dulaimi told the newspaper *al-Hayat* that the activities of al-Qaeda personnel were proof of its moral and religious bankruptcy.[181] The head of the Anbar Salvation Council declared: "We are fighting a war against the terrorists who have killed our prominent figures and shaykhs."[182] Tribe after tribe turned against ISI. In his capacity as a senior member of the Anbar Salvation Council, Sheikh Ali Hatim Suleiman al-Dulaimi said: "We are in an open war with Al-Qa'ida, particularly since it has been insulting our blood, dignity and honor for two years, something the tribes cannot remain silent about. By God, we never fought on the side of Al-Qa'ida. Al-Qa'ida was imported and came to the country when the Americans entered Iraq. Frankly speaking, we do not consider Al-Qa'ida an enemy only, but we have excluded its elements from any humanitarian or governmental law and from tribal norms."[183] As it was squeezed out of Anbar province, ISI sought greener pastures at the demographic fringes of the Sunni Arab population, in places such as Diyala, where it could pose as that population's champions by engaging Shia and Kurdish militias. Their efforts did not succeed. Diyala gave rise to the Patriotic Diyala Salvation Front, a provincial coalition of politicians from mainstream Sunni Arab political parties. Formed in early 2006, its original purpose was to confront Iranian interference and Shia militias and combat sectarianism. By early 2007, it had identified ISI as the greater threat. Its leader, Abdullah al-Jibouri, a former governor of Diyala, organized armed neighborhood watches to keep ISI at bay. As ISI's local presence continued to grow in Diyala in the spring of 2007, so did opposition to it. On April 30, the tribes of Diyala held a conference to express support for the government and its security forces.

The Salah al-Din Awakening Council (SAC) was also formed to fight the militants of the ISI. The Salah al-Din Awakening Council also generated considerable opposition among the inhabitants of Salah al-Din province, just north of Baghdad. The Salah al-Din Awakening Council held its founding conference in Tikrit, Saddam Hussein's hometown, on May 24, 2007, and its members pledged to focus their resources and manpower on fighting ISI. The conference was dominated by the Jibouri tribe, which had suffered extensively at the hands of the defunct Baath regime and of ISI. Nonetheless, the Salah al-Din Awakening Council encountered opposition from many of Salah al-Din's tribespeople. A statement attributed to Tikrit's sheikhs and notables surfaced online and accused the Salah al-Din Awakening Council of exaggerating the dire state of affairs and wishing to cause strife among the inhabitants of the province.[184] This divisiveness highlighted the fact that even among the tribes there was no consensus about ISI. Some had suffered more at its hands and wanted revenge and thus took active roles in promoting the fight against it. Other tribes had either been cajoled or bribed to work with ISI and were loath to break this relationship off. Finally, others had neither benefited nor suffered from ISI, indeed, had not witnessed an ISI presence in their territories and simply did not wish to be on anybody's "radar."

The response of ISI to the increasing prominence of the various Awakening Councils, particularly that of the Anbar Salvation Council, from 2007 onward was to wage a hostile media campaign in parallel to its physical assaults on the group. The key message was that the Anbar Salvation Council was not as effective as it claimed to be and that its support among Anbar tribes was not extensive. The campaign denounced "those who sold their religion for a few dollars and were happy to be the crusader occupier's henchmen and a poisoned dagger that stabs the mujahideen in the back."[185] The campaign referred to the Anbar Salvation Council as the Anbar Infidel Council and claimed that it was composed of murderers, highway robbers, and looters.

The tribes responded with their own information campaign. In a new twist in the bitter struggle between the Anbar tribes and ISI, the tribes accused Iran of supporting ISI. One member of the Anbar Salvation Council, Colonel Fadil Mukhlif al-Dulaimi, declared that weapons and explosives from Iran had been discovered in ISI bases in al-Sufiya, albu-Fahd, and Ramadi. If one delves deeper into the political culture of the Sunni Arabs, particularly of the tribes, it was not irrational for them to blame Iran ultimately for their woes, whether these woes were actually at the hands of the U.S.-led Coalition, the Shia community, or ISI. In the mindset of the highly nationalist Sunni Arab tribes—many of whom gave thousands of their sons to fight and die in the sanguinary Iran-Iraq War, Shia Iran is often the root cause of the problems that Iraq has faced. In their worldview, Iran supported the U.S.-led Coalition in its invasion and occupation of Iraq and, through the Iraqi Shia community, facilitated the process of subjugating Iraq. Moreover, it was conspiracy-minded but not irrational for them to believe that ISI was Iran's ally precisely because much of ISI's action in Iraq seemed to have harmed the role and position of the Sunni community.

The Islamic State of Iraq's Response to Its Rifts with the Insurgents and Tribes

While cracks had begun to appear between the Iraqi insurgents and AQI when Zarqawi led it, the tensions and episodic flare-ups of 2004 and 2005 had escalated into serious conflict and violent clashes by 2006. The first order of business of the MSC and then the new ISI was to deal with the growing opposition of a wide variety of Iraqi insurgent groups. The response of MSC and then ISI was a mixture of threats, propaganda, and assassinations of foes and at times involved efforts to shame or cajole the opposing groups back into the fold.

On September 25, 2006, the MSC released a statement attacking and threatening certain tribes and an insurgent group based in al-Qaim. It accused the leaders of the Abu Rughal tribe and the Hamza battalions, a nationalist insurgent movement consisting mainly of members of the albu-Mahal tribe, of betrayal and treason. The statement argued that it was justifiable to fight against this group because it had sided with the enemies of Islam and violated Islamic law. Its members were now subject to "traditional punishment," which included exile, amputation, and crucifixion.[186] In the fall of 2006, Abu Hamza al-Muhajir labeled the anti-jihadist movement an apostasy when it first appeared in the form of the Anbar Salvation Council, with Abu Risha as its leader. Abu Hamza al-Muhajir appealed directly to other insurgent groups to give their blessings to the ISI project and unite under its banner. He specifically addressed Ansar al-Sunna, IAI, and Jaysh al-Mujahidin, three of the most powerful jihadist insurgent groups, and praised them for their roles in the fight against the foreign forces.[187]

Stunned by the intensity of the mainstream insurgents' rejection, the MSC conducted an intense media campaign beginning in October 2006, after months of inactivity, to counteract its detractors. The intent was to establish Abu Hamza al-Muhajir as a worthy successor to Zarqawi and to promote the MSC as a leading force behind attempts to bring unity to the defense of the beleaguered Sunnis of Iraq. The post-Zarqawi jihadist leadership argued that the United States, allegedly on the verge of defeat in Iraq, was seeking to spread lies and rumors and thus create divisions between the insurgents.[188] Abu Hamza al-Muhajir offered the "traitors" amnesty if they publicly renounced the Iraqi government and publicly embraced the MSC.

The situation did not get better when ISI under Abu Omar al-Baghdadi replaced the MSC. On March 13, 2007, a jihadist website posted a delusional half-hour audio message issued by Baghdadi, titled "Say: For Me, I Work on a Clear Sign From My Lord." In a rambling speech he alleged that ISI faced a vast conspiracy hatched by the United States, the Iraqi government, Sunni Arab political parties, and insurgents of all stripes, including some jihadist groups. The goals of this "conspiracy" were to break the supposedly powerful bonds and solidarity between the ISI and its large popular base; to use jihadist groups to strike ISI; to distance the global jihadist movement from the battlefield so as to benefit more moderate and openly nationalist movements; and to eliminate the jihad in Iraq.[189]

Abu Omar al-Baghdadi addressed the enemy's military assault and the "vicious media attack" against the "honorable mujahidin" in Iraq and stressed that they were designed to drive a permanent wedge among them: "While we are in the middle of this glory, fighting the enemy and consoling our brothers and ourselves to remain steadfast in the face of an unprecedented Crusader-Safavid campaign, since the occupation, calling for unity, joining forces and agreement [among the mujahidin], everyone was taken by surprise with a multi-faceted vicious media attack against the new Islamic State....Then what are the goals of the latest media campaign against the Islamic State?"[190] First, he said, the military and propaganda assaults had been designed to "disband the strong bond and closeness between the ISI and its massive popular base," a state of affairs that existed only in his mind: there was no such bond, as the Sunni community hated ISI. Second, the media campaign was an incitement to get the other insurgent groups to take on ISI. Third, the media campaign was intended to "distance the global jihad movement from the battlefield in favor of the nationalistic movements which are more moderate and more open, and to tarnish its image to the world."[191] Finally, the media campaign was intended "to abolish jihad in the Land of the Two Rivers and put an end to the hope, which the nation see [sic] in it."[192] Abu Omar al-Baghdadi believed that the United States had come to the realization by 2007 that it had a limited time in which to win quickly or face "a Vietnamese-style defeat," arguing that this was confirmed by the "war rooster Cheney," a reference to the U.S. vice president during the G. W. Bush presidency.

The second section of the audio was a lengthy reiteration of ISI's uncompromising beliefs and determination to destroy polytheism.[193] Abu Omar al-Baghdadi cited an alleged speech by Ali Ibn Abu Talib in which he reportedly told a companion of the Prophet named Abu Hayyaj al-Asadi: "Do not leave a statue standing without removing it. Do not leave a grave raised without leveling it."[194] The Shias "are a sect of polytheism and apostasy," as they do not follow many of the Islamic principles."[195] At one point, however, Abu Omar al-Baghdadi seemed to be trying to move away somewhat from the uncompromising extremism of Zarqawi concerning "deviant" members of the Sunni faith, saying: "We do not consider a Muslim man who has prayed in the direction of our Kiblah [Mecca] to be an infidel who has committed such sins as adultery, drinking alcohol, and theft, unless he claims that is permissible."[196] On other matters Abu Omar al-Baghdadi was totally inflexible. There could be no compromise vis-à-vis secularism in Iraq and all the variants associated with it such as nationalism, communism, and Baathism. Likewise, people involved in or connected to the political process in Iraq were "infidels," and he lumped the main Sunni political party, the Iraqi Islamic Party, in the same category with the Shia parties. He put Iraqis on notice that ISI considered anyone who assisted or provided support for the occupation and its associates to be an apostate, whether "this assistance is in the form of clothing, food, medical help, or any such thing that might help them or empower them. We consider anyone doing so a legitimate target."[197]

Abu Omar al-Baghdadi argued that jihad to "liberate the land of Muslims" had been an individual obligation (*fard ayn*) ever since the fall of Al-Andalus (Muslim Spain), adding that it must be carried out by Muslims whether they stood "behind a righteous one or a sinner."[198] Failure to carry out jihad was the greatest sin after disbelief in God. Any Muslim land ruled by the laws of disbelief (manmade laws instead of sharia), he said, is itself a land of disbelief, and it was "an obligation to fight the police and army of the state of falsehood."[199] The Christian and Jewish minorities in Iraq were also enemies. According to him, they were "foes with no rights as *dhimmis*."[200] In Islam *dhimmis* are protected and subordinate peoples who are entitled to protection and safety within Islamic lands as long as they pay the tax on non-Muslims and maintain their loyalty to the state. However, because they had violated their pact to pay taxes and remain loyal, they were now legitimate targets.

Abu Omar al-Baghdadi tried to heal the rift with the other insurgent groups; he was particularly keen to reconcile with other Salafist groups in the insurgency, saying: "We consider the men of the jihadist groups who are active on the scene to be our brothers in Islam. We do not accuse them of non-belief nor sin except that they disobeyed by refusing to respond to the call of the time, which is unity under one banner."[201] However, he warned the other insurgent groups to avoid signing agreements or pacts with the occupation forces without the consent of ISI. He also tried to reconcile with the Sunni ulema whom Zarqawi had alienated in Iraq and told them that ISI respected them and would come to their aid during times of hardship, but warned: "We will expose anyone who follows the path of false idols or flatters them at the expense of the religion of God."[202] He concluded by making it clear that there would be no compromise over morals and mores, as strictly demanded by the regulations and norms of ISI: "We consider forbidden anything that encourages sin and promotes it, such as satellite dish [*sic*], and we see that women must cover their face and avoid conspicuousness and gender desegregation, and they must seek chastity and virtue."[203]

Barely a month later, Abu Omar al-Baghdadi was at it again. On April 17, 2007, a jihadist site, al-Furqan Media Production, posted an audiotape by him titled "The Harvest of the Years in the Land of the Monotheists."[204] This was essentially a propaganda tape issued to downplay the chronic problems ISI was facing. Abu Omar al-Baghdadi asks: what have the Sunnis of Iraq gained from four years of jihad? He answers that they are more religious and they have begun the implementation of a divine system of governance in the parts of Iraq controlled by them. This was manifestly untrue and glossed over the growing revulsion among the Sunnis toward the jihadists. He claimed that the mujahidin had gained a lot on the ideological, organizational, military, and political levels. Militarily, the mujahidin, "the officers of jihad in the cause of God," had attained the highest standards. Morally, the Islamic world had gained tremendously from the years of jihad in Iraq: "the US giant has collapsed under the strikes of the mujahidin during day and night."[205] Either he was trying to raise morale or he was totally unaware of what was going on operationally. There were criticisms that he was cut off from his field commanders or that they were "feeding" him "good" (fake) news.

Abu Omar al-Baghdadi moved seamlessly from mouthing his delusions to exhorting various categories of people within the Islamic world and within Iraq to remain in the fight against the enemies of ISI and Islam. He told the Sunnis: "had it not been for the mujahidin, the descendants of Ibn al-Alqami would have tortured you. You are not unaware of what they are doing in their prisons [torturing and murdering Sunnis]." He then addressed the tribal sheikhs who had begun to turn away decisively from the ISI presence in Iraq, telling them that reneging on their pledge of loyalty to ISI was "a big sin." He called upon the Iraqis who collaborated with the occupier warning them to change their ways and to understand that it was not the mujahidin who had mistreated them but the occupiers and their puppets. He also addressed the insurgent fighters who had turned against ISI, telling them that the bonds between Muslims must not be broken because of petty and superficial differences.

In April 2007, ISI released its survey of the insurgency's fourth year and argued that the establishment of ISI was a critical step toward insurgent unity under one leadership, its own. It identified the ISI's broader strategic program as thwarting Iranian expansionism in Iraq and seeking to regain the goodwill of hostile insurgent movements, especially the influential IAI. The Islamic State of Iraq warned the Sunnis that continued divisions would allow their common enemies to achieve one of their goals, "the establishment of secular entities that will circulate in the orbit of the Zionist-crusader project in the region."[206] Another point tackled the issue of the aftermath of a U.S. military withdrawal, on the need to confront the Iraqi Shias and their Iranian military patrons at the political, ideological and military levels.[207] This was, no doubt, designed to highlight the fact that the Sunnis—whatever their ideological persuasions—did face a common enemy in the Iraqi Shias and the Iranians.

This ISI "state of the union" address cited the establishment of ISI in October 2006 as a critical first step toward the goal of insurgent unity under one leadership and identified the organization's broader strategic program in five points: (1) thwarting the expansion of Iran and its Shia puppets in Iraq; (2) achieving insurgent unity under the banner of ISI; (3) implementation of sharia governance; (4) protection of the "Islamic jihadist project in Iraq from theft at the hands of those who trade in the blood of martyrs, and those with half-solutions who are prepared to lay down their arms at any time." This was aimed at ISI's bitter critic IAI. The Islamic State of Iraq warned that this possibility would allow the Crusaders to achieve one of their key goals in the umma, the emergence of puppet states of the "Zionist-Crusader" enemy; (5), after the U.S. "defeat" and withdrawal, ISI would continue the war fully against the Shias and their Iranian patron.[208]

The spirited defense of ISI by its leader and others did not stem the onslaught of the mainstream insurgents. In April 2007, after Abu Omar al-Baghdadi's speech, IAI responded, with the support of the rising Kuwaiti Salafist ideologue Hamid al-Ali, in order to demolish ISI's claims of being a state. On the contrary, the creation of ISI, argued the IAI leadership, had been a mistake because ISI did not have the requisite resources to maintain itself. Moreover, there was a time for fighting and a time for creating a state, and this was not the time to create a state because fighting should occupy the attention of the mujahidin. Finally, the emergence of this state was a divisive element, since not all mujahidin groups within the insurgency supported the creation of such a state.

In late August 2007, a jihadist website posted a statement issued by ISI titled "Between the Fundamentals of Jihad and the Methodological Deviations," in which the "state" called for solidarity among the Sunni groups and outlined its position toward the Iraqi insurgents who had turned against it and were now supporting the Americans. The statement accused the Iraqi insurgents of selling out their religion for the sake of acquiring worldly goods and seeking political positions in an "illegitimate" political system established by the Americans. By way of contrast, though, the mujahidin had understood from the very beginning the nature of the struggle between them and their enemies in the "Crusader alliance." It was a struggle to the finish, and the mujahidin relied on faith and on God to show the path to victory. This transnational jihadi counter-campaign generated little support or sympathy from the local Iraqi Salafists and other insurgents. On the contrary, they increased the intensity of their opposition and forced the leader of al-Qaeda to step into the fray and analyze it from the perspective of the "mother" organization.

Incitement against alleged apostates became increasingly fevered as the tribal Awakening gained ground first in Anbar and then in other provinces in 2007, marginalizing the extremists and driving them out of many areas. On the eve of Ramadan in early September 2007, some contributors on militant Islamic discussion forums spoke of a coming offensive against the apostates to reclaim Anbar province for the jihadists. On September 13, 2007, Sheikh Abd al-Sattar Abu Risha was assassinated, and ISI claimed responsibility for it. Two days later, Abu Omar al-Baghdadi announced his Ramadan offensive against the Awakening by justifying violence against it.[209] The disintegration in relations between the mainstream insurgency and ISI accelerated in the winter and spring of 2007. By the end of 2008, even though ISI was under extreme pressure, it was focusing its ire on the Sunni community almost as much as it did on the Shias. The Islamic State of Iraq fighters went on a campaign of targeted attacks against leading Sunni political personalities and leaders of combat units and indiscriminate slaughter of civilians.

Al-Qaeda Central's Response to the Rift: Bin Laden's Concerns

As ISI found itself increasingly at odds with rival insurgents and hostile tribes, an al-Qaeda deputy leader, Abu Yahya al-Libi, took al-Qaeda's first clear public position on the growing fractionalization of the Iraqi insurgency. He called upon insurgents to unite under the ISI banner in the face of an alleged U.S.-Saudi conspiracy to thwart what he referred to as the impending insurgent victory by using other Sunni Arab groups as a fifth column.

On October 22, 2007, AQC released the latest in a string of recent messages from bin Laden in which he addressed "our people in Iraq" and the Sunni insurgents in general. The general message was that the insurgency had succeeded against the U.S. and Iraqi forces and that the Iraqis should persevere along that path. He mentioned the problems the insurgency had faced, including strife between Sunni mainstream insurgents and jihadists and tribes' cooperation with the United States. He advised insurgents to recognize their mistakes, settle their differences amicably, and strive for unity of ranks. He called upon the tribes to avoid collaboration with the United States.

Osama bin Laden began by praising Iraq's peoples, tribes, and mujahidin for their bravery in defying the U.S. invasion. He also cited the contribution of the foreign fighters who had left their homes to come and aid the Iraqis. He explained to the insurgents that their resistance would dramatically reshape Iraq and the region: "The whole world is watching your magnificent victories, and knows that a new page of history, with major changes, has begun. With God's permission, the map of the region will be redrawn at the hands of the mujahidin, and the artificial borders that the Crusaders drew will be erased to establish, with God's permission, a state of truth and justice: the greater state of Islam, stretching from ocean to ocean."[210] Bin Laden asserted that the insurgency would unravel the region's system of states that had arisen from the partition of the Ottoman Empire after World War I. He predicted that an Islamic superstate would replace the many smaller, "artificial" (to him) states in the region, reunifying the Muslims under an Islamic order. The next section addressed the insurgents, whom he chided for their mistakes. He stated that they had taken too long to achieve "unity of ranks" and had failed to rally together under one banner. He emphasized that no one, not even ISI, was above the law. He argued that anyone who transgressed Islamic law must be brought to justice and punished accordingly. He called upon religious leaders, insurgent commanders, and tribal sheikhs to promote reconciliation to limit the effects of conflicts.

The release of a video statement by bin Laden on December 29, 2007, indicated an intensification of the effort by the leader of AQC to defend his organization and bolster its supporters in Iraq. Titled "The Path to Thwart the Conspiracies," the video was produced by AQC's media wing, al-Sahab, and posted on various militant websites like Ehklaas.org. The statement differed from previous ones in that he specifically called upon the "mujahidin" to close ranks around ISI. He also criticized the various anti-ISI Awakening Councils among the Sunni tribes and other insurgents that were cooperating with the U.S. forces. He attacked scholars and preachers who were allegedly undermining the jihad.

One of bin Laden's chief concerns was the division and disunity among the ranks of the insurgents, specifically between extremist Salafi-jihadist entities like ISI on the one hand and Iraqi Islamist and nationalist groups like IAI and Hamas-Iraq on the other. Denouncing the Awakening Councils and the Iraqi Islamic Party as "collaborators" and accusing them of dividing the insurgents' ranks, bin Laden called upon Iraqi insurgents to repent and to dissociate themselves from their leaders and to correct the course of their parties and their groups. He claimed that "America has increased its political and media efforts to deceive Muslims, and one of its wicked schemes was to seduce the tribes, buy their allegiance, and form the councils of dissension under the name of the awakening councils."[211] He also compared the situation in Iraq with that of Afghanistan, saying that the anti-Taliban Northern Alliance of Afghan groups had become supporters of America against the mujahidin in Afghanistan. Today, he continued, the situation in Iraq had witnessed Islamic groups, such as the Iraqi Islamic Party, and some fighting groups supporting "America against the Muslims."[212]

In the October 22, 2007, statement, bin Laden had attempted to pacify the Iraqi insurgents by alluding to ISI's mistakes. In the December 29, 2007, statement, he expanded on this theme by saying "that our mujahideen brothers should...be keen that their operations target the enemy according to the legal codes as far away from Muslims as they can." He then continued to promote the call for Muslim unity:

> What is obligated of us in order to foil these dangerous conspiracies which aim to abort the jihad in the land of Iraq, to prevent the establishment of an Islamic state in the land of the two rivers, to serve as support and assistance to the Islamic people everywhere, to foil America's plan for the division of Iraq, and to serve as the first line of defense for our nation? I say and stress that one of the greatest obligations is to unite the efforts of all the true mujahideen, to be able to stand as one rank to fight and uphold the words of Allah.[213]

Though bin Laden had made previous appeals for the unity of ranks among the insurgents, the December message was the first time he named Abu Omar al-Baghdadi, when he offered the ISI leader his support. Bin Laden stressed the religious obligation of unity under one emir and cited examples from Islamic history to show how Muslims had been victorious after pledging allegiance to a single leader. He asserted that "refraining from pledging allegiance to one of the emirs of the mujahideen in Iraq after their recommendation by trusted, fair persons...leads to great evils," one of which was the obstruction of the establishment of a Muslim nation under one leader.

The Iraqi foes of what had become ISI were not impressed by bin Laden's declamation. In a December 31, 2007, article in *Middle East Online*, Anbar province Awakening Council leading member Sheikh Khalid al-Alwani responded to bin Laden's statement: "it does not mean anything to us because he is making threats from a weak position." Alwani also asked: "what has [al-Qaeda] done in Iraq other than bring death and destruction to Iraqis?"[214] He also insisted that the "crimes" of those followers of bin Laden were the motive for the establishment of the Awakening Councils, not the desire for power, rank, money, or for employment in the service of others, as bin Laden suggested.

The Death of the Sunni Insurgency, 2008–2010?

By early 2008, the Sunni insurgency was in a state of disarray. The Islamic State of Iraq was defeated, or so it seemed. First, the U.S. surge of troops and support for the Sunni revolt against ISI was an important factor in the jihadists' declining fortunes. Second, a focused U.S. military response to AQI and then ISI whittled down ISI's military capabilities. The relentless night and day operations by the special operation forces of Joint Special Operations Command under General Stanley A. McChrystal were particularly effective in this regard. They had been targeting primarily top-level leaders of ISI, largely during the night; now they began targeting midlevel commanders and doing so 24/7, based on painstaking intelligence acquired from the teams themselves, captured insurgents, or the local populace. In early 2009, U.S. forces began pulling out of cities across the country, turning over the task of maintaining security to the vastly enlarged and, on the surface, now capable Iraqi Security Forces.

By the end of 2009, internecine strife within Sunni insurgent and political circles was at an all-time high. Many insurgent groups blamed ISI for the decline in the insurgency's fortunes. Others began to point fingers at the Awakening Councils and accused them of facilitating the divisions within the Sunni community and of deflecting it from the struggle against occupation. Some of the insurgents continued to fight the U.S.-led Coalition, the Shia-dominated government, and the remnants of ISI in their particular locales. Others sought to draw back from the struggle against U.S.

forces and wait out the U.S. Surge. The intention of the insurgents was to regroup, retrain, and presumably rejoin the fray later on, after the Surge had exhausted itself.[215]

In light of the diminishing fortunes of the insurgency, a number of Iraqi insurgent groups sought a level of cooperation and coordination that had not existed in the past. On October 11, 2007, six major insurgent groups announced the formation of the Political Council for the Iraqi Resistance, which they asserted was designed to "serve as the political representation of the Iraqi resistance."[216] However, this effort had come on the heels of several previous efforts by the same groups to achieve greater unity. Moreover, the political platform of the Political Council for the Iraqi Resistance proved short on specifics, and other Islamist groups accused it of being too "secular" (!) in its efforts to appeal to everyone and of being the instrument of regional powers' nefarious machinations.[217]

The Awakening Councils were also split; some of them disdained too close a relationship with the U.S.-led Coalition and distanced themselves from it.[218] The head of the Anbar Salvation Council, the chief Awakening movement in Anbar province, Sheikh Ahmed Abu Risha (who had taken over the movement when his brother Sheikh Sattar Buzaigh Abu Risha was assassinated late in the summer of 2007) had developed ambitions to enter national politics by capitalizing on his military success against ISI.[219] Other insurgent groups were simultaneously fighting against and engaging in negotiations with the U.S.-led Coalition forces.[220] Some Sunnis and Shias even joined forces at local and neighborhood levels to fight ISI.[221] Other insurgent groups decided that they would form a front to confront those whom they did not like, which included ISI, the U.S.-led Coalition, the Awakening Councils, and the Shia government in Baghdad.[222]

Relations between the mainstream Iraqi insurgent organizations and the tribes became very tense. Many insurgent groups resented the tribes for going over to the American side so readily and thus fatally weakening the hand of the "resistance" movement and its leverage over the Americans and the Shia-dominated government. Many of the anti-ISI insurgent groups were also vehemently against the Awakening Councils and the idea of working with the Americans and the Shia-dominated government. Their argument was that the Sahwa (Awakening Councils) had fatally weakened the hand of the Iraqi insurgency both against the Americans and their allies *and* against ISI. A group of insurgents who came together into the Jihad and Change Front were not very complimentary of the Awakening Councils:

The creation of the Awakening Councils is a plan of the occupation forces, established mainly to serve and line up with the occupation forces, and give power to their plans. At this point, we do not argue that the mistakes that were made in the Iraqi jihadist arena were made by the brothers in the Al-Qa'ida organization...[such as the] announcement that anyone who does not join the Islamic state of Iraq [ISI] is an apostate and must be fought. They created disorder and made the scope of the conflict larger. However, instead of focusing on fighting the occupation and its quislings, the spears were directed at the masses of people, especially the Islamic jihadist factions, simply because these factions said that the religious requirements for the establishment of the most wanted Islamic state are not fulfilled yet....There is a need for well-planned strategies and tactics in order to save the sacrifices and blood of the mujahidin and gather all forces that reject occupation and amass them against this enemy, a lineup that takes into account the religious and moral constants, and attempts to revive the concept of the nation, reject fanaticism, and strengthen fraternity around the constants.[223]

By October 2008, a number of prominent Sunni insurgent groups called upon the Sahwa to rejoin the resistance and resume the fight against the U.S. occupation forces and the Iraqi government. Several factors suggested that members of the Awakening Councils, which had played a crucial role in diminishing the combat effectiveness of ISI and in the sharp downturn in attacks on U.S. forces during the summer of 2008, might take up the insurgents on their invitation. When a decision was reached that the Sahwa militia would come under control of the Baghdad government on October 1, 2008, many members of Awakening Councils felt that the U.S. forces, by leaving them to the mercy of the Shia-dominated government of Nuri al-Maliki, had betrayed them. These fighters' discomfort was a source of considerable satisfaction among many insurgents who blamed them as much as ISI for the insurgency's disunity and ultimate downfall. The Front for Change and Jihad, an umbrella group of nationalist insurgent factions, asserted on September 11, 2008: "he who abased himself as a prop of the occupation and its aides is now swallowing the bitterness of his audacity."[224]

The situation became even more convoluted as the tribal Awakening movement itself split into two hostile groupings. The movement's success propelled the sheikhs into national politics. However, as soon as the movement began to step into the national limelight, it fractured into two groups.

The first group consisted of Anbari sheikhs who believed that Prime Minister Nuri al-Maliki could deliver what they wanted in terms of positions in municipal and national politics and resources to rebuild Sunni provinces and towns. In early November 2007, leaders of this group submitted their candidates to replace the ministers who belonged to the Accord Front, the Sunni Arab coalition headed by the Iraqi Islamic Party, which had withdrawn from the government because of growing tensions with Nuri al-Maliki.

The second group countered with its own move to reach out to Sunni tribes in Anbar who were not favorably disposed toward Maliki. These included the Anbar Salvation Council, whose most prominent personality was Sheikh Ali Hatim al-Suleiman, who had opposed AQI and then ISI but was a staunch critic of the U.S. policy in Iraq. His contention was that the U.S. occupation was both harmful and incompetent. He advocated closer ties with the moderate insurgent groups as a way to put pressure on the Baghdad government.

The intra-Sunni jockeying for power in national politics did not go far because after the American withdrawal Maliki turned on all the Sunnis collectively and reneged on his promises to integrate their fighting personnel into the security forces and to provide the Sunni regions with resources.

Like a Phoenix from the Ashes: The Islamic State of Iraq and Syria

Despite the reduction in violence and a return to near normalcy in 2008, the situation in Iraq remained very fragile. In this context, there was less talk concerning the imminence of victory, as recognition of the complex situation in Iraq began to dawn on even the fervent advocates of the U.S. Surge. Even General David Petraeus, commander of Multi-National Forces–Iraq and the intellectual spirit behind the Surge, sounded a note of caution as he transitioned out of his position in mid-September 2008. His replacement, General Raymond Odierno, sounded equally cautious. Both senior officers were correct in estimating that the gains of the Surge were fragile and potentially reversible. The year 2008 witnessed little or no movement at the national political level toward resolving some of the most pressing issues, such as reconciliation between the communities, integration of the Sunnis, and the equitable sharing of oil revenues. This state of affairs put into serious doubt the mid- and long-term prospects for an improved security climate in Iraq, as the various communities reverted to relying on their own armed organizations and militias.

To the consternation of the American and Iraqi governments, from mid- and late 2009, ISI rebounded in strength and launched a concerted effort to cripple the Iraqi government. During August and October 2009, ISI launched a series of deadly sabotage attacks on government infrastructure and terror attacks against civilians that killed hundreds. The Islamic State of Iraq suffered a significant blow on April 18, 2010, when its top leaders, Abu Hamza al-Muhajir and Abu Omar al-Baghdadi, were both killed in a joint U.S.-Iraqi raid near Tikrit. By June 2010, 80 percent of the group's forty-two leaders, including recruiters and financiers, had been killed or captured, with only eight remaining at large. This "decapitation" effort had been due to the relentless efforts of Joint Special Operations Command and the conventional forces on the ground.

This decapitation of the dual leadership of ISI set the stage for the emergence of the current and most successful leader of the organization to emerge: Ibrahim Awwad Ibrahim Ali al-Badri al-Samarrai, the individual the world knows better as Abu Bakr al-Baghdadi. A shadowy figure who seems to have arisen from nowhere, he has been the subject of a fascinating short biography by Will McCants. It is said that he is descended from the Prophet Mohammad and that he hails from the albu-Badri tribe, which is primarily based in Samarra and Diyala. While he had always been a stern and pious individual, his incarceration in 2004 increased his contact with and exposure to militant Islamist ideas and individuals and probably increased his anger against the American presence, and after joining ISI he rose steadily through the ranks (see chapter 4).

The appointment of this new leader by ISI, without prior approval from al-Qaeda, whose senior leaders knew almost nothing about the man—where he had come from, his military experience, and whether he could be trusted—caused consternation in AQC. In a communiqué seized during the raid on bin Laden's hideaway in Abbottabad, Adam Gadahn, the American al-Qaeda member and spokesman who was killed in early 2015, voiced his displeasure with ISI's lack of respect. Writing to an unspecified recipient, presumably bin Laden, in January 2011, Gadahn asked why ISI should be permitted to sully al-Qaeda's name with its indiscriminate slaughter when it could not even bother to keep in touch with al-Qaeda's leadership. "Maybe," he wrote, "it is better for them not to be in the ranks of the mujahideen, as they are just like a polluted spot that should be removed and sanitized and cleared from the ranks."[225] Less than six months after receiving the letter, bin Laden was dead, killed in a raid by SEAL Team Six of the U.S. Navy. The Egyptian jihadist intellectual Zawahiri inherited the problem of dealing with ISI, which was increasingly perceived as the wayward child of the jihad.

Turmoil in the Arab World and the Impact of the Syrian Civil War

Though watched carefully, ISI's resurgence between 2010 and 2013 in Iraq elicited little commentary from AQC, which was dealing with leadership transition from bin Laden to al-Zawahiri. It was simultaneously responding to the eruption of the Arab Spring in several countries, a state of turmoil that fascinated al-Zawahiri, who thought that al-Qaeda could take advantage of it. Iraq receded to the back burner. Al-Qaeda was definitely taken by surprise at the rapid success of revolutions that toppled entire regimes. However, it believed that these revolutions constituted an opportunity for bringing about profound change in the Arab world. Though surprised by the Arab Spring revolutions, al-Qaeda announced its support for them, hoping to benefit from the overthrow of the dictators. Zawahiri has always been interested in the fate of the Arab world, and his operational goals focused on securing a territorial foothold and generating greater support for al-Qaeda.[226] The Arab Spring reinforced his belief that al-Qaeda had to work with the local populations and win their hearts and minds, a concern he had previously addressed in his memoirs, *Knights under the Prophet's Banner*, written in 2001.

Meanwhile, the new leader of ISI, Abu Bakr al-Baghdadi, had been rebuilding, establishing alliances within Iraq, and doing his utmost to hollow out the power of the Iraqi state by destroying infrastructure and killing officials and security personnel. However, it was not long before the attention of both AQC and ISI turned toward next door: Syria, which became the scene of a profoundly violent civil war. It was the civil war there that finally brought about the complete rupture between AQC and ISI. That rupture itself increased the complexity of the civil war in Syria, leaving insurgent groups fighting one another as well as government forces.[227] The Islamic State of Iraq sought to take advantage of the deteriorating situation in Syria in 2011.

When the series of Arab revolts known as the Arab Spring broke out in Tunisia, Egypt, and Libya, Syria's young president, Bashar al-Assad, thought his country would be immune.[228] It was not, and a series of protests that broke out in March 2011 in the town of Deraa culminated in a nationwide uprising. The causes of the Syrian crisis have been the subject of extensive analysis that need not be repeated in detail here. The revolution started initially as a protest against a tyrannical and despotic system of authoritarian governance that had not kept its promises of political and socioeconomic reforms. People's anger was magnified by the onset of severe economic difficulties in the years immediately preceding the outbreak of violence.[229]

Unfortunately, since Syria is a multiethnic and multisectarian society, much like its eastern neighbor Iraq, it was not long before a seemingly national revolution became transformed into a civil war that was increasingly dominated by sectarian and religious opposition to the dominant Alawi minority, who controlled the levers of power.[230] The Alawi religion had emerged in the tenth and eleventh centuries in the Levant as a separate religion, a mixture of Islamic and non-Islamic motifs from paganism and Christianity. The key feature of the Alawi religion is the veneration of Ali, the Prophet Mohammad's cousin and son-in-law and one of the Rightly-Guided Caliphs of the umma. Often viewed as Shias—though they split from that sect of Islam hundreds of years ago—Alawis are different from the Shias (many of whom have regarded the Alawis with disdain) in that they view Ali as one of the many divine manifestations of God Himself.[231] This earned the Alawis ferocious treatment at the hands of Sunni orthodoxy, including from the noted jurist Ibn Taymiyya, whose fatwas (legal rulings) about the Alawis were tantamount to a call for their extirpation from the umma. They are not viewed any more favorably in contemporary times by Sunni orthodoxy, and particularly not by the Salafists.

The persecution of the Alawis over the centuries forced them into remote and mountainous locales they could easily defend against their oppressors. During the French colonial era after World War I, the Alawis "descended" from their regions to seek employment in low-level and menial jobs. They became exposed to modern ideologies, and the French encouraged their entry into the colonial administration and native military levies, positions that the elite from the Sunni majority disdained and frowned upon for increasingly nationalistic reasons.[232] As a traditionally persecuted minority, Alawis gravitated either toward seeking protection of the French or autonomy in order to avoid coming under Sunni control.[233] In the post–World War II years, when Syria attained independence, the Alawis became convinced that they could best further their interests and security by adhering to and promoting secular Arab ideologies that transcended potentially destructive sectarian identities within the country. Not surprisingly, they promoted secular Baathist ideology, sought an alliance with like-minded (i.e., secular and Arab nationalist) sectors within the demographically dominant Sunni community, and reinforced their position within the security services and armed forces.[234]

Almost immediately following the Alawi-dominated 1963 coup that installed the Baath in power in Syria, the Muslim Brotherhood rose up against what it considered an apostate and therefore illegitimate government in Damascus. Splinter cells such as the Islamic Liberation Movement in Aleppo (Halab) and the Fighting Vanguard (al-Talia al-Muqatila) in Hama, joined the fray.[235] By April 1964 the uprising by the Islamists had developed into a so-called religious war in Hama. The extremists erected roadblocks and stockpiled weapons and provisions. Marwan Hadid, the leader of al-Talia al-Muqatila, moved his fighters into the Sultan Mosque in Hama, where the movement positioned itself for a prolonged standoff. He believed that other militants would soon join his group, ultimately forcing a collapse of the Baathist regime. The prime minister, General Amin al-Hafiz, ordered air raids and a full-scale assault on the mosque. In all over seventy Muslim Brotherhood fighters were killed and hundreds more captured. Lack of organization, the absence of a clear message and set of goals, and lack of popular support had doomed the rebellion from the start.[236]

When Hafez al-Assad assumed power in 1970, his "Corrective Movement" renewed support for the Baath Party, whose image had been discredited by nepotism, corruption, and instability in the 1960s. A series of political and socioeconomic reforms granted the Hafez al-Assad regime a level of legitimacy unmatched in the history of the modern Syrian state.[237] His state-building strategies reinforced the exploitation of the divided Sunni community by commanding the loyalty of the urban Sunni elites through the provision of lucrative positions and financial rewards, by maintaining surveillance over the Sunni lower middle classes, who were the champions of radical and antisecular and anti-Alawi Islamist movements, and by seducing the rural poor through the initiation of land reforms.[238] Furthermore, the rise in Syria's regional and international stature following the October War of 1973, which wiped out the humiliation of the Six-Day War of 1967, lent much weight to Hafez al-Assad's version of Syrian nationalism. This did not prevent the revival of another challenge by the Islamists in the late 1970s and early 1980s, which was mercilessly put down by the regime with considerable loss of life, particularly in the city of Hama, where a Muslim Brotherhood uprising was ruthlessly crushed by armored units dedicated to the protection of the regime.

Bashar al-Assad sought to continue his father's formula for maintaining stability and power, but with attempts to implement reforms, which ultimately stalled.[239] Furthermore, the young Assad initially failed to recognize how religious Sunni society in Syria had become in the 1990s and 2000s in an ostensibly secular state.[240] Ultimately, the Syrian government tried to control the rise of Islamism by promoting a full embrace of Islam. Starting in 2000, a vast network of state-sponsored imams appeared. Their emergence led to a nickname for them: mashaykh al-sultan (Sultan's Clergy).[241] The regime allowed the broadcasting of religious programming on TV and the building of new mosques and religious schools, which alarmed a large number of secular Syrians, whether Sunni or from the minorities.[242] In their two respective large-scale encounters with the Muslim Brotherhood, the Baathist regimes of Salah al-Din al-Bitar and Hafez al-Assad found themselves mired in violence in the same city—Hama.[243] The essential characteristics of this city have always remained constant: it is the fourth-largest city and the most religiously conservative Sunni urban center in the country.[244]

In the early 2000s, observers began to notice signs of a return to Islamist politics in Syria, even though the Islamists functioned clandestinely because of fear of the state.[245] Analysts argued that the resurgence was a response to the massive American wars in Afghanistan and Iraq, impotence of the Arab world in the face of perceived Israeli mistreatment of the Palestinians, and ineffective domestic reform efforts in Syria itself.[246] A religious revival began to sweep Syria, challenging the ruling secular Baath Party to allow more Muslim influence in government and frightening many Syrians who had been schooled for decades to fear political Islam.[247] The Syrian government closely monitored this resurgence and sought to ward off the threat by paying clerics to promote a government-controlled revival of religion. The most prominent progovernment cleric, Sheikh Ahmed Kuftaro, toed the government line: "As an Islamic thinker, I am for a moderate secular state working for the religious beliefs of all.... There is no room for political Islam on our agenda."[248] His son, also a cleric, echoed his father's views, stating that only "moderate" Islam was taught in Sunni educational institutions to ensure that the Islamic Awakening was "kept clear of extremism."[249] Bashar al-Assad's efforts to maintain stability proved unsustainable. Both mainstream and extremist

Islamist movements reappeared and took advantage of the severe economic difficulties the country experienced between 1998 and 2011.[250] Moreover, the country could not insulate itself from the downward spiral faced by its neighbor Iraq. Ironically, Damascus had contributed much to the instability in Iraq through its support for insurgent groups of all stripes and colors in the period 2003 to 2009. By 2011 these radicals came back to haunt the regime that had helped spawn them.

The Syrian civil war gave ISI a chance to show its mettle. As the conflict began to intensify, Abu Bakr al-Baghdadi dispatched one of his junior officers, Abu Mohammad al-Jolani (Ahmed al-Shara), across the border in late 2011 to take advantage of the chaos. Equipped with funds, weapons, and some of ISI's best soldiers, Jolani's group quickly became one of the most formidable fighting forces in Syria.[251] Jolani formed Jabhat al-Nusra (JN) and began distancing himself from ISI as early as January 2012. Jabhat al-Nusra fought well in the battle for Aleppo in July 2012 against regime forces, and that was when it became popular. It established close links with the communities that came under its control and provided basic services efficiently and cheaply. However, it was very secretive at the beginning and did not allow its members to be photographed or give interviews or give out the names of its military commanders.[252]

We know little about Abu Mohammad al-Jolani except that he is Syrian and was a teacher of Arabic before he left to join the Iraqi insurgency sometime around 2004. He became close with Zarqawi, and when Zarqawi was killed in June 2006, Jolani left for Lebanon. While there, he worked as an organizer, providing logistics support for the Lebanese jihadist group Jund al-Sham in the northern part of that country. He then made his way back to Iraq, but he was captured by U.S. forces and interned in Camp Bucca at the same time as Abu Bakr al-Baghdadi. It is not clear that they forged their relationship during their incarceration.[253] After he was released from Camp Bucca, Jolani joined ISI as it sought to revitalize itself and recover from the serious setbacks it had received at the hands of Sunni insurgents and U.S. forces.

A 2013 interview with Jolani by Taysir Alluni of Al-Jazeera revealed a great deal about the JN leader and his vision. Jolani stated that the outbreak of the revolution in Syria had removed people's fear of the oppressive Baathist regime and provided the opportunity for the mujahidin to take advantage of the situation to confront the oppressors.[254] In response to the question of who gave the approval for the emergence of JN in Syria, Jolani answered: "of course, the approval was given by the command of

Iraq there," which could only have meant Abu Bakr al-Baghdadi; and he confirmed it by saying: "the ISI command approved our entry into the land of Al-Sham."[255] Jolani outlined JN's strategy for taking on the Assad regime and its security services. Jabhat al-Nusra focused on targeting the security and intelligence services of the government because they constituted the backbone of the regime, key divisions of the Syrian army, presumably elite units such as the Fourth Armored Division, whose main mission was regime protection, and finally officials of the government. Jolani also said that JN was not all about fighting but sought to implement Islamic governance, maintain security, and provide socioeconomic services for the population in the areas it controlled.[256]

Jolani made it clear that JN's activities were not intended to lead to a unilateral declaration of a state. Once the country was liberated from the clutches of the Baathist regime, the sharia committees, the Muslim elites, clerics, and thinkers, and the ulema would gather to consult with one another and then "draft a plan for running the country."[257] Of course, the governing of post-Baathist Syria would be done according to sharia, and the intent would be to ensure rule according to God's law and to promote justice (*'adl*). Jabhat al-Nusra did not seek to rule Syria but to help in bringing about an Islamic government.[258] While Jolani seemed to have problems with the widespread exercise of the practice of takfir by other jihadist groups, including ISIS, it would be far-fetched to refer to him and JN as "moderates." For Jolani the conflict in Syria is existential and civilizational, as it was for Zarqawi in Iraq. It is a struggle between "good and evil." Jabhat al-Nusra is on the side of "good," obviously the "righteous" Muslims, who have been faced with a pantheon of "evil" forces—Jews, Safavids, Romans, Christians, Alawis, Shias, and misguided Muslims—going back hundreds of years. The war in Syria elicited a curious interpretation from Jolani. He argued that at present a powerful constellation of these "evil" forces had formed a coalition to maintain the Alawi-dominated Baathist regime in power so as to prevent the Muslims from coming to power in Syria.[259] That this interpretation is quite colorful and inaccurate does not matter as much as the fact that it resonated with many jihadists, whether local or foreign.

By early 2013, Jolani was such a powerful commander in his own right that it is possible Abu Bakr al-Baghdadi feared that the Syrian might upstage him or seek to obtain Zawahiri's support to elevate himself as the leader of an independent al-Qaeda branch in Syria. On April 8, 2013, Abu Bakr al-Baghdadi issued a statement that would seal the fate of his relationship with AQC and its leader, Zawahiri. In an audio recording released online, Abu Bakr al-Baghdadi declared that the Nusra Front and ISI would officially become one organization. The merged organization would be called Dawlat al-Islam fi al-Iraq wa Bilad al-Sham (the Islamic State of Iraq and Syria)—more simply, ISIS, or, as the U.S. government calls it, the Islamic State of Iraq and the Levant (ISIL). The rebrand was to be effective immediately. Two days later, Jolani replied, and it was not what Abu Bakr al-Baghdadi had expected to hear. He rejected Abu Bakr al-Baghdadi's "invitation" to merge—and pledged an oath of loyalty directly to Zawahiri, appealing to the "sheikh of jihad" to resolve the dispute. Jolani acknowledged that ISI had provided money and personnel to set up JN, but he put his eggs in the al-Qaeda basket. Not long thereafter the jihadist world was embroiled in a destructive internecine war.

The Ideological Rift between al-Qaeda and the Islamic State of Iraq and Syria

In May 2013, Zawahiri wrote to both Abu Bakr al-Baghdadi and al-Jolani urging ISIS to dissolve and demanding that the original Iraqi group, ISI, focus solely on Iraq while JN would focus on Syria.[260] Verbal sparring continued, but nothing concrete happened to end the conflict. The continuing war of words resulted in yet another letter penned by Zawahiri and published online on June 10, 2013. In that letter, Zawahiri ruled against ISIS, berating Abu Bakr al-Baghdadi for announcing the annexation of JN and the renaming of ISI without consultation. Zawahiri ordered the revocation of the "merger" and stated that Abu Bakr al-Baghdadi and his organization, ISI, would take responsibility for Iraq and Jolani's JN for Syria.[261] The letter named Zawahiri's envoy, Abu Khalid al-Suri, as mediator between the two warring groups. The Islamic State of Iraq rejected al-Suri's appointment and, to add insult to injury, on June 14, 2013, Abu Bakr al-Baghdadi rejected Zawahiri's order to abandon the merger between ISI and JN.[262] Abu Bakr al-Baghdadi challenged Zawahiri's letter, questioning its authenticity and Zawahiri's use of "man-made" [Western] borders to confine ISIS to Iraq.[263] He and ISIS spokesman Abu Mohammad al-Adnani separately referred to Zawahiri's decision revoking the merger—and thus the eradication of the border between the two states, as ISIS wanted—as based in a desire to abide by the Sykes-Picot Agreement of May 1916, implemented by the European powers to establish the broad boundaries of the modern Middle East.

The ideological animosity that erupted between AQC and ISIS involved the wider jihadist world and brought the heavyweights of the Salafist universe into the fray, most notably Maqdisi and Abu Qatada al-Filistini (aka Omar Muhammad Osman).[264] Maqdisi, an eminent Salafi thinker who rose to prominence in the 1980s, became the first significant radical Islamic scholar to declare that the Saudi royal family were apostates and therefore legitimate targets of jihad. Over the years he toned down some of his radical rhetoric, and he is considered the most influential jihadist intellectual, in terms of output and global impact. Even though he has had to fend off thoroughly annoying and snide remarks about being an "armchair" jihadi—he has never carried a weapon in a field of battle—he is held in the highest regard by AQC, and his numerous books and pamphlets are required reading for Islamic militants around the world, who eagerly follow the latest proclamations on his website, the Pulpit of Monotheism and Jihad. Though not as well known as Maqdisi, Abu Qatada has been involved in his share of controversy, first in Britain, when he was deported to Jordan in 2013 for his open support and encouragement of jihadist acolytes. In Jordan he got himself in trouble after being accused of promoting terrorism. After being acquitted, he threw himself wholeheartedly into supporting Jabhat al-Nusra.

For more than a year after the fallout occasioned by the AQC-ISIS conflict over events in Syria in 2013, both Maqdisi and Abu Qatada sought to heal the rift between the two jihadist entities with a view to reintegrating ISIS into the fold of al-Qaeda itself. The effort was not crowned with success, and Abu Qatada felt that the actions of ISIS resembled those of the nihilistically violent Algerian jihadists of the 1990s, who indulged in an orgy of killings that seemed to serve no rational political purpose. During the Algerian confrontation in the 1990s, the most violent and ultimately self-destructive group was the Groupe Armée Islamique, who engaged in an orgy of killing that shocked the mujahidin (see below for Adam Gadahn's critique). Maqdisi, for his part, hoped that there could be some form of genuine reconciliation among the jihadists and that al-Qaeda and ISIS would join hands again. Some of ISIS's most senior members had already written to him in prison signaling their desire to come back into the fold.[265] Maqdisi reached out to the inner circle of ISIS in late 2013, approaching one of his former students, a Bahraini named Turki Mubarak Abdullah Ahmed al-Binali (aka Abu Humam Bakr Ibn Abd al-Aziz al-Athari) whose constant use of many aliases initially confused people as to his identity, which was probably his intention. Binali had been Maqdisi's student and protégé but had drifted away and joined ISIS. Binali rapidly rose into its highest ranks. On April 2013, Binali wrote an important piece of work titled *Madd al-ayadi li-bayaat al-Baghdadi* (Extend Your Hand in Loyalty to Baghdadi), in which he declared that the emir of ISIS had all the qualifications to become caliph. First, he was of Qureishi descent, which was not surprising for Binali to say, as he had invented a genealogical biography of Abu Bakr al-Baghdadi attesting to the validity of his supposed descent from the Prophet Mohammad's tribe. Second, argued Binali, Abu Bakr al-Baghdadi had all the other necessary qualifications: leadership, piety, knowledge, and ability to build consensus.[266] No doubt Maqdisi, recognizing Abu Bakr al-Baghdadi's growing importance, allegedly had warned Binali that unless ISIS was willing to negotiate an end to the conflict with al-Qaeda, the group risked condemnation from the world's most eminent jihadi thinkers.[267] Binali assured Maqdisi that Abu Bakr al-Baghdadi wanted to reach agreement with al-Qaeda. Eventually, Maqdisi concluded that Binali had little intention of settling the feud that was roiling the jihadist ranks. Binali apparently spent his time in arguing over frivolous ideological issues and making snide remarks aimed at Maqdisi.[268] It was clear that he was reserving his serious output to advance the rise of his chosen mentor, Abu Bakr al-Baghdadi. The polemics between the two sides went on with little letup into late 2013 and incorporated attacks on one another's ideological stances and operational methods and vitriolic personal assaults.

The deterioration in relations between al-Qaeda and ISIS accelerated dramatically in the wake of a momentous decision taken by Zawahiri: in early February 2014, he declared that ISIS was no longer a branch of al-Qaeda. Al-Qaeda, he stressed, had no organizational relationship with ISIS and was not responsible for its actions and behavior. This was the first time that AQC had disaffiliated an affiliate. Zawahiri then declared JN to be the official AQ affiliate in Syria. Abu Bakr al-Baghdadi made his displeasure and disagreement evident. On February 23, 2014, ISIS sent two suicide bombers to kill Zawahiri's friend Abu Khalid al-Suri, the mediator.[269] On April 17, 2014, Abu Mohammad al-Adnani poured scorn on al-Qaeda in an audio message, "Ma kan hadha Manhajuna wa lan yakun" (This Is Not Our Methodology nor Will It Ever Be). The path of jihad, said Adnani, was strewn with difficulties and it was not surprising that many engaged in it halfheartedly or gave up halfway. Only the mujahidin of ISIS had stayed on the true path and confronted the mightiest force ever fielded by the enemy, "with bare chests, confident of Allah's victory, determined to establish the Law of Allah. Their bodies in Iraq, their souls in the imprisoned city of Makkah, their hearts in Bayt al-Maqdis [Jerusalem], and their eyes upon Rome."[270] Al-Qaeda on the other hand was a "deviated" creed that had adopted concepts that were secular in origin and that now, "horror of horrors," argued that the mujahidin must be tolerant toward and understanding of Shias, Hindus, and Christians. The attack seemed to be aimed at the supposedly new and deviant direction al-Qaeda was taking under Zawahiri. Zawahiri was the same man, however, whom Adnani had praised as the rightful successor to bin Laden on August 7, 2011. This admiration had not lasted long. In 2013 Zawahiri had written a short pamphlet, *General Guidelines for Jihad*, in which he called for extensive preparation of the mujahidin and the civilians before fighting and for the adoption of a flexible and pragmatic stance vis-à-vis other Islamist groups and, indeed, non-Muslim populations. The guidelines advised the mujahidin to avoid provoking and targeting others just because they did not share the goals of the jihadists. This "moderate" posture, which advocated a live and let live attitude, avoiding making enemies needlessly, and focusing on the target—America and its local collaborators—must have incensed Adnani.

Barely a day after Adnani's vitriolic verbal assault, Zawahiri discussed the interjihadist conflict in an interview with AQ's media wing, al-Sahab. He claimed that the violence among the jihadist groups had been caused by the ignorant, unjust, and capricious behavior of some elements, that is, ISIS, and suggested that some kind of "anti-jihadist influence" had penetrated the ranks of the mujahidin.[271] This prompted ISIS spokesman Adnani to respond on May 11, 2014, with the release of a thirty-eight-minute YouTube video sarcastically titled "Udhran ya amir al-Qaeda" (Apologies O Commander of al-Qaeda) in which Adnani said that ISIS was following the "truth path" of al-Qaeda: "Osama bin Laden united the mujahideen upon one word, while you [Zawahiri] disunited them, split them, and dispersed them." Adnani claimed that al-Qaeda was too moderate and that Zawahiri was focused on promoting himself. Not surprising, Adnani asserted that the current al-Qaeda was different from the "al-Qaeda that we loved...al-Qaeda that we allied ourselves with...al-Qaeda that we supported."[272] This assault on al-Qaeda tested the patience of its leading supporters in the Salafi intellectual scene. On April 28, 2014, Abu Qatada, who is never at a loss in coming up with a colorful phrase, responded to the attack on al-Qaeda's leadership and accused ISIS leaders of being "misguided, liars, and ignorant" and said that they were the "dogs of hellfire."[273] On May 26, 2014, Maqdisi declared that his negotiations with ISIS were dead and that all his efforts trying to make ISIS "return to the path of truth" had been for naught. Abu Bakr al-Baghdadi, his commanders, and their religious officials were members of a rebellious "deviant organization."[274] Maqdisi advised ISIS personnel to defect to JN and decreed that no Islamic website should host ISIS's messages.[275]

The attacks by both Maqdisi and Abu Qatada on ISIS did not mean they were unaware of the serious problems within al-Qaeda itself. These were the very problems that ISIS had been able to exploit and take advantage of.[276] Zawahiri's leadership was a major problem itself; it is possible that they thought Zawahiri's "excommunication" of ISIS had simply worsened matters needlessly. Maqdisi and Abu Qatada believed that Zawahiri possessed little of the authority and charisma required to thwart successfully the threat from ISIS. From the very beginning of his tenure, Zawahiri had lacked direct military or operational control and situational awareness of what was going on within al-Qaeda's far-flung affiliates. According to Maqdisi, al-Qaeda's organizational structure had "collapsed."[277] Zawahiri, Maqdisi said, operated solely based on allegiance. There was no organizational structure left in AQC. Instead, "there is only communication channels, and loyalty."[278] In Maqdisi's and Abu Qatada's opinions, ISIS had blunted the fortunes of al-Qaeda. They believed that the events of the past decade highlighted the need for al-Qaeda to review its goals, the strategic relationship between its goals and means, and its operational methods. Review would lead to renewal. For instance, Maqdisi argued that al-Qaeda should no longer aim to recruit followers in large numbers; it needed "people of quality" who thoroughly understand Islamic scholarship, and would not merely deploy it in the furtherance of their own personal ends.

The rift between ISIS and AQC was transformed into bitter animosity after the proclamation of IS on June 29, 2014, by ISIS spokesman Mohammad al-Adnani, though the solid ground for it had been thoroughly prepared two months earlier on April 30, 2014, by the ideologue Binali, in an important piece of work in which he declared that ISIS did not have to have territory—though it did control territory—in its possession (*tamkin*, empowerment) for the faithful to pledge loyalty to Abu Bakr al-Baghdadi. After all, the faithful had pledged loyalty or allegiance to the Prophet Mohammad even when he had no state. Salafist thinkers like Maqdisi became convinced that Binali was laying the groundwork for this momentous declaration. Sure enough, the audio message by Adnani of April 17 was all the confirmation they needed. Adnani stated that it was incumbent upon all Muslims to pledge allegiance to Abu Bakr al-Baghdadi, who was now the Caliph Ibrahim. Adnani continued by stating that Caliph Ibrahim had fulfilled all conditions in Islamic law to become the new Islamic ruler and thus the state was legitimate. The Islamic State aimed to make its "state" a chosen destination for jihadists, who would come to support it in its methodology and the wars it waged in defense of Islam.

Al-Qaeda and its supporters adamantly refused to accept the declaration of the Caliphate. Abu Bakr al-Baghdadi had had himself declared caliph without the global consensus of Muslims; al-Qaeda argued that he lacked the requirements to be a caliph and was a figure previously unknown to Muslims. Every utterance of allegiance given to him was therefore null and void. Al-Qaeda has long maintained that while the establishment of the caliphate is the ultimate goal, conditions are not yet right. In their view, Muslims need to be educated about "true Islam" for many more years before the caliphate can be revived. Al-Qaeda did not consider it permissible to declare a caliphate before achieving full political capability (*al-tamkin al-kamil*), the full ability to gather a Muslim community in a defined territory and provide for its security and needs. Al-Qaeda Central did not believe that IS had such a capability over a sufficiently large portion of the umma or that IS was capable of sustaining its efforts in the long term. The Islamic State justified its proclamation of an Islamic state because a council of Islamic scholars known as *ahl al-hall wa al-aqd* (the people who loosen and bind) had "legally" sanctioned it. Al-Qaeda Central argued that this group was too small and unrepresentative to have effectively done so. In the wake of numerous lessons learned from setbacks, al-Qaeda had started to promote a strategy of Islamization of Muslim populations. It argued that without popular support first, the jihadist movement could not set up a functioning Islamic state.[279]

The Islamic State disagreed vehemently with AQC's assessments. The Islamic State saw itself as emulating the Prophet Mohammad's example, first by building up a small community of faithful followers, seizing territory from the enemy, and then expanding it by force of arms, and finally through the establishment of a state. The Islamic State's narrative, as articulated in the August 2014 third issue of its online magazine *Dabiq*—named after the Syrian location of the supposed end of days battle between Muslims and unbelievers—the establishment of the Caliphate in 2014 represented the culmination of a multiphase strategy in 2003 by its then leader, Zarqawi. According to IS, this path began with the hijra of the mujahidin to a land with a weak central authority—Anbar province—as

Mohammad and his followers had done, "to use it as a base where a *jama'ah* [organization] could form, recruit and train members." Zarqawi and his organization then implemented a strategy to create as much chaos as possible. As IS articulated in *Dabiq*, this was to "prevent any taghut (tyrant) regime from ever achieving a degree of stability that would enable it to govern and use its security apparatus to crush any Islamic movement."[280] After having destabilized the regime, the final phase of the strategy included, according to *Dabiq*, a steady campaign of more complex attacks on a larger scale, which were meant to pave the way for the claiming of territory over which the mujahidin would consolidate control.

Soon after ISIS declared the formation of a caliphate in June 2014 and changed its name to IS, Maqdisi released a statement castigating IS as an ignorant and misguided project and accused its founders of subverting and undermining the mujahidin's efforts to bring about Islamic unity. In an interview with Western journalists at his friend Abu Qatada's house, Maqdisi accused the group of having lied to him and betrayed him and said that its members were not worthy of calling themselves mujahidin.[281] Abu Qatada joined Maqdisi as one of the most prominent radicals to excoriate IS publicly. He accused IS of causing divisions within the jihadi movement and establishing a caliphate when conditions were not yet ripe. For Abu Qatada, Abu Bakr al-Baghdadi and his followers "were not our brothers."

While Maqdisi and Abu Qatada took the lead in criticizing and trying to shame IS, the fallout between al-Qaeda and IS involved a whole parade of jihadist luminaries who were able to put pen to paper and thus take an ideological stance. Some took positions supporting al-Qaeda; some argued vehemently in favor of IS. Another leading al-Qaeda personality also entered the fray, but his critique of IS has not received the attention it deserves. This was the critique of Adam Gadahn, the one-time American spokesman for al-Qaeda who was killed in mid-January 2015 in Waziristan, Pakistan. To be sure, Gadahn was not the intellectual equal of the heavyweights Maqdisi and Abu Qatada. However, as mentioned, Gadahn had already cast doubt on the actions of ISI as far back as 2011, just before bin Laden was killed. Furthermore, being a media spokesman, he was articulate and accessible, while Maqdisi and Abu Qatada often used esoteric language to attack IS's "ideological deviations" and operational methods. Gadahn's critique appeared in the guise of an interview with the al-Qaeda magazine *Resurgence* in the summer of 2015. The interview must have taken place in the latter half of 2014, after the declaration of IS and, obviously, before his death on January 19, 2015. His wide-ranging interview with *Resurgence*, which also touched upon Zarqawi, is fascinating. Though his views on guerrilla warfare are somewhat superficial and erroneous—that was not his area of expertise—his observations on the goings-on within the jihadist world and particularly his critique of IS are informative. It is his withering critique that is of relevance here because he was articulate and, being American, spoke fluent English and thus could reach a wider public.[282]

Gadahn's approach was three-phased. He started the interview by pointing out the "positive" traits of al-Qaeda; he did not, however, engage in comparing it with ISIS and its successor. He just pointed out what he saw as the positive attributes of his parent organization, such as its recognition of the importance of having good public relations and of winning the hearts and minds of the "Muslim masses."[283] This, he said, was in contrast with groups—unnamed—that rejected or belittled the idea of gaining and maintaining a popular support base.

Gadahn then proceeded to discuss the "positive" attributes and characteristics of the Islamic Emirate of Afghanistan (the Taliban), ruled by Mullah Omar. Outsiders disparaged the alleged, he emphasized, "brutality" of the Taliban without examining it dispassionately. Even the mujahidin needed to learn from it. First, it was an Afghan experience; yes, fighters from outside came to help the Afghan mujahidin, but they did not jockey for power and the top positions within the jihad in Afghanistan (unlike the foreigners in Iraq presumably).[284] Second, the spiritual leadership of the Islamic Emirate of Afghanistan was in the hands of "real" and learned religious scholars who advised the decision-makers. Third, the Islamic Emirate in Afghanistan had been careful to avoid making too many enemies and had shown prudence in not opening too many fronts.[285] This statement cannot be seen in any other way than as an implicit criticism of ISIS and IS under Abu Bakr al-Baghdadi.

Gadahn then launched into a lengthy, hard-hitting critique of ISIS's methodology and approach before it declared an Islamic state and then proceeded to dismantle its pretensions to being such a state. The leadership of Abu Bakr al-Baghdadi and his acolytes had been controversial from the very beginning, according to Gadahn, and consisted of a largely unknown group of individuals who had risen to power following the deaths of Abu Omar al-Baghdadi and Abu Hamza al-Muhajir. The new leadership had managed to enter into vicious fights with almost all other jihadist groups in Iraq and Syria, spreading fitna: jihadist infighting and chaos. The new leadership were inflexible, doctrinaire, and prone to issuing declarations and committing acts that deviated from Islam.[286]

Despite repeatedly shrugging off the stream of criticism from al-Qaeda heavyweights as irrelevant, IS became sufficiently worried by it to embark on a social media campaign against them, which was apparently sanctioned by ISIS's chief propagandist, Adnani. At first ISIS and then later IS social media accounts berated the two al-Qaeda clerics as "stooges" of the West, part of a growing conspiracy against the Caliphate. The sixth issue of *Dabiq* featured a full-page picture of Maqdisi and Abu Qatada, labeled as "misleading scholars" who should be avoided more than the devil himself. According to the *Guardian,* a series of detailed leaks from an anonymous Twitter account indicated that Binali had approached Abu Bakr al-Baghdadi with a stark appraisal of IS's vulnerable position. The Caliphate would eventually collapse if the jihad's leading scholars and veterans continued to stand against IS.[287] The project could not be sustained unless IS recruited supporters and continued to maintain its level of success on the ground.

As the verbal offensives and counter-offensives between al-Qaeda and IS proceeded apace and captured the attention of both the wider jihadist constellation and the academic observers who studied them, IS continued with its strategy of taking foreigners hostage and executing them. The American journalists James Foley and Steven Sotloff were beheaded in August and September 2014, respectively, as a "message to America." Maqdisi thought that negotiations between him and IS leaders to release its hostages rather than killing them could help bridge the gap between al-Qaeda and IS and, just as important, reverse the growing perception in both the Muslim and non-Muslim worlds that all Islam was about was violence. He tried to intercede on behalf of American hostage Peter Kassig, a convert to Islam who had been captured by IS. It responded by executing Kassig in November 2014. This duplicity outraged Maqdisi.

What followed was even worse and sealed the enmity between Maqdisi and IS, when Maqdisi realized that he had been played. On December 24, 2014, a Jordanian F-16 jet fighter crashed over IS territory near the northern Syrian city of Raqqa, and its pilot, Muadh al-Kassasbeh, was taken hostage. Maqdisi sounded out Jordanian officials about securing the return of the pilot. Maqdisi sent word to IS in January 2015 that the Jordanians would be willing to conduct a prisoner swap. In return for the pilot, they would release Sajida al-Rishawi, who was the sister of Thamer al-Rishawi, one of the first Iraqi army officers to join Zarqawi's original group years back. In 2005, Zarqawi had sent Sajida al-Rishawi and her husband on a suicide mission to Jordan to explode bomb belts at the Radisson SAS hotel as part of a coordinated series of suicide bombings in Amman, the Jordanian capital. Rishawi's device did not detonate; she fled the scene and wandered aimlessly around the city until she was arrested, tried, and sentenced to death. She remained on death row for the next decade. Maqdisi believed that IS was ready to make the trade, and he invested considerable time and prestige in trying to consummate the deal, contacting Abu Bakr al-Baghdadi and appealing to his sense of decency and self-interest.[288] People both inside and outside the jihadist world were perplexed: who was al-Rishawi? And when they became enlightened as to the identity of this inept and sad nonentity who had been languishing in a Jordanian prison, the next question was why was she so important to IS? To complicate matters, on social media, IS supporters began calling for al-Rishawi's release, which led people to finally conclude that she must be of some value to them. In reality, she was of no value. Even Maqdisi was duped.

The rest, as they say, is history. In February 2015, IS put on a spectacle that even the ancient Romans could not have surpassed in the Coliseum: they doused the orange jumpsuit-clad Jordanian pilot in gasoline and put him in a cage, and a jihadist "soldier" from a unit allegedly badly damaged by Jordanian aerial strikes lit the gasoline and burned him alive as the world watched in morbid fascination. The video of the execution was professionally done, and IS went out of its way to state that the horrific event was just reward for the Jordanian pilot's "crime of bombing innocent civilians."[289] Many Muslims were enraged by this unwarranted display of savagery, which they deemed un-Islamic; the Jordanian government, for its part, ordered the execution of al-Rishawi and a hapless male terrorist in what was incontrovertibly an act of revenge.[290] An embittered Maqdisi appeared on Jordanian TV on February 6, 2015, to denounce "these people [who] invented many bad practices" and condemn them as slaughterers who had introduced a practice, immolation, which the Prophet had specifically reserved for God.[291] The world wondered what kind of an organization was capable of engaging in such acts.

4

From Network to Organization

THE STRUCTURE OF THE ISLAMIC STATE AND ITS PREDECESSORS

THE ISLAMIC STATE has emerged as one of the world's most well-developed nonstate actors in terms of organization and structure. It was not always that way. It started small as a cadre of like-minded jihadists connected by kinship or friendship in the time period between 1999 and 2000 grouped around Zarqawi and other "Levantine" fellow travelers. In Afghanistan this network came together in a small training camp in the eastern part of the country where the Taliban commander was a sympathizer. Eventually, they called their organization Jund al-Sham (Soldiers of the Levant). It developed into a relatively potent organization under Zarqawi, called Jamiat al-Tawhid wa al-Jihad (the Group of Monotheism and Jihad) when it relocated to Iraq to fight the Americans and the Shias. When it became an affiliate of the world's best-known and leading jihadist enterprise, al-Qaeda, the group was renamed Tanzim Qaedat al-Jihad fi Bilad al-Rafidain (Organization of the Jihad Base in the Land of the Two Rivers, i.e., Iraq), often shortened to al-Qaeda fi Bilad al-Rafidain (al-Qaeda in the Land of the Two Rivers, or al-Qaeda in Iraq, in line with the American nomenclature). Its efforts to develop further after Zarqawi's death succumbed to internal and external pressures. It began to unravel and disintegrate by 2007. Effectively hounded by U.S. forces, it went to ground and reemerged in 2011 following the U.S. withdrawal. The organization that emerged as ISI and then ISIS and finally as IS (or the Caliphate) required considerable effort and resources on the part of its adherents. This chapter will trace the origins and evolution of the organization from the early difficult days to mid-2017, when it began to slowly disintegrate under the military blows of its various enemies.

As an organization, the entity we now know as IS has to be clandestine concerning its inner workings, the relationship between its various branches, and its administrative, security, and military personnel. The full story of its organizational structure will remain incomplete until outsiders manage to amass more and more documentation about its inner workings. A number of people have done a sterling job in acquiring the documentation to build a picture of IS's organization. In many cases the documentation has been handed over by people who have risked their lives to do so and then fled IS control. At other times advancing anti-IS forces would recover documentation about the inner workings of IS left behind by fleeing jihadists. A U.S. academic and policy team analyzed dozens of AQI's and ISI's internal financial and managerial documents. Captured by U.S.-led Coalition and Iraqi forces between 2005 and 2010, these include scans of typed documents as well as electronic files found on hard drives, flash drives, and other media. Among them have been spreadsheets listing the qualifications and training of hundreds of fighters, numbers of family members of fighters, details on thousands of individual salary payments, and massive lists of carefully itemized expenditures. There have also been instructions outlining geographic areas of responsibility for subunits, memos suggesting minor changes to organizational structures, and periodic management reports from personnel stationed in the various "governorates." Month by month, particularly as IS unravels as it loses control over territory and peoples, more details have been uncovered about how it was built over the years, how it is run, and how it has engaged in its pursuit of state-building and governance. This chapter is an effort in the direction of building a picture of the inner workings of IS and its predecessors going back to Zarqawi's original groups. But the full story of its organizational structure is one we will to have await for a while longer.

The Abu Musab al-Zarqawi Network and Jund al-Sham

When Zarqawi made his way into Afghanistan for the first time, he allegedly received military training at Abdullah Azzam's Sada camp, run by the Maktab al-Khidamat, or Office of Services. Zarqawi believed that his first experiences in Afghanistan contained both positive and negative elements. He pointed out: "There is no doubt that the Afghan jihad experience benefited us. The shortcomings stemmed from the nature of the situation in Afghanistan. We lived on the front and conducted a general form of jihad against the infidels. We used to spend long months on the front."[1] However, it was not all a positive learning experience, judging by this statement: "There were no organized programs to provide us with a jihadist training that would include shari'ah rules and *organizational affairs.* There was nothing of the sort. There were camps in which you got military training and then you went off to the front to fight. That was all.... Our experience was military and involved learning the arts of combat. *There was no emphasis on organizational matters."* [2] Many of the foreign fighters from the Arab countries were neophytes whose organizational and fighting skills were nonexistent and which were eventually acquired on the ground in combat rather than through prior preparation and training. This situation stood in stark contrast to the emphatic calls from some jihadists, like Abdullah Azzam, for thorough preparation and training prior to engagement in combat. However, the chaotic situation on the ground in Afghanistan and the overwhelming domination of the anti-Soviet and anti-Kabul regime jihad by Afghan mujahidin did not provide the Arabs with much opportunity to prepare and organize as well as they wanted.

Nonetheless, the Afghan mujahidin themselves were not "ten foot tall." Zarqawi was disappointed by the lack of discipline and cohesion among the various Afghan mujahidin factions, which fell out with one another following their defeat of the Soviets in 1988 and then following their overthrow of the Marxist regime in Kabul. He complained that "the various factions began to fight against each other after the fall of Kabul." [3] Some of the Afghan mujahidin, stated Zarqawi, were following a "twisted path" and accepting "secularists and communists" into their ranks. Many of the mujahidin groups, he fumed, "fought alongside the nationalists and failed from the start to distinguish between those who followed the right Islamic path and those who did not." [4] As a result of witnessing "things that contradicted the right path of Islam," Zarqawi and his close friends decided to leave Afghanistan and try to do something in the Greater Syria region, also known as the Levant and encompassing Syria, Jordan, Lebanon, and the Palestinian territories. [5]

Back home, Zarqawi's efforts to fight the well-entrenched Jordanian monarchy came to naught. He met with like-minded jihadists and with Maqdisi, who had already returned home. They planned actions against the Jordanian state for its perceived betrayal of Islam and its forthcoming peace treaty with Israel. The plans to take on the Jordanian state, Zarqawi himself admitted, suffered from amateurishness: "When we returned to Jordan, we were excessively zealous. This was obvious. We also lacked sufficient experience.... We suffered from some security gaps as a result of our lack of experience in organizational matters and our lack of jihadist experience. I am talking about my personal jihadist experience with some brothers who decided to transfer the jihadist process to Jordan. Three years in Afghanistan was not enough to give us the needed experience."[6] The Jordanian General Intelligence Department had numerous informants among the itinerant Salafist groups in Zarqa. Zarqawi and his associates, including the intellectual Maqdisi, who really was never cut out for field operations, were arrested and put on trial on charges of terrorism.

Maqdisi, Zarqawi, and others were sent to prison. Stories of Zarqawi's time in prison and his complex relationship with Maqdisi abound, and there are, of course, variations in these narratives. However, they all agree that it was in prison that Zarqawi "matured" as a jihadist. It was at that time, too, that he actually adopted the moniker Abu Musab al-Zarqawi and emerged as the "tough" of his cell block. The name Musab he took from Abu Musab Bin Umayr, a companion of the Prophet Mohammad and a Qureishi tribesman. The name Zarqawi he took to indicate where he came from, the town of Zarqa. In the dynamic of prison life, he took command and doled out chores. Khalid Abu Doma, who was jailed with Zarqawi for plotting against the Jordanian government, recalled: "He didn't have great ideas. But people listened to him because they feared him."[7] He emerged as a key and respected player within the walls of the prison, often acting as the prisoners' spokesman vis-à-vis the prison authorities (i.e., the Jordanian state, which he despised).[8]

To celebrate the accession of King Abdullah II to the Jordanian throne, Zarqawi and the others were released in an amnesty in 1999.[9] The Jordanian monarch allegedly regretted this act of clemency when the crisis over the pilot Muadh al-Kasasbeh broke. Zarqawi took off for Afghanistan again, where he ran into al-Qaeda through a well-known Egyptian militant, Sayf al-Adl, who wrote a report on Zarqawi for the senior al-Qaeda leadership duo of bin Laden and Zawahiri. The militant Islamist currents present within Egypt in the 1980s heavily influenced Sayf al-Adl, yet he managed to keep his sentiments well hidden, to the extent that he was allegedly accepted into Saiqa 777, one of the major Egyptian special operation units. He attained "expertise in explosives, counterintelligence and parachuting, earning the rank of Lieutenant Colonel."[10] His career in the special forces imbued him with discipline, as well as taught him the importance of training in effective communication and of gathering intelligence on enemy forces.[11] Training in counterintelligence taught him the importance of taking precautions to ensure operational security. He learned the importance of allocating information to junior operatives on a need-to-know basis, to prevent a large "volume of information" from falling into the adversary's hands. After an attempted assassination of Egypt's interior minister in 1987 by Islamist militants, the government, perpetually in fear of the militants infiltrating the institutions of the state, went on a massive manhunt, arresting Islamists and suspected sympathizers in an effort to weed them out from the security and military forces. Sayf al-Adl came under suspicion for Islamist activism and was put on trial, but there was little evidence against him. He was released and cashiered. He promptly left for Afghanistan.

At the time of his meeting with Zarqawi, Sayf al-Adl was also beginning to devote a considerable amount of time to security and intelligence matters within the jihadist organizations, including those who had failed due to lack of attention to security and intelligence. His booklet *The Compilation on Security and Intelligence* did not appear until much later. He probably wrote it in Iran while he was a "guest" of the Iranians after al-Qaeda cadre fled from Afghanistan in October 2001 following the American assault in retaliation for 9/11. Nevertheless, many of his ideas were already germinating at the time of his meeting with Zarqawi, and it is reasonable to assume that he imparted some of them to the Jordanian.

Sayf al-Adl himself had a great deal to say about Zarqawi. After the victory of the Afghan mujahidin against the Soviets in 1988 and the subsequent fallings-out among Afghan insurgent factions, many of the Arab Afghans who were able to do so returned to their countries of origin. Others, such as the Egyptians, could not, because of the power of the Egyptian state and its vigilant surveillance of jihadists. Some chose to go to "Sudan, Somalia, and some underprivileged African countries," places where "there were no powerful central governments and where we would have powerful alliances."[12] Adl stated that those who remained in Afghanistan decided to take measures to stop the hemorrhaging of experienced fighters. They set up al-Qaeda and began to gather information in order to reorganize the jihadist effort. They focused much of their attention on the Jordanians and Palestinians. The jihadists began to follow the military tribunals that the Jordanian State Security Court was holding against those who had returned to Jordan from Afghanistan:

> We began to gather needed information to reorganize our effort. First, we wanted to obtain old and recent information concerning all the pioneers of jihad in the Afghan arena. Foremost of them were our Jordanian and Palestinian brothers. We wanted to update our information about them.

Therefore, we followed the military tribunals that the Jordanian State Security Court held against Jordanians who returned from Afghanistan and various small Islamic groups that attempted to carry out some jihadist acts from Jordanian territories against the state of the Zionist enemy in beloved Palestine. Most prominent in the media were fraternal brothers Abu Muhammad al-Maqdisi and Abu Mus'ab.[13]

Al-Qaeda command received information that Zarqawi wanted to go to Chechnya after his release in 1999. Adl allegedly first met Zarqawi in Kandahar after Zarqawi was forced to leave Pakistan due to problems with the Pakistani authorities. Adl begins by noting: "in a nutshell, Abu Mus'ab was a hardliner when it came to his disagreements with other fraternal brothers."[14] After an extended meeting with Zarqawi in Kandahar, Adl related:

> I found that I was talking to a man with whom I shared many traits. Abu Mus'ab was a sturdy man who was not really very good at words. He expressed himself spontaneously and briefly. He would not compromise any of his beliefs. He was uncompromising but he had a clear objective, which he strived to achieve—the reestablishment of Islam in society. He did not have details regarding how to achieve this objective except for initiating tawhid, comprehending the faith thoroughly, and initiating jihad against the nation's enemy. Abu Mus'ab's life experience was not very rich. He had, however, great ambitions and defined goals. I asked him about the situation in Jordan and Palestine. He had adequate information about Jordan, but his information about Palestine was poor. We discussed points of disagreements between him and his fraternal brothers. We listened to him, but we did not argue since we wanted to win him over to our side.[15]

Adl later met with bin Laden and Zawahiri to give them a summary of his interactions with Zarqawi. The key issue discussed seems to have been Zarqawi's inflexibility and his "disagreements with...fraternal brothers":

> the controversial issues with Abu Mus'ab were neither new nor uncommon. We used to have disagreements with hundreds of other fraternal brothers who came from various regions in the world

regarding certain issues. The reason was the diverse understanding of some aspects that pertain to wala [commitment to everything God says], and bara' [abandonment of everything God hates], and the subsequent issues of takfir [excommunication] or irja [an early Islamic school of thought that was characterized by insistence on keeping an apolitical attitude and refusal to judge the faith of others].[16]

This was ironic, as many jihadists have stated that Sayf al-Adl himself was not easy to get along with. He was ruthless, unwilling to countenance failures, particularly in the realm of security and secrecy. Moreover, he loathed the jihadists from the Gulf.

One of the unanswered questions is whether al-Qaeda was looking carefully at Zarqawi at that time with an eye to having him set up an affiliate in Jordan. Some tantalizing hints of such a scenario are suggested in Sayf al-Adl's assessment of the jihadists from the Levant:

> The information we had said that Al-Qaida and its tenets did not have many supporters in Palestine or Jordan. The plan [not further defined] that the fraternal brothers agreed on underlined the importance of the presence of Al-Qa'ida in Jordan and Palestine since the Palestinian question is the bleeding heart of the nation.... The liberation of the nation is contingent on dealing a strike to the Israelis and annihilating their state. There will be no change or liberation unless Israel is undermined and eliminated.... How could we abandon such an opportunity to be in Palestine and Jordan? How could we waste a chance to work with Abu Mus'ab and similar men in other countries.[17]

It is not clear why al-Qaeda would focus so much attention on the then relatively insignificant and "difficult" Zarqawi. However, given al-Qaeda's lack of traction within the populations of the Levant—Syrians, Lebanese, Jordanians, and Palestinians—the leadership may have concluded that Zarqawi would be a means to reach out to those people, rather than the more prominent and obstreperous Syrian jihadist Mustafa Setmariam Nassar (aka Abu Musab al-Suri), who was a visceral critic of jihadist failures, including those of al-Qaeda.[18]

During his second sojourn in Afghanistan, Zarqawi managed to create the nucleus of a kinship-and friendship-based organization, meaning that it was an organization that was composed of individuals (and their families) who knew and trusted each other as a result of long years of intermarriage and family relationships or simply because they came from the same cities in Jordan, such as Zarqa, al-Rusayfa, and Salt.[19] More than three hundred men and youths left Zarqa to carry on jihad activities in Afghanistan, Chechnya, and then in Iraq with Zarqawi. The city of Zarqa provided him with some of his first recruits for the jihad in Iraq. Zarqa is important because it was the home of Zarqawi but, more important, that of Maqdisi. A large number of Salafi-jihadists emerged from Zarqa long before Zarqawi became known. A number of young men from Zarqa went off to the jihad in Afghanistan and were killed there. Zarqa is home to the Banu Hasan Bedouin tribe, from which Zarqawi hails; to Chechens and Circassians, whose forebears founded the city at the end of the nineteenth century; and to Palestinian refugees, whose families came there when they were expelled from Palestine at the end of the Arab-Israeli War of 1948.[20]

When the Chechens first built it, Zarqa was a small community and not a town. It grew after the Palestinian exoduses in 1948 and in 1967. In the 1960s, it became a poorly planned industrial adjunct serving Amman, the capital of Jordan. An oil refinery and phosphate, paper, and beverage plants were opened there. Many residents left the town in the 1970s and 1980s to work in the oil-rich Gulf States. Following the Iraqi invasion of Kuwait, which Jordan and its population tacitly endorsed, many Palestinian-Jordanians were expelled from Kuwait; 250,000 returned to Jordan, and 160,000 returned to Zarqa itself. Among them were several individuals espousing Salafist sentiments that they had developed in Kuwait under the aegis of an Egyptian cleric, Sheikh Abd al-Rahman Abd al-Khaliq, who had settled in Kuwait in the 1960s to escape Gamal Abdel Nasser's secular regime. At the same time, homegrown Salafism was also beginning to appear in Zarqa as a result of splits and disagreements within the Jordanian Muslim Brotherhood.[21]

The Zarqawi group in Afghanistan also took in Syrians, Lebanese, and Palestinians, including men such as Abd al-Hadi Daghlas and Khalid al-Aruri, both Palestinians, and Suleiman Khalid Darwish (aka Abu al-Ghadiya "the first"), a Syrian. Zarqawi refused to integrate his group into al-Qaeda while in Afghanistan but set up his own camp in Herat.[22] However, al-Qaeda provided the Herat camp in eastern Afghanistan with "seed" money to get off the ground. The Herat camp was small; according to Sayf al-Adl, it consisted of forty-two men, women, and children. It eventually increased in size. Adl also noticed that Zarqawi had changed: from the uncompromising but awkward doctrinaire, he had become more organized, more interested in global affairs, and more articulate. At one point, Adl seemed to imply that Abu al-Ghadiya "the first" had an impact on the emergence of a more polished Zarqawi: "His Syrian companion was wonderful. He possessed vast experiences and mastered several languages including English, Turkish, and some Kurdish."[23] Zarqawi's education in history (he seemed to have developed an interest in two great figures of Islamic history: Nur al-Din Zengi, the Turkish Muslim *atabeg* (ruler) of Mosul, and Salah al-Din al-Ayyubi, the Kurdish Muslim commander from Tikrit who defeated the Crusaders) and contemporary global affairs seems to have been at the hands of his more politically savvy Syrian "brothers" in arms. As Adl stated, at the dawn of 2001, Zarqawi had become a "different person," and "he began planning for the future in a strategic manner." He focused on building relations with all nationalities and races, including young Arab and non-Arab men in the Afghan arena. Initially, this group of jihadists was nothing more than a network, which is a porous and fluid entity with no established or clear-cut hierarchy and leadership; moreover, individual members have no specific skill sets or tasks assigned to them. As this network of ideologically like-minded Islamists connected by ties of friendship and kinship evolved into a simple organization with a more discernible hierarchy and functional specialization among its personnel, it came to be known as Jund al-Sham (Soldiers of the Levant).[24]

Whatever it was that Zarqawi was planning to do in Afghanistan or beyond, it was overtaken by the 9/11 attacks on the United States. Zarqawi was not in on the operation, but apparently he was brought into the discussions following the 9/11 attacks concerning their ramifications and implications, particularly the expected U.S. response. Al-Qaeda did not have a clear or defined plan for confrontation with the force bearing down upon it following 9/11. Adl stated that al-Qaeda's leadership "ultimately decided that the form of confrontation was the guerrilla warfare or the hit-and-run tactic."[25] However, the top leadership decided that it would be best if the Afghan mujahidin were to bear the brunt of this guerrilla war, as "our race and language as Arabs were not suitable for such missions."[26] Those among the Arabs who had mastered the languages and dialects of the country could elect to stay or leave with the Arab fighters. Adl added that the dispersal of the Arab fighters to other potential theaters was actually a benefit, as it "provided us with further financial and human resources that we could employ in the battle," which was now not confined to a particular area but could take place anywhere in the world.

Following the U.S. invasion of Afghanistan, Zarqawi and his nascent organization were stranded in Herat, whose largely Shia population had become increasingly hostile. The group left Herat in a massive convoy for Kandahar, the remaining safe haven of the disintegrating Taliban state. From there, Sayf al-Adl facilitated the transfer of Zarqawi and his group to temporary refuge in Iran. Iran's murky role in helping jihadists—a group whose ideology is anathema to the Iranians—has never been fully addressed. Iran might have been playing the old game of power politics in the unsettled Afghan situation before the U.S. invasion, when various groups were jostling for power and resources. It is also possible that Iran did not fully comprehend at that time the vast differences among jihadist groups—the Iranian view of the Salafists is often as distorted historically as the Salafists' view of the Shias—and did not realize the depth of animosity toward the Shias among the more militant Salafi-jihadists, such as Zarqawi and his ilk.

After the U.S. invasion of Afghanistan and overthrow of the Taliban, Iran might have thought that keeping some jihadists close to itself might come in handy in the future. The jihadists reached the decision that it would be best for Zarqawi and his Levantine colleagues to make their way to Iraq, where their "skin color and tongue would enable them to integrate into the Iraqi society."[27] Al-Qaeda's leadership and Zarqawi had apparently concluded, according to Adl, that the Americans would decide to invade Iraq and overthrow Saddam Hussein's regime. Adl added: "contrary to what the Americans frequently reiterated, Al-Qa'ida did not have any relationship with Saddam Hussein or his regime."[28] Linking Saddam Hussein and al-Qaeda, said Adl, was part of the American attempt to legitimize their war against Iraq.

The sojourn of al-Qaeda's remnants and the Zarqawi group in Iran was not easy. Iran grew ambivalent about the presence of anti-American groups, and this turned to hostility following an American media campaign against Iran that accused it of supporting global terrorism. Iran feared that it would become the target of American wrath and decided to do something about the jihadists in its midst. Adl claimed that the Iranians took action by pursuing the young men and arresting them. Iran began to deport them to their former home countries, or wherever they wished, as long as they left Iran. The sudden Iranian hostility, said Adl, "confused us and aborted 75 percent of our plan." A large number of young men were arrested, including up to 80 percent of Abu Musab's group. Consequently, Zarqawi and those who remained free needed to flee.[29]

Zarqawi and his small group made their way into northern Iraq. There, Zarqawi developed extensive ties with Ansar al-Islam (Partisans of Islam), a Kurdish Islamist group in the rugged extreme northeast of the country. Militant Islam had seeped into Iraqi Kurdistan, despite the dominance of the Kurdistan Democratic Party and the Patriotic Union of Kurdistan in Kurdish politics. Salafist thinking had had an impact on Kurdish youth and led some to participate in the "holy war" in Afghanistan against the Soviets.

After 1991, when Iraq lost control over the devastated north, Saudi "charities" moved in and funded hundreds of mosques that spread the extremist Wahhabi version of Islam.[30] Ansar al-Islam itself was the result of the merger of three small Kurdish Islamist groups on December 10, 2001: al-Hamas, al-Tawhid, and Jund al-Islam. Mullah Fatih Krekar (real name Najm-al-Din Faraj), who had formerly headed a small Islamist group called Islah, was the most prominent leader of the new group. With its headquarters in Biyarah, Ansar al-Islam set about establishing a formal organization according to jihadist sources.

The hierarchical structure of Ansar al-Islam was composed of the following:

- The emir and his two deputies: the military committee charged with developing Ansar al-Islam's mediocre military capabilities of six to eight hundred men and fending off attacks from Kurdish Peshmerga forces; most of the fighters were Kurdish Islamists, and only about one hundred were Afghan Arabs, according to Iraq intelligence sources
- The sharia committee
- The sharia court
- The information committee; media
- The security committee: counterintelligence and prevention of penetration of the group by other groups and the Peshmerga security services

This organizational structure looks remarkably like what Zarqawi developed later in the rest of Iraq. Ansar al-Islam itself began to implement an experiment in small-scale governance in the area under its control. Zarqawi himself established two small bases for his followers who had managed to follow him into northern Iraq. It is not clear that the Zarqawi group engaged in any operations in the north at the time. However, in February 2004, well into the American occupation of Iraq, Zarqawi's group claimed responsibility for a horrific terrorist attack on a Kurdish political gathering organized by the two main Kurdish parties, the Kurdistan Democratic Party and the Patriotic Union of Kurdistan.

On the eve of the U.S. invasion and subsequent occupation of Iraq in 2003, Zarqawi worked hard to rebuild his jihadist network from the small foundations already established in Afghanistan's Herat province. He realized that Iraq was going to become a battlefield of the jihad, as it was becoming obvious that the Americans were preparing to invade and occupy the country. In Iraq he began by building upon and expanding the inner circle of his most loyal followers. The most prominent among them were:

- Abu Hamza al-Muhajir (aka Abu Ayyub al-Masri), an Egyptian who took over the group for a short period after Zarqawi's demise
- Abu Anas al-Shami (aka Omar Yusef Jumaa), a Palestinian-Jordanian from the West Bank who became the group's first spiritual advisor and reportedly second in command of the Zarqawi organization until his death in late 2004
- Nidhal Mohammed Arabiat (killed February 23, 2004, by U.S. forces), another Jordanian, from the city of Salt, who was the group's top bomb-maker and thought to be responsible for most of the group's early car bombs or vehicle-borne improvised explosive devices (VBIEDs)
- Mustafa Ramadan Darwish (also known as Abu Mohammed al-Libnani), who was Lebanese
- Abu Omar al-Kurdi
- Thamer al-Rishawi, a former Iraqi military officer whose sister Sajida al-Rishawi failed in her suicide bombing mission in Amman in 2005 and was executed after IS immolated the captured Jordanian pilot Muadh al-Kasasbeh
- Abdullah al-Jibouri (also known as Abu Azzam), also an Iraqi
- Abu Nasser al-Libi
- Saad Ali Firas al-Dulaimi, allegedly a former Iraqi Special Forces officer who was responsible for operations against the U.S.-led Coalition forces in the Ramadi and Fallujah areas and for facilitating meetings of high-ranking AQI leaders to discuss strategy and operations
- Abu Osama al-Tunisi, a Tunisian who was an AQI commander or "emir," in the area of Yusufiya, south of Baghdad; he also played a key role in facilitating the arrival of foreign fighters and their integration into AQI units. His unit was vastly depleted by the time he was killed in September 2007

- Turki Badran Hisham al-Mazidi (Abu Ghadiya "the second"), an Iraqi who is not to be confused with Abu Ghadiya, "the first," Suleiman Khalid Darwish, who was Syrian, was entrusted with facilitating the flow of foreign fighters into Iraq from Syria, mainly Arabs from North Africa but also Syrian jihadists, including a cadre of older (in their forties) personnel who became what we can refer to as combat service support for Zarqawi's organization (medics, doctors, computer engineers, and IT technicians) rather than combat personnel

Almost all of these individuals were killed between 2003 and 2007, but the fact that the organization did not fall apart completely was a testament to their success in institutionalizing it by putting in place rules and regulations and a communications system to ensure relatively smooth succession from one leader to another. Because of this structure, in theory, management would continue to function in the absence of the leader and the midlevels would not be adversely affected. Of course, it did not always work that way: when counterinsurgency forces targeted management and field commanders, that is, the middle ranks and the leaders in the field, the organization began to suffer immensely.

From the start of its expansion in 2003, Zarqawi's nascent organization grew and developed quickly, and the leadership decided to give it the name Jamiat al-Tawhid wa al-Jihad (the Group of Monotheism and Jihad). It is generally believed that it was Anas al-Shami (aka Omar Yusuf Juma) who suggested giving the Zarqawi-led group in Iraq this name. There was a shura council made up of members of Zarqawi and his inner circle, but they had not yet developed any form of functional specialization or division of labor. Nobody was trained to do anything specific. Zarqawi set about changing this; he must have known that the coming battle against the considerable number of enemies within Iraq was not going to be easy. He himself had pointed out to bin Laden that the "heroic mujahidin" were surrounded by spies, apathetic people, two-faced people, collaborators, and, of course, enemies. A clearly defined structure was devised, with Zarqawi and his shura council as leaders. He had no second-in-command at the time, but he set up several committees, the most important being the military, communications, security, finance, and sharia committees.

Zarqawi developed a tightly knit leadership circle at the top. His companions had begun marrying each other's daughters even in Afghanistan and continued this process in Iraq. In the words of Sayf al-Adl, "in every respect—ideologically, socially and economically—Abu Musab and his brothers succeeded in becoming a single, interlinked and interrelated family."[31] As it evolved into AQI, Zarqawi's organization became more functionally specialized. According to a Multi-National Forces–Iraq briefing, AQI operatives were classified into three tiers. The tier 1 operatives were the key leaders and confidantes with direct access to Zarqawi. The tier 2 operatives were the regional cell leaders who planned, coordinated, and enabled attacks within assigned regions. The tier 3 operatives were the individual cell leaders responsible for the execution of attacks. Zarqawi stood as the powerful and charismatic leader maintaining the AQI network, while cells and groups maintained autonomy in organization and execution of attacks against assigned targets, in order to maintain security.[32] The regional cells executed operations within Zarqawi's operational framework and intent.

The speed with which the Iraqi military collapsed in April 2003 caught the Iraqis unprepared for irregular or insurgent warfare. To be sure, there were weapons, money, and manpower aplenty. However, there was no organizational structure, no command and control, and no higher direction from a leadership ready for post–conventional war operations. There were hundreds of Arab foreign fighters who had enthusiastically come over prior to the U.S. invasion and had been welcomed by the Baathist regime. During the invasion, some fought, many died, and others fled back home. Others remained stranded in Iraq, unwelcome among the Iraqis, and looked for patrons to incorporate them into their ranks. Zarqawi's emerging organization took in many of these Arab foreign fighters, a number of whom were from the Levant, as was the majority of his organization. Zarqawi's group managed to recruit most of the Arab volunteers into his organization. Prior to the invasion, many Arab "volunteers" had come into Iraq courtesy of the Iraqi security and intelligence services. A former Iraqi officer, "Raad," told the influential and respected Arabic-language paper *al-Hayat*: "the volunteers had originally been brought into the country through coordination with regional intelligence services and religious organizations that were active within the Salafi movement and acted as liaison groups with Al-Qaida groups in Iraq." When Baghdad fell, a number of Iraqi Islamist groups transported the Arab foreign fighters into Anbar province, where they could seek sanctuary and receive training to join the insurgency.

However, the "center of gravity"—the people Zarqawi needed to cultivate—were those Iraqis who were disgruntled with the U.S. presence and the empowerment of the Shias. After all, this was their home, they had a better understanding of the situation than the foreigners, some of them were trained military personnel, and they knew where the former regime had stashed weapons and money. Finally, working with Iraqi groups or fostering the inclusion of Iraqis within Zarqawi's organization would allow it to project its power and extend its reach far and wide into various targets within Iraqi society. Before the U.S. invasion of Iraq, Zarqawi began sorting out the Iraqis who were sympathetic and the Iraqis who had fought as mujahidin in Afghanistan.[33] The ineffectiveness of some of the Iraqi groups, suffering from poor leadership, or leaders who absconded with funds, and lack of resources, forced many Iraqis—particularly those with an inclination to adopt militant Sunni sentiments—to make their way eventually into Zarqawi's burgeoning organization. While he finally began to incorporate Iraqis into his organization, he wasted no time in "taking out" those whom he viewed as a threat or could not bring under his control.

According to Abu Anas al-Shami, Zarqawi had been waiting for a homegrown Iraqi group to emerge within which he would operate. However, while he recognized the need to absorb Iraqis into his group in order to increase its size and to "embed" it within the Iraqi social context, he was initially wary of them. He regarded them as lacking in dedication to the principles of Islam; he was particularly suspicious of the Baathists. Furthermore, the Iraqis represented a problem: while they provided the opportunity for his organization to embed itself within the larger social context, they were largely "untrustworthy" and represented a security threat. The wariness was mutual and proved to be an obstacle to solid cooperation between some of the Iraqi insurgent groups and Zarqawi. Among the first of the organized insurgent organizations was Jaysh Mohammad (Mohammad's Army), which was formed by Baathist officials and former intelligence officers in Ramadi. It was made up of several battalions: al-Awda, the Fedaiyin, the Armed Forces General Command, composed of former officers, and a unit called the Mujahidin, which was made up of Arab foreign fighters. Jaysh Mohammad did not remain cohesive for long; it collapsed when its various battalions went off on their own. "S.S.," a close personal companion of Saddam Hussein, allegedly in charge of hiding his movements and finding his hiding places, also told the Arabic-language paper *al-Hayat*: "in July 2003 the financing of the armed operations took place by several different methods, chiefly from the funds that Saddam Hussein himself had made available to fund Muhammad's Army and establish the General Command for Resistance and Liberation." According to "S.S.," Saddam Hussein instructed the groups' commanders to establish a financing and accounting system to divide substantial sums of money among the various combatant groups for their anti-American operations.

Disaster struck, continued "S.S.," when, after Saddam Hussein's capture, "we discovered that four out of the five commanders had fled with the money they received and settled in Syria....This was a catastrophe that left the organizations that Saddam had established without funding. It created an upheaval among the combatants who served under the commanders who absconded." "S.S.," described the relations between the Baathist groups and the jihadists as having been marred by mutual suspicions. Saddam Hussein had apparently advised those insurgent factions associated with the defunct regime and with the Baath Party to refrain from "coordinating their ideologies and policies" with the Islamist groups that had started to surface openly after the occupation. According to "S.S.," Saddam Hussein stressed that the insurgent factions made up of personnel of the former regime could establish a kind of ad hoc cooperation with the Islamists to conduct joint military operations until the Americans were driven out of Iraq. That is why he, "S.S.," was a "liaison officer" between the Iraqi insurgent groups and the jihadists, including the group led by Zarqawi.

As the insurgency evolved, the exigencies of the battlefield forced Zarqawi to cooperate with former regime elements. In 2004, Hazem al-Amin, an investigative journalist for *al-Hayat*, wrote a report about the interactions between jihadists and former regime elements. He interviewed Jordanian jihadists who had either fought with Zarqawi in Iraq or were extremely well-acquainted with the dynamic situation there. They explained to him that Zarqawi was relying on the expertise of the Baathists, especially in security affairs, in this war against the U.S. presence. One jihadist, "Ahmed," told the journalist that this was especially true in Fallujah, which was home to thousands of former Iraqi military personnel. Many swore allegiance to Zarqawi and disavowed the former "secular" regime.

The cooperation between the foreign jihadists under Zarqawi and their Iraqi hosts, including the Baathists and former officers, was noticeable from the first battle of Fallujah in the spring of 2004. At that time the Fallujah fighters established their Committee of the Mujahidin, which grouped the local fighters into battalions (*kataib*). The locals called on the foreign fighters, including Zarqawi's group, to come and help defend against the U.S. offensive. Zarqawi sent a group under Abu Anas al-Shami, who won over Omar Hadid, an Iraqi jihadist, and Sheikh Abdullah al-Janabi, one of the more vociferous insurgent clerics in Fallujah. The Zarqawi fighters set up their own battalion, al-Muhajirun (Emigrants). They drew their resources—weapons, ammunition, and food—from the same centralized logistics center in the city as did the local fighters, whether Islamist, tribal, or Baathist. Moreover, they would all meet to cooperate in intelligence gathering, establishing defensive points, and conducting attacks. All of this early cooperation improved the organizational resilience and sophistication of Zarqawi's group way before anybody knew by name most of the former regime officers who were later found to have cooperated with or been part of IS for a such a long time, a matter that became a big point of discussion in 2014 (see below). It seems, however, that many former officers had joined with the jihadists, particularly Zarqawi's group, in the 2003–2004 time frame, apparently including Abu Abdul Rahman al-Bilawi al-Dulaimi, an infantry officer, who joined Zarqawi in 2003 and rose to high rank in IS's military council before his death in Mosul in 2014.

Nonetheless, despite its efforts to anchor itself solidly within the Iraqi social fabric, by its own admission, the original organization, Jamiat al-Tawhid wa al-Jihad, lacked a solid base of operations and popular support. A rather revealing report by Abu Anas al-Shami stated: "We have discovered that after one year of jihad we have not accomplished anything on the ground. None of us could find a piece of land... or use as a shelter or a place to retire to safety among some members of [his] group.... We would hide at daylight and sneak like a cat at night.... Homes were raided and the heroes were chased. It was a dark picture and everyone felt a sense of terrible failure."[34] Given the jihadists' predicament, the organization decided to use the city of Fallujah as a safe haven in which to build itself. They also began to use the al-Tharthar region, with its lake, as a safe base. The region was a stronghold of a subclan of the Dulaim tribe, which subsisted by fishing. Zarqawi set up training camps and stores for weapons and explosives in the area because of its remoteness and sparse population. His fighters trained there, and the group prepared suicide-bombing operations in safe houses. Al-Tharthar's location provided easy access into Baiji, Tikrit, and Samarra.

Tanzim Qaedat al-Jihad fi Bilad al-Rafidain (Organization of the Jihad Base in the Land of the Two Rivers)

In October 2004, Zarqawi, eager to extend his authority over jihadists and to get financial resources in particular, wanted to get access to al-Qaeda's funding sources in the Persian Gulf region and decided to make a pitch for joining al-Qaeda. Earlier, bin Laden had sent a letter to the networks financing Zarqawi's group and told them to stop doing so because it was not a member of the al-Qaeda network. Zarqawi decided that he would prefer to join al-Qaeda and fight alongside them rather than in opposition to them. He pledged allegiance (*bayaa*) to bin Laden and changed the name of his organization from Jamiat al-Tawhid wa al-Jihad to Tanzim Qaedat al-Jihad fi Bilad al-Rafidain (Organization of the Jihad Base in the Land of the Two Rivers), or al-Qaeda in the Land of the Two Rivers, for the sake of clarity and brevity.

Initially, AQI experienced considerable growth as a franchise of al-Qaeda. It began to attract more Iraqi fighters as their own organizations suffered massive attrition, at the hands of U.S. forces, and depleted resources. Zarqawi later delegated more of his powers in order to guarantee that the organization would remain operational in the event of his death. He announced that Abu Abdul Rahman al-Iraqi would be his deputy. This second-in-command post occupied by al-Iraqi was created to take the sting out of the complaints that the Iraqis were not key players within the organization. Zarqawi ensured that al-Iraqi was in charge of communicating directly with the Iraqis in the group, while Zarqawi handled communications with volunteer fighters from outside Iraq. He was able to extend his network to reach the rest of Anbar province, Diyala province, and the cities of Mosul, Baghdad, and Samarra. Al-Qaeda in Iraq bought weapons on the Iraqi weapons market and acquired cars for VBIEDs from local merchants. Al-Qaeda in Iraq coordinated with certain groups that closely shared its ideological approach, such as Ansar al-Sunna, Ansar al-Islam, the Islamic Jihad battalions, and the Victorious Army Sect. Zarqawi and these groups coordinated to prepare volunteer suicide attackers from among the Arab foreign fighter contingent.

Al-Qaeda in Iraq began to achieve prominence within the insurgency by late 2004. A commander of the IAI explains the prominence of Zarqawi's group by arguing that the confusion that accompanied the disintegration of several armed groups at the beginning of 2004 was brought on by "a failure in financing, organization, and propaganda." This, said the IAI commander, allowed AQI to take credit for most of the operations planned and carried out by those other groups. This fact "helped surround Zarqawi with a special aura and attributed to his group an image of great capability" and, not surprising, allowed AQI to gain recruits. Moreover, Zarqawi and his followers, said the IAI commander, "came from societies that were proficient in the modern methods of propaganda, especially via the Internet. They exploited their online connections with Al-Qaida to propagate their ideas and messages. In contrast there was no Internet in Iraq before the occupation and the web did not enter Al-Anbar province until the beginning of 2004," because the country had been under crushing international sanctions between 1990 and 2003, which, among other things, had technologically retarded it.

Zarqawi's affiliation with al-Qaeda brought him prestige and, more important, foreign and Iraqi recruits. The recruiting procedure consisted of several phases. After establishing contact through acquaintances or at the mosque, a would-be member was assigned to a study group, where he was informed about the group's ideological and sociopolitical stance. He was then accepted into the organization on a provisional basis. A true test was considered to be a spell in prison. Next, the member was entrusted with a task in a terrorist cell, in accordance with his particular physical and mental skills. Those wishing to go to the front themselves required a reference from two long-standing members of Zarqawi's network vouching for the candidate's seriousness, competence, and reliability. Those who headed off without references or facilitation often met with tragedy on the way or faced the suspicion of the organization they wished to join.

During one daring escape from U.S. Task Force 626, who were hunting for him, Zarqawi left his laptop in his vehicle. The information it contained facilitated the arrests of around a dozen of his accomplices. The documents within the laptop gave a fascinating insight into the structure of the original organization in Iraq around 2005. The main theater of operations of Zarqawi's organization was the Sunni triangle, which was divided into nine subcommands, each controlled by a regional emir with a large degree of operational autonomy. As the organization grew, it became necessary to rely more on locals, and Zarqawi began the process of putting Iraqis in positions of authority. After volunteering for the organization, new arrivals spent time studying tactics and familiarizing themselves with several types of small arms. This training lasted for several weeks, except for suicide bombers, who learned their trade within a few days. Training in open fields, except in remote areas, was difficult because of the nearly constant American military presence. Jihadist fighters often trained in apartments, houses, and abandoned public sector factories.[35] The organization even tried to conduct operations beyond Iraq, with the most obvious target being Zarqawi's homeland, Jordan.[36]

There were several other units that had special ties to the upper echelons in the organization. The Security and Reconnaissance Battalion was responsible for vetting new recruits and gathering intelligence about targets of the organization's operations. They were also responsible for conducting reconnaissance on the U.S.-led Coalition forces and the various private contractors that provided them with security and logistical support. In addition, they conducted reconnaissance on U.S. troop movements, studied their tactics, and the future plans of both the U.S. and Iraqi governments. The battalion recruited agents within the Iraqi army and the police, as well as private contractors, and transportation contractors and other entities that had vital and sensitive positions.

The sharia committee was responsible for research and provided answers to any religious issues the organization needed addressed in order to justify their beliefs and actions. This committee issued a magazine, *Thurwat al-Sanam*, to help spread the group's doctrine. This publication described the organization's religious edicts and served its agendas. The mission of the media and communications department, headed by Abu Maysara al-Iraqi, was to issue statements and make audio- and videotapes. Propaganda played a significant role in recruiting new members.

The financial committee collected the funding required to bankroll the organization's various activities. It relied on a network of supporters who gathered donations from businesspeople and mosques not only in Iraq but all over the Arab and Muslim worlds. This committee also managed finances from the sale of battle spoils won by the organization and the various taxes levied on locals in areas under its control.

Al-Qaeda in Iraq was very keen from the beginning to make use of media resources to propagate its message, highlight the importance of the battle in Iraq, and boast of its exploits. In an interview following his defection, one AQI commander, Nazim al-Jibouri, was reported to have said that AQI "considers the media the main instrument to broadcast its ideas and ideologies and convey its messages."[37] Indeed, AQI focused on the media from the very beginning. It issued two magazines in Iraq as early as 2003. *Sawt al-Jihad* (Voice of Jihad) dealt with AQI's personnel, ideas, and aspirations and served as a forum for recruitment of foreign fighters. *Al-Battar* (The Sword) dealt with military issues, such as operations, raids, and tactics against the U.S.-led Coalition forces. Its media personnel also filmed attacks on U.S. forces and put out some extensive but initially amateurish documentaries on the war.

After 2005, AQI's media strategy and resources improved, mainly thanks to Muhannad al-Saidi (aka Abu Maysara al-Iraqi), a young energetic Iraqi convert to Salafism from Shiism. He was trained in media production by Abu Talha al-Libi, a U.S.-educated computer engineer. Abu Maysara and a small group of Arabs from the Maghreb (Algeria, Morocco, Tunisia, and Libya) who were more familiar with computers, the Internet, and media than the Iraqis, because sanctions had ensured that Iraq had remained cut off from cutting-edge developments in information technology for a decade, set up al-Furqan Media Production and another media center, al-Fajr.

The Mujahidin Shura Council and the Islamic State of Iraq

Zarqawi was killed in June 2006. His immediate successor was Abu Hamza al-Muhajir. Shortly after Zarqawi's death, Abu Hamza al-Muhajir and his colleagues in the top leadership of the organization sought desperately to widen their base of support among the Iraqi insurgent constellation. After months of wheeling and dealing, they brought several sympathetic Sunni insurgent groups into the MSC, forming the Hilf al-Mutayyabin (Pact of the Exalted) on October 12, 2006.[38] On October 15, 2006, the MSC announced the establishment of an Islamic emirate in Iraq, and thus the MSC became ISI. It claimed Iraq's western and northern provinces as its territory. The Islamic State of Iraq theoretically encompassed the provinces of Anbar, Kirkuk, Nineveh, Diyala, Salahuddin, Babil, and Wasit. The first ISI government was announced by Muharib al-Jibouri, ISI's official spokesman, and highlighted increasing Iraqi dominance within the ranks of the organization, with few other Arab and foreign elements. The preamble of this announcement declared:

> After the Kurds had secured a state in the north and the Rawafid [Shias] had won approval for federalism in the south and the center with the support of the Jews in the north and the Safawis in the south... the condition of the Sunnis has become the same as the condition of the orphans on the table of the wicked people. Therefore, it has become a must for the honorable and free Sunni mujahidin, ulema, and notables to make something for their brothers, sons and honor in light of this silly drama that is called Al-Maliki's state, in which it was regrettable that Sunni traitors took part. By doing so, they confused the religion for the people and deliberately wasted the rights of their people.
>
> Based on this, your brothers in Hilf al-Mutayyabin [Alliance of al-Mutayyabin] convey to you the glad tidings of the establishment

of the Islamic State of Iraq in Baghdad, Al-Anbar, Diyala, Kirkuk, Salah al-Din, Ninawa, and part of the governorate of Babil and Wasit to protect our religion and people so that there would be no sedition and the blood of martyrs and the sacrifices of your brother mujahidin would not go in vain.

Today, we call on all of Iraq's mujahidin, clergymen, chieftains, and Sunnis to pledge allegiance to the amir [emir] of believers, the virtuous Shaykh Abu Umar al-Baghdadi; to obey him in good and bad times and to work relentlessly to strengthen the foundations of this state and sacrifice ourselves and our precious possessions for its sake.[39]

Abu Hamza al-Muhajir filled the role of minister of war in the new "state," which was now led by Abu Omar al-Baghdadi. Initially, the United States believed that Abu Omar al-Baghdadi was a fictional leader who had been invented to put an Iraqi face on the foreign-led group. However, it subsequently emerged that Abu Omar al-Baghdadi was a real person: an Iraqi former policeman and preacher from Anbar province; his given name was Hamid Dawud Mohammad Khalil al-Zawi. On April 19, 2007, the top leadership and structure of IS was identified as follows.[40]

- Abu Omar al-Baghdadi, the emir or leader
- Abu Abdel Rahman al-Falahi, "prime minister," or deputy leader
- Abu Hamza al-Muhajir, minister of war
- Sheikh Abu Osman al-Tamimi, minister of religious institutions
- Abu Bakr al-Jibouri, minister of public relations
- Abu Abdel-Jabbar al-Janabi, minister of security
- Sheikh Abu Mohammad al-Mashhadani, minister of information
- Sheikh Abu Abdel Qader al-Issawi, minister of martyr affairs (equivalent to veteran affairs)
- Engineer Abu Ahmed al-Janabi, minister of petroleum
- Mustapha al-Araji, minister of agriculture
- Dr. Abu Abdallah al-Zaidi, minister of health

What is noteworthy in this lineup of ministries making up the new ISI is that all the members were Iraqis, except Abu Hamza al-Muhajir, who was an Egyptian, and he held the most important ministry in the nascent state, the Ministry of War. After Zarqawi's death, AQI's legitimacy deficit grew as it began to face serious resistance from Iraqi insurgent groups infuriated by the organization's behavior and tactics, including the luring of Iraqi fighters away to join it. For example, in 2006, when Abu Hamza al-Muhajir called specifically upon the IAI—whose leadership had taken a position against AQI—to pledge allegiance to ISI, apparently a significant number of IAI personnel defected to the new "state." The frustration of a large segment of the insurgency and of the tribes with ISI's behavior (described in the previous chapter) provided the United States with an opening to reach out and support these two Iraqi groups, both financially and materially, on the condition that they fight against ISI. As a result, between late 2006 and early 2007, ISI suffered considerable setbacks as the Iraqis turned against it. The most obvious manifestation was not the verbal polemics (see chapter 3) but the loss of manpower, as low-ranking Iraqi fighters deserted and Iraqi tribesmen and urban civilians began to inform on suspected ISI personnel and sanctuaries. This had a deleterious impact on the organization's ability to function on the ground. Under the pressure of the loss of manpower, coupled with the U.S. forces' impressive "24/7" targeting of ISI management personnel and fighters, ISI began to disintegrate. Its deteriorating command, control, and coordination meant that the central leadership was increasingly unable to exercise "due diligence" over the actions and activities of local leaders and military commanders on the ground. Corruption, indiscriminate killing, fraud, and gang-like behavior became rampant. The number of foreign fighters coming into the country began to decrease significantly.

The Islamic State of Iraq had an elaborate governance structure on paper. However, this was a façade; it was lying to itself even more than to the Iraqi people and outside jihadists it was seeking to impress. Its leadership was concerned primarily with fighting and with reorganizing and rebuilding the organization. In chapter 3 I described the bizarre ideological fascination of Abu Hamza al-Muhajir with the apocalypse and the fighting between ISI and a vast array of Iraqi opponents. Here the focus is on ISI's failures as an organization. It soon became clear that the emirate was a failure, mainly because the group had difficulties reconciling the diverging demands of its ideologically motivated foreign fighters with the Iraqi fighters' demands for increased political and economic influence. As ISI came under greater pressure, it found itself devoting the vast majority of its manpower to fighting a losing battle. It achieved barely a fraction of what the later IS, or the Caliphate, has achieved to date.

The Reinvention of the Islamic State of Iraq, 2010–2014

In March 2010, Iraqi forces arrested an ISI commander, Manaf Abdul Rahim al-Rawi, whom they discovered to be one of the group's main commanders in Baghdad and one of the few people who had access to the leader of ISI, Abu Omar al-Baghdadi. Al-Rawi talked and gave up the hideout of the ISI leader, which, he said, was a house six miles southwest of the city of Tikrit. After it was confirmed that Abu Omar al-Baghdadi and his deputy, Abu Hamza al-Muhajir, were present at the house, a U.S.-led raid assaulted the place. Both men detonated suicide vests to avoid being captured. Messages to bin Laden and Zawahiri were found on a computer inside the house. Much like bin Laden's safe house in Pakistan, where he would be killed a little more than a year later, Abu Omar al-Baghdadi's hideout was "off the net" and had no Internet connections or telephone lines—all important messages were carried in and out by only three men, one of whom was a man named Ibrahim Awad Ibrahim Ali Mohammad al-Badri al-Samarrai, who was known by a number of aliases. In a statement by ISI on May 16, 2010, the senior leadership announced that this man from Samarra would become ISI's emir and would be known as Abu Bakr al-Baghdadi. Abu Abdullah al-Hasani al-Qureishi would be his deputy and prime minister. Nasser al-Din Abu Suleiman, a Moroccan who had studied in Russia, had acquired his military skills in Afghanistan, and spoke Russian, Dari (Afghani Farsi), and French, would replace Abu Hamza al-Muhajir as minister of war.[41]

Who is Abu Bakr al-Baghdadi? His life story has been examined in far greater detail than that of Zarqawi and Abu Omar al-Baghdadi. He was born on July 1, 1971, to a lower-middle-class Sunni family in the city of Samarra, just eighty miles north of Baghdad. There is no need to engage here in a full recounting of his ascent, as the investigative journalists Martin Chulov and Abdel Bari Atwan, the well-known expert on IS ideology, Will McCants, and others have done this admirably. What is required is a short description of his life and the political and social contexts of his ascent to power.

Abu Bakr al-Baghdadi had an unremarkable upbringing. An introverted child, he was apparently fond of playing soccer and was quite devout from an early age. As with many Sunni families in the 1980s and 1990s, his family was caught between the obligation of serving the Baathist state and the growing tide of religiosity, even among the Sunnis during those trying decades. Two of his brothers served in the Iraqi army, and one of them was reportedly killed during the war with Iran. Two uncles served in the enormous Baathist security apparatus built to keep tabs on the military and population. The fact that the family had multiple members serving in the army and the security services was not remarkable. This was common in Sunni families during the 1980s and 1990s. Moreover, men from Samarra had always played significant roles in the armed forces and security services before they ran afoul of Saddam Hussein's paranoia in the 1990s.

However, the family was also caught up in the rising tide of Islamism among significant sectors of the Sunni population. The costly Iran-Iraq War, the devastating Kuwait War, and the punishing international sanctions imposed on Iraq for more than a decade contributed to the Iraqis' turn to religion for spiritual succor. As a young adult in the 1990s, Abu Bakr al-Baghdadi began to dabble in proscribed Islamist politics. However, his definitive entry into Islamist politics seems to have been initiated when he joined a local branch of the Muslim Brotherhood. He received a master's degree from the Saddam University of Islamic Studies (now known as the University of Islamic Studies) in Baghdad while he was a member of the Muslim Brotherhood. He seems not to have been persuaded that this group was sufficiently militant in its quest to change Iraqi society. He left in 2000 after reaching the conclusion that the Muslim Brotherhood was all words and no action.

In the early 1990s, while Saddam Hussein sought to curry the favor of mainstream Islamist movements, he tried to control the proliferation of Salafist ideology in Iraq, regarding it correctly as very subversive and incendiary. By the early 2000s the "cat was out of the bag," and followers of Salafist thinking were everywhere. Little is known about Abu Bakr al-Baghdadi's activities between 2000 and 2002, when he reportedly became a Salafist under the influence of Abu Mohammed al-Mufti al-Aali, who was one of the main ideologues of the jihadist groups in Iraq. Abu Bakr al-Baghdadi along with other followers of al-Aali formed the Salafi-jihadist Ahlu Sunna wa al-Jamaa (Followers of the Sunna and the Community) movement, which became an active insurgent movement after the U.S. invasion in 2003. As the insurgency grew in intensity and scope, Abu Bakr al-Baghdadi was a doctoral student and was not on the expanding American list of suspects, although it was inconceivable that he was not involved in anti-American activities, given his membership in Ahlu Sunna wa al-Jamaa. Unfortunately for him, U.S. forces arrested him in Fallujah in February 2004, at the house of a friend suspected of insurgent activity. He was moved to Camp Bucca, a detention facility in southern Iraq that held over twenty thousand insurgents.

According to Hisham al-Hashimi, an Iraqi security analyst, the Iraqi government estimated that seventeen of the twenty-five most important IS leaders running the war in Iraq and Syria spent time in U.S. prisons between 2004 and 2011. Some were transferred from American custody to Iraqi prisons, where a series of jailbreaks in the last several years allowed many senior leaders to escape and rejoin the insurgent ranks. Abu Ghraib was the scene of the biggest—and most damaging—breakout in 2013. Up to five hundred inmates, many of them senior jihadists handed over by the departing U.S. military, fled, in July of that year, after IS forces stormed the prison. The Islamic State launched a simultaneous raid on nearby Taji prison that was equally successful.

The story of Abu Bakr al-Baghdadi's enforced sojourn in Camp Bucca is as murky as that of his early life. When Chulov interviewed the jihadist who used the nom de guerre "Abu Ahmed," he provided considerable detail on life in Camp Bucca in general and Abu Bakr al-Baghdadi's time there.[42] "Abu Ahmed" was captured by U.S. forces and detained at Camp Bucca as a young man in 2004. He had become a senior official within IS after rising through the ranks over several years. American soldiers had captured the other detainees—insurgents of competing ideological groups—over the course of the military campaign against the insurgents. Camp Bucca allowed the Iraqi detainees from these competing groups to get to know each other; as "Abu Ahmed" put it, "we could never have all got together like this in Baghdad, or anywhere else. It would have been impossibly dangerous. Here, we were not only safe, but we were only a few hundred meters away from the entire al-Qaida leadership."[43] In "Abu Ahmed's" assessment: "If there was no American prison in Iraq, there would be no IS now. Bucca was a factory. It made us all. It built our ideology."[44] Many of those released from these prisons—and indeed, several senior American officers who ran detention operations—have admitted that the prisons had an incendiary effect on the insurgency. Senior American officers eventually concluded that the various detention centers like Camp Bucca "actually become radicalizing elements."[45] The Americans may have set up the camp and populated it with their detainees, but it was the detainees who ran things on the inside. They established hierarchies and norms, conducted classes, and meted out punishments for transgressions. The camps, in the assessment of the U.S. military, were places where incarcerated insurgents planned and organized, appointed leaders, and launched operations. The detainee "Abu Ahmed" concurred with this assessment. He claimed that the detainees spent a great deal of time assessing their failures and planning for what they would do and how they would reconnect with each other after their release. They took each other's names and numbers, reestablished contact after their release, and went back to doing what they were good at: being insurgents. He added: "But this time we were doing it better."[46]

It was at Camp Bucca that "Abu Ahmed" first met Abu Bakr al-Baghdadi. From the beginning, others in the camp seemed to defer to him, according to "Abu Ahmed." Abu Bakr al-Baghdadi was a quiet person, according to "Abu Ahmed," but "he has a charisma. You could feel that he was someone important. But there were others who were more important. I honestly did not think he would get this far."[47] Despite his seemingly timorous and retiring nature, according to "Abu Ahmed" and two other men who were jailed at Camp Bucca in 2004, the Americans saw Abu Bakr al-Baghdadi as a fixer who could solve fractious disputes between competing factions and keep the camp quiet.

Another jihadist detainee, "Abu Omar," a former IS member who was held for three years at Camp Bucca, had a lot to say about the prison and the future leader of IS: "Camp Bucca was a great favor the United States did to the mujahedeen. They provided us with a secure atmosphere, a bed and food, and also allowed books giving us a great opportunity to feed our knowledge with the ideas of Abu Mohammed al-Maqdisi and the jihadist ideology. This was under the watchful eye of the American soldiers. New recruits were prepared so that when they were freed they were ticking time bombs."[48] At Camp Bucca, "Abu Omar" met the future caliph, Abu Bakr al-Baghdadi. According to "Abu Omar," Abu Bakr al-Baghdadi often used to lead the prayers and on many occasions gave Friday sermons. However, he was not as important there as the high-profile inmates, such as Abu Mutaz, Abu Abdul Rahman al-Bilawi, and future IS spokesman Abu Mohammed al-Adnani, whom I introduced at the very beginning of this book: he was the spokesman who announced the Caliphate on June 29, 2014. At that point, Abu Bakr al-Baghdadi was not a member of ISI. At Camp Bucca, he further absorbed the jihadist ideology and established himself among the big names. He met "Haji Bakr" (then known as Samir al-Khleifawi), Abu Muhannad al-Sweidawi, and Abu Ahmed al-Alwani. These were officers in Saddam Hussein's army, and despite their Baath origins, they impressed him with their military knowledge and, above all, their organizational skills. He also influenced them with his religious background—mainly his expertise in Quranic studies. "Abu Omar" filled in other details of Abu Bakr al-Baghdadi's daily life there: "I saw him playing football with other prisoners. This is the only thing

I saw in him. I heard his speeches but he was nothing compared to Abu Musab al-Zarqawi. His words lacked power."[49]

If the stories from these two jihadist detainees are accurate, then Abu Bakr al-Baghdadi used his time in prison to learn the strengths and vulnerabilities of the various groups whose personnel were incarcerated there, to build alliances, to cement friendships, and to transform himself into a "somebody" of importance. By December 2004, the Americans deemed Abu Bakr al-Baghdadi no further risk and released him. As soon as he was released, he became a member of ISI. Outside prison, he met Sheikh Fawzi al-Jibouri, one of the influential intellectuals within the ranks of ISI. Jibouri introduced him to the organization's minister of information, Muharib Abdul Latif al-Jibouri, who used his authority to help Abu Bakr al-Baghdadi go to Syria and concentrate on his writings, on condition that he would help with media issues whenever they needed him. In Baghdad, "Haji Samir," a fellow jihadist whom he had met in prison, introduced him to ISI's second-in-command, Abu Hamza al-Muhajir. Muhajir was impressed by Abu Bakr and introduced him to ISI's emir, Abu Omar al-Baghdadi. Abu Bakr al-Baghdadi was allegedly later promoted to serve on ISI's coordination committee, whose primary mission was to ensure coordination between the emir of IS and the provincial governors ("walis," the historical term for governors in the Muslim empire). Abu Bakr al-Baghdadi was one of a handful of trusted individuals entrusted with the dangerous mission of communication with the provincial leaders. The higher he climbed up the ISI organizational ladder, the higher he was ranked on Iraq's most-wanted list. The deaths of Abu Omar al-Baghdadi and Abu Hamza al-Muhajir were a serious blow to ISI, but the roles they had so precipitously vacated were quickly filled by the alumni of Camp Bucca, whose upper echelons had begun preparing for this moment since their time in prison. When ISI lost its two senior leaders in April 2010, the nine members of the shura council voted to make Abu Bakr al-Baghdadi the emir of ISI. It had lost its leader and his deputy, and there was a dire need to choose a successor.

One of the main reasons for Abu Bakr al-Baghdadi's selection was that he was supposedly descended from the Qureish, the tribe of the Prophet Mohammad, which fulfilled one of the conditions for being selected as caliph. Abu Bakr al-Baghdadi's main mandate was to revive ISI. He started by gathering members he thought were capable of helping him achieve his goal.

The demise of Abu Omar al-Baghdadi and Abu Hamza al-Muhajir was a reflection of the immense pressure ISI was under between 2007 and

2011. It was hampered by a tribal revolt that uprooted its leadership from Anbar and shrank its presence elsewhere in Iraq, as it was militarily squeezed by Iraqi insurgents who had turned against it and hunted day and night by U.S. forces. It was at this point that ISI made an approach to the Baathist remnants of the old regime—ideological opponents who shared a common enemy in the United States and the government it backed, led by Shias. The mutually wary groups held secret meetings in various locations. By early 2008, these meetings had become far more frequent—and many of them were taking place in Syria. Syria's links to the Sunni insurgency in Iraq had been regularly raised by U.S. officials in Baghdad and by the Iraqi government. Both sides were convinced that the Syrian president, Bashar al-Assad, allowed Arab foreign fighters of all stripes, including jihadists, to fly into the Damascus airport, where military officials would escort them to the border with Iraq, where "facilitators" negotiated their entry into Iraq via Nineveh province, while Syrian border guards turned a blind eye to these cross-border goings-on. Many of the foreign terrorists would cross into Iraq through smuggling routes in Nineveh, often close to the ramshackle border town of Rabiya. They would then be handed over to the jihadist or Baathist insurgent groups in the equally unappealing dusty town of Tel Afar. There the foreign fighters would be handed over to Iraqi facilitators, who would transfer them to become part of insurgent networks in the larger cities, such as Mosul, Ramadi, Baghdad, and the small towns that dotted Anbar province.

By 2007, General David Petraeus, Commander of Multi-National Force–Iraq, was convinced that there was crystal-clear intelligence of cooperation between Syrian military intelligence and the jihadists. The jihadist "Abu Ahmed" emphasized the Syrian connection to Iraq's insurgency: "the mujahideen all came through Syria. I worked with many of them. Those in Bucca had flown to Damascus. A very small number had made it from Turkey, or Iran. But most came to Iraq with the help of the Syrians." To be sure, the United States had every reason to highlight the "perfidy" of the Assad regime, which the Bush administration viewed as hostile to U.S. goals in the region. By the same token, however, Damascus had every reason to thwart the U.S. project for Iraq and to ensure that the Americans were ensnared in Iraq in a no-win situation. As early as 2004, some of the Islamist elements, including jihadists and the Iraqi Baathists, had decided to shelve their ideological distaste for one another and work together against their common enemies, as I briefly described earlier.

The Syrian government reportedly facilitated this cooperation, which seemed to have deepened over time. According to Martin Chulov, Major-

General Hussein Ali Kamal, the director of intelligence in Iraq's Interior Ministry toward the end of the first decade of the 2000s, was convinced that Syria was heavily involved in destabilizing Iraq, an assessment that was based on the interrogations of jihadists his troops had captured. Strong evidence existed of a tripartite cooperation between Syria, jihadist elements in Iraq, and some groups and senior individuals from the Iraqi Baath Party. As ISI activity ebbed in Iraq, he had become increasingly concerned about two meetings that had taken place in Syria early in 2009 that brought together Iraqi jihadists, Syrian officials, and Baathists from both countries. Kamal obtained transcripts of recordings made at two secret meetings in Zabadani, near Damascus, in the spring of 2009. The attendees included senior Iraqi Baathists who had taken refuge in Damascus since their patron Saddam had been ousted, Syrian military intelligence officers, and senior figures of ISI. Kamal told Chulov that the Iraqi government had a source who reported back on a key meeting between Baathist and Islamist personnel. The Baathists' and Islamists' aim, according to Kamal's source, was to launch a series of spectacular attacks in Baghdad and thereby undermine Maliki's Shia-majority government and thwart its efforts to bring security and stability.[50]

Until then, jihadists and the Baathists had been fierce ideological enemies, but the rising power of the Shias—and their backers in Iran—brought them together. Why did these two starkly different ideological groups cooperate? What did each side expect to gain? Who was using whom in this seemingly odd relationship? And finally, what was the end result of it?

The Baathification of the Islamic State or the Salafization of the Baathists?

In 2014 and 2015 a major debate erupted concerning who exactly was responsible for the revival of ISI and who was leading it. Samuel Helfont and Michael Brill point out, in this seemingly endless and unresolved debate, that there is a small but vocal group who argue that Saddam Hussein's deliberate policies in the last years of his rule promoted Salafism in Iraq. This allowed a large number of Baathist officials and Iraqi military and security personnel eventually to make their way into AQI and then to take over control of its successors.[51] Among the most prominent proponents of this view are the British blogger Kyle Orton and the Israeli academic Amatzia Baram, a globally recognized expert on Iraq. Helfont and Brill argue that "these depictions are inaccurate and dangerously misleading…

our rigorous study of those records has found no evidence that Saddam or his Baathist regime in Iraq displayed any sympathy for Islamism, Salafism, or Wahhabism."[52] Neither view is entirely correct or fallacious.

Saddam Hussein and those closest to him, like Taha Yasin Ramadan, a senior official of the Baathist regime, Barzan al-Tikriti, the ruler's half-brother, and Tariq Aziz, the former regime's highest ranking Christian member and what passed for an intellectual in the regime, went to their deaths still believing in the principles of Baathism. Both Barzan and Aziz had warned Saddam Hussein of the dangers of trying to rein in Islamists by accommodating them or tactically allying with them. However, the logic of the situation on the ground in Iraq, even before the American invasion, had led many to move silently toward greater religiosity. Just because Saddam Hussein and his closest circle may have felt one way about "political Islam," this does not mean that the majority of Iraqis—materially impoverished by international sanctions and psychologically impaired by a brutal regime—felt the same way. Naturally, they opted to keep their views to themselves. Moreover, following the downfall of the regime, the security apparatus was no longer there to censor proscribed political and ideological movements, of which Salafism and the Muslim Brotherhood represented two distinct strands. During the early stages of the insurgency, it looked as if the Baathists and nationalists would dominate; there was even some cooperation between the secularists and the Islamists.

Over the course of time, a number of officers, officials, and enlisted men migrated into the jihadist ranks because their own insurgency organizations had crumbled, lacking finances and other resources, and because a number of them began to think that AQI was making a greater impact against the occupation and was more successful—even though in reality, given the myriad number of insurgent groups, AQI itself was responsible for a fraction of the attacks. Some of the former regime personnel who joined the Islamists and then rose to such high levels that they were able to shape the organization and structure of ISI may have become "born-again Muslims." But the question that cannot be easily answered is whether an equally important number are instrumentalists in their approach rather than true believers. Baathism was not only an ideology; it was also an instrument of control. It was organized hierarchically and sought to extend control into the depths of society for purposes of surveillance, control, and ideological indoctrination. It sought to organize society in a disciplined manner in order to achieve the goals of its ideology. It looked to the Soviet Union and East Germany not for *ideology* but for *instrumentalist* reasons having to do with inner organization of the party structure and the organization of and control over the state.

Naturally, as the Baathist state eroded in the late 1980s and the 1990s, this totalitarian edifice disintegrated. The ideology no longer motivated people; the instruments of control and surveillance were beginning to fray due to lack of resources and personnel's increasing lack of belief in what they were doing. Saddam Hussein himself blamed the party for allowing too many unscrupulous, untrained, and unmotivated individuals to join it. He lodged withering criticism of the party qua ideology and instrument of control after the Shia rebellion in 1991 was put down. His regime set up instruments of control over the Shia slum of Medinat al-Sadr (known during his time as Medinat Saddam and before that as Medinat al-Thawra), the sprawling Baghdad slum of 1.5 million souls. The slum had been a stronghold of the Iraqi Communist Party (one of the best disciplined and organized Marxist parties in the Middle East). Over the course of time, as a result of work by the Shia clerics, communist sentiment was eroded by rising religious sentiment. Shia Baathist cadres were assigned to watch over each neighborhood block there. As the regime became more and more decrepit, these cadres reported less and less to their superiors across the river about the rise of political Shiism within the ranks of the population.

The regime's surveillance of Sunnis in the military and security services focused primarily on preventing these cadre from threatening the regime by trying to seize power by means of a coup d'état. Religious radicalism was not believed to be as widespread or as dangerous among the Sunnis as it was among the Shias. Moreover, many Sunnis turned a blind eye to their kin's involvement in Islamist politics and often would fail to report illicit political activity. It is not clear, however, whether the regime knew how much Sunni Islamist sentiment had filtered into the lower rank and file of the armed forces, the security services, the Popular Army (al-Jaysh al-Shaabi, or in Iraqi bitter humor, al-jaysh al la-shaabi, the "Unpopular Army"), and the Saddam Fedaiyin (Men of Sacrifice, a Baathist paramilitary group, many of whose personnel were déraciné, or uprooted elements from rural roots, and what Marx referred to as the lumpenproletariat, from urban areas).[53]

The issue of murky Baathist-Salafist interactions goes beyond having similar views about the "distressing" situation prevailing in Iraq—Shia hegemony and the American and Iranian presence—or even a growing affinity for Islamism among some Baathists. What drew many of these former regime elements was their belief that they had a lot to offer the

Islamists in the fight against their common enemies, especially in the areas of organization, intelligence gathering, counterintelligence, surveillance, and methods for seizing and maintaining control of a region and its population. Despite the recognition by the jihadists of the importance of personnel with these skill sets, they knew their ranks were woefully lacking in these areas. Moreover, given their problems with Iraq's obstreperous Sunni Arab tribes, the jihadists were particularly interested in furthering their own understanding of how the former Baathist regime had managed to achieve a mutually beneficial relationship with these denizens of rural Iraq and the small tribally based conservative Sunni towns.

One of Abu Mohammad al-Maqdisi's close associates in Jordan, "Raheem," a personal aide to Zarqawi, allegedly had an inside view of the group's transformation after the end of the first decade of the twenty-first century. In an interview, "Raheem" described the men running the revitalized organization as different from the original cadre. According to "Raheem," when Zarqawi was in charge, it was his unofficial policy to exclude anyone from the secular nationalist Baath Party. Zarqawi firmly believed that Iraqis in general, and Baathists in particular, lacked piety and were untrustworthy. "Raheem" stated: "There were very few Iraqis who were exposed to other ideas. They were nationalists and were highly influenced by the Baath."[54] The former Baathists, who had run Iraq for decades, were invaluable new recruits for ISI as it sought to revitalize itself following the deaths of Abu Omar al-Baghdadi and Abu Hamza al-Muhajir in 2010. Saddam Hussein's former military officers knew the vulnerabilities of the Iraqi army. His former intelligence officials knew the power brokers in each town and village. Since the regime's overthrow, these men had lost their incomes and their authority; now ISI would serve as a means for them to regain their status.[55] According to "Raheem," a former officer, Colonel Samir Abd Mohammad al-Khleifawi, (aka "Haji Bakr," about whom I will say more), brought an entire Baathist unit with him when he joined the group. "Raheem" alleged that it was largely these men—former Baathists who became senior members of ISI—who nominated Abu Bakr al-Baghdadi as the organization's new leader in 2010.

"Haji Bakr" may or may not have been as instrumental in the elevation of the relatively unknown Abu Bakr al-Baghdadi to leadership of ISI, as "Raheem" would have us believe, but he certainly was key in the revitalization of its organizational structure and its ability to take control of territory and people. At the time of Abu Bakr al-Baghdadi's rise to power, "Haji Bakr" was already a key military commander, allegedly the chief of staff, within ISI's ministry of war, which was ultimately renamed the military council. He became the head of the military council in early 2011.[56]

In 2012, "Haji Bakr" was back in Syria for the second time in his career as top military commander for ISIS; his trip was part of the effort to heal the rift between the Iraqi organization under Abu Bakr al-Baghdadi and JN. "Haji Bakr's" approach to conflict resolution included an unusual way to heal a rift: killing opponents of ISIS's stance on the internecine conflict. However, "Haji Bakr" had his eyes on bigger things than low-level operational skulduggery. The military council was the powerhouse behind the efforts to rebuild ISI's organizational and administrative structures and its combat capabilities in the wake of its serious battering between 2007 and 2010. One could conceivably argue that "Haji Bakr's" mission in life was to figure out how to effectively implement Abu Bakr Naji's *Management of Savagery* and the ISI-produced booklet for action, "Strategic Plan for Reinforcing the Political Position of the Islamic State of Iraq" (both of which I will discuss in chapter 6). Programmatically, "Haji Bakr" was focused on (1) revitalizing ISI as an organization; (2) establishing a sanctuary in Syria as a springboard into Iraq; (3) causing mayhem and chaos to undermine the Iraqi state; (4) "neutralizing" groups or communities within the Sunni population who were deemed hostile and seeking allies or even cajoling or coercing groups to join the jihadists.

In 2015 the German investigative journalist Christoph Reuter, of *Der Spiegel*, revealed the major role played by "Haji Bakr" in the transformation of ISI and then its successor, ISIS.[57] When "Haji Bakr" was killed in January 2014 in a firefight with anti-IS Syrian insurgents, he left behind a treasure trove of secret information: the blueprint of the steps and techniques for IS's making a comeback and seizing power. Syria would be the beachhead for springing into Iraq in a major comeback. To be sure, Syria would not be ignored in the battle; once ISIS consolidated its position in its home, it would be back to fight the "atheist" regime in Syria. It was in Tel Rifaat, north of Aleppo, where he took up residence in an inconspicuous house, that "Haji Bakr" sketched out the new structure of ISIS and the mechanics of seizing power. (In 2013, Tel Rifaat would become IS's stronghold in Aleppo province, with hundreds of fighters stationed there.)

The blueprint was implemented quickly and with astonishing accuracy in the ensuing months. It would begin with the stealthy and unobtrusive infiltration of a village or neighborhood. The organization would open a Dawah office, an Islamic missionary center, which would recruit followers to come and listen to lay preachers' proselytizing. The real purpose of the

"Dawah office" would become apparent when some of the recruits would be enlisted or encouraged to "provide information" on their villages, communities, and neighborhoods. Specifically, "Haji Bakr" wanted to gather useful information, and he thus compiled lists such as this one:

- List the powerful families
- Name the powerful individuals in these families
- Find out their sources of income
- Name and estimate the size of armed units in their village or community
- Find out the names of their leaders, who controls the armed units, and their political orientation
- Find out the illegal activities taking place (according to sharia), which could be used to blackmail individuals or communities if necessary
- Uncover "dirt" about people—criminality, homosexuality, adultery—for purposes of blackmail

"Haji Bakr" added that several "members" would be selected in each town to marry the daughters of the most influential families, in order to "ensure penetration of these families without their knowledge."[58] The infiltrators, who would report to the organization's military and security councils, were to find out as much as possible about the target villages, communities, and towns: who lived there, who was in charge, which families were religious, which Islamic school of religious jurisprudence they belonged to, how many mosques there were, who the imam was, how many wives and children he had, and how old they were. Clerics were a particular target of attention. "Haji Bakr" wanted to know their religious and political orientations. "Bakr" also wanted answers to questions like: Does the imam earn a salary? If so, who pays it? Who appoints him?

The agents were to inform their superiors about the vulnerabilities and jealousies, as well as age-old faults that existed within the deep fabric of society. Such information could be used to divide and subjugate the local population. There was no shortage of recruits for such work, as many individuals were in dire need of money. The informants included former intelligence spies and young men and adolescents. Most of the men on "Bakr's" list of informants, such as those from Tel Rifaat, were in their early twenties, but some were as young as sixteen or seventeen.

"Haji Bakr" and others, mostly former regime security officials, were most likely responsible for setting up and expanding the security council, which was quite distinct from the military council, which was to all intents and purposes ISIS's and then IS's "department of defense." "Haji Bakr" was obsessed with gathering information about opponents and counterintelligence to prevent enemies from penetrating the organization. He had no compunction about kidnapping and assassinating opponents. From the very beginning, the plan was to have the intelligence services operate in parallel, even at the provincial level. A general intelligence department reported to the "security emir" for a region, who was in charge of deputy emirs for individual districts. A head of secret spy cells and an "intelligence service and information manager" for the district reported to each of these deputy emirs. The spy cells at the local level reported to the district emir's deputy. The goal was to have everyone keeping an eye on everyone else. Those in charge of training the "Sharia judges in intelligence gathering" also reported to the district emir, while a separate department of "security officers" was assigned to the regional emir.[59]

The jihadists' strategy for a comeback after 2010 required them to rebuild their military capabilities to capture territory. Maintaining control over people and getting them to do what you want even in the face of opposition required other skills, including sinister ones. "Haji Bakr's" program for the seizure of power for the jihadists came out of the Baathist playbook. To impose itself on Iraqi society in the 1970s, the Baathist regime learned from the best, namely the East German Stasi—security service—and the Soviet KGB. Over the course of their tyrannical rule in Iraq, the Baathists tailored these models to fit their own society. The Baathists' surveillance of society and the fear they inspired among Iraqis were without peer in the Middle East. This system began to break down in the 1990s after the virtual collapse of the Baathist state's mechanisms of surveillance and enforcement. The skills did not disappear; and the Baathist cadre had plenty of skills that the jihadists needed but did not have in abundance.

Although Iraq's dominant Baath Party was secular and IS was Islamist, the two systems, in Christoph Reuter's view, shared a conviction that control over the masses should lie in the hands of a small conspiratorial elite who knew better than the masses because it had a grand design, legitimized by either God, for the Islamists, or Arab or Iraqi nationalism, for the Baathists. In Reuter's view, "the secret of IS's success lies in the combination of opposites, the fanatical beliefs of one group and the strategic calculations of the other."[60] This is very plausible but also suggests that the Baathists viewed the Islamists in purely instrumentalist terms and had not imbibed any of the Islamist ideology. Given the Islamization campaign under Saddam Hussein, the infiltration of radical Islamist ideas into Iraq—Salafism had made an entry in the 1970s and was stamped out, and then reentered from 1983 onward—and the decline of the appeal of pure nationalism, it strikes me as unlikely that many of the former regime's personnel were not influenced by radical Islamism. To many, radical Islamism seemed to be pretty much the only effective ideology of resistance against the United States and its perceived machinations in the Arab and wider Islamic worlds.

It is also important to recognize the fact that some of the more militant Arab nationalist and Islamist motifs, as were briefly described in chapter 3, were strikingly similar. Both see the United States as an exploitative neocolonial power out to extract the resources of the Arab and Islamic worlds for its benefit. Both see the United States as having a design to fragment the Arab and Islamic worlds into small mini-entities that can be more easily controlled and would not pose a threat to America's "creation," the "Zionist" entity. Both ideologies excoriate Iran, "the Safavids," which they believe has a long history of expansionism and covetousness (*atma*). When it comes to Iran, some subtle differences *do* appear, though. Traditionally, the Baathists hated Iran on a nationalist basis; and when religion entered into the equation, the Baathists derided the Islamic Republic of Iran's arrogation of a primary role for itself within Islam. On the contrary, argued the Baathist regime, God delivered Islam to the Arabs first so that they may propagate it globally, and He did so in Arabic.[61]

In addition, originally the Baathists did not cast aspersions on Shiism; instead they went out of their way to distinguish between "Arab Shiism"—as practiced in Iraq—and "Iranian Shiism." The latter was marred, they hinted, by pre-Islamic Iranian elements. During the early insurgency (2003–2009), the Baathists, as can be gathered from their statements, did not attack the Shias on religious grounds. However, this did not prevent the Baathists from viewing the Shias as having betrayed the country on behalf of the "direct" invaders—that is, the United States—and the more insidious "indirect" invaders, that is, the Iranians. Over time, the Baathist view of the Shias turned more sinister and closer to that of the radical Salafist groups, such as AQI and then ISI. This darker and more religious turn in the negative view of the Shias was not surprising, as the political situation in Iraq was totally transformed: the Sunnis viewed themselves as being disenfranchised, deprived of their property, their livelihoods, their nation, as members of their community were killed en masse by triumphant Shia militias and Iranian intelligence operatives. Finally, one must not forget the impact of the Sunni clerical establishment in Iraq in influencing people within the Sunni community to view the Shias in dire and uncompromising terms as the enemy of Islam, created to destroy it from within, in cooperation with the infidels, who are the outsiders.[62]

"Haji Bakr's" efforts to rebuild the organization went a long way in making it easier for Abu Bakr al-Baghdadi and the other members of the senior leadership to create a management and administrative structure as the stepping stone toward building the Caliphate. By mid-2017, much of this structure was in disarray and probably no longer functioning as IS, in effect, transitions from being a state to controlling territory and ruling people and to being an insurgent terrorist organization focused on survival, fighting, and seeking to make a comeback yet again.

The Structure and Management of the Islamic State
The Caliph

The caliph is the ruler of the Islamic state. The literature on the caliph and the governance structure of the caliphate, both medieval and modern, is voluminous. The doctrinal premises upon which ISIS's senior officials justified the formation of their state, as well as the requirements and conditions to be met by candidates seeking the job of head of state, were the same ones that medieval Muslim jurists, such as al-Mawardi, had laid down for the caliphate. Taking the Prophet's flag as their own is not the only way in which the jihadists have sought to emulate him; they also adopted his state in Medina as the blueprint upon which the Islamic state should be modeled.

The caliph is required to be well versed in sharia, to claim descent from the Qureish tribe of the Prophet Mohammad, and to be of sound mind and able-bodied. He has absolute power over all religious and worldly affairs in Sunni Islamic political history and Islamic jurisprudence. As the religious and political leader, the caliph has the absolute obedience of his followers after being chosen by the shura council and those who hold binding authority within the organization (*ahl ul-hal wa al-aqd*). Abu Bakr al-Baghdadi, the current leader, further developed that structure on the basis of allegiance and obedience, thus solidifying the organization's centralized nature and the caliph's ironclad control.[63] He has direct authority over so-called councils, a term he employs as an alternative to the term "ministries" used by his predecessor, Abu Omar al-Baghdadi.[64] These councils are IS's central leadership pillars. Abu Bakr al-Baghdadi has sweeping powers to appoint and remove the heads of councils, after consulting with the shura council, whose role seems to be primarily advisory. All final decisions lie in his hands.

Abu Bakr al-Baghdadi ensured that there was a strong Iraqi presence in all key positions of the organization, such as the shura, information and communication, and recruitment and fundraising councils, while confining Arab and foreign members to support functions. He retained semiabsolute authority in war and hostilities. He kept sole control of the key organizational functions, such as security, intelligence, day-to-day management, the shura and military councils, the information and communications department, spiritual guidance, and finance. He also had the power to appoint leaders and emirs in the Syrian and Iraqi provinces under the control of the new "state." Under Abu Bakr al-Baghdadi, the organization became more security conscious than before. Once he took over, he restructured the organization, putting former Iraqi army officers, such as Samir al-Khlefawi and Abdul Rahman al-Bilawi, in charge of the military, turning the military structure into a more professional, cohesive entity.

At the same time, Abu Bakr al-Baghdadi used Arab and foreign jihadists for spiritual functions, especially those who came from Gulf states, such as Abu Bakr al-Qahtani, from Saudi Arabia, Abu Hammam al-Athari (also known as Turki al-Banali or Turki Bin Mubarak Bin Abdullah), from Bahrain, and Osman al-Nazih al-Assiri, a Saudi national. Abu Bakr al-Baghdadi put Turkmen from the northern town of Tel Afar into key security positions, most prominently Abu Ali al-Anbari, and put Arabs and foreigners in charge of his media machine, which was led by Abu Mohammed al-Adnani, the Syrian spokesman for IS who was killed in late August 2016 while on the front lines in Syria. Even though Abu Bakr al-Baghdadi increasingly began to integrate more Arabs and foreigners into the leadership of IS since declaring himself caliph in June 2014, Iraqis still dominate the highest, most sensitive positions in IS's upper echelons.

A "cabinet" of deputies, who manage IS's administration and military operations, helps Abu Bakr al-Baghdadi. His predecessors, including Zarqawi, kept power very centralized in their own hands and among their very close trusted deputies. This was possible because the extent of territory and the amount of resources under Zarqawi's control were limited, allowing close oversight. The ambitions of ISI, then ISIS, and now IS were broader; its presence was felt over a sprawling expanse of territory; and it had greater resources at its beck and call than Zarqawi's original group ever did. "Caliph Ibrahim" assigned deputies to manage the intricate work-ings of the organization and then IS. Abu Abdul Rahman al-Bilawi, the IS military chief for Iraq, who was killed in a raid, was found to have a flash drive detailing some of the workings of the organization. There were reportedly one thousand top- and middle-ranking field commanders, most of whom had technical, military, and intelligence expertise.[65]

The Shura Council

The shura council is one of IS's most important structures. Despite the orga-nization's various changes since Zarqawi's leadership, the shura institution has remained significant from the era of Abu Omar al-Baghdadi into Abu Bakr al-Baghdadi's reign. Headed by Abu Arkan al-Ameri, the council grew or shrunk as circumstances and needs dictated, with members usually num-bering between nine and eleven of IS's senior leaders, appointed by Abu Bakr al-Baghdadi on the recommendation of emirs and provincial rulers.

The council convenes to debate current affairs, critical decisions, and policy-making. In theory, it has the power to depose the caliph, although it is certain that Caliph Ibrahim would not take too kindly to such a move. It would be interesting to know what debates occurred, if any, when his wounding in northern Iraq by a U.S. air strike led to rumors about his death. The council supposedly offers Abu Bakr al-Baghdadi advice on strategic and political matters, but its advice is nonbinding. Shura was confined to day-to-day affairs that were not explicitly covered by specific texts in the Quran and Sunna, because Islam states that where a text is available, there is no place for debate, or shura, unless the debate is about how the said text should be interpreted. The shura council also recommended candi-dates for governor positions and memberships of various councils. The spiritual council enjoys special status within the shura council, given IS's theological nature. It is headed by Abu Bakr al-Baghdadi himself and is made up of six members. Two of its basic functions are to monitor how other councils adhere to sharia and recommend new caliph candidates in the event the current caliph dies, is captured, or is somehow no longer able to run the organization and the state due to illness or disability.[66]

The Sharia Council

The sharia council is one of the most important entities within IS. Abu Ali al-Anbari was formerly responsible for security and spiritual guidance, but this council is now headed by Abu Mohammed al-Ani. Abu Anas al-Shami was the first to head the sharia council in the Zarqawi era. Under Abu Omar Al-Baghdadi's leadership, it was held by Osman Bin Abdul Rahman al-Tamimi.

This council issues ideological tracts, writes Abu Bakr al-Baghdadi's speeches and statements, and provides commentary for the organization's videos, songs, and other media. There are two departments within the council: one acts as the judiciary, which runs sharia courts and the judiciary system at large, handles litigation, mediates in disputes, dictates punishments, and manages the promotion of virtue and prevention of vice. The other department is tasked with preaching, guidance, recruitment, and propagation and monitoring of media. The sharia council's staff consists mainly of non-Iraqi Arabs, particularly from the states of the Arabian Peninsula, and other foreigners. Despite the council's key role, Abu Bakr al-Baghdadi was allegedly declared caliph without its consent. Consequently, this council apparently suffered a large number of defections of clerics and scholars shortly after his elevation to caliph.[67]

The Media Council

Mass communication is a significant focus for IS; it is one of the few jihadi organizations that gives considerable attention to the Internet and mass communication. Since its early days, it has recognized the value of the media in spreading its political message and Salafi ideology. The media council was first headed by Abu Maysarah al-Iraqi. During the advent of ISI in 2006, Abu Mohammed al-Mashhadani was minister of information, while Abu Abdullah Moharib Abdul Latif al-Jibouri was spokesman for the state. In 2009, Ahmed Al-Tai became minister of information. A large committee headed by Abu al-Atheer Amru al-Absi ran the council.

The media council of IS has undergone considerable development in form and content and has extensive support. Al-Furqan, an institution for media production, is older and more influential than many of the newer media production entities that belong to the organization. This group also publishes a number of Arabic- and English-language magazines, such as *Dabiq* and *al-Shamikhah*, and has established local radio stations, such as al-Bayan in Mosul and another in the Syrian city of Raqqa. The organization runs online blogs in Russian and English. Media productions are translated into various languages, including English, French, German, Spanish, and Urdu. The organization controls several websites and online forums, which offer a vast array of literature about its ideology, discourse, methods of recruitment, fundraising, training, covert activities, battle tactics, bomb-making, and everything jihadists need to know about combat, gang warfare, and attrition.

The quality of videos and other material produced by institutions like al-Furqan and al-Etisam reveals significant changes in IS's structure, resources, violent tactics, and terrifying strategies of warfare. It has produced a series of professional-grade videos, often showing beheadings or executions in graphic detail. After IS took control of Mosul in June 2014, it released a series of horrific videos that depicted brutal beheadings. The first of these, "Message to America," showed an IS member beheading American hostage and journalist James Foley. On September 2, 2014, a second video, with the same title, showed the beheading of another hostage, American journalist Steven Sotloff. On September 14, 2014, the organization ran a third video, "Message to America's Allies," in which IS members were shown beheading British hostage David Haines, followed by yet another video on October 3 that showed the beheading of a second British hostage, Alan Henning, with threats to behead a third American hostage, Abdulrahman (Peter) Kassig. Kassig was subsequently beheaded as well in November 2014. Several other IS videos were widely viewed on YouTube, including "Kasr al-Hudud" (Smashing Borders) uploaded on June 29, 2014, and Abu Bakr al-Baghdadi's address in Mosul on July 5, 2014. The organization also uploaded a series of videos under the title "Rasail Min Ard al-Malahim" (Messages from the Land of Epics) that documented the victories and operations of the organization, with more than fifty episodes uploaded so far. Another series of videos is titled "Fa Sharrid Bihim Min Khalfihim" (Scatter Them from Behind). Part 1 covered the battle in which Raqqa's 93rd Brigade base was captured on August 23, 2014, and part 2 covered the takeover of the al-Tabqa airbase on September 7, 2014. The video "Laheeb al-Harb" (The Flames of War) is one of IS's highest-quality productions and one of the most terrifying. It includes coverage of many of IS's battles, as well as a message to the countries of the U.S.-led Coalition.

The group has magnified its use of mobile electronic devices and social media as important weapons of war. Tweets of beheading videos and posts of gruesome images have led to Twitter's suspension of two important IS pages, al-Itisam and al-Hayat. For years, jihadists recognized the multifaceted role that images, audio messages, and videos play in psychological warfare and recruitment. Zarqawi's Internet jihad began in the pre-YouTube and -Liveleak era, when posting videos online was difficult and time consuming. Zarqawi's network had to rely on jihadi online forums and on trusted members to upload and disseminate videos and media releases. Videos such as the infamous beheading of Nicholas Berg took hours to upload and several more to download. Soon after the video was posted on the jihadi forum Ansar al-Islami, the site crashed due to the volume of downloads. In spite of such difficulties, Zarqawi persisted in his use of the Internet as his main media outlet. Nowadays, smartphones and social media accounts are all that is needed to share material in real time with tens of thousands of jihadists.

The organization adopted these tools and has been utilizing the latest Internet technologies and social media outlets to maintain massive, sophisticated online media campaigns used to promote jihad, to communicate, to recruit, and to wage psychological warfare.[68] Twitter became an important tool for the jihadists because of its ease of use and ability to provide rapid updates to an unlimited number of viewers. Some jihadists became active to the point of "live" tweeting during fighting, reporting on injuries or deaths of fellow fighters and battle outcomes without any censorship.

The organization maintains an organized and well-coordinated online network, with several official accounts on Twitter for its central leadership. Some of these pages are used to release messages from its central leadership; others focus on recruiting and networking in order to gain followers and attract skilled professionals, such as doctors and engineers, to "migrate" to IS, where their skills were needed.[69] Al-Itisam, which Twitter suspended on June 13, 2014, had fifty thousand followers and served as ISIS's information clearinghouse. Ajnad tweets religious and Quranic citations to its 36,500 followers. Al-Furqan, the official IS media wing, has a dedicated Twitter page where it posts messages from the IS leadership, as well as videos and images of beheadings, to its nineteen thousand followers. Al-Hayat Media Center focuses on recruiting Westerners and provides media in English, French, German, and Russian. The Islamic State also maintains several official local pages, focusing on the state's activities in various provinces. These are aimed at winning the hearts and minds of Sunni Muslims in Iraq and Syria. In addition to its own pages and media, IS is supported by thirty other online media groups. For example, al-Battar Media Group, with thirty-two thousand followers, constantly works to mobilize Twitter members to support IS by translating IS releases. In June 2014 ISIS launched a social media campaign to highlight its military campaign. It posted on Twitter photos of captured Iraqi security personnel along with threats and messages warning surrounding towns that it was approaching. In its Twitter feeds, ISIS gave extensive details of its operations, including the number of bombings, suicide missions, and assassinations it has carried out.[70] By way of contrast, al-Qaeda and its affiliates primarily used jihadist forums, such as Shamoukh and Fidaa, to release information. These were password-protected forums that required users to log in and used proxies to disguise the names of Internet service providers. These methods also required computers, which were not always readily available or accessible.[71]

The Finance Council (Bayt ul-Mal)

Finances are the sinews of war and state-building. Finances were critical to the rebuilding of the organization, its fighting capabilities, and its efforts to build a state. The Islamic State emerged as the wealthiest organization in the history of jihadi movements. Its wealth exceeds even that of al-Qaeda and its regional branches. Since the Zarqawi era, the organization has successfully built a vast fundraising network with many varied sources of financing. An effective financing committee has existed since the days of JTJ. The committee relied on a network of fundraising activists who collect funds from individual businesspeople and from mosques, especially in wealthy Gulf Cooperation Council states and Europe, in addition to collecting money within Iraq and administering spoils gained from conquering new ground and levying various taxes. As the organization's power grew, it announced its first cabinet during 2006, with several "ministries" being tasked with controlling revenues from oil and other natural resources. In 2009, the leadership announced the formation of a second cabinet, in which Yunus al-Hamdani was appointed "minister of finance." Under the current IS, Abu Bakr al-Baghdadi oversees the management of Bayt al-Mal (literally "House of Wealth"), which was headed by Mowaffaq Mustafa al-Karmoosh. The organization's finances increased considerably with Mosul's June 2014 fall and as it gained control over vast swathes of territory in Iraq and Syria.[72] Captured documentation has shown that IS earned several million dollars per day from a diverse financial portfolio. The organization had several income sources at its disposal; these are the most important:

- *Donations and grants*: News organizations have reported that individual Gulf citizens are large donors to the group in Iraq and Syria. It also enjoyed a windfall from wealthy Iraqis who inflated its coffers after the fall of Mosul.

- *Charity, donations, and zakat (alms)*: During 2011 and 2012, supporters used mosques and the media to urge Muslims to dedicate their zakah and charity money to jihad and resistance in Syria. These funds quickly and easily found their way to ISIS.

- *Ransom revenues*: The organization has created an entrepreneurial enterprise of kidnapping foreign nationals, employees of international organizations, and Western journalists and then extorting millions of dollars in ransom money from their families and home countries.

- *Expropriation*: Taking possession of resources and goods in conquered areas: hospitals, shopping centers, restaurants, and power and water utilities in these areas have provided millions of dollars in revenue every month.

- *Revenues from natural resources and mining*: IS took possession of oil and gas resources in Iraq and Syria. At the height of its power and territorial extent, more than eighty minor oil fields were under its control whose products were sold either locally or internationally through traders. Revenues were estimated at $8–10 million a month from oil at the height of IS's power in 2015.[73] This was reduced considerably over the course of 2016 and 2017 as IS lost territory, and thus oil fields, and as outsiders reduced their trading with IS.

- *Taxes and stipends*: Businesspeople, farmers, industrialists, and the wealthy in IS-controlled areas are some of the most important sources of funds. The organization also collected *jizya* (money collected in exchange for protection) from non-Muslims, as well as monthly taxes from local businesses, whose level began to fluctuate in 2015, as business owners shut up shop and fled or the amount of commercial activity declined due to violence and tighter restrictions imposed on traffic going in and out of IS-controlled territories.

- *Government funds*: Many people have alleged that IS seized cash estimated at tens of millions of dollars from banks and government institutions after Mosul's fall, including one-half billion dollars from the central bank in Mosul. The latter story is folklore, has become a cliché, and was repeated ad nauseam whenever the matter of IS finances came up.

- *Agricultural revenues*: IS controls large swaths of wheat and produce fields in Iraq and Syria, with as much as a third of Iraq's wheat production at its disposal.

When ISIS transformed itself into IS in June 2014, it hoped that its revenue stream would allow it to fund its state and its personnel, to fight its wars, and to proceed along the path of establishing and governing a state and providing services for the populace under its control. While IS was definitely more professional and better run than ISI was under Abu Omar al-Baghdadi, which was highly dysfunctional, it began to show its administrative and bureaucratic vulnerabilities in 2015, when evidence of corruption, fraud, and graft multiplied. This affected not only the financial stability of the organization's structure but also its fighting and state-building enterprises. The most embarrassing episode, though certainly not the largest in scale, was the disappearance of Abu Fatima al-Tunisi, an emir in the region of eastern Deir ez-Zor, with $25,000 in zakat funds, accompanied by his tweet "What state? What caliphate? You idiots."[74] In addition to the corruption that pervaded IS's administration and reduced its efficiency, it faced the enormous costs of running a war and providing services and goods to the population under its control while its infrastructure and sources of finance were under relentless attack by the U.S.-led Coalition both from the air and from the ground (see chapter 6).

Between 1999 and this writing (mid-2017), the entity we now refer to as IS evolved from a network of individuals grouped around Zarqawi into a formidable organization that survived considerable hiatuses in its organizational structure. By late 2012, not only had ISI developed into an organization with a system of management, it had also developed into a fighting organization. The formal administrative capacity of IS was a substantial strength, which it inherited and built upon from its predecessor organizations, AQI and ISI. Its administrative capacity also has an important side effect: a massive paper trail dating back years, to long before the group's current incarnation, that is only just beginning to be studied.

Zarqawi started with setting up an organization and then ensuring that it had sufficient structural stability and management capabilities to survive in a very adverse environment. His immediate successors faced immense problems, and the organization was nearly extinguished during the combined U.S. military campaign and Sunni uprising against what became ISI. After its near defeat, ISI went underground to "lick its wounds" and to revitalize its organization and its military capabilities. It reemerged as ISIS and then as IS. The main goals of the revitalized organization were

5

"Organizing to Fight"

THE EVOLUTION OF THE JIHADIST WAY OF WAR IN IRAQ

Ways of Warfare

This chapter will address the evolution of and changes in a specific jihadist way of war in Iraq that is associated with Zarqawi's original organization and then those of its successors after his death in 2006. During the American occupation of Iraq between 2003 and 2011, many different entities were fighting one another. The post-Baathist Iraqi state and the Americans—until they left in 2011—fought various insurgent and militia groups, including the predecessors of IS. Each party involved in the conflict in Iraq had its own way of war, which was determined by ideology, goals, organizational structure, training, geographical reach, and weapons and resource availability.

The same holds true today in the current conflict that erupted from 2012 onward and was still going strong in mid-2017. The Americans returned, albeit with a smaller footprint, primarily as advisors, trainers, and operators of complex weaponry. This time the Kurdish Peshmerga forces were more heavily involved in this internal war than they were in the first iteration of it between 2003 and 2011. The Iraqi Security Forces found themselves saddled or aided, depending on one's perspective, by the vast presence of Shia militias.

After many ups and downs, the post-Zarqawi jihadist entity that emerged as ISIS and then as IS managed to develop the most formidable and most resilient military machine possessed by a nonstate actor in Iraq. The victories of this military machine in 2013 and 2014 alarmed regional governments and the international community. This military machine, however, has not been able to sustain itself effectively, and IS has found its way of warfare being steadily constricted and eroded from 2015 onward. By mid-2015 IS was forced onto the defensive and began to lose ground steadily to its enemies. Yet IS's ability to defend effectively and stubbornly in built-up areas stymied the best of Iraq's forces for months. The urban battle of Mosul, which started on October 16, 2016, and was in full swing well into the summer of 2017, has proven to be one of the largest, bloodiest, and significant urban battles since World War II.

How did a "state" that nobody recognizes, except its supporters, create offensive and defensive capabilities that have unsettled two countries, Iraq and Syria, the wider region, and the international community? The answer is that IS developed and implemented a way of warfare that has been unique within the jihadist world.

The concept of "ways of warfare" has a long pedigree going back to the interwar period between World Wars I and II, when the noted British strategic thinker Basil Liddell Hart opined that there was a *specific* British way of warfare that deserved further analysis.[1] Not surprising, the thesis set off a wide-ranging debate about the existence and validity of a British way of warfare. Judging by the continuing commentary, the discussion has still not abated.[2] It is also not surprising that the concept was adopted and then became widely used to understand how and why each nation fights the way it does. Strategic analysts and military historians applied the concept to a number of nations and analyzed the American, German, and Russian ways of war.[3] A second generation of analysts began to write about the ways of war of more middle powers or of those in the Global South. Thus, from the late 1990s to the present there have been extensive studies of the Arab or even generalized Islamic, Chinese, Israeli, and, most recently, Pakistani ways of war.[4] Little work to date has been done on the ways of war of nonstate actors, particularly the various jihadist entities such as IS. Recently the term "jihadist way of war" has appeared in connection with the emergence of IS in 2014 as a significant fighting force, but such a way of war has not been adequately analyzed.

The jihadist way of war is not equivalent to the so-called Islamic way of war. Some thinkers have argued that there is an Islamic way of war whose origins can be traced to past Islamic theory and practice; others have vehemently disagreed with the notion of an all-encompassing Islamic way of war. In support of my argument that the jihadist way of war should not be conflated with an Islamic way of war, since the jihadist way of war is a product of contemporaneous conditions, I put forth four points. First, the jihadist way of war can be regarded as a particular and idiosyncratic interpretation of an Islamic way of war as perceived by Salafi-jihadists. Of course, the Salafi-jihadists universally claim that they are the only true and righteous followers and interpreters of Islam and that their way of war *is* the Islamic one. Second, it would be wrong to believe that the jihadist way of war is a self-contained corpus of military knowledge or theory and tactical, operational, and strategic practice. As many observers and strategic analysts have pointed out, the jihadi theorists and practitioners of war have also borrowed from the enormous body of non-Islamic ways of war. Third, there is more than just one jihadist way of war; what this chapter addresses is the specific jihadist way of warfare associated first with Zarqawi and then his successors. One of the key but as yet unexplored factors behind the rift between IS and al-Qaeda is the fact that their perspectives have differed on how to wage war on their common enemies.

Fourth, the Islamist militants have known for a long time that a jihadist way of war in a particular theater of operations cannot mimic the jihadist way of war in another front. That is another reason why there is more than one jihadist way of warfare. Physical geography (terrain), human geography (demography and its characteristics), the nature and strength and weaknesses of the opposing force, and many other things have a profound impact on ways of warfare. In other words, fighting in Afghanistan is very different from fighting in Iraq, and both are profoundly different from fighting in Saudi Arabia. Decades ago, Mao Zedong recognized the fact that different environments require different ways of war or modifications in principles of war. In contemporary times, jihadist thinkers on and practitioners of war have stated the same thing. Similarly, fighting in a rural environment is very different from fighting in an urban environment, just as fighting on open desert terrain is different from fighting in jungles or mountains.

The Jihadist Way of War in Iraq

When the United States invaded and occupied Iraq in 2003, the jihadist world recognized the importance of that country as a critical front in their war against what they habitually referred to as the "Zionist-Crusader" alliance. Individuals affiliated with al-Qaeda were particularly vehement in their condemnation of the U.S. action. For the ideologues, clerics, and strategic thinkers of al-Qaeda and the jihadist world in general, the American invasion of Iraq in 2003 became the most important threat to the security and well-being of the umma, and they discussed ways and means to combat it.

Matters were no different for the small group around Zarqawi who found themselves in Iraq after being ejected unceremoniously from Afghanistan in 2001. They recognized the importance of Iraq as a front in its war against the United States, but they entered Iraq with little in the way of military capabilities. Zarqawi also recognized the vast disparity in military power between his novice organization and that of the powerful coalition led by the United States. Caught up in a fierce and deadly combat environment, Zarqawi and his organization had no time to immerse themselves in intensive intellectual pursuits concerning warfare. They needed to come up with an immediate and viable military response to the Americans and their local allies on the ground in Iraq.

The first premise of Zarqawi's approach to war was the recognition of the manifest imbalance of power between his forces and those of his enemies. As he explained:

> We are fighting a battle that is not equal in any sense. There can be no comparison between our capabilities and the enemy's resources. Hundreds of our brothers are fighting hundreds of thousands of the enemy. As to military equipment, it is no secret that the enemy possesses huge military resources, on land, in the air, and at sea. What the mujahidin possess cannot compare with the enemy's resources. The brothers possess their firearms, some mortars, and some rifle-propelled grenades against tanks, armored vehicles, and aircraft. The land of jihad in Iraq is different from Afghanistan and Chechnya. The brothers in those two countries are helped either by forests or high mountains where they can hide from the enemy and prevent him from reaching them. Iraq is flat without mountains, wadis, or forests.
>
> Another problem is that the battlefront is a close engagement. The brothers are fighting one of the fiercest battles in human history.... They are fighting a fierce battle while lacking many supportive conditions. They have no strategic depth or an area unattainable to the enemy. The enemy is behind them, in front of them, on their right, and on their left.[5]

In this illuminating statement, Zarqawi was pointing to an age-old problem of the weaker side facing a stronger enemy. Indeed, this statement is eerily similar to one uttered by Luis Taruc, the leader of the anti-Japanese Filipino resistance movement, the Hukbalahap, which later became a potent anti-Manila government insurgency after World War II.[6] In the case of Iraq, the enemy (the United States) outmatched the mujahidin quantitatively and qualitatively by a wide margin.

The second premise of Zarqawi's approach was that the enemy could only be dealt with effectively by the waging of "unrestricted warfare." The term is ambiguous and has been uniformly misunderstood. "Unrestricted warfare" for Zarqawi and his jihadist followers meant implementing a way of warfare not limited by constraints, legal or moral, and making use of whatever means available to them to fight their enemies. It may seem incongruous and paradoxical to associate "unrestricted"—which conveys an image of an entity having boundless resources—with an embryonic organization that arrived on the ground in Iraq *lacking* the resources seemingly required to wage "unrestricted warfare." This would be a one-dimensional understanding of "unrestricted warfare." To be sure, the more resources an entity has, the greater range of options available to it with which to wage war. However, in the context of Iraq, Zarqawi understood that fighting the Americans *directly* was not possible. Targeting Iraqi personnel, civilians, and society was not only possible but also eminently desirable and required. Zarqawi's ideas about the efficacy of "unrestricted warfare" derived from his uncompromising ideology and his recognition that Iraq's sociopolitical fragility and fissures could be exploited to stymie the United States' goals and thwart the growth of Shia power. The indiscriminate violence by means of "unrestricted warfare" had another important goal: to rouse the "slumbering" Sunni population whose support in this cosmic struggle the jihadists needed. By attacking the Shias indiscriminately, Zarqawi hoped to provoke them into attacking the Sunnis indiscriminately in return. The Sunnis would then turn to the jihadists for succor. In conclusion, war's cruelty had to be brought directly to the vulnerable civilian population with whatever means that were available in order to take advantage of Iraq's fragile political and social structure so as to ensure the failure of the United States' efforts to stabilize Iraq and implement its goals there.

In pursuit of his goals, Zarqawi waged a jihad that left a trail of death and destruction within Iraq. Even with their limited "strategic weapons" of the early years, the jihadists came close to bringing Iraq to its knees and also dealing the United States a costly failure. The strategic weapons of the insurgency included improvised explosive devices (IEDs), suicide bombings, and the recruitment, integration, and extensive use of foreign fighters.

The Effectiveness of Improvised Explosive Devices

During the first insurgency between 2003 and 2011, IEDs in all their forms constituted the biggest threat to the U.S.-led Coalition and to the

Iraqi civilians. In principle, any explosive weapons not originated from an industrial production line may be classified as IEDs.[7] They can be divided into several distinct categories: roadside or buried bombs, which are essentially improvised land mines; static vehicular car bombs that were known as vehicle-borne improvised explosive devices (VBIEDs), and explosive-laden vehicles driven by suicide drivers to their targets, which were known as suicide-vehicle-borne improvised explosive devices (SVBIEDs).

The roadside IED was the most common device in the first nine years of the war in Iraq, often referred to as the first insurgency (2003–2011). All the insurgent groups, including the jihadists, used IEDs. However, the IED was more often the primary weapon of the local Iraqi insurgent groups, both Islamist and non-Islamist. Its attraction was that it often allowed insurgents to attack their opponents remotely, avoiding exposing the them to the superior firepower and tactical skills of a modern force.[8] By mid-2004, insurgent roadside IEDs had begun to take a toll against the U.S.-led Coalition forces, especially American military personnel in Anbar province. On an average day in 2005, forty so-called IED events occurred in Iraq. A U.S. intelligence report in 2006 calculated the basis of current usage that there were "enough stocks of illegal explosives to continue the same level of attack for 274 years without re-supply."[9]

The United States was unable to find effective countermeasures quickly enough to outsmart the insurgents' ability to modify the specifics and tactics of their IEDs.[10] A technological fix as a solution proved to be elusive, so the United States began to focus on taking down the IED-manufacturing cells and their workshops. Though most IED cells "belonged" to the various insurgent groups, they were given considerable leeway to act independently and autonomously of the main insurgent force.[11] The IED cells were key elements of insurgent groups' firepower, but they neither mingled with nor were generally known by members of the main force, for purely security purposes. Other IED cells were independent entrepreneurs who advertised their deadly skills online and "rented" themselves out to insurgent groups who lacked the requisite resources or manpower to have their own IED cells.[12] The IED cells were also purposely kept small, not only for better security but also for ease of movement to avoid detection and takedown, and to enable them to provide their "services" across the country.

Improvised explosive devices were simple to make, easy to employ, and very effective. They were planted in everything—in trash on the side of the roads, in soda cans, in dead animal carcasses, in cars, on people. Their initiation devices used everything from remote car alarms to garage door openers to long-range cordless phones (no cell phones had been used up to this point), with remote car alarms being the most numerous. The roadside IED was primarily a forte of the local Iraqi insurgent groups, particularly those composed of former military and security personnel.

Unlike the jihadists, whose primary target was civilians and Iraqi Security Forces, the local Iraqi insurgents preferred to target the American military convoys and patrols. Given the insurgents' weaknesses in small unit engagements, the easiest and least costly method for them was the roadside bomb. Moreover, while the jihadists developed a small cadre of bomb-makers, their primary mission was to develop bombs for the various types of suicide bombing missions described below. The primary mission of the local Iraqi insurgent bomb-makers, usually explosive ordnance disposal specialists from the former Iraqi military, was the development and emplacement of roadside IEDs. The cost to U.S. troops was quite heavy. By early January 2007, roadside IEDs accounted for 45 percent of all U.S. fatalities from enemy action. Of the twenty-three thousand U.S. military personnel wounded by the same date, almost 50 percent were wounded by IEDs.[13]

The VBIED was the jihadist choice of IED weapon because their target set were primarily civilians in urban areas or the newly reconstructed Iraqi military and police, who had less force protection capabilities than the American forces. The VBIED carried more explosives than a roadside bomb, and initially, because "innocuous" passenger sedans were used, they did not raise suspicion when they were parked by a marketplace or building where young Iraqi men turned up for recruitment into the security forces and police. The vehicles were often acquired from the huge secondhand car markets in Baghdad and other Iraqi cities. They were transformed into weapons in "bomb-producing" workshops in Baghdad and Fallujah. As the jihadists' bomb-making skills grew and as they acquired more explosives, they graduated to the use of large-vehicle-borne improvised explosive devices (LVBIEDs), which included trucks, oil tankers, and dump trucks. These were devastating in their effects on the hapless civilians in Iraqi cities.

Suicide Bombing Tactics

Zarqawi's organization relied heavily on suicide bombings, beginning with individual suicide bombers whose logistical requirements were not too onerous. To put it briefly, the requirements were an individual willing to die in the commission of his attack, a suicide vest with explosives, a safe house, and a small cell of minders who prepared the individual for the mission. As Zarqawi's organization grew, it acquired more resources and personnel; this allowed it to develop the more deadly SVBIED.[14]

Eventually, the jihadists managed to manufacture and use the more deadly SVBIED, which a specially designated individual, willing to be vaporized in the process, drove to or *into* the target. The Zarqawi network targeted a wide variety of groups, including the Iraqi Security Forces, political and religious figures, civilians, foreign civilian contractors, and United Nations and humanitarian workers. Between 2003 and 2010, according to the prestigious British medical journal the *Lancet*, suicide bombings killed twelve thousand civilians but "only" two hundred soldiers in the U.S.-led Coalition, the vast majority of them (175) U.S. military personnel.

Zarqawi justified suicide bombing as the most effective operational method for the jihadists: "The brothers' most effective weapon, after relying on God and praying to Him for success, has been martyrdom operations. It is the brothers' unanswerable weapon for which the enemy can find no remedy. The enemies cannot prevent such operations. As we said, the enemies are present among the population and place their bases among the people's houses. They do so cunningly to place barriers between them and the mujahidin. Hence these martyrdom operations have played a big role in weakening the enemy and making it reach this level of despair, confusion, defeatist spirit, and psychological collapse."[15] Kurdish radical Mullah Krekar of Ansar al-Islam, an ally of Zarqawi, reportedly stated: "martyrdom operations...are effective because our losses are little and the opposition's losses are great."[16]

Zarqawi and his immediate successors were never able to produce SVBIEDs (or for that matter VBIEDs) on the industrial scale that ISIS and then IS were able to do much later on. However, it was the suicide bombing operations that ultimately allowed Zarqawi and his organization to frustrate the American effort to stabilize post-Baathist Iraq and to ignite the civil war between the Sunni and Shia communities in Iraq. His organization made its presence known as early as August 2003, when they began their "offensive" campaign. They first bombed the Jordanian embassy in Baghdad. The truck bombing of the United Nations headquarters in Baghdad, which killed twenty-three personnel, including the United Nations special representative for Iraq, followed on the heels of the embassy attack.

Zarqawi also initiated offensive attacks in August 2003 against the Shias, when he targeted the Imam Ali Mosque in Najaf, killing seventy-five worshipers and the leader of the Supreme Council for the Islamic Revolution of Iraq, Ayatollah Mohammad Baqr al-Hakim. Zarqawi's attacks ranged from single suicide bombers to large-scale complex attacks spanning multiple cities. He followed attacks with Internet-based media campaigns explaining the intent behind the attacks and encouraging jihadists to join AQI in the fight against the U.S.-led Coalition and the Shias. His organization claimed responsibility for or was credited with attacks against Shia mosques, markets, and cities, including Kadhimiya, Najaf, Samarra, Howaidar, Baquba, and Shia areas of Baghdad. Despite the wide target set, his suicide bombers' preferred target set was Iraqi civilians.[17] In February 2005, a suicide bombing in the largely Shia city of Hilla killed 125 people, mainly recruits for the security forces. In January 2006, a string of suicide bombings killed scores of people in the holy city of Karbala. The most notorious event, which helped ignite an unofficial civil war, was the bombing of the al-Askariya Mosque in Samarra in February 2006. The mosque is an important Shia shrine that houses the tombs of the tenth and eleventh imams of the Shia faith, Ali al-Askari and his son Hasan al-Askari. Outraged Shias went on the rampage against Sunnis, and ethnic cleansing began in earnest. A year and half later, in June 2007 the jihadists bombed the mosque yet again in order to preclude any attempts at reconciliation between Sunnis and Shias.

When the Sunni–Shia civil war was in full swing, the jihadists, by now known as ISI, sought to emerge as the leader in defending the Sunni community from the intercommunal violence that they themselves were responsible for igniting. When multiple Sunni insurgent groups united to plan, coordinate, and execute joint offensives against Shia targets in Baghdad, ISI sought to take the lead. In November 2006, the IAI, which by now had fallen out with ISI, attacked government and Shia targets in the capital.[18] In an effort to prevent Baghdad from becoming a Shia city, ISI sought to contribute to this campaign.[19] It is not clear, however, that there was much coordination between the two Sunni groups, as the differences had become too great. Nonetheless, in early January 2007, in an attempt to diminish the growing intra-Sunni frictions, ISI issued a statement about a "Baghdad defense plan." It proposed a joint Sunni insurgent and civilian defense against Shia assaults on Sunni neighborhoods. The plan suggested first a defense against the Shia onslaught and then going on the offensive. It proposed a division of labor, with locals of neighborhoods setting up self-defense units, while the insurgent units mounted offensives. The plan also recommended dividing the neighborhoods into sectors, with each responsible for its own immediate defense.[20]

The Sunnis were not buying it, and ISI, largely through its own ideological logic and military action, found itself in the unenviable situation of fighting the Americans, the Shia community, and a majority of the Sunni community. A concerted and coordinated Sunni effort against the Shias' quest for revenge was not going to succeed in light of the growing chasm between ISI and the vast majority of the other Sunni insurgent groups. As soon as the Sunni insurgents and tribes turned against ISI, it added significant elements of the Sunni community to its target set. In Anbar province, ISI increased attacks on Sunni civilians by 57 percent between February and August 2006, which strongly suggests that ISI was meeting with some form of resistance or reluctance on the part of the people to toe the ISI line. Prominent Sunni politicians, insurgent commanders, and tribal leaders were targeted for assassination; sometimes this even extended to threatening or killing their families.[21] This was a war ISI could not sustain.

The Foreign Fighters

Foreign fighters were both a boon and a bane for the insurgency. First, they constituted a source of badly needed manpower for Zarqawi's group when it was still largely a foreign entity that was competing, and only sometimes collaborating, with the local Iraqi insurgent groups. Second, though many of the foreign fighters were not militarily trained and often did not know one end of an AK-47 (Kalashnikov) from the other, they were useful for static defensive positions and as suicide bombers.

Most could not be used as messengers or as part of the logistics network because (except for the longtime resident Palestinians and Egyptians) they did not know their way around and their accents gave them away. At the higher reaches of Zarqawi's group, foreigners controlled the organization's intelligence and counterintelligence branches.[22] Though Zarqawi's distrust of the Iraqis dissipated at a later stage, when he allowed them to join his group, he did not relax so far as to include them in one of the most important branches of the organization: intelligence and counterintelligence. His view of the Iraqis was that they were indifferent to the struggle, collaborators, spies, and Baathists. This is, of course, in stark contrast to the situation later, when it was Iraqis who began to populate the ranks of the successor organizations ISI, ISIS, and then IS.

However, the foreign fighters could be a problem. Many Iraqis resented them because of their airs of superiority and the efforts of the fanatics among them to impose strict Islamic mores. As mentioned, they were outsiders, and Iraqis were more ready to inform on them than on their own insurgents, a tendency that was reinforced by the fact that they were readily identifiable as outsiders. What infuriated the Iraqis was the tendency of the foreigners to act as if the Iraqi resistance to the American presence was insignificant or even totally irrelevant to what the foreigners saw as the greater transnational battle being waged on behalf of Islam. It was this "proprietary" Iraqi attitude that prompted Zarqawi to admonish the Iraqis for believing that this was "their" war and not that of the whole of Islam against its enemies. The presence of foreign Arabs in the ranks of the top leadership of the jihadist movement under Zarqawi was a source of friction with Iraqis, both within the ranks of AQI and outside of it. The fact that they were Arabs also did not mean they understood the specific cultural tribal dynamics of Iraqi society. The Saudis were particularly disliked partly because they lacked the most basic military skills and partly because they seemed more concerned with global jihad against the "infidels" rather than the specific goal of "liberating" Iraq from the "occupiers."

The number of foreign fighters and the roles they played in the first Iraq insurgency during the time of Zarqawi were vastly dwarfed by their level of participation in jihadist activities from 2012 to the present (mid-2017) in both Iraq and Syria. Following Zarqawi's death and the increase in the pressure on AQI and then ISI, the jihadists exhorted more foreign fighters to come over to join the war. This time it wanted individuals who could man front line combat units. As ISI began to face heavy attrition of units and destruction of its cells by U.S. forces and Sunni opponents, it began to call upon foreign fighters to bring equipment and weaponry that they could use to augment ISI fighting units and even provided instructions on tactical preparation for the various combat environments they were going to encounter in Iraq. The jihadists also produced a "field manual" for foreign fighters heading to Iraq.

On April 19, 2007, a jihadist website posted a booklet entitled *Instructions to Jihadists before They Go to Iraq*, which provided advice and instructions on what fighters needed to know and what they needed to bring into Iraq. The article pointed out that operational art in urban and rural areas differed substantially, arguing that a fighter's military equipment was closely associated with the type of missions to be entrusted to him and with the nature of the field in which he would operate. The instruction manual stressed the notion that the guerrillas (mujahidin) were an army that needed to be constantly on the move with a lean logistical tail. In short, the guerrilla had to have all the equipment he needed to execute his mission "without depending on other individuals or units."[23] A guerrilla fighter could not be like a soldier in a regular army, who operated in conjunction with others in terms of equipment and combat. Often the individual mujahid or fighter had to be the commander, the navigator, the shooter, and the communications or reconnaissance man. This, of course, put a lot of stress on flexibility, fitness, and initiative, which most foreign fighters did not have coming into Iraq.

The booklet provided an extensive list of equipment, weapons, and supplies that a "mujahid" needed. The list is quite similar to that of a regular soldier, for example, an automatic weapon, a load-bearing belt to carry grenades and four magazines, a night-vision scope, a handgun (usually a Russian- or U.S.-made 9m) and two magazines for it; appropriate military attire, boots, a Kevlar helmet, and a knife. The "noncombat" requirements were also extensive and were in accord with the fact that the mujahid had to maintain a wide variety of logistics equipment and supplies ready at hand—in a secure area—such as navigation and communications equipment, compass, flashlight, pickaxe, saw, water bottles, collapsible cot, combat rations, first aid kit, and rope.

The booklet emphasized the importance of fieldcraft, combat skills, and physical fitness. The Saudi jihadist guerrilla Yusuf al-Ayiri, who is quoted in the manual and whose articles on guerrilla warfare circulated among insurgents in Iraq, wrote that field skills and fighting skills were the "crux of combat operations."[24] He defined field skills as the "ability to adapt to the field, move efficiently in it, and take up positions by using all forms of camouflage methods."[25] A "mujahid" must be able to develop field skills for different terrains. Fighting skills constituted proficiency in combat operations, and again each type of terrain required the development of its own particular method of combat; for example, combat skills for desert or mountain fighting were different from one another, just as they were different from those required for urban combat.

What this manual highlighted was the jihadists' growing need for combat personnel by 2007 and the fact that ISI did not want foreign fighters just to be suicide bombers. Severe losses and massive desertions by Iraqis coupled with the rising hostility toward the jihadists among Iraqi insurgents themselves meant that there was a need for combat personnel to maintain ISI's shrinking options.

Strategic Weaknesses and Vulnerabilities

Even though Zarqawi and his immediate successors used their "strategic weapons" extensively to cause mayhem in Iraq, their weaknesses and vulnerabilities cannot be overlooked.

Small-Unit Firefights: The Achilles Heel of the Insurgency, 2003–2011

Small-unit firefights are tactical engagements between small units (squads, teams, platoons, and even companies). They can result from ambushes, from one side attacking the enemy and the enemy defending, or from both small units blundering into each other. A high level of training of the individual soldier, the quantity and *quality* of firepower, the presence of initiative, and quick decision-making play critical roles in the small-unit firefight. One side wins the firefight through fire superiority, which is a situation where one side is able to lay down a volume of accurate and sustained fire on the other side, thus "suppressing" or "pinning" them down, rendering them unable to respond. This allows the side winning the firefight to move forward—to fire and maneuver—and to kill or capture the "suppressed" or "pinned" enemy unit or force it to flee.

While the Americans had the aforementioned qualities in abundance, neither the Iraqi military of the defunct Baathist regime nor the insurgents were good at small-unit firefights. First, both Iraqi basic training and advanced individual training was exceedingly poor. When the Iraqi army went to war with Iran in 1980, the proficiency of its small-unit skills left much to be desired, though they improved over the course of that war.[26]

Second, the Iraqis lacked an effective noncommissioned officer corps, which constitutes the backbone of an army and the core personnel for building cohesion within small units, leading them, and exercising command, control, and coordination during small-unit engagements. Initiative and flexibility on the battlefield were not encouraged among the junior ranks within the Iraqi army.[27] This is not unique to them among Middle Eastern armies but seems to affect Soviet-trained Arab armies more than Western-trained ones.

Third, poor weapon serviceability and maintenance contributed enormously to the execrable small-unit performance of the Iraqi insurgents (and the U.S.-trained Iraqi Security Forces). Locally made weapons such as the NADER (Iraqi RPG-7) averaged a very high rate of failure due to poor serviceability, lack of maintenance, and the insurgents' poor marksmanship, which resulted in a poor shoot-to-hit and hit-to-kill ratio.

Similarly, the small-unit tactical proficiency of most of the insurgent fighters in the years 2003–2011 was for the most part nonexistent. Many of the insurgents were former Iraqi military and exhibited a distinct lack of flexibility and skill in small-unit firefights. Others, including foreign fighters, had little or no basic military skills. The limited number of secure territorial sanctuaries prevented all the insurgent groups from setting up training bases to teach fighters the requisite skills. Training was believed, correctly, to be of paramount importance in the raising of combat skills. A wide range of jihadist strategic thinkers and practitioners emphasized this point, while others sought ways to overcome the structural inability to create and maintain permanent training facilities.[28] The insurgents were notorious for underutilization of weapon systems capabilities in combat. In the early days of the insurgency, the average insurgent or jihadist fighter was not effective past fifty meters with his weapon because he did not aim his weapon and expended a large volume of fully automatic fire against U.S. forces. This was ineffective and was known among U.S. troops as "spray and pray," a problem that also afflicted the U.S.-trained Iraqi military forces.

The disparity in training and firepower between the insurgents and the U.S. forces ensured that small-unit encounters were not worth it for the insurgents. Attacks against defensive outposts manned by U.S. soldiers and marines were suicidal. Instead, the insurgents launched attacks with indirect fires (mortars), which were a popular tactic due to the insurgents' determination to strike U.S.-led Coalition bases. Among the myriad insurgent groups, the jihadists between 2003 and 2011 were usually inept with indirect fires, as they displayed a marked lack of the technical knowledge required for the use of mortars. Usually there was little or no adjustment of the rounds, and they were unable to hit anything accurately. They often used mortars in baited ambushes, that is, placing IEDs in a location where they could easily be found. Once U.S. troops arrived on site and attempted to disarm the IED, the insurgents would fire some mortar rounds targeting them.[29]

For any combat organization, whether it is a conventional or insurgent group, the development of small-unit tactical skills requires training bases. For the Iraqi insurgents, including the jihadists, the setting up of secure and safe training bases could not be guaranteed.

Inability to Consolidate Control of Territorial Sanctuaries and Bases

Zarqawi and his organization focused much of their efforts on the ground looking for secure and safe sanctuaries and bases. This, as he himself recognized, was not an easy task. After his death, his successors, Abu Omar al-Baghdadi and his deputy, Abu Hamza al-Muhajir, redoubled their efforts when they transformed the organization from AQI to ISI.

Initially the insurgents sought to establish safe bases within cities like Fallujah but were unable to do so in the face of their poor skills in urban warfare and U.S. firepower, which succeeded in dislodging them from cities (see below). Though some insurgents filtered back into Fallujah even as early as December 2004, the effective loss of Fallujah and manpower forced Zarqawi to transfer his activities to Diyala, northeast of Baghdad, a province with many remote areas and rugged terrain that enabled the Zarqawi organization to build sanctuaries and train its forces, especially small units able to conduct firefights. Later, after Zarqawi's death, Diyala province became a main arena of war between ISI and its various foes. It originally established itself in this demographically diverse province as part of the struggle for Baghdad and the wider sectarian war. As tribal and Iraqi insurgent opponents deprived ISI of its traditional stronghold in Anbar province, Diyala became the new center of its operations. Diyala's geography made it useful for militarily engaging the Kurds and Shias, threatening Baghdad to the south, and claiming to be confronting the perfidious Iranian enemy, as Diyala borders Iran. Increased interest in Diyala became evident in late 2006, as the wave of retaliatory sectarian violence between Baghdad's Sunni and Shia neighborhoods spilled over into Diyala, which had a similar demographic mix. It was also in Diyala that the organization began to lay the foundations for its "state." Its operatives took over the Sunni mosques in this ethnically mixed and very poor rural region so as to impose their strict Islamist decrees. Many imams fled rather than comply, as did most of the Shia people in mixed communities.[30]

In early 2007, Diyala assumed more significance as part of the ISI's strategy to thwart Baghdad's security plan to stop insurgent attacks and the bloodletting between the sects, named "Fardh al-Qanoon" (Enforcing the Law). The "Plan of Nobility," ISI's own security plan, involved falling back on the provinces ISI claimed as its territories. In addition, Diyala's Shia population made the province attractive as a target-rich area where the militants could seek revenge against the Shia community for what Shia militias had done to the Sunnis in Baghdad. Diyala's rural character and hilly topography made it useful as an insurgent base. Reportedly, ISI developed a strong presence along key routes through Diyala to Baghdad, such as the area of al-Hadid, which earned the name "Diyala's Triangle of Death." Insurgents there made IEDs, car bombs, and suicide vests for use both in the province and in Baghdad. Along the key roads, they set up checkpoints, planted IEDs, conducted ambushes and abductions, collected tolls, and looted commercial traffic. Diyala became increasingly important to ISI, evolving from a secondary theater in the battle for Baghdad into a centrally located base from which ISI could confront multiple foes.[31] However, even in Diyala it became increasingly difficult by the end of 2007 for ISI to maintain a secure sanctuary or safe training areas.

The most important political reason for the decline of ISI was the organization's falling out with the Sunni community and the Sunni fighters. This, of course, had military implications for ISI as well, as did the vast improvement in U.S. counterinsurgency operations. However, the reduction of ISI territories that it could use as safe havens or sanctuaries cannot be underestimated in contributing to its diminishing power. All together, these politico-military factors brought about the military decline of ISI.

Urban Warfare: "Above Their Comprehension"

Urban warfare, or "military operations in urban terrain," is universally abhorred by conventional militaries. It is costly in terms of manpower and materiel, it requires specialized skills and tactics, and it is often fought in the middle of a civilian population. Furthermore, the enemy is sometimes indistinguishable from the civilians if they are not wearing uniforms. Those defending urban terrain against an attacker have some advantages. If it is home territory, they know the layout of the city, and this enhances their ability to maneuver in the urban terrain relative to their attacker. If they have been afforded time before an assault, it is assumed they will have prepared formidable defenses that will exhaust and attrite the attacking force. It is not uniformly the case in urban warfare, though, that the defender, whether a regular or insurgent force, is adept at defensive urban war. To be sure, the nature of the urban environment breaks up the attacking force into smaller units, which makes them vulnerable to the defender. However, the defender is not a priori endowed with urban tactical skills and knowledge of defensive configurations for urban warfare. The defender has to learn these tactical skills and build these defensive configurations.

If the defender does neither, the urban battlefield is not the level playing field it should be for him.

During the first insurgency, the insurgents—jihadists and nonjihadists alike—proved to be quite inept at or unprepared for urban warfare, largely but not solely due to their low skills in small-unit tactics. To be sure, the urban environment does equalize the battleground for less trained units, but even here such units will need to develop proficient small-unit tactics and capabilities if they are to prevail against or fight off more professional forces such as the U.S. Army and U.S. Marine Corps.

Zarqawi's organization was also involved in the myriad urban battles that took place in Iraq during the first insurgency (2003–2010). However, in this arena the jihadists had to compete with other Iraqi insurgent groups who were usually fighting in or near the same turf. The conduct of urban warfare by both insurgent and counterinsurgent requires skill, patience, training, stamina, and resources. During the first Iraqi insurgency, the insurgents simply did not have a surplus of these factors in their confrontation with U.S. Army and Marine units. The two Fallujah battles of April 2004 and November 2004 highlighted the Iraqi insurgents' profound weaknesses in urban battle at that time. The number of insurgent factions operating in Fallujah in early 2004 was a microcosm of the factions operating throughout much of the country. The Fallujah insurgents did not have a clear chain of command. U.S. Marine intelligence estimated that there were seventeen rival groups with twelve key leaders.

The first battle of Fallujah, "Operation Vigilant Resolve," was fought between April 5 and 30 in 2004. Despite the fractious nature of the insurgency, the United States concluded that it did not have sufficient forces at the time to clear the city. The U.S. decision to halt a forcible assault into the city in the wake of the murder of four American civilian contractors led the insurgents to view the situation as a victory. The offensive ended with a bizarre agreement to cede security to former Iraqi military personnel: the al-Fallujah Brigade. The setting up of the al-Fallujah Brigade should have meant an end to the insurgents' dream of controlling the city, as the agreement stipulated that they hand over their heavy weapons to the brigade. However, the al-Fallujah Brigade was disunited and was composed of mutually feuding factions. This allowed the insurgents to reassert control over Fallujah again.

Zarqawi's group began an extensive campaign of kidnapping and assassinations against the local police force and attacked members of the al-Fallujah Brigade.[32] Between April and November 2004, dozens of "new" groups sprang up in Fallujah who engaged in a wave of kidnappings, sabotage, and assassinations. Some of these groups were linked to Zarqawi but fought independently of his organization. Zarqawi's relations with these local groups within Fallujah were often marked by tension over turf and resources and Iraqi resentment of foreigners' presence within the ranks of the insurgency.

The second battle of Fallujah at the end of 2004 was better planned and implemented by U.S. forces. The insurgents had also learned some lessons from the first battle, but they were still outclassed by better-trained and better-equipped U.S. soldiers and marines. While they proved to have learned how to be ingenious in constructing defensive positions in buildings and in constructing booby-traps, the insurgents built them in the wrong place. They expected the Americans to attack from the southern edges of the city as they had done in the first battle in April 2004. Instead the American assault came in from the north, while units at the southern edges of the city conducted probing attacks from the south to focus the attention of the insurgent units on that particular sector and make them think that the main effort was coming from the south.[33] Urban battles are sharp small-unit engagements at short range, led by noncommissioned officers and junior officers, such as lieutenants and captains. The better-trained and more skillful belligerent who is able to deliver more firepower has the advantage. The insurgents in Fallujah could not bring to bear the same intensity of firepower as the Americans did and invariably lost the firefights. They proved unable to move as coherent small units to fight U.S. soldiers and marines; rather, they careened en masse down streets, firing wildly in all directions, instead of using fire and maneuver and cover and concealment as effectively as their opponents.

The insurgent losses against the U.S. forces in Fallujah were substantial; the United States estimated that twelve hundred had been killed.[34] In June 2006, insurgents were launching nearly thirty attacks a day in Ramadi alone. By June 2007, that had come down to fewer than one a day. The flow of foreign fighters was reduced significantly.[35] This meant there were fewer individuals to fill the ranks of the jihadists and to conduct suicide bombings. By mid-2007, the situation in Anbar province was showing improvement because many insurgent groups and the tribes had turned against the extremists. As for Anbar province itself, the rate shrank from roughly five hundred attacks a week to barely a third of that. Discoveries of weapons caches, based largely on tips from civilians, had skyrocketed nearly 190 percent.[36]

The Military Decline of the Islamic State
of Iraq, 2008–2011

The ability of ISI to move freely came under severe pressure as Iraqi civilians and certain insurgent elements began to provide useful information to U.S. forces, who used it effectively and quickly to take down ISI leaders and cells. In early November 2007, U.S. forces raided an insurgent hideout in Balad and found a diary of an ISI "emir" (commander) named "Abu Tariq." Apparently mostly written in October 2007, the diary catalogues the decline of ISI in that sector. "Abu Tariq" once commanded six hundred fighters, a substantially sized ISI brigade, as most were smaller. By October 2007 he was down to twenty men. He blamed the Sunni turnaround against ISI for ISI's demise: "We were mistreated, cheated and betrayed by some of our brothers. We must not have mercy on those traitors until they come back to the right side or get eliminated completely in order to achieve victory at the end."[37] "Abu Tariq's" diary, which was redacted by the U.S. military to remove names, is worth quoting in part to highlight the catastrophic decline in ISI combat capabilities: "there were almost 600 fighters in our sector [al-Mashahdah sector near Balad] before the Tribes changed course 360 degrees under the influence of the so-called Islamic Army [IAI; "Abu Tariq" called this formidable opponent "Deserter of Jihad"] and other known believer groups. Many of our fighters quit and some of them joined the deserters."[38] The tribes in his sector proved to be untrustworthy and two-faced, according to "Abu Tariq." Speaking of one particular clan, "Abu Tariq" claims that they feigned friendship but "later on we found that those people were nothing but hypocrites, liars and traitors and were waiting for the right moment to switch sides with whoever pays them the most and at the end they fought against us and they tried to prevent us from attacking the al-Sahwah [Awakening] groups."[39] Another ISI emir highlighted the predicament of the organization in a letter found in a safe house in Samarra in November 2007: "We find ourselves in a circle not being able to move, organize or conduct operations. There was a total collapse in the security structure of the organization."[40] American operations and the turn against the jihadists by the Iraqi Sunni insurgents and the civilian population eventually constricted ISI's ability to find safe sanctuaries and to plan and execute operations.

By early 2008, U.S.-led Coalition and local security forces had killed two thousand ISI personnel and taken almost nine thousand prisoners.

That the pressure on ISI was severe and relentless was quite obvious by 2008, as indicated by intelligence reports and the seizure of internal memos by ISI leaders concerning the dire situation in which their "state" had succumbed. In January 2008, an internal communiqué surfaced into the open or was seized by U.S. or Iraqi Security Forces. Signed by Abu Hamza al-Muhajir, it read, in part: "Dedicate yourself to fighting the true enemy only, in order to avoid opening up new fronts against the Sunni Arabs. Do not close the door of repentance in the face of those Sunnis who turned against us."[41] Riyadh al-Ogeidi, a senior ISI emir, was even more directly revealing of ISI's collapse in Iraq: "We do not deny the difficulties we are facing right now. The Americans have not defeated us, but the turnaround of the Sunnis against us had made us lose a lot and suffer very painfully. We made many mistakes over the past year."[42] By 2009, the United States was funding one hundred thousand Sunnis to fight ISI. This was too vast a force for ISI to fight off, and its counterintelligence service, such as it was, proved incapable of ferreting out double agents and preventing information from leaking to their Sunni foes. The Sunnis then passed it on to the Americans, who were relentless in mounting operations that were peeling ISI apart layer by layer. By mid-2010, ISI had more or less disintegrated, and thirty-four of its forty-two senior leaders had been killed or captured.[43] In mid-2011, Leon Panetta, then U.S. secretary of defense, testified before the U.S. Congress that only one thousand ISI fighters remained active in the fight. By December 2011, when the United States withdrew from Iraq, the number had allegedly declined to seven hundred.[44]

The decline in ISI's military fortunes forced it back down to the lower end of the spectrum of violence. As the pressure grew, ISI devoted considerable efforts to maintaining or even increasing the tempo of its suicide bombings against Iraqi civilians and security forces in 2010–2011.[45] Even under pressure, ISI was somehow able to maintain the production of VBIEDs and SVBIEDs at a level that allowed them to keep up a deadly intensity in operations, including the launching of multiple attacks almost simultaneously. For example, on April 6, 2009, ISI launched *six* nearly simultaneous VBIED attacks on Shia civilians in Baghdad, killing forty people.[46]

The Military Rebirth of the Islamic State of Iraq, 2012–2015

The December 2011 U.S. withdrawal signaled the end of ISI's decline. The Iraqi Security Forces simply did not have the training, flexibility, and energy to plan and execute fast-paced operations against the jihadists of the kind the Americans were capable of conducting. Throughout 2012, with ISI facing less pressure, the number of attacks by its personnel rose significantly. By late 2011 and early 2012, ISI was rebounding from defeat.

The "Breaking the Walls" and "Soldiers' Harvest" Campaigns: Building Capacity and Gaining Experience

In July 2012, ISI began the first of two intensive insurgency campaigns that paved the way for its operations of 2014.[47] The first, "Breaking the Walls," involved a growing wave of high-explosive truck bombings designed to provoke Shia retaliation against the Sunni community and to hit soft targets such as markets. It lasted for a year and involved several phases. The second, "Soldiers' Harvest," which began in July 2013, was a more targeted campaign of assassinations and bombings against the security forces. These campaigns were well resourced, prepared, and executed and showed a high level of flexibility on the part of the ISI fighters. This indicated that ISI's military organization had moved from being a largely terrorist outfit, which used suicide bombers, assassinations, and car bombs, to one that could fight effectively along a spectrum ranging from terrorism to more complex operations involving the command and coordination of different types of units and weapons.[48]

It was in April 2013 that ISI changed its name to ISIS because of its decision to become involved in the increasingly bloody civil war in Syria against the regime of Bashar al-Assad. Its presence in Syria allowed ISIS to develop into a more functionally specialized military organization able to wage war at the higher end of the violence spectrum—for example, guerrilla warfare and semiconventional mobile warfare. It put this combat structure to good use in mid-2014 but still dedicated considerable efforts and resources to its terrorist capability. Thus, even when the group was reconfigured as ISIS, there was no lessening of the terrorist assaults on civilians, largely Shia, back in Iraq. The terrorist capability had been revitalized because ISI was no longer under the relentless 24/7 "gaze" of U.S. intelligence and special operation forces that had previously managed to unhinge the organization's terrorist operations. Second, ISI had begun to transform its suicide bombing enterprise from a small-scale effort producing suicide belts and vests for individuals, fitting passenger cars with explosives for the deadly VBIEDs, in small workshops, to more industrial-scale production that would eventually also be able to rig large trucks and captured military vehicles with explosives. Third, ISI sensed the growing disenchantment among the Sunni community with the Shia government of Nuri al-Maliki. The killing of Shia civilians by ISI was designed to provoke reprisals by the government and Shia militias so that the Sunni community might run to ISI for protection. In the final analysis, both opportunity and increased capabilities were responsible for ISI's terror wing ratcheting up suicide and car bombings against civilians.

Between 2011 and early 2014, ISI and then successor ISIS's suicide bombing infrastructure, wreaked physical and psychological havoc on the Shia population. The organization's terrorist wing worked overtime to kill Shia civilians at bus terminals, markets, and during rush hour traffic in urban areas where they could strike at Shias. For example, in late May 2013, on one day ISIS detonated eight car bombs parked in public areas, in Baghdad, Basra, and Babil, killing close to one hundred civilians.[49] The Iraqi Security Forces were not spared either; for example, on July 22, 2013, an SVBIED struck an army convoy in the small town of Kokchali in Nineveh province, killing twenty-two soldiers.[50] On August 28, 2013, in Baghdad alone, ISIS detonated fourteen car bombs, two IEDs, and one individual suicide bomber, killing thirty people and wounding close to two hundred.[51] In September 2013, in a daring assault on Abu Ghraib Prison near Baghdad, ISIS fighters sprung five hundred prisoners, including, it was alleged, twenty important former ISIS commanders. In January 2014, ISIS attacked a government institution in Baghdad, an adjunct of the Ministry of Transport. A VBIED was detonated in front of the building, and in the ensuing mayhem six suicide bombers rushed into the building itself.[52] These attacks were not just terror attacks for the sake of terror. They were a part of a rational strategy (1) to provoke the Shia community and Iraqi army to launch revenge attacks on the Sunnis, who would then presumably turn to ISIS for protection, and (2) to force the Iraqi forces to spread themselves thinly throughout the country and thus be unable to respond effectively to ISIS's coming offensives.

The "Blitzkrieg" Advance of ISIS in Iraq and the Seizure of Mosul, January–June 2014

The growth in the military power of ISIS, including the emergence of large numbers of VBIED and SVBIED units, the creation of small units for direct assault, and the development of robust logistics capabilities, enabled it to develop a capability to engage in assaults on defended military bases and even against garrisoned cities. The military capabilities of ISIS in Iraq were evident in the spring of 2014 even before its "blitzkrieg"— lightning advance—to seize Mosul. The ability to conduct multiple simultaneous attacks—a skill developed in Syria—was evident in late April 2014 when ISIS launched coordinated predawn attacks near the town of Qara Tepe, a Turkmen town northwest of Kirkuk. The organization blew up two bridges, detonated an explosive-carrying fuel tanker at a police base, and killed twelve soldiers in another attack. Its fighters then proceeded to attack four other Iraqi security outposts the same day.[53] The Iraqi military took out its frustrations on the locals, judging by the comments of a local farmer: "the security forces are weak, and they are putting the responsibility for their weakness on us. They are not professional."[54] The commander of the Iraqi Twelfth Division, then based in Kirkuk, General Mohammed Khalaf Said al-Dulaimi, exaggerating somewhat, exposed major weaknesses in his force, stating: "We're facing a good, well-trained enemy. The attacks in this area [in Qara Tepe and Anbar province] were huge. The security forces were surprised that the militants were better equipped than the security services. Our soldiers didn't have anything more than AK-47s."[55] The reason the jihadists were better equipped was because corruption and poor logistics capabilities ensured that the Iraqi soldiers did not receive the weapons, ammunition, and materiel allotted to their respective units.

The ISIS units were helped by a variety of local Sunni insurgent units in their assault in the north. The Sunni units were not as well equipped as the ISIS units. They ranged from small groups to groups, similar to localized units, that had turned against the Americans and then against the Shia-dominated Iraqi Security Forces, and to groups like Jaysh Rijal al-Tariqa al-Naqshabandiya, which included former officers of the Iraqi army and were more cohesive and were put together by the Baathist senior official Ibrahim Izzat al-Duri. In an effort to promote closer integration of the myriad insurgent groups, including armed tribesmen disgruntled with the Maliki government, an umbrella group referred to as the General Military Council of Iraqi Revolutionaries emerged in December 2013. Its violent activities in Anbar province, while not necessarily coordinated with ISIS, ensured that government forces would become overstretched, thus allowing ISIS to filter back into a province from which it had been ejected. The support provided to ISIS was more of an alliance of convenience for many of the groups, while others collaborated more closely. The Sunni insurgent groups provided ISIS with information, logistical support, and flank protection as the jihadists advanced to breach the defenses of Mosul in June 2014.

In order to conduct reconnaissance and to disrupt the movement of Iraqi forces, ISIS infiltrated forces into key areas of the city. By then ISIS had developed a relatively effective combat support infrastructure, which included mortar and rocket units that conducted attacks on command and control headquarters. Outside the limits of Mosul, ISIS assault forces seized the Qayyara airbase and the Sharqat airport, limiting air support against their assault on Mosul. When assault forces entered the Mosul, they occupied key infrastructure, specifically Mosul General Hospital, the Nineveh provincial government building, the Mosul airport, the Regional Army Headquarters, police stations, and private banks. Exploitation forces then entered the city and defeated remaining isolated enemy units. Iraqi forces did not immediately capitulate, initially conducting clearing operations supported by air assets. Multiple forces coming in from different directions hit defending Iraqi forces simultaneously.

To disrupt the movements of Iraqi forces and force them into kill zones, ISIS placed obstacles and numerous IEDs. The ISIS units displayed effective battlefield tactical skills. Its forces displayed a high degree of mobility and flexibility on the battlefield, in contrast to the Iraqi forces, who were slow in their movements and unable to react quickly to the fast-paced and dynamic nature of the fighting. The ISIS disruption and defense forces utilized camouflage, cover, concealment, and deception to improve survivability. So that there would be no dead ground for Iraqi forces to take cover in, ISIS's battle positions provided overlapping fields of fire. The ISIS fighters placed crew-served weapons effectively in order to provide concentrated fires into a kill zone or zones. Reserve units were concealed or camouflaged in battle positions slightly to the rear and thus were readily available to senior ISIS leaders' use in reinforcing battle positions, responding to Iraqi attacks, and/or reacting to other offensive actions.

It took five days for ISIS to take control of Mosul.[56] The assault began with a series of suicide bombings in the Mushayrafa area, west of Mosul, which enabled the ISIS units to breach the security barriers erected by the Iraqi Security Forces. After the breach, the security forces withdrew to their headquarters, and the jihadists were able to rapidly seize many neighborhoods. The Iraqi Security Forces used helicopters to strafe and bomb residential areas where they suspected ISIS fighters had broken through. However, this tactic killed dozens of civilians, which did not win the Maliki government in Baghdad much favor with the Sunni population of the north. The Nineveh Operations Command had different brigades operating almost independently of one another in the city of Mosul. Command, control, and communications between Iraqi forces broke down almost completely. The behavior of the security forces toward the civilians of Mosul and the increasingly apparent lack of combat-worthiness of those units forced the Sunni Arab governor of Nineveh province to call upon Mosul's inhabitants to take up arms to defend their city.

New and Improved: The Jihadist Way of War, 2012–2015

The development of a more proficient jihadist way of warfare under Abu Bakr al-Baghdadi following his elevation to leadership and then caliph was due to a number of changes that unfolded over the course of 2012 and beyond.

First, one of the most important factors was the creation of a more professional and institutionalized ISI military council in 2012, whose main mission was to turn around ISI's declining military fortunes. In the early days of the jihadist way of warfare, Zarqawi was both the emir and the head of the military council, though at one point he did appoint a subordinate to the post. Nonetheless, Zarqawi was very much hands-on when it came to the "military operations" of his organization. When he was killed, the organization decided to separate the top leadership role from that of military commander, or "minister of war," whose sole purpose was to develop the organization's military capabilities.

The first minister of war was Abu Hamza al-Muhajir; he occupied the role until his death in 2010. He was not particularly effective as minister of war or supreme military commander. Though he was not fully responsible for ISI's declining military fortunes, he either chose not to communicate with or lost command and control over lower echelon provincial commanders. The effectiveness and success of some commanders, like Mohammad Momou (aka Abu Qaswara), the ISI military commander in the north with operational responsibilities for Nineveh, was not due to Abu Hamza al-Muhajir's flair for supreme command. Rather, Momou proved to be an effective commander possibly partly due to his own aptitude but most likely due to having some of the best-trained military personnel in the north available to him and the availability of funding. Momou's stint as an effective commander was short-lived, however, as U.S. forces killed him in 2008. When Abu Hamza al-Muhajir was killed in 2010, Numan Mansour al-Zeidi (aka Abu Suleiman-Nasser al-Din) replaced him as war minister or supreme military commander. Abu Suleiman was more energetic and more brutal, but his tenure was also short-lived, as he was killed in May 2011.

"Haji Bakr" (aka Samir Abed Mohammed al-Khlefawi) then became military commander. It is generally acknowledged that he was the man most responsible for revamping ISI as a military organization and not just as a vast revitalized organization, as detailed in chapter 4. It was during his tenure that ISI managed to spring veteran personnel out of the infamous Abu Ghraib Prison on the outskirts of Baghdad. Estimates of the number of veterans released, including former Baathist and ISI commanders, vary but range as high as five hundred.[57] "Haji Bakr" was responsible for setting in motion the development of the functionally specialized units (branches with specific or specialized skills, discussed below), which his successors continued. After "Haji Bakr" was killed in Syria in January 2014, he was succeeded by Abu Abdul Rahman al-Bilawi (aka Adnan Ismail al-Bilawi), who was killed in June 2014. He was followed as leader of the military council by Abu Muslim al-Turkmani (aka Fadl al-Hayyali from Tel Afar), who was killed at the beginning of 2015.

The leadership of the military council then devolved upon Omar al-Shishani (aka Tarkan Batirashvili), of Kist ethnic background, from Chechnya. He was allegedly the military mastermind behind ISIS's operations in Syria (at Deir ez-Zor and the Menagh airbase) and assault on Mosul. Unlike the vast majority of the foreign fighters, who had not experienced military service, he had served in the Georgian army and fought the Russian invaders of Georgia in 2008. He was discharged due to illness and later made his way to Syria when the violence erupted there. He was either wounded or killed in a U.S. air strike on March 4, 2016.[58] The rapid turnover or "decapitation" of the top leaders or ministers of war did not prevent ISIS from creating a relatively formidable military capability.[59] The senior military command in the council allowed the delegation of military authority and military capabilities to subordinates such as the regional commanders. The regional commanders controlled military sectors throughout the Caliphate, with each sector consisting of three battalions of 300–350 fighters. Each battalion was made up of several companies containing one hundred or so fighters. When the terms "battalion" and "company" are mentioned in the context of IS, they should not be confused with battalions associated with regular armies, which ordinarily contain anywhere between three and six hundred personnel. The IS's battalions were lighter, smaller, and more mobile than those of regular militaries. The "decapitation" of the operational field commanders in each defense sector had a greater impact on the offensive and defensive capabilities of IS.

Second, IS recognized that warfare encompassed not just "kinetic" military action against opposing military forces but also revolutionary political war activities on the ground.[60] (I have discussed in chapter 4 the origins of this program as it was implemented by "Haji Bakr.") Revolutionary political warfare action requires profound knowledge of the sociopolitical and economic environment on the ground. Operationally, such action consisted of a broad integrated campaign of shaping the environment with actions such as assassinating key enemy figures; bribing or encouraging other key figures and competing Sunni movements to join the jihadists conducting an information operations campaign to "enlighten" the Sunni community about their plight under the Shia-dominated government in Baghdad; and extorting resources from commercial enterprises and businesses. As the Sunni protests against Nuri al-Maliki's government took root, ISIS sought to shape the political environment by openly calling upon the community to take up arms under its helm. It also tried to lure in former Iraqi insurgents and tribal members of the Awakening Councils by offering cash incentives to take up arms again. Many accepted the offer, and indeed, ISIS could not have marched on Mosul in 2014, as mentioned above, without the support of Sunni insurgent movements in Nineveh. A clear example of ISIS's seductive power in shaping the environment in its favor prior to and during the battles of 2014 is the fact that among the Sunni groups involved was the IAI, which had been one of the most vehement opponents of ISI when it was headed by Abu Omar al-Baghdadi prior to 2010. In June 2014, IAI leader Sheikh Ahmed al-Dabash acknowledged that the IAI was fighting alongside ISIS and would march with them to Baghdad.[61]

By way of contrast, the founding father, Zarqawi, was never able to set up an effective revolutionary political warfare capability. When Zarqawi began his war in Iraq in 2003, initially he had little knowledge or situational awareness of the sociopolitical, economic, and cultural environment on the ground. However, judging by the lengthy letter he wrote to Osama bin Laden discussed in chapter 3, he learned quickly what constituted the vulnerable sociopolitical fissures. However, his organization simply did not have the capability, resources, or mindset to shape the environment in his favor. The preferred method was the "kinetic" assault on enemies in the hope that it would have an effect in rousing supporters.[62]

Third, IS military structure became functionally specialized, with different types of units and branches that trained to fight together and actually got experience fighting together. As ISI rebuilt itself, it created branches with different specializations.[63] First, it developed a dedicated combat branch composed of men who could conduct small-unit firefights. However, the skill levels varied widely, from those who were or became well-versed in such semiconventional operations to "combat" outfits that were used largely for guard duties, patrolling, and garrison duties. Among the best units in the combat branch were the Chechens and the *inghimasi* suicide commandos, or suicide assault teams, which included local Syrians and Iraqis as well as foreign nationals. The *inghimasi,* literally the "penetrators" or the "plungers into," must not be confused with suicide bombers who blow themselves up via a suicide vest/belt or vehicle. The *inghimasi* are special assault or storm troops who carry out difficult missions, such as the storming and breaching of fortified enemy positions. The *Inghimasiyun* wear explosive belts that they trigger if they are surrounded or about to fall prisoner. However, their missions, unlike those of true suicide bombers, do not require their ultimate sacrifice. Indeed, despite their high mortality rate, they can live to fight another day, which is why calling them assault or storm troopers is more appropriate than thinking of them as battlefield suicide bombers.[64]

The Islamic State has adopted and applied the effective use of sappers in its offensive operations, going so far as to dig trenches to move them closer to enemy positions and attack points. This use of trenches in the attack is a classic sapper maneuver. The lesson here is that IS tacticians and troops are able to counter high-tech threats, such as air power and other technology, by taking a more difficult but effective low-tech route, even if it requires additional time and energy. Their employment of sappers to approach the enemy's position, prepare attack lanes, pinpoint key defenses, and prepare the way for follow-on assault forces also demonstrates their ground commanders' tactical patience and maturity. The Islamic State has learned to coordinate artillery and mortar fires with assault "troops," which they have done on a number of occasions, especially against Syrian military bases.

The military units of IS also built armored hunter teams that fighters deployed against the Syrian and Iraqi tanks that supported the troops opposing IS. These teams were only armed with RPGs but were trained to a high standard to overcome the fear of the tank that ordinarily afflicts infantry. Dismounted troops were often available to provide some distraction and covering fire for RPG teams as they maneuvered to engage Syrian or Iraqi tanks. The use of special teams (sappers, assault or storm troops, antitank teams) is a characteristic of an organized, professional military force: an army in which every element understands the bigger picture and its part in accomplishing the mission.[65] The outbreak of the Syrian civil war allowed ISIS to further develop its military capabilities, particularly those associated with urban combat and the assault of fixed enemy military positions.[66] To be sure, ISIS's small-unit assaults were not uniformly successful either in Syria or in Iraq, and they made many tactical errors. However, their assaults showed greater flexibility, operational initiative, and ability to adapt to changing and fluid circumstances than their opponents' troops had.

Fourth, IS created its Committee for Military Manufacturing and Development, an entity with several missions assigned to it. The committee built an infrastructure for the effective categorization of the arms and ammunition in the IS inventory and for the efficient distribution of them to the various units throughout the Caliphate. The seizure by ISIS of a wide range of high-grade military equipment from the Iraqi and Syrian armies in 2014 allowed it to build a quasi-conventional mobile force that even included an armored battalion and artillery units. A force that had once been lightly armed, IS came to be far more comprehensively equipped, thanks to its raids on the depots of the Iraqi army's Second Mechanized Division in June 2014, of the Syrian army's 121st Artillery Regiment on July 24, and of the Syrian army's Ninety-Third Brigade at Ain Issa near Raqqa, IS's "capital," on August 7, 2014.[67]

The committee was also actively involved in modifying weapons systems or vehicles and even in constructing hybrid and peculiar weapons systems that have been the source of enormous commentary in the media and on specialized blogs. The most important output of IS's arms infrastructure and production capability was its industrial-scale production of VBIEDs and SVBIEDs. Neither Zarqawi nor the ISI under Abu Omar al-Baghdadi were ever able to produce these deadly implements on such a large scale. Moreover, the SVBIEDs were no longer tactically used just against vulnerable civilians in soft targets like public buildings and marketplaces but also now against troops in IS offensives and defensive operations. This required them to up-armor the SVBIEDs by welding steel plates on their fronts and sides to ensure survivability until the suicide driver reached his designated target. To produce VBIEDs and SVBIEDs on an industrial scale and then to be able to modify them required obtaining a large amount of materiel and setting up workshops. The Islamic State did not lack vehicles or explosives, and after 2014 its capture of huge quantities of military vehicles allowed it to transform armored personnel vehicles and even armored bulldozers into monstrous explosive machines. Its consolidation of control over territory in northern Iraq and eastern Syria allowed it to build workshops where work continued uninterruptedly on production and modification of arms until the Iraqi offensives of late 2016 and early 2017 began to uncover and destroy these workshops.[68] However, the sheer scale of production can be seen in the fact that between October 16 and November 31, as Iraqi forces advanced on Mosul, IS launched 632 VBIEDs, or fourteen per day.[69]

The military manufacturing and development industries that IS owned also developed a drone warfare capability for its fighting forces. Initially, as early as 2015, IS "engineers" were only able to produce very primitive drones for surveillance and reconnaissance purposes. These drones were off-the-shelf or modified ones that, nonetheless, proved useful, as they provided IS's ground forces with imagery of enemy fortifications prior to or during the assault phase of an operation. Later, IS began using drones to guide SVBIEDs to their targets or to provide their artillery and mortar units with target coordinates of enemy forces. The most ominous development came on October 2, 2016, when an IS drone rigged with explosives crashed onto Peshmerga and French special operation forces, killing two Kurdish fighters and wounding two French SOF soldiers. Not surprising, IS progressed to using drones to drop small bombs or grenades on Iraqi troops and armored vehicles. While the damage was limited, due to the small payload, the psychological impact was considerable. The Iraqi army's assault on Mosul, which disrupted much of IS's arms production and modification, including its Air Observation Unit, in charge of drones, ensured that the jihadists were unable to progress further in the evolution of drone warfare in the current fight.[70]

The success of ISIS's and then IS's offensives in 2014 should not be taken to mean that the jihadist fighters were "ten feet tall." Indeed, over the course of the fighting between IS and its enemies from early 2015 onward to mid-2017, comical failures in the skills of IS's fighters were evident and appeared on YouTube almost as often as videos showing these fighters' prowess in their offensive operations, particularly when they seized military bases. Nonetheless, the success of ISIS in the battles of 2014 must also be explained by examining what has historically been referred to as "the other side of the hill": the status of the opposing forces.[71]

Failing Foes: The Iraqi Army and the Kurdish Peshmerga

The success of the jihadist way of war benefited from the incompetence of their enemies, the Iraqi army and the Kurdish Peshmerga forces. Neither the army nor the Kurds had any tactics, techniques, and procedures to counter the revised and improved jihadist way of warfare.

The disaster that befell the Iraqi military in Mosul raised numerous questions about its military effectiveness. The United States had spent about $25 billion to train and equip Iraq's security forces and provide them with installations and bases. Iraq spent billions of dollars of its own money to buy F-16 fighter jets, M-1 Abrams main battle tanks, and Apache helicopter gunships. Despite the sterling efforts of U.S. military trainers, the problems of the Iraqi army were starkly evident even in the four years before the United States' exit at the end of 2011.

The post-Saddam American-trained Iraqi Security Forces and military were suspect from the very beginning, despite the heroic efforts of the American military trainers. Before the Americans left in 2011, observers noted that the Iraqi forces suffered profoundly from sectarianism, poor motivation, and a deep gulf between officers and men and between the rank and file of different sects and ethnic groups.[72] As politico-military advisor, I noticed this as early as 2005. Sunnis and Shias and Arabs and Kurds spoke disparagingly of each other in both mixed and nonmixed units stationed in Tel Afar, where the Iraqis were ostensibly helping the U.S. Third Armored Cavalry Regiment to liberate Tel Afar from the grip of a mix of insurgents that included particularly nasty foreign jihadist fighters. It was politically incorrect to voice disparagement of Iraqi forces at the time. In fact, they were not much help to the Third Armored Cavalry Regiment. The Kurdish troops were perceived as spending much of their time helping themselves to Iraqi territory that was not theirs and sneering at the "poor quality" of the troops from the south, whose officers, in turn, castigated the Americans for "imperialist" behavior and for "secretly aiding" the Kurds. A fervently nationalist young Iraqi Shia officer, who seemed diligent and efficient, responded to my statement that the Kurds surely deserved their own homeland by saying: "We know what the Kurds are up to. They can leave if they want, but we won't allow them to take more of Iraq." This was in August 2005. Watching from the sidelines were the Sunni Arab troops, enlisted for the effort so as to make the offensive look like a national enterprise. The Sunni troops had, by then, developed a seeming inscrutability on the surface—it was impossible to elicit any political comment from them in my discussions with them—but it was clear that they were boiling with fury and rage. They were probably sympathetic to the insurgents and their former comrades in the old Iraqi army, whom Tel Afar, as well as Mosul, contained in abundance.

The logistics of the Iraqi armed forces were poor or were riddled with corruption even when the Americans were in Iraq in force during the first decade of the twenty-first century.[73] They collapsed almost entirely after the Americans left in 2011. Corruption, poor leadership, a vast gulf between officers and enlistees, low morale, broken equipment due to poor logistics, and even worse maintenance practices ensured that the Iraqi army remained subpar.[74] Moreover, with the American departure came a sharp decline in training and accountability. None of the ethno-sectarian communities represented within the forces located in the north had any sense of national commitment to fighting the advancing ISIS fighters. Many divisions suffered from the existence of a phenomenon the Iraqis refer to as *fadhaiyin* ("spacemen"), that is, personnel who exist only on paper, allowing senior officers to pocket the pay of these nonexistent soldiers. In addition, often officers would make a deal between themselves and enlisted men allowing the latter to remain permanently absent. The conspirators would split the paychecks of the absent men, who would then take up civilian jobs. In some units, "spacemen" constituted half the force. Officer ranks were often bought and sold. Soldiers were issued shoddy or nonfunctioning equipment. With such rampant corruption, morale among the rank and file plummeted.[75]

As a legacy of the U.S. rush to build up the Iraqi Security Forces, almost one-quarter of the Iraqi army failed to meet its own minimum qualifications for soldiers in 2009. About 24 percent were not qualified, based on army criteria for enlistment—poor health and age restrictions—and approximately 15 percent were illiterate.[76] Most units operated at 75 percent strength in 2009 and suffered from a severe shortage of competent leaders. The forces' logistics, intelligence, and engineering capabilities were woefully inadequate in 2009; judging by the events of 2014, they did not get better.

The Iraqi army also suffered from severe politicization. The government purged the upper levels of the military on suspicions of disloyalty to Prime Minister Nuri al-Maliki. He fired anyone seen as having been too close to the Americans and many Kurds and Sunni Arabs.[77] An Iraqi Special Forces soldier remarked: "These were the most competent leaders, trusted by the Americans and loved by their men."[78] Not surprising, this soldier deserted sometime in 2014. The Iraqi collapse in northern Iraq, especially the loss of Mosul on June 9, 2014, was also due to intelligence failures brought on by Maliki's refusal to accept intelligence from Sunni and Kurdish sources in the north that ISIS was "up to something."

From January through May 2014, Iraqi forces were battered in clashes with ISIS: six helicopters were shot down, twenty-eight Abrams tanks were damaged, and five sustained full armor penetration by antitank missiles. General Mohammad Khalaf Said al-Dulaimi, the commander of the Twelfth Division in Kirkuk, lamented in April 2014 "that he was facing a well-trained enemy that launched multiple large-scale attacks."[79] Raids by heavily armed ISIS fighters probed Iraqi army positions in intense firefights that often led to the Iraqi units deserting their positions. When Mosul fell to ISIS's combatants in June 2014, large numbers of Iraqi military personnel discarded their weapons, changed into civilian clothes, and fled the city. Four of Iraq's fourteen divisions abandoned their posts. The divisions that collapsed were made up of a mixture of Sunni, Shia, and Kurdish troops. Logistics support for troops proved to be one of the biggest problems the army faced; this meant that food, ammunition, water, and weapons were always in short supply.[80] In October 2014, the forces of the new Caliphate seized a series of army bases, including that of the Seventh Division, in the town of Hit, despite air strikes by U.S. planes in support of the Iraqi ground forces. An anonymous Iraqi officer complained: "We don't have any leadership. We could have kept our base with some simple reinforcements and ammunition."[81] Distrust between soldiers of different ethno-sectarian backgrounds worsened in 2014 and thereafter in parallel with the growing ethno-sectarian gulfs between the various communities.

After capturing Mosul and humiliating the Iraqi Security Forces, ISIS turned its attention toward the Kurds who stood in the way of the ISIS march south toward Anbar province and Baghdad. It was imperative for ISIS to weaken the Kurds and push them back from their forward positions close to ISIS's path of advance southward. The Kurdish forces, the Peshmerga, were traditionally known to be a highly motivated and skilled force who had been fighting for decades against the central government in Baghdad. However, when ISIS forces fell upon the forward-based units of the Kurdish security forces, they routed the Peshmerga and forced them to retreat into the Kurdish autonomous region in disarray.

Why were the Peshmerga defeated so easily? The simplest surface explanation is that they were not combat ready; they had not engaged in major combat since 2003. A more profound explanation is that the

Peshmerga were a guerrilla force who had trained to deal with a large organized army, like the Iraqi army, seeking to snuff out their quest for autonomy or outright independence, which required advancing on Kurdish strongholds. The Peshmerga fought in rugged terrain in their mountains, and there they were formidable. In the words of Tahsin Qalan, a retired Peshmerga commander who fought the Iraqi army in the 1980s: "We need to lose the name peshmerga and [become] a modern regional army. In the past, we would fight in the mountains, forming security belts around our bases. *We rarely had front lines.*"[82] Nihat Ali Ozcan, a Turkish strategic analyst, further highlighted the fact that the Peshmerga's organizational structure and culture as it existed was more geared toward guerrilla fighting. With the rise of ISIS, the Kurds were forced to confront new strategic and military realities:

> They now had to assume a static role defending a geographic region and a people, rather than hitting and running. In other words, it became essential for them to transition into a "regular army." This meant that they had to become an army of the country and not the party, an army in which strict rules prevail, logistics are centralized, a formal hierarchy is in effect, and an army that is capable of waging a symmetrical war. This new form meant budgets, patience, values, laws, training, and time. In other words, the establishment of institutional culture and values would require many years and resources.[83]

The Kurds had not even made the slightest efforts in restructuring and modernizing their forces before ISIS hit them in mid-2014. Since the downfall of Saddam Hussein's regime, they had only been in garrison duty along the de facto border between Iraqi Kurdistan and the rest of Iraq. The main Peshmerga missions had been to prevent the infiltration of terrorists and of Arab refugees into their homeland. When they faced ISIS fighters on the open plains of Nineveh province, they found themselves dealing with a totally new situation.

The Peshmerga were nonplussed by ISIS's way of warfare, which was something new and very different from that of their traditional foe, the conventional Iraqi army, whom they had been fighting since the early 1960s. Like all conventional militaries, the Iraqi army, whether under the previous pre-Baath republics or under Saddam Hussein, was a large and rigid force incapable of effectively confronting adept guerrillas in mountain terrain.[84] The ISIS way of war incorporated terrorism, guerrilla hit-and-run attacks, and semiconventional warfare, used in parallel. The jihadist fighting machine could fight the Peshmerga on their own terms and, because of its mobility and flexibility, proved better in 2014. It also confronted the Peshmerga with semiconventional war. The mobile forces of ISIS could concentrate wherever they wanted to and quickly launch surprise attacks against the overstretched border units of the Peshmerga, who were seeking to protect Kurdistan's borders from lesser threats than jihadist forces. By using such tactics, ISIS was able to attain battlefield superiority before Kurdish reinforcements arrived. Even the weapons ISIS used were very different and vastly superior. The fighters of ISIS were well-equipped with heavy modern weaponry and armored vehicles, partly as a result of the ease with which they had routed the U.S.-trained and -supplied Iraqi army and plundered their supplies. That equipment, much of it American-made, included tanks, armored vehicles, artillery, and huge supplies of ammunition.

By way of contrast, Peshmerga forces were equipped mainly with Soviet-era weapons looted from the Iraqi army during the 2003 U.S.-led invasion. Ammunition was also in short supply. Most of the veterans had decided to retire after the downfall of the Baathist regime and had entered into politics or business, both of which were more lucrative than military service. The newer recruits had little or no experience in battle.[85] They lacked modern military infrastructure and had problems with coordination and a lack of operations centers, information sharing, air support, and satellite imagery. They were not prepared for a large-scale attack. A lack of professionalism was pervasive too. Salaries were ridiculously uncompetitive, forcing many Peshmerga to moonlight and work side jobs. Stories circulated of ammunition and even arms being sold to supplement income and, conversely, of men having to buy their own ammunition and rifles. In addition, rivalries between the Peshmerga units of the competing Kurdistan Democratic Party of Masoud Barzani and the Patriotic Union of Kurdistan reduced Kurdish effectiveness.[86]

The Islamic State of Iraq and Syria Marches South

Following the crushing of the Iraqi and the Kurdish forces in the north, the jubilant ISIS fighters marched south toward the heart of the country. They struck Tikrit, Saddam Hussein's birthplace, and Ramadi, the capital of Anbar province and one of the biggest cities in Iraq.

At 1400 hours on June 11, 2014, ISIS forces entered Tikrit with a small forward unit of just thirty trucks, without firing a shot. Though ISIS was far from invincible, its use of information operations to promote its victories and use of terror as a psychological weapon contributed to facilitating its march south. Its cells had already infiltrated the city months before and had succeeded in extorting money from commercial enterprises and in assassinating or forcing government officials to flee. As a journalist put it: "Fear alone was enough to induce surrender and retreat of Iraqi forces."[87] The government forces in Tikrit should have been adequate to repel an ISIS advance. Three police regiments of four hundred policemen each were dedicated to the city alone, including a heavily armed SWAT force. Most were seasoned officers who had fought a wide variety of insurgent forces over the years. Outside the city, at Camp Speicher, a former U.S. army base, were three brigades of the Iraqi army whose primary goal was to protect the vast network of oil pipelines from attack by insurgent and criminal elements.

The Iraqi forces in Tikrit had numbers on their side, and tactically they had the advantage of defending a fortified city from a weaker ISIS force that was bearing down on them. However, they were weaker than their numbers suggested. They were poorly organized and crippled by corrupt and ineffective leadership. They were also not prepared for a force that was quite different from their previous experiences with insurgent cells; ISIS was fighting like an army. The largely Shia Iraqi army units at Camp Speicher did not provide the police units with support to fight ISIS. Most of the police officers who were intimately familiar with the situation in the city saw its defense as suicidal, since ISIS cells were already inside the city providing intelligence and waiting to rise up in support of the approaching ISIS columns.

On June 11, 2014, the local Iraqi military units were facing a rising tide of desertion, and the police called upon the army to deploy into Tikrit. By the afternoon, ISIS moved into Tikrit as Iraqi forces fled. The first priority of the ISIS invaders was to kill any remaining Iraqi security and government personnel. The details of the mass surrender at Camp Speicher are unclear, but hundreds of soldiers walked out of the base in civilian clothes and surrendered en masse to ISIS, naively believing that they would be let go. Instead they were marched to the Qusoor al-Raisiya area in the city center, where they were segregated by hometown and sect. Sunnis from local provinces—Nineveh, Salah al-Din, and Anbar—were released, while the Shias and Sunnis from Baghdad and other parts of the country were executed en masse. The only real resistance in the city came from the suburb of Hayy al-Alam, a stronghold of the Jibouri tribe, who had large numbers of men in the police force; ISIS crushed the tribal resistance by rounding up and massacring members of the tribe. Simultaneously, ISIS released hundreds of detained terrorists and criminals who readily joined its ranks.

The provincial capital of Anbar province, Ramadi, was a prize target for ISIS because it had been a center of the Iraqi insurgency between 2003 and 2011 and had taken a lead in reviving Sunni resistance to Prime Minister Maliki's policies after 2011. When clashes erupted between disgruntled Sunni residents and the Iraqi Security Forces, ISIS saw an opportunity to insinuate itself within the city. A fierce struggle for total control of the city ensued between the government and ISIS, which by then had declared the Caliphate and evolved into IS. Determined to seize Ramadi, IS launched an offensive in October 2014. The battle proved to be a bruising slugfest between the IS fighters and Iraqi military forces, who were more motivated than in the past. The Iraqi government turned to the Sunni tribes for help to prevent IS's fighters from taking Ramadi. However, the Sunnis suffered from a severe shortage of arms and ammunition, and by December 2014 it was clear that they no longer had the wherewithal to prevent IS's further advance toward Ramadi.

In March 2015, IS launched a coordinated attack on government-held areas in Ramadi, involving seven almost simultaneous suicide car bomb attacks designed to breach the Iraqi forces' defenses. In their assault on Ramadi IS also used tunnel attacks to devastating effect. On March 11, 2015, IS forces detonated a tunnel bomb under an Iraqi army headquarters. The blast consumed seven tons of explosives in an eight-hundred-foot tunnel that had taken two months to dig.[88] In late April 2015, IS forces were ready to launch an offensive to take Ramadi.

The commanders of IS executed a complex battle plan, outwitting a larger force of Iraqi troops. The commanders evaded surveillance and air strikes while bringing reinforcements to their front lines in Ramadi by using civilian vehicles and traveling in small convoys. After mid-April victories in the albu-Faraj and Sijariya neighborhoods, IS issued a military order hundreds of miles to the north in Aleppo, calling for a redeployment of some of its best fighters to the front lines in Anbar and Salah al-Din provinces in Iraq. During its Ramadi surge IS displayed a high degree of operational security by silencing its social media and propaganda teams. By converting captured U.S. military armored vehicles designed to be impervious to small-arms fire into megabombs, IS also churned out dozens of deadly new makeshift weapons. At the height of the battle, over the course of a three-day surge, IS fighters launched 27 SVBIEDs that destroyed the Iraq military units' defensive perimeters and crumbled multistory buildings.

On May 5, 2015, IS fighters launched an attack on Ramadi's city center, but Iraqi helicopters and the elite counterterrorism special operation force called the "Golden Division" repulsed the advance. To counter the fire-power of the entrenched Iraqi units and the support they received from the air, IS launched its surge by sending a single armored bulldozer to clear a path through the concrete barriers placed in front of the Iraqi forward defensive lines. Covered by suppressive fire, the bulldozer worked unimpeded at removing the barriers. Once a clear path was secured, IS suicide drivers drove six SVBIEDS, including an armored Humvee and an armored dump truck, into the Iraqi defenses, including the provincial government complex, which served as headquarters for the security forces. The IS offensive was relentless, and over the course of the next three days it set off another twenty SVBIEDs and VBIEDs. Iraqi morale collapsed, and the IS fighters took the government complex on May 15. The group launched another wave of SVBIED attacks on May 17, preventing Iraqi reinforcements from entering the city. The "Golden Division," the elite unit that bore the brunt of the urban fight, retreated from the city. Once IS's black flag began flying from Ramadi's city center, IS lifted its information blackout and celebrated its victory.

Role Reversal: The Revival of the Iraqi Forces and the Peshmerga

Stunned and embarrassed by the magnitude of their defeats in 2014, the Iraqis and Kurds began to address seriously the factors behind the humiliating showings of their respective forces. No military establishment or its political masters like to believe that there is something wrong with their military. Furthermore, it is difficult to make the requisite changes, for they challenge tried methods and entrenched constituencies. Moreover, changes in the military organizational structure, including personnel changes, have political implications. The dire threat to political stability in Iraq and Kurdistan that ISIS's offensives in 2014 represented and the decision of Western and other states to lend ground advisory support, provide weapons, and conduct aerial strikes forced the Iraqis and Kurds to implement changes in their respective military structures. The implementation of these changes was not smooth or devoid of errors and setbacks.

The Recovery of Tikrit (March–April 2015), Ramadi (January 2016), and Fallujah (May 2016)

The effort to retake Tikrit constituted the first trial for the reconstituted and retrained Iraqi forces. More than two weeks after the fall of Tikrit, Baghdad launched an offensive to recapture it. The campaign began with air strikes, in coordination with local tribes, that won part of the city back. The fighting in Tikrit showed that the Iraqi Security Forces had a Herculean task ahead of them. A few hundred IS fighters held off a 24,000-strong Iraqi government force for two months. Only after U.S. forces began bombing IS positions from the air did the government finally seize the city.[89] The government was able to fully retake the city only a year later, in April 2015, and even then it was not the glorious victory the government made it out to be as that offensive highlighted the security forces' continuing deficiencies.[90]

This time, however, there was an added complicating factor, in the shape of the presence on the battlefield of Shia militia forces, whose relationship with the Iraqi army units tasked with recapturing Tikrit were tense. The Iraqi army and the Shia militias were very uneasy partners in the effort to retake Tikrit from IS's fighters.[91] The Shia militias' approach to the captured IS fighters or their Sunni allies was generally to "hear their confessions" and execute them out of hand.[92] This vengeful attitude of the Shia militias did not go down well in Sunni-majority areas, whose inhabitants admitted to seeing no difference between the bloodthirsty IS and its Shia militia foes.

Some analysts have argued for some time that Arabs fight better as guerrillas, insurgents, or fighters in semiregular outfits. The converse is that they do poorly as regular soldiers, as reflected in their poor showings or defeats in battles against a variety of opponents. The failures and defeats of the Iraqi army, not only in previous wars but also in 2014, seem to have proven the point. This is reinforced by the fact that the Shia militias have allegedly done so much better. This is a specious argument. The failures of the Iraqi army are a reflection and microcosm of the failures of Iraqi society. If these are not fixed, it is unlikely that they will ever field an effective military. In the frantic efforts to defeat IS, Baghdad and, by default, the international U.S.-led Coalition have relied on the Shia militias, in addition to the regular military forces. Since militias are not directly under the control of the state—indeed, sometimes they owe allegiance to a foreign patron—they often weaken the state further because their existence erodes the state's monopoly over the instruments of violence.[93]

The various Shia militias who have joined the fray against IS have shown courage and motivation and a flexibility that the Iraqi army did not have well into 2015.[94] However, they also have committed serious violations against Sunnis in areas where it has regained control, leading to a backlash against them in Sunni areas and a reluctance to join the government side against IS. The poor training of al-Hashd al-shaabi (Popular Mobilization)— an umbrella organization of numerous Shia militias—units was confirmed by a number of its members who had fought against IS units and even been badly wounded. Colonel Salah Rajab, who was deputy commander of the Habib Battalion, a three-hundred man unit from Karbala, of the Ali Akbar Brigade of the Hashd, related his own experiences to a Western journalist. A former professional army officer who resigned in 1999, he said: "I joined the Hashid [sic] to defend my country against foreigners and I had been fighting in Baiji city for 16 days when a mortar bomb landed near me, leaving two of our men dead and four wounded." Himself seriously wounded, Rajab explains the weaknesses of his men: "there is a lack of experienced commanders who know how to direct an attack." There is also a general lack of training for the volunteers: "they get a maximum of three months' training when they need six months." The Hashd is not good at communications security: "Daesh is continually hacking into our communications, finding out what we are doing and inflicting heavy losses."[95] The Shia militias have been imbued with more fervor and piety, sentiments that have allowed them to attack IS positions with little fear of death. It is inaccurate to assume, as many have, that the Shia militias are uniformly well trained or well disciplined. Most are not, and that fact is precisely one of the key reasons why they are such a problem in Sunni areas and ultimately a danger to the viability of the Iraqi state.[96] They have managed to create a form of "bifurcated sovereignty" within Iraq, where the government's control over armed forces has eroded significantly in recent years.

The influx of Shia volunteers into the army and the increase in the size of Shia militias worried politicians in Baghdad. Hamid al-Mutlaq, a Sunni parliamentarian, argued: "We can't solve such problems with this sectarian mobilization. We can't just include untrained fighters in a war on terror."[97] Local residents in Sunni Samarra were frightened by the presence of Shia army volunteers who openly wore arm- and headbands bearing the insignia of Shia militias. Poorly trained Shia volunteers were given perfunctory training and then sent into battle against veteran insurgents. Not surprisingly, they did poorly against IS fighters in Tel Afar in June 2014. The air strikes arrested the progress of IS expansion on the ground.

There are no official figures on the number of Shia militiamen fighting alongside the Iraqi army.[98] Most of the militiamen are volunteers from the population who joined up after Ayatollah Ali al-Sistani called upon ordinary Iraqis to defend the country against IS in June 2014. He later clarified his statement, recommending that anyone who wanted to defend the country could also do so by joining the regular military.

Tension between the official security forces and the militias had a negative impact on military morale and operations. Iraqi officer Mohammad al-Saadi elaborated on this: "Everyone thinks that the Iraqi army is the main force fighting the IS group and that the Shiite militias support the army. But the reality on the ground would suggest that the army doesn't actually have any authority over these militias and that the militias make their own decisions."[99] The militias did not trust the army and often had their own intelligence units. They did not share information and often carried out operations without informing the army or disrupted supposedly jointly coordinated operations by "going off and doing their own thing." According to one Iraqi officer, some of the Shia militias—especially those affiliated with Iran—refused to cooperate with the army when planning for or executing operations. They preferred to come up with their own plans and choose their own targets, which were at times at variance and in conflict with army operations.[100] Relations improved somewhat by 2016, and as a result so did coordination between the regular forces and the militias.

Another factor that affected regular military morale was that many Iraqi soldiers indicated that they would rather join the militias. Iraqi regular army officer Colonel Jassim al-Mamouri opined that this was due to a number of things: (1) they have a better leave policy: for every ten days of combat, the militiamen get ten days of leave; (2) if militiamen get defeated or make battlefield mistakes, nothing happens to them.[101] By way of contrast, Iraqi army soldiers are subject to draconian punishment. Unsurprisingly, soldiers have been known to resign from military service and join the militia outfits. The poor image of the Iraqi army among the Iraqi population has not helped its morale or dedication to the fight. The Iraqi government's ability to fight IS effectively was degraded not only by the tensions between the regular army and the militias but also by tensions among the several militias making up the Popular Mobilization. Their disagreements are not purely or even primarily over military matters but over political and economic issues. The Shia militias can be divided into three categories, all three of which are different in terms of strengths and weaknesses, weapons they possess, how they are funded, and their independence vis-à-vis the Iraqi government.[102]

Following the success in Tikrit, the recapture of Ramadi in 2016 showed some major improvements, as well as lessons learned by the Iraqi army and its U.S.-led Coalition allies.[103] The campaign to recover Ramadi saw much closer coordination between troops on the ground and Coalition air power than in the past. Air strikes killed at least 350 IS fighters in the days before the ground offensive began. Nonetheless, Iraqi forces some ten thousand strong were needed to defeat no more than one thousand IS fighters. The fight for Ramadi was a long slog, led not by the army, known as the Iraqi Security Forces, but by an elite counterterrorism force coupled with some forces from the Iraqi Eighth Division.[104] They were only able to beat IS with U.S.-led Coalition air strikes launched from the Taqadum airbase, located southeast of Ramadi.[105] The majority of the Iraqi ground forces involved were incapable of taking the lead in the assault but served in a support role, pointing out IS positions for air attacks and holding the roads that led to the city center. Iranian-backed Shia militias, who have often been in the vanguard of the fight against IS, were largely excluded from this battle. This was at the insistence of the Americans, who wanted to encourage a Sunni uprising against IS like the one they fomented against its predecessor, AQI, in 2006. The results were patchy because the Shia government in Baghdad blocked Anbari Sunni tribes from receiving any meaningful supplies of weaponry.[106] Nonetheless, the Sunni inhabitants of Ramadi also welcomed the absence of the Shia militias, because the bigger the role they played in the fight, the greater was the Sunni perception that the Shias were waging a sectarian war against them.

The battle was complicated by IS's defensive posture. The fighters of IS had time to construct a multilayered defense based on booby traps and a network of tunnels that allowed small units and suicide bombers to move around the town unseen by surveillance drones. As a result, the Iraqi army had to spend months encircling the city and slowly cutting IS off from outside help.

The battle in Ramadi also showed that the Iraqi military still had a long way to go before it could wage sustained combat against IS. The battle showed that the elite units were not large enough to bear the burden of liberating cities and holding them against the threat of an IS return. Iraq's elite forces had no choice but to learn how to conduct urban warfare—often the hard and deadly way—but the bulk of Iraq's conventional forces lacked even basic tactical skills. Even when Ramadi was recovered, the victory remained incomplete because roughly 30 percent of Ramadi remained under IS control for some time thereafter.[107]

Buoyed by the Ramadi success, the government began to prepare for "Amaliyat Kasr al-Irhab" (Operating Breaking Terrorism), which was designed to retake the strategically and symbolically important city of Fallujah. This would be the third battle for Fallujah since 2004. The city is important because it sits on a transportation network that allows access to Baghdad as well as to Jordan through the desert and to the north and south. Fallujah had also been a stubborn center of insurgents, including jihadist groups, from 2003 onward. Finally, it posed a threat to Baghdad that the government could not ignore: Fallujah's IED workshops produced explosive-laden vehicles that the jihadists used in their terrorist offensive against the capital.[108]

The Iraqis kicked off the offensive on May 22, 2016. The Iraqi advance was hesitant, even though the Iraqis threw four divisions as well as the controversial Shia militias into the fray. Fallujah is located in the middle of a dense agricultural region, with many villages along the approaches to the city. The IS fighters had turned some of the villages into fortified redoubts designed to slow down the Iraqi advance. Furthermore, the Iraqi forces had little or no contact with the tribes of Fallujah. This was in contrast with the situation in Ramadi, where, despite the tensions between the government and the Sunni Arab tribes of Anbar province, the two sides had established contact and a kind of modus vivendi, due to the presence of Sunni politicians from Ramadi at the center of power in Baghdad. In other words, the Iraqi forces' "human terrain" understanding of Fallujah was inadequate.[109]

As the Iraqi Security Forces were undergoing training by practicing in their bases and by fighting entrenched IS fighters in cities, the retraining and restructuring of the Kurdish Peshmerga also proceeded with considerable urgency from the autumn of 2014 onward. The training of the Peshmerga proceeded with less of the baggage that attended the retraining of the Iraqi forces, for a number of reasons. The Iraqi Security Forces were much larger, and the impact of the divisions between the regular forces and the Hashd had to be taken into account. On top of these issues was the growing sectarian chasm between Sunnis and Shias as the Iraqi forces were reconstructed and sought to prevent the sectarianism from affecting operations on the ground. To be sure, there were similar issues within the Peshmerga between the units of the Kurdistan Democratic Party and the Patriotic Union of Kurdistan and between the older generation of guerrilla

fighters and the younger more professional generation, who were impa-
tiently angling for a united and modern army. Many premier Western militaries, ranging from that of the United States to those of Great Britain, France,
and Germany, were at the forefront of the effort to transform the Peshmerga
from a militia into a (national?) modern army. The overall aim was to transform the Peshmerga, with their vaunted reputation as mountain warriors,
into a force better prepared to face the brutal and battle-hardened militants
in the largely desert terrain and urban areas they had seized. The more specific goals were to improve command and control within the Kurdish
forces, to improve coordination between the two rival Peshmerga forces of
the Kurdistan Democratic Party and the Patriotic Union of Kurdistan, to
provide basic ground warfare skills, and to provide training in the new
weapons that the Western powers gave the Peshmerga from 2014 onward.[110]

The Battle for Mosul, October 2016–June 2017

Everybody knew that Mosul was the prize.[111] Though not IS's official capital, it was clear that Iraq's second largest city, steeped in history, had to be
retaken from IS for symbolic and strategic reasons. The so-called Caliph
Ibrahim (Abu Bakr al-Baghdadi) had declared the rebirth of the Caliphate
in a historic mosque in Mosul. It was in Mosul that the Caliphate had to
be dealt its decisive defeat.

Given the state of the Iraqi military and its associated security forces, it
also became manifestly clear that it was going to take many months to
prepare Iraq's still struggling military for a long-anticipated assault on IS's
biggest stronghold in the country. It was clear to the Americans and Iraqis
that they could not wait for the entire Iraqi Security Forces to reach the
highest standards of training and reequipment across the board. The
focus was on improving the existing best units, which was a rational
approach. However, the drawback was that the battles against IS would
"chew up" these units and many of the "second echelon" forces were simply not up to the task of extensive and intensive urban combat.

For example, the elite counterterrorism force the "Golden Division"
was designed for small team operations against terrorist targets and was
not initially optimized for high-intensity sustained urban operations.
However, because of its high standard of training and esprit de corps, this
force was assigned to urban operations, which meant larger scale operations involving three or four battalions at a time. The division rose to the
challenge because, in the words of one of its senior commanders, Brigadier

Haider al-Obeidi, "there's a weakness in the army and other forces which has increased the pressure on us."[112] This lopsided reliance on the elite forces meant that their attrition rates were high, and this factor worried the Iraqi government, because most of the regular units were not ready for that kind of high-intensity urban warfare.[113]

As the United States and its allies worked to train thousands more troops for the enormous task of retaking Iraq's second largest city, IS fighters began waging a diversion campaign of bloody suicide attacks in Baghdad and elsewhere. Their aim was to force Iraq's already overburdened security forces to spread even thinner to protect the capital and other cities rather than preparing the Mosul operation. It took some time to get the forces for the assault on Mosul and its environs in place for the offensive to recapture the city.[114] The U.S.-led Coalition and Iraqi officials estimated eight to twelve brigades, or an estimated 24,000–36,000 troops, were needed for the operation to capture Mosul. In preparation, 2,000–3,000 Iraqi troops were deployed at a base at Makhmour, a major staging ground for the Mosul assault, located forty miles (sixty-seven kilometers) southeast of the city. Under political pressure to show victory, Iraqi prime minister Haider al-Abadi repeatedly vowed to liberate Mosul in 2016. The Iraqi military's few competent, battle-tested units were scattered throughout the country in 2016, helping to hold various front lines against IS in the country's central and western provinces or tied down controlling cities and towns retaken from the militants because other security forces are not capable. Iraq's elite counterterrorism forces had to station units near Tikrit and Baiji in central Iraq and Habbaniya in the west. In Ramadi, capital of the Anbar province, a counterterrorism unit had to remain because local police forces could not maintain control. ISIS would often come back and recapture terrain that thinly stretched Iraqi Security Forces had spent months taking from them.[115]

Another issue that plagued the government was overwhelmingly political in nature.[116] The Iraqi "coalition"—the government in Baghdad, the anti-IS Sunni political and armed groups in Nineveh, the Kurds—were all mutually suspicious of one another's agendas.[117] To be sure, Iraqi prime minister Haider al-Abadi and Masoud Barzani, one of the key leaders in the Kurdish region, had drawn closer together because they were besieged by enemies on their respective domestic fronts and there seemed to be some coordination and cooperation between Iraqi forces and Peshmerga. This was undoubtedly tactical and fell short of unity against a common enemy. In the field the two forces continued to be disparaging of one another.[118] Abadi's relations with the Sunni Arabs were not on solid ground either. The Sunnis continued to suspect him of being ineffectual, unwilling to arm them, and unable to rein in the Shia militias who were running amok. Indeed, another major unresolved issue concerned the continuing tensions between Abadi's government and its regular military force, on the one hand and the myriad Shia militias on the other.[119] These tensions had only been exacerbated by the "unsavory" actions of the militias in the field against Sunni civilians.

Despite the existence of a less than optimal situation on the ground and politically, the Iraqis commenced the operation to liberate Mosul, dubbed "Qadimun ya Naynawa" (We are Coming, Oh Nineveh), on October 16, 2016.[120] The city is split into two halves by the Tigris River, and the thrust of the initial assault was to liberate the eastern more modern bank first and then to thrust into the western half, where IS was deeply ensconced. By early November 2016, after a methodical advance, which included setting up a number of forward operating bases and well-stocked logistical depots, the Iraqi forces breached Mosul's city limits along the eastern half of the city.[121]

From 2015 onward, it was no longer easy for IS forces to conduct operations or conduct spoiler attacks to derail enemy offensives. The air power of the U.S.-led Coalition devastated IS's formations in open terrain, and IS's enemies had learned how to conduct operations more effectively due to better training and more firepower at their disposal.[122] Indeed, by the time the Mosul offensive was under way, IS had not been able to mount a successful offensive of its own since May 2015. Furthermore, whenever they had mounted counteroffensives after that date they were invariably smashed with heavy casualties.[123] The heavy casualties IS suffered were initially borne by its best combat personnel, who invariably were at the forefront of the IS offensives. Their replacements did not have the requisite skills, and given IS's concern with current operations, there was no time to train personnel effectively. Furthermore, as IS's financial resources dwindled due to the loss of territory and destruction of revenue-generating infrastructure, such as oil fields, the salaries of fighting personnel fell precipitously; in some cases there were situations where fighters did not receive their pay.[124]

In anticipation of the Mosul offensive, the IS forces turned some outlying villages into fortified positions in which they stationed SVBIEDs whose purpose was to attack advancing Iraqi and Peshmerga forces. Between October 31 and December 1, 2016, a total of six weeks, IS managed to set off 632 VBIEDs and SVBIEDs, a staggering total of fifteen per day.[125] However, the IS tactic of sending SVBIEDs headlong into the open against enemy forces was effectively countered by new tactics and weapons. Iraqi and Peshmerga forces dispersed their units more as they advanced into the open, while forward screening forces were tasked with providing warning about SVBIED assaults. Better coordination between forward air controllers on the ground and aircraft allowed coalition air power to take out many SVBIEDs before they reached advancing ground forces. Finally, Iraqi and Peshmerga forces were now equipped with antitank missiles, which were used to take out the SVBIEDs.

The situation in built-up areas evened the imbalance between IS and its enemies. It was clear that the IS fighters were waiting for the opportunity to do damage when the Iraqi forces approached Mosul city proper. The urban battlefield is fluid and dynamic, as is, of course, the open battlefield, but the urban battlefield is "fuzzy," in that battle lines are not distinct and clear-cut and close-quarter combat is the norm, placing a premium on the skills of the small-unit fighting force, the danger to which could emerge from any direction. Civilians could be intermingled with the terrorists. In Mosul, initially the presence of civilians was a particular problem because, unlike Ramadi, where many districts were leveled by Iraqi forces and U.S.-led Coalition air power after civilians fled, in Mosul most civilians stayed put (or were forced to stay put), and there was an effort to try to ensure that civilian casualties were minimized. As the intensity and scope of the fighting in Mosul proved unbearable, many civilians began a mass exodus out of the city.[126]

The IS forces were able to use VBIEDs and SVBIEDs more effectively because the dense urban maze allowed these vehicles the possibility of concealment until the moment of attack, in contrast with the situation in open terrain. The urban maze also broke up Iraqi forces into smaller units as they advanced up booby-trapped streets and searched booby-trapped homes. Snipers and mortar attacks proved to be a problem in many areas, slowing down the Iraqi forces and inflicting heavy casualties. Tanks and other armored vehicles proved vulnerable to IS attacks if they were separated from supporting infantry, and in many cases there were not enough infantry trained in urban combat to support the push by armored forces.[127] In southeast Mosul the Iraqi Ninth Armored Division faced a nightmarish battlefield with little support from infantry units as it advanced into a fluid situation where terrorists commingled with civilians and any vehicle that was not recognizably part of the advancing Iraqi units represented a dire danger.[128] The urban terrain, which provided concealed avenues of approach, also allowed IS small units to emerge from their underground hideouts and launch short and sharp but ferocious assaults and ambushes.[129] In these built-up areas Iraqi losses began to mount, as small groups of IS fighters launched ambushes of Iraqi soldiers.[130] The lack of sufficient forces to consolidate control over liberated urban sectors meant that small groups of IS fighters and suicide bombers were often overlooked in the dense urban maze, and these left-behind jihadists were the ones who launched assaults on the flanks and rears of Iraqi units. Moreover, since it was the elite forces that were leading the charge into the city and getting involved in bitter close-quarter combat, they suffered the greatest number of casualties.[131]

However, IS leadership could not view the situation in the Mosul urban environment with equanimity. A paranoid "state" by definition, IS began lashing out even more indiscriminately than before as the Iraqi forces slowly approached Mosul.[132] As IS began experiencing a shortage of seasoned troops, it was forced to begin using younger and inexperienced fighters to defend its strongholds. Some IS fighters fled their positions, and on occasions firefights broke out between different factions, most notably between local and foreign personnel. Finally, while there was no massive uprising by an increasingly resentful population, IS had to take into consideration and guard against the revival of opposition by Sunni insurgent groups who had been erstwhile allies in 2014 but by 2017 had turned against IS and were engaged in a "low-level insurgency" that distracted IS's fighters.[133] In mid-October 2016, just before the Iraqi offensive began, Jaysh al-Rijal al-Tariqa al-Naqshabandiya had started attacking IS, exhorted the people of Mosul to rise up, and for good measure warned the Iraqi government not to let the Shia militias be a part of the liberation of Mosul.[134]

The eastern half of the city was secured in early 2017. In February 2017, Iraqi forces began probing the forward defenses of IS in the western half of the city, across the river, and by the end of the month had secured some important victories, including the recapture of the Mosul airport, despite fierce resistance by IS. By mid-March 2017, Iraqi forces had consolidated themselves firmly on the western side of the city and had begun probing the rabbit warrens of the old city, which was an IS stronghold.[135] The fighting in this sector was essentially close-quarter combat between opposing infantry squads. This should have been a more equal battle for IS fighters. However, despite the horrendous casualties suffered by the Iraqi special operation forces, it was clear that IS's capacity for defensive operations was being steadily eroded as it lost veteran personnel. The IS fighters suffered significant casualties in February and March 2017, including the loss of several middle-ranking commanders (emirs) and skilled fighters. Fighting grew in intensity as Iraqi forces edged bit by bit into the old city neighborhood, which is difficult to negotiate for either tracked or wheeled military vehicles and which the IS fighters had turned into what seemed like their final stronghold. However, the local IS fighters, including younger, less trained recruits from the rural areas outside Mosul, began to desert, leaving only foreign fighters—described as mainly Saudis, Yemenis, Uyghurs, and Central Asians—who had nowhere to go and were easily recognizable if they tried to escape the cordon around Mosul.[136]

Under Pressure: The Islamic State "Returns to Terrorism"
The Terrorism Offensive: 2015–Present

Because IS could not expand by being on the defensive, it returned to its tried and tested offensive operational method—terrorism. From late 2015 to the spring of 2016, IS increased the rate at which it conducted suicide operations against civilians in Iraq and spoiler attacks against concentrations of Iraqi Security Forces.[137] The workshops of IS produced all types of IEDs on an industrial scale, with significant supply chains and funding lines. This allowed IS to employ IEDs in a variety of ways—in defensive and offensive military operations and in terrorism against civilians—and on a scale never seen before.[138]

In response to setbacks in Ramadi, IS stepped up suicide attacks. On January 3, 2016, five suicide bombers killed at least fifteen security personnel and wounded twenty-two others outside a former U.S. base in Tikrit. A few days later, on January 11, IS gunmen wearing suicide vests detonated their explosives inside the Jawhara shopping mall in Baghdad. Not far from that target, IS operatives set off a VBIED, killing eighteen people. This was only in Baghdad; other terrorist suicide attacks took place in Muqdadiya and Baquba.[139] On February 28, 2016, a suicide bomber at a funeral in Iraq's eastern province of Diyala killed at least forty people, while a suicide blast at a security checkpoint in Baghdad's western outskirts killed eight members of the Iraqi Security Forces.

A larger attack in Muqdadiya, fifty miles (eighty kilometers) northeast of Baghdad, killed six local commanders of the umbrella group of Shia militias Hashd al-Shaabi; they were attending the funeral of a commander's

relative. A further fifty-eight people were wounded. The killing of these commanders, four of whom were from the Asaib ahl al-Haq militia and two
from the Badr Organization, was designed to inflame sectarian tensions
in the mixed province. Dozens of angry Shia militiamen went into the
streets vowing revenge. On March 6, 2016, at least fifty people were killed
and seventy others were wounded in yet another IS suicide attack in the
largely Shia city of Hilla, capital of the Iraqi province of Babil, south of
Baghdad.[140] In mid-May 2016, a relentless wave of suicide bombings and
car bombings wreaked havoc in Baghdad; in three consecutive days of
SVBIED and VBIED attacks, IS killed one hundred civilians. The goal was
to put pressure on the beleaguered government of Prime Minister Abadi
and to provoke the Shias.

The carnage continued well into early 2017. It was a clear reflection of
IS being forced back to its more primitive form of warfare (terrorism) to
show that it still had an offensive capability that could cause significant
damage.[141]

Expansion of the Theater of Operations

The Islamic State wished to show the world that even under pressure its
offensive terrorist capabilities would extend beyond its primary theater of
operations, Iraq and Syria. The terrorist carnage in Iraq and Syria was
relentless. However, it was not only those two hapless countries that were
subjected to IS's terrorist onslaught. Relentless shrinkage in the Caliphate's
control over territory resulted in an IS determined to "punish" the outer
ring of enemies: the countries providing the material aid to the Iraqis and
Kurds.[142] The Islamic State looked for ways to strike further afield beyond
Iraq and Syria.[143]

As a result of the large number of European Muslims who have gone
to fight in the "jihad" in Syria and Iraq, European authorities had grown
seriously worried by 2014 of the potential threat posed by battle-trained
and hardened returnees coming back to cause widespread mayhem.[144]
The Islamic State had a ready instrument for waging terrorist assaults in
Europe: the European foreign fighters who were mobilized by the IS's
"External Operations" Department to undertake terrorist actions in Europe.[145]
The European authorities' fears were realized when IS fighters launched
a complex multitarget assault on Paris on November 12, 2015, and then on
Brussels on March 22, 2016, in which thirty civilians were killed by jihadists
associated with IS. These attacks followed a number of similar failed

attempts and represented progress in an evolving IS strategy, as well as a steep change in the intensity of the attacks. Although several attacks have been carried out across western Europe in the past two years between 2015 and 2017 by actors claiming affiliation with IS, the Paris operation, involving well-trained, armed, organized, and coordinated teams of attackers, suggested a key shift in the group's European operations. However, the attacks can also be interpreted as the successful culmination of a strategic progression IS had been attempting to effect for almost two years.

As well as attacking France, IS and its regional affiliates have also targeted Saudi Arabia (the bombing of a mosque in Asir on August 6, 2015, killing 13 Saudi security officers); the Kurds in Turkey (October 10, 2015, bombings at a pro-Kurdish rally in Ankara, killing 102); Russia and Egypt (October 31, 2015, Russian plane crash over the Sinai, killing 224); Jordan (November 9, 2015, shooting at a Jordanian police academy, killing 6, including two Americans); and Hezbollah in Lebanon (November 12, 2015, suicide bombings in a Shia neighborhood in Beirut, killing 43).

The patterns of IS attacks outside its core areas of Iraq and Syria show that its external activity is designed to target states and groups confronting it militarily or conducting counterterrorism campaigns against it. The aim of these attacks has been to show the consequences of confronting IS and to demonstrate these states' inability to protect their own people. They were also intended to undermine social cohesion, for instance by polarizing relations between Sunni and Shia communities in Saudi Arabia and Lebanon. The Islamic State has also aimed to provoke an intensification of operations against it in order to promote support of its narrative of an apocalyptic confrontation and to increase recruitment to its cause.[146]

Breaking with Tradition

The primary focus of this chapter has been to address the jihadist way of warfare from the early days of the Iraqi insurgency to the IS way of warfare in early 2017. The aim has been to put forth a conceptual narrative that describes the tactics, techniques, procedures, and characteristics of this way of war. When a nonstate actor or, as in the case of IS, a nonrecognized state decides to fight, it must decide how it is going to do so and who it is going to target.[147] The repertoire of targets and tactics of an entity such as IS are shaped by ideology (who is the enemy), are restrained (or not) by moral and ethical considerations (do we target civilians and how?), and are circumscribed or enabled by a host of structural factors.[148]

First, insurgents require an operating budget: waging war requires money. Lack of money restricts one's repertoire of tactics and targets; the converse, availability of money, allows the organization to recruit, train, and acquire weapons and ammunition. For example, setting up and maintaining an IED infrastructure required skilled personnel, vehicles, safe houses, and bomb-makers. Money allows one to develop makeshift arms production facilities and to innovate with new tactics and weapons. From the time of Zarqawi to the present (2017), the level of funding available to them has shaped the jihadists' way of war in Iraq. Times of financial constraint have invariably limited the repertoire of tactics.

Second is the issue of the number and quality of personnel: it is clear that a small size and a limited number of quality personnel greatly circumscribe a fighting organization's ability to do much. A greater number and better quality not only allow it to do more but also allow it to develop functionally specialized units, and each one of these can be further trained to develop one particular skill set. Third are the nature and ways of war of the opposing side. To paraphrase the German thinker Carl von Clausewitz, the enemy has a vote. As a fighting organization, IS and its predecessors were acutely aware of the strengths and vulnerabilities of those who had faced them over the course of the past fifteen years (2003–2017) and tailored their ways of warfare to offset their opponents.

Fourth, one of the most important factors in furthering a nonstate actor's military capabilities and effectiveness is the ability to hold and consolidate control over territory. This is essential not only for state-formation (one of the organization's ultimate goals, of course) but also for military purposes. Control over territory allows the nonstate actor to build bases, to experiment out in the open with little fear of disruption, and to evolve from simpler or more "primitive" methods of warfare, such as terrorism, to more advanced methods, such as guerrilla warfare, and ultimately to mobile semiconventional warfare.[149] In short, it is clear that the development of military power beyond mere terrorism by insurgents is highly dependent on securing control over territory.[150]

Theorists and practitioners such as Mao Zedong in China and Vo Nguyen Giap in Vietnam argued for the necessity of sanctuaries and control over territory to enable the upward development of their military capabilities. In traditional insurgency theory and practice, insurgents move up the spectrum of violence from simple terrorism to more advanced and "legitimate" ways of warfare as they became more developed. However, insurgents in the late twentieth and early twenty-first centuries do not give up on their more primitive ways of war, terrorism, and guerrilla warfare even as they acquire territory to develop their operational methods. As a result, these contemporary insurgents, such as the jihadists, will continue to operate across a large spectrum of violence, oscillating between a robust terrorist capability and semiconventional warfare, depending on the enemy and its capabilities.

This is what happened in Iraq with the evolution of Zarqawi's group. In the early years, it struggled to develop its capacities from pure terrorism to guerrilla warfare. Over time, however, Zarqawi's group began to emerge as the leading insurgent group—it received more funds and fighters than its competitors within the insurgent constellation. However, control over territory was tenuous, and the improvement in the enemies' tactics finally reduced Zarqawi's successors, AQI and ISI, to a kind of seminomadic existence moving from one sanctuary to another while fighting a losing battle. This ultimately forced the group back into resorting to terrorism, because it was simply incapable of mounting effective guerrilla attacks or semiconventional assaults.

Reflecting the operational methods of twenty-first-century insurgents, ISI returned to rebuilding its organizational structure and its fighting capabilities as the pressure on it lessened following the United States' withdrawal from Iraq in 2011. Between 2012 and 2016, ISI and its successor, IS, displayed an alarming capability to pursue new tactics associated with advanced insurgent organizations and armies (to attack defended positions, to defend positions itself), to produce existing weapons systems on an industrial scale (car bombs), to develop new weapons (armed light drones), and to adopt subterranean warfare practices copied from other theaters of operation.[151] Many of these new capabilities required the ability to exercise control over territory for an extended period. From late 2015, as IS's territorial control shrank, IS units were reduced to just two operational methods: terrorism (increased attacks against civilians and enemy military forces through car bombs and suicide attacks) and urban defensive warfare (holding defensive positions till death in an attempt to sufficiently attrite the attackers).

By the spring of 2016, IS fighters in Iraq were under significant pressure from the Iraqi Security Forces on multiple fronts.[152] Due to the increasing effectiveness of U.S.-led Coalition air strikes in coordination with the advance of ground forces, IS could no longer conduct offensive operations.[153] It proved resilient on the defense but lost every urban battle from mid-2015 onward. The fact that IS has come under intense pressure on the ground in military operations has forced it to quickly adapt its military posture.

When IS was on the offensive in 2013 and 2014, its units moved in large semiconventional formations. The beginning of air strikes by the United States, however, had a negative impact on IS's quasi-conventional mobile military arm and large-scale patterns of movement on open ground.[154] The group now began preparing for the defensive. Once the air strikes began, they adapted, ditching conspicuous convoys in favor of motorcycles and ordinary cars.[155] They also reduced the number of checkpoints and cut back on mobile phone use to prevent interception of their communications. The commanders dispersed their command centers and began to rely on couriers for communications between units. Furthermore, IS fighters disappeared from streets, and IS redeployed weapons and fighters and cut down its media exposure.

In perhaps the most obvious indication that its combat units feared air power and its impact, they took to digging trenches in and tunnels under the cities they occupied.[156] They emptied out their bases and training installations and thinned out their presence in government buildings they had previously occupied. They also took cover or set up their installations within neighborhoods and planted their black flags on civilian homes in order to confuse planning for air strikes.[157]

Being forced onto the defensive after three years of offensive operations constituted a significant setback for an entity that prided itself on its motto of "baqiya wa tamadud" (remaining and expanding). Rather, it is disappearing and contracting. However, losing territory due to consistent air strikes and the improved fighting prowess of its opposing ground forces was not enough to dismantle or destroy IS. It has proven to be extremely resilient, and its survival in the face of recent setbacks is largely due to the fact that it has operated across the spectrum of violence—ranging from terrorism to semiconventional warfare and back to terrorism. Even as IS showed immense flexibility and innovativeness in the military arena, mercifully this was not paralleled in its governance and state-formation activities in Iraq.

6

Organizing to Build Caliphate 3.0

STATE-FORMATION AND NATION-BUILDING
UNDER THE ISLAMIC STATE

ON JUNE 29, 2014, ISIS declared the establishment of the Caliphate (IS). At the time it was not clear whether the declaration was a stroke of genius or a monumental blunder. By declaring the Caliphate (IS), the organization had upstaged its rival al-Qaeda and was able to draw growing numbers of adherents. The proclamation of the Caliphate was a momentous event, and it resonated with a large number of people throughout the Muslim world for whom religious unity under a caliphate remained a desirable goal. Others were perplexed or bemused. Most Muslims did not understand the divisive debates within jihadist circles concerning the sustainability and desirability of a caliphate at that juncture.[1]

From the vantage point of mid-2017, the declaration looks like a monumental blunder. Setting up a state with a "footprint," including territorial control and governance, allowed the Caliphate's enemies to target it. Instead, some jihadists argued that the focus should have been on fighting and on slow but steady incremental progress toward the ultimate goal.[2] Al-Qaeda's ambivalence stemmed not from an ideological antipathy toward the aspirational goal of a caliphate but largely from the fact that it was not feasible. Zawahiri, the head of al-Qaeda, had clearly declared years back in his memoir, *Knights under the Prophet's Banner*, that the jihadist movement must seek to control a portion of land in the heart of the Islamic world, where it would establish a territorial entity, which would function as the base for the struggle to restore the caliphate. There was also an increasingly pragmatic tendency within al-Qaeda that seemed to believe that if the infidels were kicked out, "apostate" Muslim rulers overthrown, and the various Muslim states became Islamic, that is to say, ruled by sharia, without joining together as a suprastate, that was victory enough. Moreover, given that the Caliphate that Abu Bakr al-Baghdadi and his colleagues had built was on the path toward collapse due to external and internal pressures that had been steadily mounting against it from 2015 into mid-2017, it was not surprising that many, including in the wider jihadist world, began to see it as a failed experiment. The end of the Caliphate will not necessarily mean the end of IS, but it will not be a "state" after the collapse in Syria and Iraq, merely a terrorist-cum-insurgent entity, albeit a strong and ruthless one, in a sea of such entities in both countries. However, as long as these two countries are not "fixed," IS will undoubtedly seek a comeback.

The intensified pressure that IS has come under between 2016 and mid-2017, which included substantial loss of territory, reduced financial capabilities, and a greater focus on fighting desperately merely to *exist*, has effectively meant the end of its state-formation and nation-building enterprises. After all, when faced with a fight for its life with increasingly limited resources, the governance enterprise fell by the wayside. In this context, one could conclude that addressing this joint state-formation and nation-building enterprise is now of merely historical interest. It is, however, important to examine, both as an example of IS's determination to create a state ruled by divine law and as a case study of rebel governance.

What facilitated the establishment of IS in 2014? The vulnerabilities and failures of the Iraqi and Syrian governments, which were occasioned by civil conflict and internal war, provided the *opportunity* for ISIS to exploit the situation to its advantage. However, mere opportunity is not enough. The leadership of ISIS capitalized on the unfortunate situations within both countries and formulated and implemented a proactive strategy specifically designed to take advantage of fissures and fragility within a state and society and that enabled it to move forward toward establishing IS.

Why the Caliphate was established, how the Caliphate rules, what its vulnerabilities are, how successfully it handled resources and opposition, and how successfully it earned legitimacy (or failed to) are important questions. By the end of 2014, IS was functioning like a state, having established an administrative infrastructure and extended its rule over the population under its sway.[3] From day one, IS tried to convince itself, the population under its control, and the outside world that its state-formation and nation-building efforts were doing well, judging by the amount of propaganda it put out to show its achievements in these areas and to entice Muslims to migrate to it.

As time went by, the facts on the ground highlighted the enormous complexities of state-formation and nation-building, particularly under conditions of external pressure, in the shape of constant warfare. The state-formation enterprise of IS failed because its "primitive" economic base was unable to sustain its war machine, constant war against its enemies, and provision of social services all at the same time.[4] In the history of state-formation, some entities succeed in managing these complex tasks, and indeed, as many political scientists and sociologists have pointed out, war in many instances has promoted the emergence and consolidation of states.[5] But it was increasingly evident by mid-2017 that it was not happening in this particular case.[6]

The Islamic State's nation-building enterprise of creating an "Islamic nation" of believing Muslims failed for many reasons. It was not able to create and sustain legitimacy among its "citizens," which resulted from its failure to provide social services after its brief euphoric "moment" of mid- to late 2014, its capricious and terroristic behavior, and, last but not least, the fact that many of the local "citizens" in Iraq and Syria were not so much attracted to its ideology as they were repelled by their own respective governments. Many local citizens were appalled by IS's version of Islam, specifically its intolerance, its perception of the world in terms of black and white, and its brutalities. To be sure, the foreign migrants were attracted to IS because of ideology for the most part, and indeed, this difference between an increasingly ambivalent local population and the migrants caused social friction that exploded into violence. In the final analysis, though, IS did not face severe internal pressure in the shape of an unmanageable insurgency against it either in Iraq or Syria or in both at the same time. However, a sullen and seething population that IS increasingly could not trust was not a good thing to be faced with when fighting your external enemies.

A Failing Iraq: Setting the Stage for the Caliphate

What helped facilitate the establishment of IS was the rot within the Iraqi body politic; always below the surface while the Americans were the dominant force, it burst forth into the open when they left at the end of December 2011.[7] On December 14, 2011, just two weeks before the American withdrawal, President Barack Obama told a military audience at Fort Bragg, North Carolina: "We're leaving behind a sovereign, stable and self-reliant Iraq. The war in Iraq will soon belong to history."[8] His words have proven to be just as misplaced, though not as well known, as President Bush's infamous "mission accomplished" banner at the "end" of "Operation Iraqi Freedom" in May 2003. As a state and a nation, Iraq continues to fail due to catastrophic decisions taken by people both foreign and Iraqi. While the Americans failed in their state-formation and nation-building efforts between 2003 and 2011, the failures between 2011 and 2017 were almost entirely the fault of the Iraqi government and people.[9]

The Trials and Tribulations of Nuri al-Maliki

When Nuri al-Maliki became prime minister of Iraq in 2006, the Americans were understandably wary of a man whom they knew little about, and what little they knew did not inspire confidence.[10] He seemed slow and indolent, though that seemed to be a function of trying to appease many conflicting constituencies. The Sunni community suspected him of being too close to Iran and of being discriminatory against the Sunnis because of his own personal experiences at the hands of Saddam Hussein's regime.[11] United States officials thought he would not be able to deal with the armed groups and vocal political parties emerging in the country. He seemed to have assuaged their worries by taking decisive political action against obstreperous groups, such as the Shia militia of the mercurial Moqtada al-Sadr, leader of a militant Shia faction, even though the Iraqi army had to be bailed out by the Americans. Maliki also said the right things about his commitment to democracy and continuing Iraq's relationship with the United States. Yet the Americans continued to read Maliki incorrectly. He stood up to the United States by refusing to sign a new Status of Forces Agreement, which would have allowed a limited number of U.S. forces to remain in his country to ensure a smooth transition to a secure Iraq. Once the Americans withdrew, it was left to the Iraqis to build their new country or fail in trying. They would no longer be able to pin all the blame on the "external presence," the Americans. However, Maliki failed to give Iraq its much-needed lease on life, and the efforts of his successor, Haider al-Abadi, to do so are not guaranteed to succeed, despite the costly but successful offensive to retake Mosul.

Maliki was no democrat, but to be fair, neither were many of those who opposed and despised him. His rule over Iraq proved authoritarian and sectarian.[12] Unsure of his power base in a fragile and traumatized country, Maliki created and sought to maintain a highly personal and centralized system of government, which alienated a large segment of the Iraqi political elite and population. He tightened his grip over the military and security services, which he reorganized as a source of patronage, purged them of their more competent elements in favor of individuals loyal to him, and supplemented his power with sectarian Shia militias.[13] It was these political actions, among other things, that contributed to the dismal performance of the Iraqi military described in chapter 5. As of mid-2017, three mutually exclusive enterprises were at loggerheads: the Shia-dominated Iraqi central state, the stealthy but steady efforts of the Iraqi Kurds toward de facto freedom from control by the central government in Baghdad, and the efforts of IS in parts of Iraq and Syria.[14] The government was buoyed by its defeats of IS in 2016 and 2017. However, it was clear that there were going to be issues to resolve with the Kurds. As the Iraqi state teetered on the edge of a precipice in 2014 after its stunning defeats, the Kurds, who were fighting for their lives against IS, could not conceal their glee. They saw the impending collapse of the Iraqi state as their opportunity to claim independence, particularly after they seized land that did not belong to them.[15] However, reality set in as the Kurds realized quite quickly that they were not prepared for independence; their "armed forces" were dilapidated and in serious need of restructuring. Kurdish officers complained about the state of the Peshmerga, and politicians in the Kurdish region realized that they had to work with Baghdad to deal with the dire threat IS posed.[16] But this was nothing more than an alliance of convenience.

Maliki's authoritarianism and the persistent problems with the Kurds were not the only destabilizing factor. He had a serious Sunni problem.[17] The government would not commit to promises it had made to the Sunni militias who had turned against AQI and then ISI years earlier. Maliki had promised to integrate the Sunni insurgent groups and tribal fighters, known as the Sahwa (Awakening), who had turned on the jihadists, into the official security forces or find them alternative employment. Members of these Sunni armed groups complained that the government only begrudgingly paid them and had integrated only a few hundred of them into security services. In fact, the security services began to harass or even arrest leaders and foot soldiers of the Awakening movement. As the pressure on the Sahwa mounted, the Americans turned a blind eye to its problems with the Iraqi government. As a result, the Sunni community and the Sahwa fighters, who could have been useful in the fight against IS, grew wary of both Maliki and the Americans.

Maliki's government was in no mood to bargain with the Sunni community. It did not feel the need to "reward" the former Sunni insurgents for fighting the jihadist extremists of AQI and then of ISI. By the late summer of 2008, Maliki seemed bent on delegitimizing the Sahwa as much as possible.[18] In Diyala, hundreds of members of the movement were arrested as part of large-scale security operations by the Iraqi Security Forces.[19] The government itself claimed that it could not continue to support or justify the continued existence of armed nonstate actors, though it conveniently ignored the dangers posed by the Shia militias. Sunnis were not convinced by the comments of Jalal al-Din al-Saghir, an influential Shia member of Parliament, who stated: "the state cannot accept the Awakening. When the government attacked the Mahdi Army, it sent the message to all the militias including the Awakening that their days are numbered."[20] When the Sunnis inconveniently pointed out that certain Shia militias aligned with the government or protected by Iran were not harassed, Baghdad had no answer. An Iraqi army brigadier, Nasser al-Hiti, commander of the Fifth Muthanna Brigade, referred to the Awakening fighters in less than flattering terms: "These people are a cancer, and we must remove them."[21] Iraqi insurgent groups that had not joined the Sahwa movement pressured the tribal militias to join them in opposition to the Maliki government. Indeed, a number of the Sahwa fighters began preparing for a return to confrontation with the government and reached out to their Iraqi colleagues in the insurgency who were also readying for violence.

In his effort to "dump" Sunnis from sensitive positions within the government, Maliki launched a new round of de-Baathification—removing from power those with links to the defunct Baathist regime—thus reopening a divisive political issue. On October 24–25, 2011, two months before the American exit, over six hundred individuals were arrested across the country. Most were accused of being part of a Baathist plot aimed at toppling the political system. Some 140 administrators and professors at the University of Tikrit were expelled from their positions on de-Baathification charges.[22] Less than twenty-four hours after the last convoy of U.S. troops left Iraq in December 2011, Maliki ordered the arrest of Vice President Tariq al-Hashimi, the highest ranking Sunni Arab politician in the government. The government accused Hashimi of running a death squad that assassinated police officers and government officials. Hashimi fled to the Kurdish autonomous region, where the Kurds were delighted to grant him asylum. Maliki used the draconian antiterrorism laws to detain tens of thousands of Sunni men, many of them for years and often without access to lawyers or their families.

As relations between the Baghdad government and the Sunni provinces deteriorated, the Sunnis launched a protest movement. Sunni protestors set up "protest camps" in Ramadi and Fallujah.[23] Their existence alarmed Maliki, all the more so because of the provocative statements that emanated from rather excitable Sunni ringleaders, many of whom fancifully thought that the hour of the Sunni Arab return to power was at hand. Maliki himself was paranoid and did believe that the Sunni goal was to return to power and that the community had the means to do so. The fact that the Shias—the majority of the population—were now firmly ensconced in power did not reassure this insecure leader. He was determined to show the Sunnis who was boss, and he massed security forces to shut down the protest camps.[24] Anbar province erupted in violence. Maliki escalated by surrounding Fallujah and Ramadi—the epicenters of Sunni discontent since 2003—with troops and beginning to shell them. Fifty Sunni parliamentarians resigned, and the Sunni police in both cities deserted en masse. The government ordered the army to leave, which then opened the doors for ISI fighters to move into the Sunni cities.[25] The Sunnis accused the government of using Shia sectarian militias to massacre members of the Sunni community and suggested that the current leadership had not learned from former Iraqi rulers' mistreatment of other communities.[26]

The Rage of the Dispossessed: Iraq's Sunnis under the Shia

It would be remiss to concentrate only on Maliki's failures without addressing those of the Sunni community as well, which for the longest time, from the early days of the American invasion and occupation, refused to acknowledge its demographic minority status in Iraq and accept its reduced political clout.[27] By 2012, some within the Sunni community became acquainted with reality and even promoted the idea of an autonomous Sunni region.[28] It was, however, hard for the Sunnis to become accustomed to minority status or even the status of a religious sect, having been acculturated for decades to see themselves as the majority and as simply *Muslims*. The Sunnis viewed the concepts of autonomy or even federalism with suspicion.[29]

As protests gathered pace, the Sunni community became more mobilized politically, and the former insurgents vowed to take up arms again, there was a sense that the time had come to deal the Shia-dominated government a major blow.[30] The idea of autonomy was submerged in the euphoria with which many within the Sunni community—even those who had no love for ISIS—greeted the jihadists' easy trouncing of the Iraqi government's forces in 2014. For many Sunnis it seemed that the recovery of Baghdad was within reach. As ISIS flung its forces against the hapless Iraqi military in the summer of 2014, delusional Sunnis within Baghdad, mostly associated with the insurgency of 2003–2011, actually thought that their time to rise up against the Shia government in Baghdad was at hand and were dismayed that the ISIS forces stopped in Salah al-Din province north of Baghdad.[31] The hopeful Sunni would-be rebels betrayed their ignorance of professional military considerations. Having outrun its supply lines, ISIS thought better of launching a hasty onslaught on Baghdad without preparation. The ISIS leadership ultimately realized that seizing Baghdad, which was protected by a roused Shia population who believed they were in an existential battle, was never going to be an easy proposition.

Sunnis' frustration, and indeed, susceptibility to ISIS and then IS, was compounded by their weakness in local and national politics, where they were the weakest of the three communities that made up the majority of the Iraqi population. The promises made by the myriad individuals who claimed to represent them never came through. Sheikh Ahmed Abu Risha, one of the major players in the Sahwa, told Dubai TV in late 2008: "Political work means rallying the people to participate in the elections and bring forth efficient and trustworthy people who are known for their experience, competence, good governance, and integrity. Furthermore, we will be capitalizing on our social relations with the tribes and sponsoring the resolution of their disputes and conflicts in order to turn them into a strong support structure for these politicians we intend on nominating to the electoral process."[32] A tribal coalition that came to power in Anbar in early 2009 did nothing for the people living there.[33] The provincial elections at the end of January 2009 were supposed to enfranchise people in the province and address their demands.[34] The provincial politicians, including the tribal leaders, who were basking in the glow of new-found importance as the victors over the jihadists, "talked the talk" about honest representation in Baghdad and new socioeconomic projects in the Sunni areas.[35] The provincial government of Anbar received hundreds of millions of dollars for reconstruction and economic recovery. However, these projects never materialized, and the Sunni politicians only enriched themselves.[36] An Anbar businessman referred to the provincial politicians as "thugs" rolling in money.[37] As a result, the Sunni Sahwa leaders lost a lot of their support within the Sunni community.

Maliki's paranoid style and divisive policies and the pusillanimity of Sunni leaders provided the opportunistic opening for IS to insinuate itself again into the sympathetic Sunni provinces. However, the issue was much deeper than Maliki's style and Sunni failures. What the neat previous explanation ignores is the reality that newly found Shia chauvinism and paranoia came headlong into conflict with deeply established Sunni chauvinism and revanchism. For the Shias, any set of meaningful concessions to the Sunnis raised fears about the longevity of the Shias' new hegemony in Iraq. For the Sunnis, it was inconceivable that the Shias could represent Iraq, and, for many of them, any meaningful political solution could only come with their return to power, though a number were increasingly realizing that the dream of a return to hegemony was delusional and put them in the uncomfortable position of agreeing with some of the more rabid anti-Shia rants of the Islamists and sharing some of the "centralized state" delusions of the Baathists and hardcore Arab nationalists.

Instead, these more pragmatic members of the Sunni elite considered the idea of promoting greater autonomy and self-governance for a wide Sunni region in Iraq. Before the notion could get much traction, the jihadists pounced and set about establishing their vision of an Islamic state. Some Sunni groups aided the jihadist campaign in the forlorn hope that they could use the jihadists and emerge as the eventual victors in a marriage of convenience with them. Others watched from the sidelines with considerable foreboding, recognizing that the jihadists were hijacking the Sunni revolt or, more accurately, using it against Maliki so as to come to power.[38]

"The Administration of Savagery": Plotting the Reemergence of the Islamic State

Watching gleefully from the sidelines as the Sunni community and Maliki feuded was the revitalized ISI under its new leader, Abu Bakr al-Baghdadi. *Opportunity*, reflected in the rampant dysfunction within the Iraqi body politic just described, coincided with the adoption and implementation of a new *strategy* by the jihadists, which propelled them to statehood in June 2014 as IS.

The Management of Savagery

Understanding the foundation and strategic rationale behind IS's approach to establishing the Caliphate is important.[39] A jihadist strategic book written by one Abu Bakr Naji heavily influenced the jihadists in Iraq. The tract, *Idarat al-Tawahush: Akhtar Marhala Satamurru biha al-umma* (The Management of Savagery: The Most Dangerous Stage through Which the Umma Will Pass), appeared in 2004 to great acclaim in jihadist circles as offering a way to fight a set of enemies who were much stronger. Naji's main focus in his book was on the strategy for attaining an Islamic state in the face of violent opposition from powerful foes. Planning and waging war for him was a "function of practical reason, not religious law."[40] There were a number of states in the Islamic world, wrote Naji, against which the mujahidin forces should concentrate their political and military efforts.[41] Incidentally, at the beginning of the book, he presented a list of countries that did not include Iraq; however, later on he cited approvingly the hard-hitting blows being delivered there against the enemy. Presumably he was referring to the actions undertaken by Zarqawi and his organization in the period 2003–2004.

The "priority group" (of targeted states) that Naji listed should be subjected, he said, to the "power of vexation and exhaustion," that is, constant small or medium-sized harassment operations to "vex" the targeted government, annoying and forcing it to overreact, and "exhausting" its forces by forcing it to spread them thinly throughout the battle arena. Why were these "priority states" so designated? The geography and topography of each provided an environment in which the jihadists could operate. *This was not the case, as Zarqawi complained, in Iraq.* Each of these priority states, Naji said, suffered from structural weaknesses, including lack of elite consensus, weak legitimacy, and the state's inability to enforce its writ over periphery regions. In those countries the jihadist fighters would be aided by the existence of sympathizers and other jihadist forces. While the geography and topography of Iraq were not conducive to guerrilla war, the Iraqi state's structural weaknesses and demographic divisions did provide opportunities for causing problems for the Iraqi government and its patron, the United States.

According to Naji, the incumbent state's forces would have to disperse over a wide area in order to deal with these small and medium-sized attacks. Ultimately the effects of these sustained attacks would compel the exhausted government forces to withdraw from remote and untenable regions and to concentrate in safer areas. By then the ability of the central government to "project power" into its more peripheral regions would be sufficiently attenuated. These small jihadist victories would attract more youth to the jihadist enterprise. These peripheral regions would be subject to chaos and mayhem—"savagery"—since the writ of the state would no longer exist. The jihadists must then move in to establish control, implement the divine law (sharia), impose their governance, and provide the people with basic services, security, and stability.

The jihadists would have to "administer the regions of savagery" and be ruthless and determined in their methods. Jihad, or fighting, was about violence; it was not about Islam. Those who studied jihad "theoretically will never grasp this point well," wrote Naji. The youth in the contemporary umma, he emphasized, "regrettably do not understand the nature of wars." Hence they must be introduced to and immersed in violence with all its ugliness. In this context, the jihadist "prestate" must establish a fighting society with a high level of combat efficiency. However, he warned, setting up a state was not all about fighting. The jihadists must train a cadre of managers and administrators with specialized skill sets. This "prestate" or entity must also set up an intelligence structure whose goal would be to infiltrate its enemies and the institutions of the state, such as the security services and police, political parties, media, and economic institutions. It was permissible for the embryonic jihadist entity to seek allies and establish coalitions with other groups as long as they pledged allegiance to the embryonic state. The emerging state must have a media strategy designed to attract the masses to its side and to foment dissent and defeatism among enemy forces.

Naji's work appeared in hard copy in 2004; it circulated among jihadist circles and then appeared online in 2005. Zarqawi had already started waging a form of warfare in Iraq in 2003, which seems to have strongly hewn to what Naji said in his book. This suggests one of two possibilities: Zarqawi was already familiar with Naji's ideas before they appeared in print, or Naji's ideas of war were a combination of lessons learned in Afghanistan during and after the Soviet interlude (including the rise and fall of the Taliban regime) and formed Zarqawi's modus operandi in Iraq *between 2003 and 2004*. However, given the chronological timeline, it is not clear to me that Naji's book influenced Zarqawi at the beginning of his savage assault on Iraq. It may have reinforced him in the righteousness of his strategy when it was published in 2004.

At any rate, the influence of Naji's book on Zarqawi's successors has been established. According to Hassan Hassan, a well-known expert on jihadist strategic theory and practice, IS personnel have confirmed that the book has been part of IS's curriculum.[42] Hassan Hassan cites an unnamed IS cleric who claimed that Naji's book was widely read among military commanders as a way to justify their strategy on the ground and the widespread use of savagery (brutality) against their enemies. Another member, said Hassan Hassan, gave a list of books and ideologies that influenced IS, which included Naji's book. The article "Hijrah to Khilafa" in the first issue of IS's glossy propaganda magazine *Dabiq* states that the "goal of establishing the Khilafa has always been one that occupied the hearts of the mujahidin since the revival of Jihad this century," adding that the question of how to achieve it has long remained unanswered. The Islamic State proposes a militant path, which must begin with hijra to a land with weak central authority "to use as a base where a jamaa—group—can form, recruit members and train them."[43] Specifically, the article lists Yemen, Mali, Somalia, Sinai Peninsula, Waziristan (Pakistan), Libya, Chechnya, and Nigeria, as well as remote parts of Tunisia, Algeria, Indonesia, and the Philippines. This is quite similar to what Naji stated in his huge tract, leading one to conclude that the *Dabiq* article's list was taken from his book.

If a land with a weak central authority is not available, the article suggests, such a place can be formed through a long campaign of *nikayah* (vexation) attacks carried out by underground mujahid cells, which will compel "apostate forces" to partially withdraw from rural territory and regroup in major urban regions. Accordingly, the goal of these attacks is to allow the jihadists to "take advantage of the situation by increasing the chaos to a point leading to complete collapse of the regime in entire areas."[44] The jihadists can fill the vacuum by managing the state of affairs to the point of developing a full-fledged state and continuing to expand into territory still under control of the regime.[45]

Implementation of Savagery

The effort to implement "savagery" began in 2008, even as the entity pursuing it at the time, ISI, was failing. A letter found in a raid on an ISI hideout in March 2008, by an operative named "Abu Sufyan," outlined a strategy to destabilize Iraq by targeting Sahwa members, economic infrastructure, and Shias. Dozens of Sahwa fighters and their leaders were killed in 2008 and 2009. In 2010, as ISI was struggling, it published an operational booklet, *Khouta Istratigya li Taaziz al-Mawqif al-Siyasi al-Daw-lat al-Islamiya fi al-Iraq* (A Strategic Plan to Improve the Political Position of the Islamic State of Iraq), which seemed to build on Naji's strategy for attacking the enemy. The strategic plan to "improve the position of Islamic State; [so that] therefore it will be more powerful politically and militar-ily . . . so the Islamic [State] project will be ready to take over all Iraq after the enemy troops withdraw," required the implementation of several steps simultaneously.[46] The plan called for the unification of the mujahidin's efforts under a united leadership that would be able to reinforce and sustain IS. It also called for military operations against the "Crusader" forces and the Iraqi Security Forces and the assassination of important political and military leaders. Finally, it called for the jihadists' own Sahwa (Awakening), which would seek allies among the tribes and exploit the grievances of the disgruntled Sunni community.

Not surprisingly, mayhem reappeared in Iraq with the reemergence of ISI. The organization resorted to terrorism against civilians both Shia and Sunni, attacks on infrastructure, and assassinations of Sahwa personnel. The head of ISI issued a call for the Sunnis to return to the fold or to face certain death. By 2012, ISI began to attack Sunni members of the Iraqi Security Forces as well, and as its capabilities grew, it launched small-unit assaults against police stations. A jihadist suicide bomber killed a leading anti-ISI tribal leader from Fallujah, Sheikh Aifan al-Issawi, in January 2013. A sniper killed the mayor of Fallujah, Adnan Hussein al-Dulaimi, in the neighborhood of al-Shuhada on November 13, 2013. Further north, in Nineveh province, a string of assassinations of provincial officials succeeded in gutting the administration of the province long before the jihadists' sudden sweep of it and seizure of Mosul in 2014.[47] This was crowned by the infliction of a mass atrocity on the albu-Nimr Sunni tribe in Anbar province: a massacre of seven hundred males in October and November 2014.[48]

The Emergence of the Caliphate

The Islamic State would have us believe that we have witnessed the rebirth of the caliphate. I choose to call their enterprise Caliphate 3.0 to indicate that there have been three major historical episodes of the caliphate. The first encompassed the Rightly Guided Caliphs, who followed the Prophet Mohammad after his death in 632 AD, and the not so rightly guided caliphs who ruled right up to the Mongols' bloody destruction of the caliphate in 1258. The second caliphate, after a period of dynasties competing for the legitimacy it provided, came when the rising Ottoman power seized the mantle for itself in 1517 and held it until 1924, when it was "finally" abolished by the founders of the modern secular Turkish state, to the dismay of a large element of the umma.

It was Zarqawi's dream to establish a caliphate. It was left to his successors to realize his ultimate goal and ambition. They began setting the stage shortly after his death. On November 14, 2006, the jihadist website Keepers of the Promise posted an article, "Al-Qa'ida between a Past Stage and One Announced by Al-Muhajir," by "Yaman Mukhaddab," analyzing a November 10, 2006, statement made by then ISI deputy commander Abu Hamza al-Muhajir. This statement announced the dividing line between two stages in AQI's jihad in Iraq: "We announce today the end of one stage of jihad and the beginning of a new, important stage in which we lay the first of its bricks to inaugurate the project of the Islamic caliphate and restore the glory of the faith." In this new stage, AQI, now rebranded ISI, was going to lay the foundations for the reemergence of the caliphate. Under Abu Omar al-Baghdadi, ISI would restore God's sovereignty on earth by establishing Islamic rule, liberate Muslims from "enslavement," and guide them back to their religion.

With the formation of ministries and the appointment of governors to areas under its control as a reflection of its "statehood," ISI sought to adopt a more institutionalized formula to achieve its ideal caliphate. However, ISI under Abu Omar al-Baghdadi was a weak entity. The "state" ISI was so keen to establish lacked legitimacy, as it was viewed with derision by Iraqis, insurgents, and others. Al-Qaeda Central poured scorn over Abu Omar al-Baghdadi's aim to set up an Islamic state, and the nearly imperceptible ideological crack that had arisen under Zarqawi turned into a yawning chasm. Al-Qaeda Central was a little concerned by what it perceived as a precipitous declaration of a state, given ISI's lack of resources, solid control over people, and tenuous territorial jurisdiction.

The Islamic State of Iraq was nowhere near moving toward the ultimate goal of a caliphate. The "state," such as it was, was also facing collapse due to pressures from Sunni insurgents, the U.S. special operation forces, and the Iraqi government's security forces.[49] The biggest problem facing ISI was the lack of personnel to run the state or fight. Its personnel were either on the run, dead, captured, or fighting for their lives and did not have the time to run a state. The creation of elaborate ministries— including a Ministry of Fisheries, which was hardly a priority—was a façade. Furthermore, the military pressure being brought to bear on ISI was slowly but surely attenuating its territories and killing its personnel, whether military or administrative. The organization found itself squeezed out of the Sunni provinces of Anbar and Salah al-Din and mixed provinces like Diyala. Furthermore, the death of Zarqawi did not lessen the jihadists' reign of terror, which massively alienated potential supporters. The loss of support from the Sunni tribes and Iraqi insurgents accelerated because of ISI's brutality, its attempts to muscle in on Sunni economic enterprises, and its propensity for messing around with Sunni tribal mores and customs. The first Islamic state project was a colossal failure; it was not surprising, then, that it was never going to be the solid foundation for moving forward toward the establishment of the Caliphate.

Ultimately ISI remnants retreated to the north to Nineveh province, where they continued to be subjected to devastating attacks by U.S. forces that further decimated their ranks. Abu Omar al-Baghdadi's efforts to lay the ground for the third historical stage of the caliphate proved a catastrophic failure. The "state" did not have the trappings or institutions required of a state. It was hardly the stepping stone to the return of the caliphate.

The surviving cadre reformulated their strategy for re-creating the Islamic state and the necessary administrative structures it would need to sustain it. To plot its return as a state, ISI adopted a diabolically clever strategy of state-formation inspired by Abu Bakr Naji. The real change for ISI occurred under the leadership of Abu Bakr al-Baghdadi who took over after Abu Omar al-Baghdadi's death in 2010. The opportunities for revival were increased by the start of the Syrian civil war in 2011, by the U.S. withdrawal from Iraq at the end of 2011, and by the growing alienation of the Sunni community in Iraq.

Rebranded as ISIS, the leadership also began to think in grandiose terms. They intended to set up a caliphate. The doctrinal basis for the establishment of the Caliphate was laid out a year in advance in "Madd al-ayadi li-bayaat al-Baghdadi" which was released on July 22, 2013. Written by Sheikh Turki Binali, this work describes the traditional conditions of eligibility for a male individual to become the caliph and lays out Abu Bakr al-Baghdadi's alleged fulfillment of them: membership in the Qureish tribe, piety, sound mind and body, wisdom, jihadist experience, and so on. Senior Salafist thinkers, including Maqdisi, concluded that the organization's leadership was preparing for the declaration of the Caliphate under Abu Bakr al-Baghdadi. The recognition that ISIS was thinking of taking this momentous step roiled the jihadist world. Other Islamist groups, from al-Qaeda to the mainstream Muslim Brotherhood, have argued that the umma has to be prepared and educated through a long process of proselytization (*dawa*) before the ideal Islamic state can be founded. For ISIS and its leadership the establishment of the Caliphate has a more immediate time frame and requires the use of force to overthrow all apostate governments. ISIS wanted to establish a state as the prelude to the end of days. This event is supposed to take place in the insignificant Syrian town of Dabiq (former population four thousand), where the Romans (Christians) and the remaining "true" Muslims will fight each other in the apocalyptic battle to herald the end of days.[50]

What is this caliphate that all shades of Islamists talk about and aspire to? The term "caliphate" (*khilafa*) derives from the word "caliph" (successor), referring to those who ruled as successors to the Prophet Mohammad. The different trends of political Islam seek to reestablish what they see as a glorious past in which the historical caliphate was a global power ruling over the umma.[51] However, historically there has been no consensus among Islamic philosophers and thinkers concerning the qualifications of the caliph and his "job description." Ironically, the thinker the Salafi-jihadists admire greatly, Ibn Taymiyya, actually did not discuss the caliphate and its tasks in detail in his various writings. He stressed that governance in Islam was needed to maintain, protect, and further the religion. By way of contrast, Abu al-Hasan Ali Ibn Habib al-al-Mawardi (972–1058) waxed lyrical about the caliph's qualifications and "job description" in his work *Al-Ahkam al-Sultaniyya* (The Ordinances of Government).

The setting up of an Islamic state required the setting up of the administrative and regulatory instruments required to create an Islamic society ruled by divine law, to control the population and ensure that they did not deviate from the path of righteousness, to defend the caliphate against its enemies, both internal and external, and to provide public services.[52] The concept of *al-siyasa al-shariyya* authorized the caliph and his subordinates to determine the manner in which sharia should be administered in the real world and particularly in the contemporary world, where situations existed with which sharia was not familiar. Within the formula of *al-siyasa al-shariyya*, the ruler and his subordinates were authorized to implement any measure, enact policies, and follow rules that they deemed in the interest of the state (*maslaha*), as long as it did not violate sharia.[53]

State-Formation and Nation-Building

Less than a month after the announcement on June 29, 2014, of the establishment of the Caliphate, Abu Bakr al-Baghdadi began the process of legitimizing, sustaining, and building the "state." History shows, as the political scientist Charles Tilly has pointed out in numerous studies, that state-formation and nation-building enterprises are not bloodless activities. Following from Tilly, other noted observers have pointed out that these twin activities involve efforts to consolidate control over territory and people, and even expand, and to enforce legitimacy internally. The process involves monopolizing the growing entity's control over the instruments of violence by taking them out of the hands of competitors. State-formation requires providing services and protection for the population, driving out or killing those who are "different" or who do not conform, and last but not least, fighting off external threats. These are complex tasks that require financial resources.

The first objective of IS was to acquire territory. Closely connected to this objective was to ensure that the state remained (*baqiya*), consolidated, and then expanded (*tamaddud*) its borders. Achieving this objective required following the example of the Prophet Mohammad and using military force to defeat those who resisted the establishment of the Caliphate. Following this reasoning, IS considered it permissible to use its military force against a broad range of adversaries, including Sunni Muslim rivals as well as the obvious enemies within the territories of the Caliphate. This approach enabled IS to expand its territory into new areas, where the imposition of its own rules, the enforced co-optation of local groups, and the provision of some form of local governance were typically the first steps undertaken to consolidate its control. The broader objective of IS was to expand the borders of the Caliphate. This territorial expansion of the Caliphate was not subordinate to its consolidation of power; rather, the two projects of remaining and expanding were to be undertaken simultaneously. The thinking was that the more the Caliphate consolidated, the better it was placed to expand. The more it expanded, the more people and resources it could acquire. The more people and resources, the more permanent the Caliphate would be. The logic is impeccably Cartesian. Abu Bakr al-Baghdadi stated that the objective was to reclaim all the places where Muslims' rights had been usurped: China, India, Palestine, Morocco, Somalia, the Arabian Peninsula, Iran, Pakistan, Tunisia, Libya, Algeria. Although IS recognized that expanding their state would require time and perseverance, they believed in creating chaos in order to establish themselves elsewhere in the Middle East and North Africa. The spreading of chaos would eventually destabilize the enemy regime and allow the organization to fill the vacuum by starting to develop a full state and continue to expand into further territory under the enemy regime's control.[54]

The territories IS brought under its control were divided into administrative units called *wilayat* (the traditional name for geographically designated units within the Islamic empire), and an appointed official (wali) governed each *wilaya* (province). Senior officials under the wali's command were called emirs. The emir was the highest authority in his sector. Under him were subordinate leaders with specific functions: sharia emirs, and military and security emirs, for example. The emirs oversaw the administration and set up sharia courts, local police, and economic administration and took over the following services: education, health, telecom, and electricity. Initially, in contrast with its predecessor, ISI under Abu Omar al-Baghdadi, IS strove to avoid a proliferation of "unnecessary" or redundant emirs. However, despite the hierarchical nature of the organization, control at the lower provincial levels was not as stringent, and large numbers of unscrupulous and opportunistic individuals emerged as emirs and contributed enormously to the rise of corruption and fraud. The corruption and opportunism within IS's official ranks, particularly at the provincial levels, widened the gap between the state and its population, since it was the population who suffered from the exactions of the unscrupulous "officials."

To argue that IS and other movements like it are essentially urban phenomena, in that they draw much of their support from disgruntled denizens of urban areas—whether in the Middle East or elsewhere—does not mean that IS ignored the importance of the semiurban and rural areas in their strategy of state-formation. To be sure, urban areas like Mosul or Raqqa are of strategic and symbolic importance; cities are centers of gravity around which the core of a state is built. They are also economic and commercial centers and thus the source of wealth, a share of which could be directed IS's way.

However, the jihadist way of warfare and state-formation enterprise has never ignored the hinterland: the semiurban and rural areas. By "semiurban areas" I mean here the numerous villages and small towns on the outskirts of a major urban conurbation, like Mosul or Baghdad, or even a midsized city, like Fallujah or Ramadi. First, control of these areas was vital for IS, as it allowed them to recruit from them; many of the "local" IS fighters in Mosul came from the close outlying regions and were despised by the city's inhabitants, who viewed them as a form of Sunni lumpenproletariat motivated by promises of loot and bounty. Second, IS used outlying villages and small towns to form defensive screens that were often fortified with trenches and tunnels in order to slow down attacking forces advancing toward a major city controlled by IS. Finally, IS placed considerable importance on the rural areas that were under tribal control. Here, given its past history, IS knew it was on shaky ground, which is why its post-2010 leadership devoted so much time to figuring out how to avoid the mistakes of the first insurgency (2003–2010), when the tribes in Iraq rose against them.

The second objective of IS was people to populate its territory. People were the most important tangible resource (along with territory and financial resources). To be sure, the lands of the Caliphate already contained people; it is not as if the jihadists seized empty lands in Syria and Iraq. However, the jihadists needed to call upon more Muslims from all over the world to migrate to the land of the Caliphate in order to reinforce its legitimacy and allow it to benefit from the skills these Muslims had. The July 10, 2014, issue of *Dabiq*, "The Return of Khilafah," included excerpts from speeches by Abu Bakr al-Baghdadi in which he declared that it was a *wajib ayni* (individual obligation) for all Muslims to undertake *hijra* (emigration) to the new land of Islam from lands controlled by unbelievers, and he urged "judges, experts in jurisprudence, people with military, administrative and service expertise, and medical doctors and engineers" to come and help build the new state. The specific reference to hijra is no accident. It is a specific historical event in Islamic history: the migration of the Prophet Mohammad and his followers from Mecca to Medina in 622 AD in order to escape persecution and certain death in Mecca. The date on which they fled also represents the starting point of the Muslim calendar. It means to move from a non-Muslim place of abode to a place where Islam rules. For IS, *hijra* applies to Muslims who leave a place where there is Islam but where the rulers, although nominally Muslim, are deemed un-Islamic because they are not governing under sharia. According to this interpretation, if the conditions for rebellion against such rulers are missing, hijra to an Islamic abode is necessary. *Hijra* is also a call to Muslims who live in non-Muslim lands, such as the Western countries where they supposedly cannot or are not allowed to "practice" Islam freely and thus are not able to be good Muslims to migrate to a land where Islam prevails. For IS, *hijra* has major strategic import, as it refers to the need for jihadists worldwide to emigrate to their Caliphate to support it materially, militarily, and morally. *Hijra* was an essential part of the state-building enterprise of IS.

The third objective of the Caliphate was to provide for its "flock" and to govern in accordance with sharia. In its fourth issue of *Dabiq*, IS stated that a "state cannot be established" unless it looks after both the "worldly and the religious needs of Muslims." With this goal in mind, IS entrenched itself in the daily lives of the residents of its "state," particularly in the fields of justice, social services, education and culture, and health. The Islamic State successfully consolidated its hold on the judiciary by establishing Islamic courts in the areas under its control. To strengthen its hold over the judiciary, IS forced lawyers to take courses in sharia. The enforcement of sharia strictures against homosexuality, "improper dress," smoking, music, and so on led to the infliction of punishments, often in public, and generated resentment. The courts provided general judgments based on sharia; a specific unit claimed to act on complaints against IS personnel who committed abuses against the population. However, this was more to show, for propaganda purposes, a judicial impartiality that IS did not have much beyond the first few months of its remarkable victories. As IS came under attack from external enemies or suspected internal resistance from recalcitrant forces within the state, its paranoia increased, and this was reflected in IS personnel committing atrocities with impunity.

At the beginning when it was flush with money and faced no sustained military pressure, IS devoted a considerable number of personnel and resources to keeping essential services like electricity, water, sewage, and basic services, including post offices, functioning.[55] In order to feed the populations in Syria and Iraq, IS tried to keep the local wheat mills and bakeries open. In one issue of *Dabiq*, IS tried to convince people that its health system—run by an entity known as the Health Diwan—was second to none: "the Islamic State provides the Muslims with extensive healthcare by running a host of medical facilities including hospitals and clinics in all major cities through which it is offering a wide range of medical services from various types of complicated surgery to simpler services....This infrastructure is aided by a widespread network of pharmacies run by qualified pharmacists."[56] It was masterful, but it was far from the reality.

The efforts of IS to revamp education and culture and create a fully Islamic society through cultural homogenization—that is, its ideological vision was the only one allowed—in line with its worldview were some of the most frightening aspects of its state-formation efforts. It terrorized, killed, enslaved, and drove from their homes hundreds and members of hated and minority sects, including Shias, Yazidis, and Christians. While reprehensible, this brutal behavior has not been unique in history; other state-formation and nation-building enterprises of whatever ideological provenance and irrespective of time period have been as unforgiving of those who "do not fit."[57] What seems unique, however, is IS's single-minded focus on attaining ever higher levels of bestiality in its pursuit of terrifying people and achieving cultural homogenization and total obedience.

Cultural homogenization did not only entail getting rid of those who were recognizably different; it also meant the total homogenization of the remaining population in accordance with the ideological precepts of the state. The Islamic State established Islamic schools in the areas it captured and eliminated courses in science, history, physical education, and geography. It also aimed to remove the Western notion of the nation-state from education. Discussions of democracy, nationalism, racism, and geographical divisions were banned.

Despite its misogynistic attitudes toward women and oppression of them, women were clearly important to the Caliphate. Women had specific roles as bearers of children, the young generation that was the future of the Caliphate, as mothers, and as wives and supporters of the mujahidin.[58] It did make a call for white-collar professional women to migrate to it so that its women could benefit from their services. In segregated classrooms, only women were allowed to teach girls. The Islamic State also made the youth, particularly the very young and susceptible, a major focus of its attention.[59] It introduced paramilitary-style training as part of its school curriculum and established youth camps for the ideological indoctrination and military training of the young, because it knew that skilled, believing youth represented the best chance for its longevity.[60] Ominously, as the Caliphate came under increasing pressure, its administrative personnel rushed to intensify the indoctrination of the youth under its control in both Syria and Iraq so as to ensure that the ideology, at least, would remain embedded in the minds of the future generations.[61]

Cultural homogenization of the "citizens" was not only a matter of implementation of the measures to ensure the process succeeds; it also required the "policing" of the people. Most citizens' main interactions with IS were with its brutal and ubiquitous police and security forces, especially the *Hisba*, whose main purpose was to ensure that Islamic law, mores, and beliefs were followed to the letter. This morality police had enormous powers of control over people's daily lives in territories over which the IS held sway. Transgressions were dealt with swiftly, often on the spot. The *Hisba* swiftly punished individuals for any deviation from IS's religious norms, including bans against smoking, failure to pray or not knowing how to pray, "deviant" forms of entertainment like pool, shaving of beards, smuggling of prohibited items, and failure to impose modest behavior and attire for women. Though the political philosopher al-Mawardi stated hundreds of years ago in his ordinances on government that the *Hisba* in an Islamic state can only step in when it sees open and public infraction of the *hudud* (punishments as stipulated under sharia) and cannot push its way into homes or private areas, IS's *Hisba* did. It established a totalitarian system of "busybodies" with a network of informants and agent provocateurs. This totalitarian police force scared most inhabitants into resigned acceptance of IS's control in the urban areas.[62]

Having learnt many lessons from the first time around, IS realized that its enterprise was not just about acquiring land and causing chaos. Therefore, it proactively engaged in propaganda, or the use of information operations, to raise support and enthusiasm for the Caliphate and to get people to "buy into it" as an entity that would remain and expand. Whenever IS conquered new land, it "encouraged" the locals to pledge allegiance to the Caliph Ibrahim, as Abu Bakr al-Baghdadi was now called, through intensified mobilization and propaganda campaigns. The Islamic State sought to define and position itself as defender of the Sunni population. In Syria, it stated that it was fighting the forces of Assad when, in fact, on many occasions it focused its energies on fighting other groups opposed to his regime. In Iraq, IS portrayed itself as the protector of the Sunni population from attack by Iraqi government forces and Shia militias. When retaking areas from IS, Shia militias routinely committed atrocities against Sunni civilians, allowing IS to capitalize on these abuses, highlighting the threat of Sunni "extinction." Physical destruction also played a large part, with IS propaganda chronicling the destruction of government offices, border posts, and destruction of pre-Islamic (*jahili*) historical heritage sites. The Islamic State recognized the value of propaganda and sought to portray life in IS as normal and calm, with ongoing construction and people using its services. It reminded potential foreign recruits that it was not infallible, explaining that some things need improvement, but that the war must take priority. Following the establishment of IS, it adopted an "either with us or against us" mentality. This included discrediting other Syrian opposition groups, including the Islamic Front and Zawahiri's al-Qaeda.

As discussed in chapter 4, IS's global media operations were designed to provoke the United States and its allies, to terrorize IS's local opponents, and to recruit foreign fighters from the Middle East and further away. However, IS's media also had another mission: to portray how wonderful life was in the Islamic utopia. As a result of IS's venture into governance following the capture of large swathes of territory in Syria and Iraq after 2013, it deployed its media to portray itself as a group capable of leadership of a state. In an effort to win the hearts and minds of locals, as well as gain further funding from donors, IS media showed the "merits" of living under sharia.

The twin state-formation and nation-building enterprise required financial resources. The fact that this twin enterprise was being conducted simultaneously with fighting a war ensured that extraction of resources—financial and otherwise—occupied much of IS's time and energies.

"Show Me the Money"

Programmatically, the priorities of IS were to gain control over territory, people, and resources in the bid to build the Caliphate, fight off foes that threatened this enterprise, and begin administering the new state. Access to financing is one of the key factors—alongside ideological coherence, civilian support, organizational resilience, and operational and tactical skills—that determine an insurgent group's ability to maintain itself in the face of efforts by an enemy state to end it. Finance can be used to recruit, extend territorial control, and improve military resources. Well-organized, resilient, and reliable funding allows insurgents to access arms, provide basic services to areas under their control, provide administrative infrastructure, procure supplies, and pay wages to personnel.[63] An insurgent organization relies on a continuous flow of arms, ammunition, medicine, food, shelter, fuel, transport, and provision of basic services to maintain civilian support.[64]

Awash in Money

Prior to its lightning offensives of 2014, IS appeared to have built a large war chest. Even before its seizure of Mosul in June 2014, it was, as ISIS, collecting, or rather extorting, monthly taxes from business and commercial enterprises in urban areas.[65] This netted it between $6 and $8 million a month.[66] With its seizure of more territory in 2014 and more resources, its gross domestic product grew to an estimated $6 billion.[67] Business boomed in the early months of IS.[68] Sheikh Abu Saad al-Ansari, a senior IS religious figure in Mosul, revealed in 2015 that IS's annual budget for that year was $2 billion.

The Islamic State's diverse funding streams included kidnapping, human trafficking, extortion, taxation, confiscation of property as punishment, sale of antiquities, and sales of oil and gas.[69] Contrary to popular perceptions, donations from sympathetic individuals or "charitable organizations" in the Middle East accounted for a very small part of IS's financing.[70] The organization deliberately moved away from the whims of private donors from the Persian Gulf.[71] Saudi Arabia was not a major source of private donations, despite its ideological mindset being incontrovertibly similar to that of IS. The Saudi government's outlawing of any expression of support for IS has ensured that any donations that come from the Gulf flow from Qatar and Kuwait, both of which wish to avoid angering powerful domestic interests and possibly causing trouble for themselves.[72] As another revenue earner, IS levied taxes on all vehicles and trucks bringing goods into Mosul. A large truck paid a tax of $400, small trucks $100, and private vehicles $50 if they were bringing goods for retail into the city.

While IS gained notoriety for its criminal enterprises, such as drug dealing, kidnapping for ransom, and the sale of antiquities, it developed more mainstream funding sources. Black market oil sales generated in the order of $1–1.5 million a day. In the course of 2013 and 2014, ISIS took control of oil production in the Euphrates valley that had previously been run by other armed groups and local businesses and tribes. Their total production was about 120,000 barrels per day. Most of the fields were mature and in decline, requiring investment to enhance production, such as water injection, to sustain output. The Islamic State's output declined due to air strikes, inability to continue with water injection due to lack of technical skills, and the recovery of many oil fields by anti-IS forces.[73] When IS swept through northern Iraq in June 2014 it seized four small oil fields. Near Mosul, IS took over the Najma and Qayyara oil fields, while it overran the Himreen and Ajil oil fields near Tikrit.

These oil fields are modest compared to the giant oil fields near Kirkuk and in the south, which are under Kurdish and central government control. However, the monopoly over fuel in the territory IS captured gave it leverage over other armed Sunni factions that sought to threaten the Caliphate's dominance in the Sunni regions.[74] The Islamic State began transporting oil from Qayyara to be processed into low-quality gasoline and gasoil in mobile refineries in Syria and then brought back for sale in Mosul, a city of two million people. Gas stations in Mosul were selling fuel supplied by traders working with IS charging between $1 and $1.50 per gallon, depending on quality. This was a huge increase on previous prices, when the central government was in charge, allegedly triple the price, but residents of Mosul had to buy it because subsidized government fuel had stopped. Large shipments of crude from the Najma oil field were sold via smugglers to Turkish traders at vastly discounted prices, according to Iraqi government officials. Qayyara, which had estimated reserves of 800 million barrels, had been producing seven thousand barrels per day of heavy crude before IS took the field and a nearby refinery that produced sixteen thousand barrels per day. Qayyara oil field continued pumping after IS asked Iraqi employees to stay at their posts, promising safety. Oil revenues drove the Caliphate's efforts at state-formation. In September 2014, outsiders estimated that IS generated $2–3 million per day in oil sales, producing approximately seventy thousand barrels at a time when the price of oil was $90 per barrel.[75] Four months later, with the air strikes by the United States and its allies destroying the majority of oil fields and small refineries under IS's control, production dropped to twenty thousand barrels. The deleterious drop was magnified by the equally stunning collapse in oil prices.[76]

The Islamic State managed to fund its victories of 2014 with a labyrinthine oil-smuggling operation from oil fields first seized in Syria. The organization's personnel tasked with its "oil portfolio" refined the oil in makeshift refineries and then sold it to various customers, including its enemies.[77] The Islamic State's oil revenues became a persistent target of air strikes; much of the focus of attention was on the modular mobile oil refineries that IS had set up to exploit the seized oil fields.[78]

The man in charge of IS oil and gas, "Abu Sayyaf" (aka Fathi Bin Awn al-Murad al-Tunisi), whom the Americans killed in May 2015, was responsible for building up a vast network of traders and wholesalers of Syrian oil that tripled energy revenues for IS.[79] To be sure, he superimposed his network on an existing one made up of organized criminal elements and tribesmen, but he expanded the network and made it more efficient in terms of production and distribution and less corrupt in its day-to-day dealings. Spreadsheets and Excel files showed that "Abu Sayyaf's" division contributed 72 percent of the $289.5 million in total IS natural resource revenues over the six months that ended in February 2015. The head of the Diwan al-Rikaz (Ministry of Natural Resources), "Haji Hamid," put "Abu Sayyaf" in charge of the Syrian oil fields that IS captured, which were among the most lucrative: Deir ez-Zor and Hasaka. His 152 employees included white-collar professionals from Arab countries who had joined IS out of ideological sympathy. They included a Saudi who managed the oil fields, an Iraqi who ran maintenance, an Algerian who was responsible for refinery development, and a Tunisian who was in charge of refinery operations. "Abu Sayyaf" retained many Syrian oil industry veterans by offering them high salaries. The Islamic State oil managers demanded cash payment in U.S. dollars from the traders, and tasks such as accounting were assigned to IS operatives from outside the region where the oil fields were located to discourage embezzlement to family and tribal kin.

However, things began to go awry. Air strikes by the U.S.-led Coalition dampened oil production and destroyed infrastructure, which "Abu Sayyaf's" Saudi deputy, Abu Sarah al-Zahrani, worked assiduously to fix. An increase in fuel prices forced the IS leadership to instruct "Abu Sayyaf" to keep prices down and put a ceiling on the profits of the traders. The traders were not happy and accused "Abu Sayyaf" and his team of overcharging them and engaging in embezzlement. They also complained that the team showed favoritism toward certain traders and sellers. The Islamic State launched an investigation, but its General Governance Committee concluded, unsurprisingly, that there was no corruption.

The Tide Recedes

After 2014, the financial resources of IS were to prove insufficient to build a state and nation and at the same time fight a war against a wide range of enemies. The Islamic State needed financial resources to fund its war-fighting and its state-formation and nation-building efforts. The political economy of IS simply could not generate the requisite resources to do all of what was required for state-formation and nation-building in the midst of war.[80] Most of IS's revenues began to go to fund its war-making capacity, which left less for the provision of services and the construction of a state. Several of the initial sources of revenue that IS exploited—bank robberies, looting, confiscation of property, sale of antiquities, and kidnapping— were either one-time revenue sources or prone to depletion over time. The primary sources of IS's revenue became—in rough order of importance— taxation, oil and natural gas sales, and donations from foreign sponsors. These were also subject to structural problems that ultimately acted to limit the revenue stream.[81] Beyond its revenue streams, IS relied on a logistical facilitation network, subject to close monitoring, that distributed its revenues throughout the Caliphate.

However, there was no direct way for outsiders to prevent the Caliphate's financial authorities from wringing money out of the millions of people who lived in the regions under IS's control, in the form of new taxes and fees or confiscation of property. The Islamic State knew everything from its spies and from the data it plundered from banks, land-registry offices, and money-changing offices. It knew who owned which homes and which fields; it knew who owned many sheep or had lots of money. The extortion of the population by means of "taxation" ultimately proved a self-defeating enterprise. It impoverished people, and in the end they had little left to give. Moreover, as IS began losing territory to its advancing enemies, it lost people and resources that it could "tax."

As for taxation as a source of revenue: IS imposed taxes from $300 for a load of foodstuffs and $400 for electronics to a flat fee of $800 per truck at various crossings. The Islamic State imposed taxes on a variety of commercial activities, including telecommunications. Companies with relay towers in IS territory had to pay taxes. Raqqa's Credit Bank functioned as the city's tax authority, with employees collecting $20 every two months from business owners in exchange for electricity, water, and security. Indirect taxation of 10–35 percent on items such as medicine was imposed. One source of revenue for IS was the tax it levied on the salaries of government employees who were still drawing wages from the central governments in Damascus and Baghdad. Experts estimate that IS, which imposed tax rates as high as 50 percent, may have collected hundreds of millions of dollars in this manner. In an apparent bid to stem this revenue stream, Iraq's Council of Ministers announced on August 6, 2015, that it was suspending payment of salaries to employees working in areas controlled by IS. Between April 2015 and April 2016, IS's total revenues dropped by almost 30 percent. Around 50 percent of its revenues had come from taxation and confiscation of property, while 43 percent came from oil revenue. As IS lost territory, it lost revenues from taxation and confiscation of property.[82]

The Islamic State fed off the local economies in a parasitic manner. It plugged into the financial nodes of every village and city it seized in Iraq and Syria, controlling transportation, commerce, electrical power, food— in short everything that had monetary value.[83] However, IS managed to sustain commercial relations with its enemies. This was particularly evident in Syria, where IS allowed the movement of prohibited goods such as cigarettes and alcohol, taxing them in order to get revenue.[84] The Islamic State began imposing onerous "taxes" on commerce at "border" crossings between territory it controlled and territory its enemies controlled. In efforts to extract revenue as the stream from other sources dried up, IS began imposing taxes within the state on almost everything: on road traffic, rent for buildings, income, crops, cattle, and cash withdrawals from banks and on the Christian minority (*jizya*).[85] The Islamic State levied fines for smoking or for wearing the "wrong" clothes. It demanded a cut of the profits small businesses earned.[86] When it began to lose territory, it lost villages and towns from which it derived revenues. As it lost control of territory and its economy began to suffer from the impact of military operations, its revenue stream began to take a major hit.[87]

At the beginning of March 2015, the fortunes of IS seemed to be riding high, despite some losses, such as in the battle of Kobane (September 2014–February 2015) in Syria, in which hundreds of fighters were killed in a fierce urban battle against a dogged Syrian Kurdish defense. But IS was still on the offensive; it would take Ramadi in May 2015. The IS spokesman Abu Mohammad al-Adnani felt compelled to inform the world of the Caliphate's accomplishments and its "bright" future: "O people, are you amazed at the Islamic State's victories? Are you amazed at its perseverance despite its weakness and its scarce amount of resources?... The Islamic State remains upon its path with insight, with firm steps, alone in its trench.... Its tower continues to rise high and grow stronger and firmer day after day."[88] Adnani went on to exhort Muslims to migrate to the Caliphate, waxing lyrical about life there:

Come forth, O Muslims, to the land of the Caliphate. For you to be a shepherd over a flock of sheep in the land of Islam is better for you than to be an obeyed leader in the land of disbelief. Here, tawhid [monotheism] is actualized. Here, wala and bara [the principles of allegiance and disavowal] are embodied. Here, there is jihad for the cause of Allah. There is no paganism here, nor any idols, no ethnic partisanship nor nationalism, no pagan democracy nor infidel secularism. There is no difference here between Arab and non-Arab, nor between black and white. Here, the American is the brother of the Arab, the African the brother of the European, and the Easterner is the brother of the Westerner. There is commanding of good and forbiddance of evil. Here, Allah's Sharia is implemented.... Here is the land of Islam. Here is the land of the Caliphate.

Adnani was describing a utopia that was allegedly already in existence and was marching toward an ever more glorious future. The reality was very far from what he was articulating in his speech. Despite being on the offensive against its enemies, IS was declining internally when he made his speech, and he continued to witness and preside over efforts to justify that rapid decline, until his death in August 2016 spared him from trying to explain the collapse in Mosul in 2017.

"Something Is Rotten in the Kingdom of God"

When IS was announced in June 2014, it made a promise to the people it now ruled over that it would be the state for the Muslims, including the oppressed of them, the orphans, the widows, and the impoverished. Today, exactly three years later, IS has come face-to-face with a reality painfully familiar to any newly empowered government: it is a lot harder to keep promises, especially economic ones, than to make them. The honeymoon between IS and its "flock" in Syria and Iraq did not last long. By early 2015, the inhabitants began to realize that it could not deliver on its promises.[89]

The Islamic State has proven as vulnerable as, if not more than, the states it has been trying to displace or defeat. From the vantage point of mid-2017, it is clear that IS's state-formation and nation-building enterprises have all but collapsed. First, it was clear even in early 2016 that IS was not expanding but was contracting due to military reverses. One needed to fast-forward only a year, to early 2017, to see that IS's remaining in existence was also doubtful. Second, the state-formation and nation-building enterprises were failing even in 2015, partly because the cost of the military campaign against opponents that were getting the measure of IS had sucked up considerable resources, leaving little for managing the affairs of state, and partly because IS's brutal governing enterprise had not created the legitimacy it sought.[90]

By the end of 2015, its state-building efforts appeared to be crumbling, as living conditions deteriorated across the territories under its control, exposing the shortcomings of a group that devoted most of its energies to fighting battles, enforcing strict rules, and meting out horrific punishments to those who violated its rules or were deemed treasonous or sinful.[91] The outside world knew that things were not going as smoothly as IS liked to portray in its propaganda. Videos depicting functioning governing offices and the distribution of aid failed to match the reality of growing deprivation, disorganization, erratic leadership, and rampant corruption. Residents of the Caliphate managed somehow to inform the outside world that services were collapsing, prices were soaring, and medicines had become scarce. Schools barely functioned, doctors were few, and diseases were on the rise by 2016. Residents of Mosul, the largest city under IS's rule, complained that they were "living in a giant prison."[92] Mara Revkin, one of the world's leading analysts of IS's governance, pointed out in late 2015 that anecdotal evidence of IS fatigue among the civilian "citizens" of the Caliphate had increased due to its shortages, capriciousness, and brutality. The sentiments expressed by people who had fled or secretly and surreptitiously made their views known suggested a change in perception, but they could not be the basis for an uprising. Attitudes toward IS's governance were positive at the beginning because it restored law and order, which had disintegrated under the Iraqi government. It also provided services.[93] When it was ISIS, its first priority was to restore security and provide basic social services. Gradually, and particularly after the proclamation of the Caliphate in June 2014, IS began to regulate public morality and religious practices. It then began to demand tax payments in exchange for protection and security. In the early days of the euphoria associated with the jihadists' victories in Iraq, civilians compared IS's governance favorably to what had come before it. Many Moslawis, as inhabitants of Mosul are known, reportedly welcomed IS as "liberators." In both Syria and Iraq, the jihadists "only needed to perform slightly better than the alternatives in order to be perceived as the lesser evil." The Islamic State's governance became the "new normal," and people adjusted. The cost of IS's services became too onerous over the course of time; this was to be expected in times of war. However, as the costs of IS's war against a wide variety of enemies mounted, the services provided became shoddy and more erratic. At the same time, their costs mounted, in the shape of increased taxation and fines, often enforced capriciously.[94]

In Raqqa, the first major city to fall under IS's control and the de facto capital of the Caliphate, the discrepancy was most conspicuous. A Raqqa businessman who traveled to Mosul said Mosul was in far better shape than his own city, where people were being driven away by the specter of hunger and devastating Syrian government bombing raids that had killed mostly civilians.[95] Water and electricity were scarce by 2016. Government workers who helped sustain what was left of the crumbling infrastructure were initially paid by the Syrian government in Syrian areas controlled by IS and by the Iraqi government in areas in Iraq under IS control. By 2016, this was no longer the case. The Islamic State simply did not have enough personnel to run its cities, and machinery was either grinding to a halt or working inefficiently. The United States' air bombardments played a big role in straining the infrastructure, such as the administrative buildings, the command and control headquarters, and the small refineries that provided the oil that fueled the "state" and civilian economic activities.

Social relations were far from harmonious within the Caliphate. In 2015 tensions increased between the foreign fighters and the Syrian civilians and local Syrian fighters. Foreigners were paid in dollars, while Syrian fighters were paid in local currency. The Islamic State personnel were treated in their own field hospitals, while civilians had to make do with treatment in collapsing government hospitals lacking doctors, nurses, and medicines. The local fighters in Syria and Iraq—the *ansar* (helpers)—suffered disproportionately more casualties than the foreign fighters. Many of the locals were veterans of the insurgencies in both Syria and Iraq. For example, many of the Syrians who fought in Iraq during the insurgency went back home when the civil war erupted there. Conversely, Iraqis who went to Syria to help the Syrians fight the Assad regime returned home to make up part of the main striking element of IS's military. The stories of individuals who deserted IS after the initial euphoria of joining it make for stark reading about the reality of the Caliphate.[96]

Many parts of IS were plagued by rampant inflation, with prices of staple goods nearly doubling; the price of cooking kerosene quadrupled after IS took over. To sustain the image of a justice-based state, critical to its legitimacy, IS had to keep its promises. The inability to establish a sound financial and economic structure hindered that effort. The Islamic State had to cut back on its system of charities and provision of electricity, wheat, and medicines due to economic disruptions.[97]

In addition to dwindling financial and material resources, by early 2015 it appeared that IS faced recruitment problems. In July 2014, six thousand fighters joined IS.[98] The rate of recruitment dropped by more than half in February 2015 compared to a *month* earlier. Casualties were heavy due to the fighting in Syria, particularly around Kobane, against highly motivated Syrian Kurdish anti-IS forces. Air strikes by the U.S.-led Coalition killed a substantial number of personnel, and the number of foreign fighters from the West dropped.[99] In order to increase the number of personnel and raise morale, IS experimented with several tactics. It resorted to the recruitment of local residents who had no military experience or interest in fighting; it was a tactic that bred resentment. It released documentaries, such as *Flames of War*, boasting of its exploits. It attempted to mobilize Syrian Arabs against the Kurds ahead of the battle of Tel Hamis. It offered cash and female slaves to tribal sheikhs in order to get them to declare *bayaa* (allegiance) and provide manpower. Indoctrinating youth and establishing military training camps, such as Sharea Ashbal and Maahad Ashbal al-Khilafa, was another way to increase the fighting ranks. Targeting youth helped break down allegiance to family and tribe and reestablish it in favor of IS. As IS lost many combat veterans, it began to rely on less trained personnel, and the awe in which its military exploits had been enveloped declined. A number of its personnel deserted and escaped to tell outsiders not only of malfeasance but also of growing tactical and operational ineptitude.[100]

Contrary to its promises, IS did not distribute much-needed money to the poor. Islam is a politico-religious system, which from the very beginning made an implicit demand for better and more *equitable* governance.

Bringing social justice is at the core of the religion (see Quran 93:6–10).[101] There seems to have been precious little social justice in Abu Bakr al-Baghdadi's Caliphate. Furthermore, the absence of social justice led to polarization between the disparate members of the flock. As the Caliphate's poor got poorer, the fighters—who were increasingly from other countries—continued to enjoy comparatively comfortable standards of living: "I can see there are two different lives in Raqqa," said "al-Raqqawi," a resident secretly detailing life under IS, adding: "the [foreign fighters] have become the residents, and the residents have become the foreigners."[102] Ordinary people could not afford to use the city's fast-food joints, restaurants, or Internet cafés. The Islamic State fighters, who were not taxed on their salaries, according to al-Raqqawi, used these places almost exclusively.[103]

Despite its decreasing revenues, IS tried to continue to pay its fighters comparatively high salaries, peaking at $1,000 a month for some foreign fighters, for as long as it could. Based on these figures, paying its fighters may have cost IS up to $360 million per year. To put this in perspective, the Rand Corporation, a nonprofit research organization based in California, estimated that in 2014 the group's total earnings were $1.2 billion. Many of the local fighters, the Syrians and Iraqis, resented the huge benefits that the foreign fighters got, as well as their perceived arrogant and dangerous behavior toward the local fighters and the local communities from which they stemmed. The foreigners had no qualms about committing acts of brutality and inflicting draconian punishments, as they had no ties to the locals they were abusing, even though the end result was that IS lost the hearts and minds so desperately needed. The disparity between what IS said and what its leaders and personnel did became steadily apparent to the Sunni population that it held captive. As described by one observer, IS turned into an "apartheid" state in which "the militants have created a brutal two-tiered society, where daily life is starkly different for the occupiers and the occupied."[104]

The Islamic State succeeded in creating and sustaining a narrative that seduced a large number of people. As more and more local people, the "citizens" of the Caliphate, became aware of the conditions within their state, the narrative ceased to fool them. Recruitment of outsiders stayed steady for some time well into the Caliphate's existence due to IS's savvy exploitation of the media, which succeeded in attracting outsiders. Once there, many apparently began to recognize that the reality bore little resemblance to the narrative. The truth was that despite putting out appeals for professionals to run hospitals, industries, electricity, and the oil infrastructure, the vaunted

Caliphate remained woefully short of skilled labor. This forced it to put unskilled people in charge.[105] Services failed because of poor maintenance and because IS's economic and commercial enterprises were not profitable; IS squeezed the private sector and overtaxed businesses. The result was that many gave up their businesses and fled. This in turn deprived IS of the finances it needed to fight its wars and build the state. The fact that something was rotten in the kingdom of God led to resentment and acts of defiance and violence against IS, putting it in the ironic position of a nonrecognized state that itself was an insurgency but was fighting against manifestations of discontent within its own territories. However, IS did not face a serious insurgency from its internal enemies, which would have forced it to conduct a counterinsurgency campaign within its own state.[106]

One of the biggest complaints was that despite IS's claims about the equality of all Muslims, the foreign migrants to the state received better treatment and bigger salaries than the local fighters and the native inhabitants. A Syrian who defected in December 2014 stated: "The Syrian fighters feel they've been treated unjustly in comparison to the foreign fighters." This favoritism and IS's brutality prompted him to desert and flee.[107] By mid-2015, IS was struggling to maintain unity, cohesion, and discipline amid growing internal rifts, dissension, and declining recruitment.[108]

In late 2015, IS mounted an information operations campaign to discourage people from fleeing from its territories. A substantial number of videos and articles were put out aimed particularly at the large wave of refugees from Syria and Iraq seeking to make their way to Europe via Turkey. This was embarrassing for IS, whose raison d'être was to create a land for Muslims that would be ruled by sharia. The Islamic State excoriated the refugees for fleeing to the land of infidels, atheists, and drug addicts.[109]

The Islamic State used terror as an instrument to terrify its enemies, to destroy or force out of the Caliphate communities it regarded as beyond the pale, and to keep the Sunnis within its territory in line.[110] As one comment astutely put it, the aim of the savagery was to break the population living under IS psychologically so as to ensure absolute allegiance to the Caliphate; in short, "under ISIL rule there are no options. If you obey, you live. . . . For their enemy, there is no quarter."[111] Early on during its state-formation practices, many among the Sunnis in Syria and Iraq who were under its control viewed it as a more palatable alternative to their respective governments, which they regarded as corrupt, murderous, and capricious.[112] The Sunni "citizens" of IS in Syria viewed it as better than most of the other rebel or jihadist organizations, which were not disciplined and were often in cahoots with or part of organized criminal networks that preyed on the hapless population in areas where the writ of the state, never strong to begin with, had eroded completely. Similar sentiments were expressed in northern Iraq, particularly in Mosul, in the immediate years preceding the seizure of the city by ISIS forces and during the first few months of IS rule. The capricious behavior of Iraqi security and military forces in Mosul earned them the enmity of the population. The ISIS practices of extortion from businesses in Mosul, which had been going on for years, as well as the assassinations of opponents, was conveniently forgotten. Nonetheless, IS's terror began to weigh heavily on the population. Initially, many thought that it was a rational instrument being used by IS to consolidate control and to get rid of the state's obvious enemies. People thought: "if I keep my head down and do not engage in any of the countless trespasses that could get you punished or worse," life would continue "normally." The problem with IS's kind of terror, as indeed with all other kinds of revolutionary terror, is that it inevitably draws you into its web as spectator, as a person complicit in its practice, or as victim.

Things began to go downhill economically as early as December 2014. Prices soared in IS-held territory. The start of winter coincided with increased shortages of gasoline and kerosene. Food and fuel prices rose sharply; for example, a fifty-kilo sack of rice cost 75,000 Iraqi dinars, or $65, in December 2014, up from 10,000 dinars, or $9, only three months earlier.[113] In order to raise money, IS began bending its ideologically rigid rules in many areas. Once smokers were flogged publicly, but by early 2015 IS was fining smokers up to $65 for smoking. The shortfall transformed IS, once flush with cash, from trying to establish a supposedly legitimate state with a taxation system into the clichéd organized criminal enterprise—which had seen better days—shaking down its "citizens" for cash. Oil revenues were estimated to have dropped to $300,000 by February 2015, a far cry from the $1–2 million it had been making per day in 2014.[114]

The budget of IS showed that its priority was warfare. Getting an accurate picture of IS's finances and revenue stream is "fiendishly complex," as the *Financial Times* has pointed out. The Islamic State operated a centralized budget that was run from Mosul and dozens of regional budgets that were managed by the provincial governors. The *Financial Times* estimated that approximately two-thirds of IS's annual revenues were "ploughed into its fighting forces."[115] At one point, about $20 million was spent every month on the state's major combat forces, which were made up of the foreign fighters. It spent a further $15–20 million on local fighters and auxiliaries. Tens of millions of dollars were spent each month on weapons and ammunition. The state's security apparatus cost it a further $10–15 million. Meanwhile, social services, such as health and education, received less than $10 million per month.[116]

When ISIS seized the Syrian city of Raqqa in January 2014, its inhabitants expressed relief that they were finally getting firm and disciplined governance after several years of instability. Even as some people grumbled about some of its inflexible and puritanical laws, ISIS provided food and social services.[117] The positive image of the jihadists did not last for long.[118]

By mid-2016, IS seemed to be facing severe internal administrative and governance problems: corruption, financial embezzlement, and bureaucratic infighting.[119] The state faced problems managing cash as its ranks and operations expanded, with more and more emirs emerging to direct various administrative departments. Many of these regional or local emirs proved to be lacking in integrity and ethics; a number absconded with thousands of funds. The differences in pay and distribution of war booty created tensions within the rank and file. Foreigners got more pay and better quarters than locals in either Syria or Iraq.[120]

Outside observers were baffled that the "citizens" of the Caliphate in the Iraqi region, as reports and refugees fleeing the Caliphate indicated that they were increasingly disgruntled, did not rise in a mass insurrection. After all, there were many armed groups within Iraq, including the country's powerful Sunni tribes. Moreover, they had risen up successfully against the Caliphate's predecessors, AQI and ISI, less than a decade earlier.

Why No Anti–Islamic State Insurgency among the Sunnis?

As IS's fortunes declined in 2016, there was a growing recognition that it was not "ten feet tall." What surprised many observers was the failure of the captive population to rise up in a sustained manner against it. In Syria the proliferation of well-armed and well-trained Sunni groups offered an alternative to IS. However, even in Syria, there was reluctance to cross IS. When an estimated seven to nine hundred members of the Shaitat tribe mounted an attack on IS in Deir ez-Zor province, to the east of Raqqa, they were slaughtered in large numbers in full view of the world's indifference, much to the anger and disgust of the Shaitat. Following the massacre, a prominent member of the tribe told a Western reporter: "When you see your relatives being slaughtered, you will be forced to accept compromises you would otherwise never been prepared to accept. And when you see the world has abandoned you, you will do nothing about it."[121] Not surprisingly, any talk of an anti-IS uprising elicited caution. Following the massacre of the Shaitat, an anti-IS tribal commander stated: "We saw what the Americans did to help the Yazidis and the Kurds. But they have done nothing to help the Sunnis against the Islamic State."[122] A sheikh of the Baggara tribe of Deir ez-Zor province, Fawaz al-Bechir, claimed that the Syrian government had asked him to rally the tribe to fight IS. His response was: "I told them, 'For decades you did everything to undermine our authority and weaken us and now you want us to help?'"[123] By way of contrast, a sheikh of the Shammar Jarba discouraged his people from participating in the protests against the regime of Bashar al-Assad, saying: "visibility was poor so to speak, and we couldn't tell where things were headed."[124] In any event, the feeling in Syria among the Sunnis is that time is on their side; and when (if) they do win, there will be bloodletting not only against their perceived enemies but also within Sunni ranks. At the same time, the fact that poverty, loss of jobs, families, and hope in a future have impelled more and more young Syrians into the ranks of radical organizations or entities such as Jabhat al-Nusra or IS does not augur well for a return to stability. Having stared into Nietzsche's proverbial abyss for so long, Syria's people are willing to stare a little bit longer in their determination to settle scores against one another.

In 2014, the Sunnis of Iraq were divided into a number of different groups as they witnessed the rise of ISIS and its transformation into a state following its victories of January–June 2014 against the Iraqi Security Forces. First, there were the Sunni insurgents who had helped ISIS in its advance. This is a different category from the former regime officials who had joined ISIS outright and transformed it into an effective entity. No matter how effective ISIS had become in 2014, it could not have swept to power without the combat, information, and logistical support provided by its de facto allies. Second, there were the Sunni armed groups—insurgents and members of the Awakening movement—who initially did nothing and then tried to prevent ISIS from taking over their areas. Third, there were those, particularly among certain tribes, who had tasted the viciousness of ISIS's predecessors. They took up arms right away when ISIS raised its head in their areas, and some towns, like Haditha, managed to hold out against the jihadist advance. Unfortunately for the anti-ISIS tribes, they had neither the wherewithal nor government support to sustain their resistance. Finally, there was the mass of the Sunni population. Initially, many of the Sunnis in Iraq seemed to be in favor of ISIS because it had defeated their tormentors, the Iraqi Security Forces, and because it seemed to represent protection against the Shia militias. In the Sunni areas of northern Iraq, Iraqi army personnel and units from the south were particularly detested. The Sunnis' joy at being "liberated" from the Shia-dominated government and its security forces did not last long. A significant element of the Sunni population sat on the fence and delighted in Maliki's humiliating comeuppance in 2014—once again, a stance that turned out to be unwise. This was doubly so in light of the fact that already in 2013 and early 2014, before ISIS seized Mosul, the Sunni community had tasted its savagery and draconian measures, even before IS was a reality.[125] As ISIS provided convincing evidence of its military prowess from early to mid-2014, just before declaring the Caliphate, tribe after tribe surrendered their weapons and pledged loyalty. In late June 2014, tribal elders in al-Alam decided to open their town to the jihadists after realizing that they did not have the weapons and ammunition to oppose them successfully. One of the leaders bitterly accused the government of letting them down and forcing them to surrender.[126] One of the Sunni tribes in Anbar province who did take a stance against IS in the autumn and winter of 2014 were the albu-Nimr, who lost over seven hundred men in their struggle against IS, including five hundred who were simply massacred.[127]

The jihadists of ISIS and the Sunni insurgents who took Mosul from the government were far from united.[128] Theirs was a marriage of convenience between ultrahardline religious zealots, which included former Baathists who had gone over to ISIS, and more pragmatic but distinct and separate, though equally nasty, Sunni insurgents. Their unity rested on two pillars: the groups' common membership of the Sunni minority and a conviction that the Sunnis had been marginalized and persecuted by the Shia government of Maliki.

Once ISIS had become a state, IS, and was at the height of its power, resistance became more difficult. Fear of draconian punishment stopped people in their tracks. The Islamic State viewed armed rebellion against it, the "legitimate" government, as *fasad fi al-ard* (corruption on Earth) and deserving of severe punishment. A palpable lack of alternatives deterred the people. The capacity of IS for violent retribution against opposition cannot be underestimated as a force in the staying of Sunni hands. There

were incidents of violent resistance here and there, as people living under
IS rule expressed their rage by launching what were essentially "lone wolf"
attacks on IS fighters and personnel in urban centers.[129] In Syria, a group
of anti-IS fighters referred to as the White Shroud started launching lightning strikes on IS units and individual fighters in Deir ez-Zor province in
late 2014. Its leader, "Abu Abboud," declared that his group did not take IS
prisoners since they deserved to die because of their brutality toward and
savage oppression of the Syrian people.[130] Furthermore, as more people fled
from the Caliphate—and IS exhorted people not to leave—the remaining
population remained more loyal, out of weakness, lack of an alternative, or
even ideological support among the committed.

There was no unified Sunni stance in favor of or against IS. The Sunnis
could not act to thwart the IS project of state-formation. At the same time,
their ambivalence and weakness vis-à-vis IS did not help IS in consolidating and sustaining a state without genuine popular support. The divisions
within the Sunni community weakened it against IS's dramatic advance,
continued to weaken it in the face of the Caliphate's tightening grip in the
period 2014–2015, and weakened it vis-à-vis the Shia-dominated government in Baghdad. It is not surprising that a Sunni tribal leader, Sheikh
Wissam al-Hardan, blamed his people as much as the Iraqi government
for IS's gains: "Sunnis dug their graves with their own hands. We lost our
homes and we may not go back.... There is nothing called a Sunni community any more." Nonetheless, he attacked Baghdad for not providing his
Aithawi tribesmen with arms to fight IS as they had fought its predecessor
a decade ago.[131] However, in a stark reflection of the existing divisions
within the Sunni community, other Sunnis disagreed with Sheikh Hardan,
who showed himself willing to work with the Shia militias of al-Hashd al-
shaabi. Another leader, Sheikh Ziyad al-Suleiman, had no intention of
working with the Shia militias because "the Hashad [sic] and Isis are two
sides of the same coin. They both loot and burn Sunni homes, kill our
young men and our leaders. Even if the government or the US gave us
more arms and money, I would not work with the Hashad [sic].... These
militias are a way for Iran to control our country."[132]

When Haider al-Abadi took office as prime minister, he was regarded
as a moderate Shia politician who could win over the powerful Sunni
tribal sheikhs to fight IS. By late 2014, Sunnis viewed Abadi with deep
skepticism because he had failed to deliver on promises. In October 2014,
he held a televised meeting with Sunni tribal sheikhs in which he appealed
to them for support. The sheikhs listened in stony silence. One senior

tribal leader, Sheikh Lawrence al-Hardan, expressed the frustrations thus: "We're bewildered by Abadi's policy toward Anbar. We want to live in peace and bring back displaced families and stop the bloodshed. But the big question is will Abadi be able to tackle these issues? The answer is no. What's happening in the country is beyond Abadi's ability and capacity."[133] Another, Sheikh Ali Hatem Suleiman, complained about the Shia militias, arguing that if Abadi was serious about seeking Sunni help to defeat IS, he should rein in the Shia militias, forcibly if need be. This was a tall order for a prime minister who came in with promises of a technocratic cabinet that would implement reforms, reconcile with the Sunnis, and take decisive action against IS. His government proved unable to break the deadlock in Iraqi politics, was slow in revitalizing the Iraqi army, took no action to reign in the Shia militias, and was faced with considerable rage from a significant segment of the Iraqi Shia population in the spring of 2016 due to its lethargy, political deadlock, and inability to move the country forward.[134]

Sheikh Ali Hatem Suleiman, a former leader in the Sunni Awakening, asked: "Why is IS here? Why are some Sunnis joining? Because of the sectarian policy of the government and the oppression this province [Anbar] faced."[135] Even when Sunni tribal fighters cooperated with Shia militias to fight IS, the mutual suspicions were never far below the surface, despite the protestations of goodwill on both sides.[136] There were few Sunni tribes in Anbar province willing to fight for a government they viewed as beyond the pale. Exceptions included the albu-Risha in Ramadi, who took a leading role in coalescing the Sunni front against AQI and its successors in 2006 until the American withdrawal in 2011. However, after 2011 the albu-Risha did not seem to have the clout or deference they had had in the past. Moreover, the perennially suspicious Shia government in Baghdad was loath to arm Sunnis to fight IS.[137] The government was faced with the problem that if it used the Shia militias extensively in Sunni areas, it would run the risk of alienating the Sunnis even further and ensuring that they would not fight for the government. The tension between the government and the militias concerning the former's participation in key battles was often resolved in favor of the militias when the government backed down and allowed them to enter Sunni areas to battle IS.[138] The government calculated that it was less of a problem to alienate the Sunni community than to alienate the powerful Shia militias and their backers.

Because of the tribes' belief that they were betrayed after the Americans left at the end of 2011, tribal distrust of both the Americans and the Iraqi government runs deep. In October 2014, Amnesty International reported dozens of cases of abductions and killings of Sunnis in Diyala by Shia militias who had accused them of collaboration with IS. At the same time, there were reports that Sunnis in this province had opposed IS and suffered the consequences.[139] To be sure, Sunni and Shia militias had fought IS together, particularly during the retaking of Tikrit in March 2015. However, suspicions between the two sects and their respective fighters were still rampant.[140] Emad al-Jumaili, a Sunni from Anbar, told a Western reporter: "I have always said I would much prefer to be killed by a Sunni terrorist organization than a Shiite terrorist organization." Yet, miles away, another member of the Jumaili tribe, Mohammad al-Jumaili, told the same journalists: "Daesh is the bigger threat. The joining of Shiite brothers into our fight will be a turning point in Iraq, the basis for the first real national army."[141] The Sunni tribes of Anbar were split between opposition to, neutrality towards, and support for IS. In such a highly fragmented community, any mission of building an effective strategy against IS was fraught with difficulties. A Sunni veteran politician and member of Parliament, Mishaan al-Jibouri, expressed his frustration with the tribes' seemingly fluid views and ambiguous stances: "They agree with you on one thing in the morning, and by night it's like you never spoke."[142]

The Sunnis in Iraq continued to move forward without vision as the Iraqi government mobilized itself to fight IS between 2014 and 2016. The Sunni elite elites were fractured and incapable of coming up with a unified vision for their community, and thus, not surprisingly, they did not know what they wanted.[143] Sunni divisions and rivalries complicated the efforts to maintain the gains the Sahwa had made in the previous "war" against IS's predecessor. Sheikhs competed with one another for influence and state patronage. This weakened their power and that of the Sunni community vis-à-vis Maliki, who naturally welcomed and encouraged this divisiveness within the Sunni community, whom he distrusted immensely. For him, the Sunni community was the vessel within which Sunni extremists, whether Baathist or Islamist, were conceived and grew to be a danger to the "new" Iraq. The failure of the Baghdad government to train and arm tribal militias to fight IS in Sunni areas served only to reinforce the suspicions of the Sunni tribes.[144] When the government belatedly set up a Sunni tribal militia program, it proved to be ineffective. The tribes' entreaties to their armed cobelligerent insurgent groups to provide them with arms fell on deaf ears; indeed, those insurgent groups, having fallen out with IS, were now using their weapons against the jihadists and waiting for the day when they would have to face the Iraqi Security Forces and Shia militias again.

Despite this internal divide between Sunnis and Shias, IS came under severe challenge from the Iraqi government and its militias and the Kurdish Peshmerga from 2016 onward. The turn of the tide against IS came at immense cost to the Sunni regions. Ramadi was reduced to rubble when it was liberated from the clutches of IS. Furthermore, the policy of the government and of Shia militias of creating buffer zones cleared of Sunni civilians was met with outrage by the Sunni community and was not a foundation for reconciliation. This scorched earth policy was first implemented in Jurf al-Sakhr, a Sunni town south of Baghdad, in November 2014, when the Iraqi army scored a minor victory by ejecting IS from its foothold there. The town was near a highway that would be packed with Shia pilgrims going south to Karbala to commemorate the martyrdom of Imam Hussein, the Prophet Mohammad's grandson. Local fighters associated with IS would often attack the pilgrims or use this small town as a base to stage attacks on Karbala itself.[145] The government offensive succeeded, whether by design or by accident, in forcing the population out. In the words of one forty-five-year-old farmer from the town, "they hit us with aircraft and mortars and artillery and rockets. This is what made us leave. It became a military area. We did not bring anything with us—we escaped with our lives."[146]

The same strategy was repeated with the recaptured city of Baiji, north of Tikrit, a drab city that is home to Iraq's biggest oil refinery. Often towns once occupied by Sunnis out of which IS has been driven are left empty. "There are some areas where they can't be allowed back," said Hadi al-Ameri, the military leader of the Shia militia umbrella Hashd al-Shaabi.[147] He argued that if the Sunni population returned to the towns that were reclaimed from IS, IS would return with them. Ameri takes care not to blame the Sunnis en masse. "The citizens are forced to deal with Isil, otherwise Isil will kill them."[148] Nonetheless, Sunnis are being punished collectively for the sins of IS, with the ensuing risk of deepening sectarianism still further. In short, the Iraqi government's approach to defeating IS is likely to result not in effective state-formation and nation-building by Baghdad but in the perpetuation of a fragile and unstable country with a large and disgruntled minority.[149]

A Sunni rising against IS between 2014 and 2017 was not an easy proposition. Desultory anti-IS attacks and localized resistance do not an insurgency make. As Aymmen Jawad al-Tamimi, who has studied both the Sunni insurgents and IS extensively, wrote in mid-2014, "resistance movements to IS are localized and do not yet constitute a wider, coordinated

Sunni Arab rebel movement against IS."[150] Three years later, a Sunni insurgency against IS had not progressed much beyond Tamimi's initial analysis that they were engaged in nothing more than desultory and localized attacks. In mid-December 2014, Sunni fighters in the town of Wafaa in Anbar province were forced to give up their positions to advancing IS fighters because they had ran out of ammunition. The locals complained bitterly that the Iraqi government did not wish to arm them because it did not trust them and it wanted its own forces, particularly the Shia militias, to take credit for any thwarting of the IS advance.[151] Assassinations of IS members by "mysterious" gunmen, that is, Sunni insurgent cells, started in late 2014, when gunmen killed IS commander Abu Anas al-Iraqi. In 2015 Moslawi gunmen killed a senior IS commander, Abu Dujana al-Saudi, and in March 2016 they disposed of Abu Furqan al-Misri.[152]

Recognizing their collective weakness vis-à-vis IS, the leaders of several influential Sunni tribes proclaimed their support for IS in June 2015. In a combined statement they condemned the Iraqi government and claimed that the only way to regain peace in Anbar province was through support of IS. It is difficult to gauge how much of this stemmed from genuine feelings of support for IS, a sentiment that would imbue IS with legitimacy, or from fear of what IS would do if they abstained from declaring loyalty, or from resignation because there simply was no alternative for them. Whatever compelled Sunni tribes to express their support for IS, it did not augur well for efforts to dismantle IS from the ground up. The fact that Sunni tribes who were fighting IS felt that it was at best difficult and at worst a hopeless task to dismantle IS under the current circumstances made it that much more difficult to enlist this crucial community in the fight. The end result was that some Sunni tribes supported IS, while others stayed with the government, however reluctantly. The conflict not only divided tribes but also caused divisions within tribes.[153]

For the lack of weapons in the hands of the tribes one sheikh blamed the "sectarian" government in Baghdad, which, he said, believed that when weapons were given to Sunni tribes, they would be "handed over to Daesh."[154] Unsurprisingly, he concluded that most of Anbar's tribes were sitting on the fence: "the first group believe in the Daesh doctrines. The second group hates Daesh, but they saw what happened to the tribes who fought al-Qaeda between 2006 and 2008. Afterward the government turned against them and arrested them. Most have been killed or jailed."[155] The words of Sheikh Abdullah Humeidi albu-Issa resonate with a lot of Sunnis in Anbar province, particularly with those who helped the Americans defeat al-Qaeda in 2010: "We blame President Obama for not keeping his promises. Sunnis have been displaced. They are being slaughtered. He misled us. The Americans have no credibility. We no longer trust what they say."[156]

The Islamic State did not care about the disintegration of Sunni morale, in fact, it profited from it.[157] The more the Baghdad government showed indifference or turned a blind eye to the atrocities of Shia militias, the more susceptible the Sunnis were to the siren song of IS, because they would have no alternative but to seek IS's protection. However, at the same time, IS massacres of Sunnis proliferated, just to show the Sunnis who was the boss and to thwart rebellion. Dozens of Sunnis suspected of collaborating with the central government were reportedly burnt alive in the town of Baghdady in Anbar province in 2015, and IS fighters made a habit of abducting Sunni Muslim tribesmen.

The Iraqi and U.S. governments hoped that a revival of the loyalty of the tribal sheikhs to the state would bring them around to pursuing another Sahwa against IS was founded on wishful thinking. The sheikhs' authority in tribal areas was shattered, due to poor and weak leadership, loss of economic clout, the rise of sectarian entrepreneurs among armed groups, and the rise in the influence of young militant clerics, as happened in Fallujah. Salafist preachers began to fill in the vacuum resulting from the decline of tribal authority and the decline in national identity. Sunni Arab identity became subject to a process of reinvention, one that evoked Islamist beliefs, not always necessarily Salafist, and an Arab nationalism of narrowed horizons, one that most definitely excluded the Shia Arabs of Iraq.

The stated hope of the United States and the Iraqi government was that the Sunni civilians in the provinces were capable of throwing out the "foreign" presence of IS if properly motivated and armed. This was fatally flawed. Although such a campaign did succeed against a much smaller and less competent incarnation of the current IS in 2007–2008, that "awakening" relied on huge U.S. cash subventions to the insurgent organizations and tribal fighters. This did not happen between 2015 and 2017 when the Sunnis began to recognize the depravity of IS. The United States was no longer in Iraq, as it had been previously when it had mentored them, befriended them in a way the Baghdad government could not, trained them, and paid them. The Shia government was unlikely to give them cash or weapons, light or heavy. Baghdad banked on the Shia militias and Iran, while it rebuilt the army. The increased presence of vengeful Shia militias—many of whom see the world in dire black-and-white terms that are remarkably evocative of what the Sunni jihadists see, albeit through a different ideological lens—in Sunni areas made matters worse. The mutual sectarian hatred was palpable and had almost been "ethnicized," where Sunni Arabs questioned the Arab identity of the Shia Arabs and the latter derided the former's "chauvinistic" definition of what it is to be Arab.

From the beginning of the current crisis, Sunni Arabs did not display any keenness to help the government in Baghdad. As Sheikh Raad Abdul Sattar Suleiman, a member of the Dulaim tribe, said in an interview: "Iraqis are prepared to accept help from any party in order to defeat the gang that is Iraq. We are Iraqis. We can change Maliki and his rule, and we will change the whole political process in Iraq."[158] Many may have hated IS with a passion, but they hated (and continue to hate) the Shia government as much; and as they came into greater and closer contact with Shia militias dominated by lower-class Shias of both rural and urban provenance—the *shruggis* (colloquial for "easterners," seen as scum)—they extended that hatred to the overall Shia community. In 2008–2009, as they defeated ISI with American aid, many of the Sunnis thought they would be able to get a good deal brokered by the Americans. This was unlikely to happen the second time around (2015–2017); and the prevailing sentiment among the Sunnis is, indeed, that they are unlikely to get a good deal from Baghdad after the defeat of IS.

Sheikh Wissam al-Hardan, a cofounder of the Sahwa, lamented that he was hampered along the way by U.S. policy-makers who were hesitant about giving support to armed Sunni factions that might include former insurgents and by Shia leaders of the Baghdad government who were reluctant to finance and arm their rivals. Sunni leaders overestimated their capacity to deal with IS militarily. Hardan was convinced that only the Sunnis of Iraq could truly break IS: "We know Daesh's secrets, where Daesh moves and how they operate. We know the weaknesses of Daesh."[159] Hardan claimed that many young men "have revenge in their hearts" against IS. However, having feelings of revenge is not sufficient to take on IS with its heavy weapons and its ruthlessness. Former Awakening members who were ready to take up arms complained that, in addition to a lack of resources, there had been little opening to allow for the reemergence of political groups that represented the interests of those Sunnis who were otherwise susceptible to IS influence. For over a decade, the political class in Iraq has constantly only promoted their own narrow agendas. In addition, the central government has yet to deliver on promised reforms that would signal to the disgruntled Sunni community that they had a place in the new Iraq. Attempts by Prime Minister Haider al-Abadi to roll back rules that exclude former members of Saddam Hussein's Baath Party and to stem the rising power of Shia militias have gone nowhere. Many Sunnis blamed the fall of Ramadi in May 2015 on the failure of the government to arm the local Sunni Arab tribes to fight IS.[160]

Nonetheless, the Sunnis tried to show their hatred for IS by rising up in some places. In February 2016, Sunni fighters attacked IS in Fallujah, overrunning and burning one of its headquarters, allegedly after a scuffle between locals and IS fighters in a queue. However, it is difficult to conceive of Sunni "flare-ups" against IS in its strongholds as signs of insurgency. Scuffles, real or alleged, are not planned and do not constitute a prelude to insurrection. In Fallujah the flare-up involved a mix of tribal militia and groups of disaffected young people.[161] The Fallujans were fed up with IS's violation of tribal and family mores and its arbitrary taxation.[162] The dynamics in Anbar allowed IS to dominate the situation on the ground. The government's reluctance to arm the Sunni Arab tribes contributed to the ease with which IS took over the region. A number of Sunni tribes announced that they did not like either IS or the Shia government; however, they disliked IS even more and declared their readiness to fight it. This included the albu-Risha, albu-Fahd, and albu-Nimr tribes, who had fought the predecessors of IS.[163]

The complicated situation in Nineveh province has essentially split the Sunni Arab tribes, who seem to be bereft of any strong or centralized leadership or party organization to represent their views vis-à-vis Baghdad or the Kurds. They are armed but are politically adrift and are caught between three competing forces. First, there was IS: it needed the support of the tribes but did not trust them, and its leadership held to the old urban Arab adage "You will never be able to buy a Bedouin, but you can rent him," which suggests a fickle, commercially minded, and mercurial "ally" who can abandon you when the circumstances merit it. Nineveh has been important for Daesh because it became a sanctuary when they were kicked out of Anbar, Diyala, and Salah al-Din. The Sunni Arab tribes there did not have strong militias or political representation, as did the tribes in Anbar in particular. Most of the opposition to the American occupation in the north was found in cities like Mosul, and that was where IS managed to obtain support and has faced the greatest opposition. Second, there is the advancing Kurdish entity, which doesn't want Arabs in its domain but is willing to incorporate those at the periphery of the Kurdish lands. Third, there is the Shia government in Baghdad, which views the Sunni Arab tribes with suspicion.

The confusion of the Arabs in Nineveh has been reflected in two differing sentiments expressed by tribal sheikhs. A sheikh of the Arab al-Haddadin tribe suggested to the Kurdish government that his region, which is outside the Kurdish autonomous region, be made a part of Iraqi Kurdistan. In Mosul, another tribal sheikh was quoted as saying: "We won't accept the entry of either the Shiite Muslim militias or the Iraqi Kurdish forces into Mosul. We will fight alongside the extremists [IS] to deny them. Just wait and see how fierce we will be in battle."[164] For the most part, the Arab tribes in Nineveh complained that the Kurds had seized their lands as part of their strategy of creating Kurdistan irredenta. One sheikh of the Shammar tribe, one of the largest in the area, complained: "Local Arabs are being displaced and prevented from cultivating their land. The Kurds are blackmailing the Arabs, promising them they will allow them to return back to their houses if they declare their support for the annexation of their areas to Iraqi Kurdistan."[165]

Many Arab leaders in Nineveh province preferred not to have a Shia government liberate them from IS. As a result, some began to draw closer to Iraqi Kurdish leaders, and some asked that their areas be annexed to Iraqi Kurdistan.[166] If this were to happen, it would change the political and social dynamics in northern Iraq irrevocably. In Nineveh, the government would have the hardest time convincing the Sunnis to fight alongside it, though the region has witnessed the emergence of shadowy Sunni insurgent groups conducting hit-and-run raids on IS positions, as well as the breaking of ranks between IS and Sunni insurgent groups that had helped it come to power. The inexorable encroachment of the Kurds into territory that is Arab and Turkmen might be the only factor that might compel them to seek Baghdad's aid.

A Sunni insurgency or "reawakening" against IS proved difficult to get off the ground between 2014 and 2017. The original Sahwa (Awakening) of 2006–2009 succeeded because of two factors: (1) the Sunnis who came over to the American side were supported by the U.S. military with arms, advisors, and training; (2) the Sunnis believed that they would be integrated into the security services and the political process.[167] Conditions have changed since then. First, there was no need for a "sahwa" in Diyala province, where IS had been squeezed by Kurdish, government forces, and the Shia militias without Sunni help, even though IS eagerly sought Diyala as a sanctuary. In Anbar, the Sunnis may detest the extremists, but they loathe the government and the Shia militias almost equally. Conversely, the Baghdad government did not wish to arm Sunni militias in Anbar province or elsewhere because it felt that would empower them too much. The Islamic State fighters are better equipped and trained than the Sunni tribal or insurgent fighters.

Second, the ambivalence of the Sunni population and of anti-IS militias or fighters made it difficult to take decisive steps in opposition to IS. As early as 2014, a number of Sunni militias and their leaders indicated that they would turn on IS but this time they wanted international guarantees that substantial concessions would be granted the community.[168] In the words of one Sunni tribal militia commander, Abu Mohammad al-Zawbai: "we want a real political solution, which the US should impose on these people it installed in the Green Zone."[169] This was not forthcoming at that time, simply because nobody thought that IS would have such traction on the ground in the Sunni areas and it had already proven difficult for the United States to influence the situation in a meaningful manner in Baghdad after its withdrawal in 2011. In fact, al-Zawbai admitted that in 2014 the Sunni tribal militias had chosen to stand down and not confront IS because they were not ready and because they wondered who and what they would be fighting for.

The resignation of Nuri al-Maliki, whom the Sunnis detested, and his replacement by Haidar al-Abadi did not inspire confidence in the government among Sunnis. In the words of al-Zawbai: "appointing someone from the same Dawa party to succeed Maliki is like appointing a Baathist to replace Saddam Hussein."[170] Secret talks between Baghdad and Sunni militias and political groups, including even former members of the Baathist regime, went nowhere. The mutual suspicions were just too deep-seated; and this does not augur well for post-IS Iraq, as it will put into doubt post-Mosul efforts by the Iraqi government to rebuild the Iraqi state and nation in a manner that would encompass all of its peoples, or at least the majority of them.[171] The alleged poor treatment of Sunni refugees by Shia militia and Iraqi military following the liberation of towns in Anbar province, particularly of Ramadi, served only to embitter the Sunnis further.[172]

The Demise of the Caliphate 3.0

As 2017 progressed, following the slow but steady erosion of the IS stronghold in Mosul, the question that loomed was whether Iraq would be able to mend itself politically in the post-Caliphate period. Many astute observers of the Iraqi scene began to consider this critical matter during the first

quarter of 2017; most reached pessimistic conclusions, and it was not difficult to see why.

First, IS's twin state-formation and nation-building enterprise will disappear, at least as currently configured in Iraq and Syria, but IS itself—it
will definitely have to rebrand itself again—will not disappear as long as
these two countries continue to be in political turmoil. The Islamic State
will reside within the interstices of the body politic, ready to strike whenever the opportunity presents itself. Its adherents are going to adapt and
claim that their current failure represents the Islamist version of the Leninist
method of "two steps back, one step forward."

Second, the Sunnis played a relatively insignificant role in the liberation from IS; this is an important point that will leave them with little
leverage vis-à-vis a disgruntled Baghdad government and vengeful Shia
community. To be sure, the Sunnis could claim that they had little choice;
but the fact that they facilitated IS's success and some joined it, hoping to
control and ride the tiger to victory, will not be forgotten. The stage will be
set for another cycle of revenge and counterrevenge.

Third, it is not clear that much in the way of efforts will be directed at
rebuilding and reintegrating the Sunni provinces in any meaningful way
anytime soon. Baghdad is strapped and will most likely focus on improvements in the Shia areas. It is not clear how much leeway the government
will have to make any progress in the Sunni areas, given the power of the
Shia paramilitaries and Iran's influence. The more the Sunnis push for
autonomy and regional security forces, the more the center will push
back. There have already been rumblings in favor of reviving the notion of
Sunni autonomy for the provinces where they constitute a majority.[173]

Fourth, enter the Kurds, who will continue to act as spoilers in order to
increase their freedom of action as they move stealthily toward greater
independence from Baghdad. Yes, there are tremendous obstacles standing in the way of outright independence, and the Kurds have recognized
that since the heady and euphoric days of 2014, when many gleefully
thought that IS was finally unraveling the Iraqi state. The fact that IS had
trounced them also did not finally translate into an existential threat. The
rebuilding of the Iraqi military and the rise in Shia power, reflected in
their capacity to fight, endure, suffer, and come out victorious against IS,
has been observed with unease by the Kurds, who now worry that the Shia
militias might engage them in a wider Arab-Kurdish battle after the end of
the Caliphate. Once again, this situation of conflict might provide an
opportunity for an IS comeback.[174]

In conclusion, by 2016, IS's twin state-formation and nation-building enterprise was facing profound disarray, and in 2017 it was in free fall, as IS was no longer engaging in any substantive state-formation or nation-building activities. It was fighting for its life, due to the massive reduction in its financial resources coupled with the military pressure being exerted on it from outside. The situation was worsened by the fact that IS's financial resources, already squeezed, were devoted largely to funding its war rather than the provision of services for its population. The decline in legitimacy due to the failing state-formation and nation-building enterprise did not help matters, but IS did not face a serious internal uprising, as its predecessor had between 2009 and 2011. It is not clear, however, that Iraq will be able to savor this victory unless it makes an effort at political reconciliation. Even then, much of Iraq's internal stability will still rely to some extent on resolution of the Syrian crisis.

Conclusions

IT IS MID-2017, and we are standing at a crossroads where every interested observer and participant in the drama in Iraq and Syria is wondering whether the demise of IS is around the corner. The Islamic State all but lost Mosul in late June 2017 after a long and bitter urban battle. Given the immense pressure that the large and unwieldy U.S.-led Coalition has been exerting against IS since 2016 and into mid-2017, the downfall of the Caliphate, such as it is under "Caliph Ibrahim," is a foregone conclusion. The effort to liberate Mosul from the clutches of IS was followed by more robust efforts to defeat it in Syria. There is no doubt that it will succumb to defeat there, too, unless, of course, its apocalyptic battle at the end of days in Dabiq, Syria, takes place soon with Jesus Christ leading the remnants of the true believers to eventual victory over its myriad enemies.[1] Since this is a fantasy, logically it will not become reality.

However, when Caliphate 3.0 ceases to exist, that will most likely not be the end of the entity known as IS. The history and contemporary structural conditions of the region provide the opportunity for IS to rise again (and indeed possibly for its equally dangerous rival, al-Qaeda, to revive its own fortunes at the expense of IS), while the fallible actions and decisions of human beings prove to be fertile grounds nourishing extremist violence.

The complicated trajectory of modern and contemporary Iraqi history, particularly the trajectory of state-formation and nation-building enterprises in a fragile ethno-sectarian environment, are critical for understanding why IS and its predecessors have been able to advance their own goals and agenda. History resonates in the region, and ideology can be used to create a historical narrative that many find believable.

Nonetheless, the more recent Iraqi political, socioeconomic, and international environments and the beliefs and actions of key personalities have provided sufficient factors to explain the rise, decline, rise, and now possible decline of IS. Saddam Hussein's Baathist regime was a brutal and execrable failure that merely succeeded in laying the groundwork for the emergence of ethno-sectarian divisions and violence in Iraq. The

United States cannot escape censure for its failures during the invasion and occupation between 2003 and 2011. George W. Bush may have genuinely believed that the United States was a force for good in the world and that its values were universal. He believed that the war in Iraq would install a democracy there and that would serve as a demonstration effect, bringing about democracy in the rest of the region. Where did these ideas come from? The terrorist attacks of 9/11 impelled him to articulate a narrative that the United States was fighting evil. He was influenced by the neoconservative power elite who dominated the top reaches of his administration, who were looking for more "amiable" leaders in turmoil-ridden Middle Eastern countries, and who claimed that they wanted to bring democratic governance to the downtrodden peoples of the region, beginning with Iraq.

However, for many Iraqis and other foreign observers, all the Bush administration succeeded in doing was to manufacture and implement institutionalized sectarian politics in the country by focusing on referring to "Sunni Arabs," "Shia Arabs," "Kurds," and other minorities.[2] What the Americans succeeded in doing was not state- or nation-building from the outside but precisely the opposite: state or nation disintegration in the worst possible way. And for the conspiracy-minded in the region, that was the plan all along. While the Americans are not innocent of what transpired in post-Saddam Iraq, their failures were not unique. Neither the Ottomans nor the British, and certainly not postindependence Iraqi regimes, had been averse to playing the sectarian card. And more recently, one cannot deny that IS is a pathologically sectarian entity in its quest to kill, drive out, or subjugate Shias, Christians, and Yazidis. Indeed, IS capitalized on the institutionalization of sectarianism and ethnic politics in Iraq to promote itself as the defender of the Sunnis, a line that also defends the Arabness of the Sunni Arabs, despite IS's strictures against nationalism.

Whatever the motivations for the invasion and occupation, the event led to a massive but disjointed insurgency beginning in 2003, which actually was never decisively defeated before the Americans left in 2011. The country had been unraveling due to years of misrule under Saddam Hussein and brutal international sanctions that had sapped the life out of the country and contributed to the strengthening of religion in a multiethnic and sectarian society. The vacillations and pusillanimity of Iraqi leaders in post-Saddam Iraq and U.S. mistakes did not help matters. Unsurprisingly, the outcome was a persistent Sunni insurgency beginning in 2003, which metastasized into a vicious civil war between Iraqi Sunnis and Shias. The Sahwa (Awakening) witnessed a rebellion within the insurgency in which several insurgent groups and tribes of the Sunni province of Anbar and the mixed province of Diyala turned against the most "extreme of the extremists," AQI. This insurgency within the insurgency, along with the arrival of more U.S. troops—the Surge—helped turn the tide of the war.

Many Iraqis felt elated in 2010 after this alliance of U.S. troops, Sunni insurgents, and the Iraqi Security Forces of the Shia-dominated government in Baghdad had routed AQI's successor, ISI.[3] For a brief moment thereafter it looked like Iraq was headed toward national unity and democracy. In reality, Iraq's trajectory from the end of the insurgency and the withdrawal of the Americans was toward greater authoritarianism, greater intolerance, and a Shia-dominated sectarian state. So what happened in Iraq to betray the promise of a brighter future and plunge the country into its present straits?

The Iraqi prime minister Nuri al-Maliki faced significant problems, not least of which was his own unbending and paranoid personality. Though a Shia himself, his standing among the Shia community was not uniformly positive, but he managed to skillfully outmaneuver some of his more serious rivals. Nonetheless, the endless bickering between various Shia groups, coupled with Shia Iran's looming presence, which he professed to be suspicious of, took up much of his energy. He botched relations with the Kurds over the nature of Kurdish autonomy, over their right to develop oil fields independently, and over the disputed city of Kirkuk. He made enemies of the Kurds when he needed them most to shore up the Iraqi state against the rising threat of a revitalized ISI, the more potent successor to AQI.[4] His ineptitude allowed the Kurds to promote and solidify their own distinct state-formation and nation-building enterprises, primarily by the expedients of seizing non-Kurdish territories from the wider Iraq, by rebuilding their deteriorating military forces, and by virtually concluding that Iraq had no viability anymore. However, the Kurds themselves are suffering from political and socioeconomic turmoil, corruption, and petty rivalries that have cast a shadow on the narrative they and their American supporters have created concerning their stability as contrasted with the rest of Iraq.[5]

The biggest source of worry and threat emanated from the disgruntled Sunni community, and Maliki's tussles on his Shia and Kurdish flanks complicated his ability to deal with this large minority community that was once at the top of the system and continued to entertain a sense of entitlement. The Sunnis rose in revolt once again because Maliki broke his promises. He did not integrate Sunni fighters into the new Iraqi Security Forces and did not provide the Sunni-majority regions with sufficient economic and development aid due to them by dint of Iraq's oil wealth. His government proved to be not only ineffective but also corrupt, well beyond even expansive regional standards. Maliki's Iraq was a state of maddening ideological contradictions and policies. The prime minister's "wooden" character—reflected in his inability to transcend sectarian politics and his proclivity to see Baathists from the former regime lurking behind every opposition move against him—succeeded in actually making him real enemies within the body politic.[6] To be fair to Maliki, it is possible that nothing he could have done would have satisfied those who opposed him. He was both a prisoner of and a willing participant in the rough and tumble of post-Saddam politics.

The turmoil in Iraqi politics provided the opportunity for ISI to make a comeback. And what a comeback it was between 2012 and 2016. To be sure, by mid-2017, when this book was finished, IS's gains were slowly but surely being reversed, but at tremendous cost to Iraq and the stability of the region. The Islamic State will be "knocked down" in 2017 when it loses Raqqa—its de facto "capital"—and Mosul, its biggest prize. But is anyone willing to bet that this will be the definite end of it? We now know that ISI was not thoroughly defeated or rooted out at the end of the first Iraqi insurgency in 2010. The Sunni uprising against ISI, as it came to call itself from 2006 onward, was neither as successful nor as extensive as it was made out to be. ISI was relentlessly battered by a variety of enemies; however, it simply went to ground, learned from its mistakes, rebuilt its organization, and established alliances with key local Sunni groups, whose suspicions of Maliki had by 2013 proved fully justified in their eyes. The ISI returned to the fray and subjected Iraq to further carnage by means of a relentless campaign of terrorism against civilians, whether Sunni or Shia. In April 2013 alone, suicide bombings killed seven hundred people, and on one day, May 20, seven car bombs went off in Shia neighborhoods of Baghdad.[7] This is but a slice of the steady uptick in violence at that time. The purpose of these attacks was to show that ISI was back, to promote recruitment to the cause, and to polarize relations once more between the Sunni and Shia communities.

From 2011 onward, the carnage of the Syrian civil war next door added fuel to the fire in Iraq. Despite President Bashar al-Assad's initial optimism that his country was immune from the revolutionary turmoil that had hit pro-Western authoritarian Arab regimes, Syria was roiled by popular discontent not long after the Egyptian Revolution of January 2011. This turned to revolutionary outrage as the regime lashed back with frightful violence, simply because it could and because that was the default reaction of an authoritarian regime beginning to feel besieged. Before long, Syria was embroiled in a bloody nationwide civil war featuring an incredibly diverse internal and external cast of characters.

Fighters of ISI infiltrated from Iraq and used the Syrian battlefield to improve their fighting skills. They also succeeded in bullying and defeating other rebel groups, including jihadists associated with al-Qaeda; carved out territory; and brought large numbers of Syrian Sunnis under their control. The Syrian element formed a group under their leader Mohammad al-Jolani called Jabhat al-Nusra. The new Iraqi leader of ISI, Abu Bakr al-Baghdadi, claimed that Jabhat al-Nusra was a subsidiary of his group. This set off a conflict with al-Qaeda's top leadership as well as with al-Jolani. Transformed into ISIS, and having expanded their combat manpower, the Iraqis, along with numerous foreign fighters, returned to Iraq and, after allying themselves with Sunni insurgents in Nineveh province starting in June 2014, conducted a lightning-quick advance. Former officers of the old Iraqi army helped ISIS in this "blitzkrieg" or rapid advance into other Sunni-majority provinces.[8] Having brought most of the Sunni-dominated regions in Iraq under their control, the jihadists declared IS, or more accurately, the Caliphate, on June 29, 2014.

Now that the early euphoria associated with this state-formation and Islamic nation-building enterprise is in the past, we are in a better position to see IS's façade and structural weaknesses more clearly. First, it may be an ideological entity, as has been mentioned throughout the book, but how ideologically committed to it is much of the population it controlled or "ruled"? To be sure, IS was welcomed in many areas initially because it replaced a hated government that provided little or no services or security, it brought "law and order," however strict, and its personnel were well behaved. Moreover, foreign fighters flocked to the cause at the height of IS's successes. As it settled into administering the territories it had acquired, the mask of civility and civilized behavior did not remain in place for long. The minorities knew who and what IS meant, and if they did not, it was not long before they found out the hard way. The Sunni Arabs and Turkmen should have known, as they had experienced its predecessor's mercies during the first insurgency. However, perhaps because of increasing ideological conviction among some of them, hatred for the Baghdad government, or fear, many jumped on the IS bandwagon, even if the oaths (bayaa) of some of the tribal sheikhs might have been nothing more than bending with the wind.

The Islamic State was able to take control over large swathes of territory, particularly in Sunni regions. It advanced rapidly in Sunni areas in

Iraq because they represented a "natural habitat." In Syria the "natural habitat" was theoretically larger because the majority of the population—roughly 75 percent—are Sunnis, but in Syria IS faces formidable Sunni opposition groups who are fighting it and the Assad regime. Iraq is where ISIS survived after its defeat in 2009 and subsequently revived, and where the fate of IS will be ultimately decided.[9] Much of IS's limitations stem from the irrevocable logic of the structural situation in which it finds itself; or as Faisal Itani put it: "the local demographic, geographic, and military realities of Iraq and Syria stand in the group's way, placing natural limits on how much it is likely to expand."[10] That is undoubtedly true. Not too many people on the ground in those two countries are willing to fight for or join the Caliphate. It does not make sense either for minorities or for the Kurds or Shias.

Second, despite its seemingly large number of personnel, IS simply did not have the capacity or resources to engage in large-scale war and state-formation simultaneously at the current juncture. The combination of war and state-formation ate up resources and personnel faster than IS could replace them. Many of the veterans, commanders, and ranks have been killed. War chews up money, and expenditure on the war has been the biggest cost, leaving precious little for effective governance and services, particularly as IS spends more money on retaining the loyalty of its core personnel even as their salaries are cut. Weapons lost and ammunition used are not easily replenished: the enemy—Iraqis, Kurds, and Syrians—are not running away as in the recent past. In the final analysis, IS remains a largely predatory economic structure—moving like a swarm of locusts from one source of income or resources, as it is exhausted, to another to exploit—rather than an institutionalized and stationary economic structure that is extracting resources in an efficient and rational manner.

Of course, IS could have dropped its aspirational goal of *tamaddud* (expanding) and focused on *baqiya* (remaining), which would have meant consolidating control over existing territory and people. This would have also meant evacuating untenable territory and losing some people. Much of IS's presence on the ground in Syria and Iraq constituted nothing more than tenuous control of swaths of territory.[11] An Islamic state that is in the state of remaining (*baqiya*) is as dangerous as one that also seeks expansion (*tamaddud*). If IS had focused on remaining, it would have conserved resources, rationalized its borders, and defended them more easily, and it could have deepened its legitimacy among the people it controlled, who would have felt they had no alternative but to "legitimize" IS's rule over them. However, mere consolidation without expansion went against the ideological grain of IS.

By the autumn of 2014, clear front lines between IS fighters and their opponents had taken shape. The aerial campaign by the United States and a motley crew of countries slowed down and, in many places, reversed IS's gains. The anti-IS forces on the ground, particularly the Iraqi Security Forces, the militias, and the Kurdish Peshmerga, improved largely thanks to battlefield lessons learned and intensive retraining by Western military advisors. By mid-2016, IS had lost upward of 30 percent of the territory it had conquered in Syria and Iraq. The process of territorial loss continued irreversibly well into mid-2017. By late 2016, the IS leadership began preparing for the eventuality that the Caliphate, established with so much fanfare in mid-2014, might be destroyed. A significant number of its commanders were killed, and in August 2016 an air strike on al-Bab in Aleppo province killed Abu Mohammad al-Adnani (aka Taha Sobhi Falaha), IS's senior spokesman and a senior operational commander whose portfolio had included commanding external terror operations against Europe.[12] In retaliation for the international U.S.-led Coalition's military actions, which had succeeded in loosening IS's control over territory, IS reverted to one of the key capabilities in its arsenal: terrorism.[13] Attacks in France, Turkey, and Belgium, either by IS itself or by those who claimed adherence to it, seemed to have woken up the international community to the changes in IS's strategy and the serious threat it represented. Its losses on the ground in conventional and semiconventional war have not significantly lowered its allure, which may stem from its continued ability to conduct terrorist strikes in a wide variety of locales around the globe.[14]

Lost in the growing confidence that the tide has turned against IS is the fact that the military defeat of it in Iraq and Syria should be one pillar of a comprehensive strategy to rebuild those two countries. This will require that the regional states and the international community address the grievances of various communities, including but not limited to those who provided succor, voluntary or forced, to IS.[15] Multilateral counterterrorism efforts must be proactive so as to ensure that IS remnants do not ensconce themselves in Libya, Somalia, or Yemen. These three countries represent serious problems for regional stability, as they suffer from catastrophic political, socioeconomic, and communal divisions. Both regional and international powers have found themselves being slowly sucked into the violence in Libya. In Libya, IS came under increasing pressure in late 2016 from its opponents. It is clear that more is required in terms of rebuilding the Libyan state than mere tactical victories on the ground. Yemen's viability as a state has taken a severe beating because of the bloody war between the Houthi rebels and a Saudi-led Arab coalition; however, as of the end of 2016, IS had little traction in that hapless country. Information about IS's presence in Somalia remains tenuous and unverifiable.

This book was completed in mid-2017. The tide turned against IS in the last quarter of 2016. The Iraqi military began its long-heralded offensive to liberate Mosul from the clutches of IS in mid-October 2016. The going was tough because IS's fighters proved to be resilient and willing to fight to the death. The bulk of the fighting in "Arab" Iraq in the north was borne by a small number of elite units who got "chewed up" badly, even if they invariably emerged victorious against IS. There were tensions between Iraqi military and Kurdish Peshmerga units, as well as between Iraqi military and Shia militia groups. By early 2017, the eastern and more modern part of Mosul had been liberated from IS. The immense task of liberating the western half of the city began in February 2017. The saga will continue well into 2017. Two important considerations come to mind as we ponder what could happen for the remainder of 2017 and possibly well into 2018.

First, while IS lost Mosul in 2017, this defeat is unlikely to be the end of this nettlesome entity. Fighting the group and undermining its legitimacy will be difficult and complex, even if it loses the Caliphate in its current configuration sometime in 2017. Reversing the attraction of IS among would-be or existing adherents will be more difficult than chipping away at its territory. We should do well to remember that outside observers were too ready to consign its predecessor, ISI, to oblivion around 2009–2010. Like a phoenix rising out of the ashes, it came back again stronger, more genocidal, and better prepared.

While it was losing its Caliphate steadily in 2016, the full defeat of IS will be a long time in coming.[16] Indeed, it may eschew the state-building enterprise for a while, shelve it, and focus on fighting a terrorist and mobile guerrilla war. Despite the defeats of its personnel on the ground in Syria and Iraq and the resulting slowdown in the flow of foreign fighters, it is not clear that the constellation of jihadist sympathizers around the world is drying up. In order to maintain support among adherents and induce fear in enemies, IS had no choice but to expand, both spatially and symbolically, its grotesque repertoire of violence.[17] To be sure, some of IS's fighters, chastened by the brutal and brutalizing experience of IS, may "bleed back" into or join for the first time al-Qaeda, a more decentralized entity, which may welcome them. In the final analysis, this is a chameleon-like and dynamic paradigm of war. Both Iraq and the international community need a new strategy to deal with it.

Second, once the fighting in Mosul is over, Iraq will not be safe, as it is likely that the next round of fighting or ethnic cleansing could engulf the feuding ethno-sectarian communities that make up Iraq.[18] In this later fight, IS remnants will always be there, lurking in the shadows, to take advantage of any opportunity to make a come-back. The Iraqi victory in Mosul could be the beginning of the country's post-IS headaches, and these will be severe.[19] Sunnis' fears of Shia revanchism will be paralleled by their growing desire to get a Sunni region with full powers of autonomy. They would, no doubt, demand the exclusion of the presence of the Shia-dominated security forces from their region. If Baghdad does not heed possible Sunni demands for a greater say in their affairs, and particularly their insistence on keeping the government military and Shia militias out of Sunni regions, the result could be a recurrence of violence between Sunnis and Shias, and the cycle of Sunni insurgency could start all over again.

It is possible that the Kurds and the Sunni regional powers, such as Turkey and Saudi Arabia, could egg on the Sunnis in their endeavor to attain greater autonomy. The Kurds could encourage the Sunnis to demand greater regional autonomy in order to weaken the Shia-dominated government in Baghdad and get it to focus on the Sunnis rather than refocus its attention on the Kurdish entity's slow but steady "creeping toward independence and de jure *statehood*." Many Kurds are afraid that the government in Baghdad will seek to reverse the opportunistic territorial gains the Kurds have made as IS has lost territory.[20] To be sure, the Kurds and the Sunnis—Arab and Turkmen—in the north may get involved in their own altercation over the division of territories after IS is expelled. The result may be significant bloodshed. The Kurds would have the upper hand because of their better equipped and now more experienced forces. However, a Sunni-Kurdish altercation would likely involve the Iraqi and Turkish governments, seeking to thwart wider Kurdish aspirations.

In short, the defeat of IS in Iraq in 2017, symbolized by the loss of Mosul, is likely to be the close of one chapter and the opening of another in the long saga of the battle against IS. The world should be prepared for the next phase of its evolution.

Notes

CHAPTER 1

1. The quote from "Caliph Ibrahim" is from Cole Bunzel, "From Paper State to the Caliphate: The Ideology of the Islamic State," Brookings Institution, Analysis Paper 19 (March 2015), 31.
2. On the saga of the caliphate and its destruction in 1258 by the Mongols and its abolition in 1924 by the new post–World War I Turkish state, see the extensive analysis of Mona Hassan, "Loss of Caliphate: The Trauma and Aftermath of 1258 and 1924," Ph.D. diss., Princeton University, 2009.
3. For a review of the major books on IS to date, see Gareth Stansfield, "Explaining the Aims, Rise and Impact of the Islamic State in Iraq and al-Sham," *Middle East Journal* 70, 1 (Winter 2016), 146–151.
4. These were extensively reviewed; see, for example, Steve Negus, "ISIS: Inside the Army of Terror, and More," *New York Times*, April 1, 2015, http://www.nytimes.com/2015/04/05/books/review/isis-inside-the-army-of-terror-and-more.html.
5. Ben Fishman, "Defining ISIS," *Survival* 58, 1 (2016), 179–188.
6. This section relies heavily on the following works: Renate Mayntz, *Organizational Forms of Terrorism: Hierarchy, Network, or a Type Sui Generis?*, Discussion Paper 4, Munich: Max Planck Institut fur Gesellschaftsforschung, 2004; H. Brinton Millward and Jorg Raab, "Dark Networks as Organizational Problems: Elements of a Theory," *International Public Management Journal* 9, 3 (2006), 333–360; Jacob Shapiro, "Organizing Terror: Hierarchy and Networks in Covert Organizations," August 23, 2005, unpublished manuscript.
7. Mary Jo Hatch, *Organizations: A Very Short Introduction*, Oxford: Oxford University Press, 2011, 1.
8. Paul Tompkins and Robert Leonhard, eds., *Undergrounds in Insurgent, Revolutionary, and Resistance Warfare*, 2nd ed., Laurel, MD: United States Army Special Operations Command and Johns Hopkins University Applied Physics Laboratory, January 2013.

9. This brief foray into the definition of ideology is largely based on John Gerring, "Ideology: A Definitional Analysis," *Political Research Quarterly* 50, 4 (December 1997), 957–994.

10. See Jacob Shapiro, *The Terrorists' Dilemma: Managing Violent Covert Organizations*, Princeton: Princeton University Press, 2013, especially 26–62; Zachariah Mampilly, "Stationary Bandits: Understanding Rebel Governance," Ph.D. diss., University of California, Los Angeles, 2007.

11. I have been teaching and reading about "small wars," guerrilla warfare, insurgency, etc. for the past fifteen years, and the brief discussion of them in the main body of the book is a distillation of this knowledge. However, I also benefited immensely from two recent books as I was writing: William Urban, *Small Wars and Their Influence on Nation States: 1500 to the Present*, Barnsley, Yorkshire: Frontline Books, 2016, and Simon Innes-Robbins, *Dirty Wars: A Century of Counterinsurgency*, Brimscombe Port Stroud, Gloucestershire: History Press, 2016.

12. Eli Lake, Jeanie Dettmer, and Nadette Visser, "Iraq's Terrorists Are Becoming a Full-Blown Army," *Daily Beast*, June 11, 2014, http://www.thedailybeast.com/iraqs-terrorists-are-becoming-a-full-blown-army.

13. The literature on hybrid warfare is now enormous. Though I have adopted a somewhat different set of premises concerning nonstate actors, I have benefited primarily from the writings of Frank Hoffman, a former U.S. Marine Corps officer, for the development of my ideas of IS's hybrid warfare capabilities and styles: Frank G. Hoffmann, "How Marines Are Preparing for Hybrid Wars," *Armed Forces Journal*, March 2006, http://armedforcesjournal.com/how-marines-are-preparing-for-hybrid-wars/. Frank G. Hoffmann, "Lessons from Lebanon: Hezbollah and Hybrid Wars," Foreign Policy Research Institute, August 2, 2006, http://www.fpri.org/article/2006/08/lessons-from-lebanon-hezbollah-and-hybrid-wars/. Frank G. Hoffmann, "Hybrid Warfare and Challenges," *Joint Force Quarterly* 51 (2009), 34–39; Frank G. Hoffmann, "Hybrid vs. Compound War, the Janus Choice: Defining Today's Multifaceted Conflict," *Armed Forces Journal*, October 2009, http://armedforcesjournal.com/hybrid-vs-compound-war/.

14. Margaret Coker, "How Islamic State's Win in Ramadi Reveals New Weapons, Tactical Sophistication and Prowess; Examination of Ramadi's Downfall Reflects Complex Plans and Weapons," *Wall Street Journal*, May 25, 2015; "Offensive Manoeuvres—The Islamic State Advances on Kurds in Northern Iraq," JTIC Brief, *Jane's Terrorism and Security Monitor* 14, 8 (September 1, 2014); Lizzie Dearden, "ISIS Making Deadly Suicide Bombs and IEDs Using Freely Available Components from Around the World," *Independent*, February 25, 2016, http://www.independent.co.uk/news/world/middle-east/isis-deadly-suicide-bombs-ieds-legal-civilian-components-from-world-islamic-state-daesh-a6893856.html.

15. Siobhan Gorman and Julian Barnes, "Middle East in Turmoil: U.S. Strikes Alter the Battlefield in Iraq—Intelligence Shows Attacks Curb Islamic State Fighters, but Shift Makes Them Harder to Target as Campaign Expands," *Wall Street Journal*, September 15, 2014, A8.

16. See Andrea Kathryn Talentino, "The Two Faces of Nation-Building: Developing Function and Identity," *Cambridge Review of International Affairs* 17, 3 (October 2004), 557–575.

17. Stacy Erin Pollard, David Alexander Poplack, and Kevin C. Casey, "Understanding the Islamic State's Competitive Advantages: Remaking State and Nationhood in the Middle East and North Africa," *Terrorism and Political Violence* (online), December 2015, 1–21.

18. I have relied heavily on Heather Rae, *State Identities and the Homogenisation of Peoples*, Cambridge: Cambridge University Press, 2002, 14–54.

19. Youssef Cohen, Brian Brown, and A. F. K. Organski, "The Paradoxical Nature of State Making; The Violent Creation of Order," *American Political Science Review* 75, 4 (December 1981), 901–910.

20. As I did not intend to get bogged down in theory for this study, I have kept it short. Nonetheless, my understanding of state-formation and nation-building has benefited enormously from the writings of Otto Hintze, Charles Tilly, and various other scholars. See Felix Gilbert, ed., *The Historical Essays of Otto Hintze*, New York: Oxford University Press, 1975; Charles Tilly, "Reflections on the History of European State-Making," in Charles Tilly et al., eds., *Formation of the National States in Western Europe*, Princeton: Princeton University Press, 1975; 3–83; Charles Tilly, *Coercion, Capital and European States, A.D. 990–1992*, Cambridge, MA: Blackwell, 1992.

21. Zeljko Branovic and Sven Chojnacki, "The Logic of Security Markets: Security Governance in Failed States," *Security Dialogue* 42 (2011), 556.

22. Jeremy Weinstein, "Resource and the Information Problem in Rebel Recruitment," *Journal of Conflict Resolution* 49, 4 (2005), 598–624; Ethan Bueno de Mesquita, "The Quality of Terror," *American Journal of Political Science* 49, 3 (2005), 515–530; Mark Irving Lichbach, *The Rebel's Dilemma*, Ann Arbor: University of Michigan Press, 1995.

23. Here I have relied on Jennifer Marie Keister, "States within States: How Rebels Rule," Ph.D. diss., University of California, 2011, 25.

24. Ibid., 32.

25. Margaret Levi, *Of Rule and Revenue*, Berkeley: University of California Press, 1988); Margaret Levi, "The Predatory Theory of Rule," *Politics and Society* 22, 1 (1981), 431–466; Tilly, *Coercion, Capital and European States*.

26. This is an academic book that models itself explicitly on four other academic books, which I have kept by my side like "bibles": Jeremy Weinstein's *Inside Rebellion*, Noriyuki Katagiri's *Adapting to Win*, Jacob Shapiro's *The Terrorists' Dilemma*, and Paul Staniland's *Networks of Rebellion*. They provided the inspiration for me to adopt an academic approach to the study of ISIS and IS, but this is not a heavily theoretical work.

27. I have found several blogs of immense use; the most helpful were *Pietervanostaeyen*, *Jihadica.com*, *Oryx Blog*, and *Jihadology*. Many of the Arabic-language jihadist and Iraqi insurgent sources I have used were downloaded several years ago

when I wrote my first two studies, and many of the sites may now be inoperative. Similarly, the voluminous number of unclassified documents I have used from the Open Source Center—a Central Intelligence Agency resource that is invaluable—was available from my government days; though these are not classified documents, access to the site is password protected and open only to U.S. government employees and contractors.

28. Ariel Ahram, "Iraq in the Social Sciences: Testing the Limits of Research," *Journal of the Middle East and Africa* 4, 3 (2013), 251–266.

29. Daniel Milton, "The Islamic State: An Adaptive Organization Faces Increasing Challenges," in Mohammad al-Ubaydi, Nelly Lahoud, Daniel Milton, and Bryan Price, *The Group That Calls Itself a State: Understanding the Evolution and Challenges of the Islamic State*, West Point: Combating Terrorism Center, December 2014, 36.

30. For details of Todenhöfer lengthy negotiations with IS personnel to gain access to the Caliphate, see Jurgen Todenhofer, "Into the Heart of Terror: Behind ISIS Lines," *Guardian*, April 4, 2016, https://www.theguardian.com/world/2016/apr/04/behind-isis-lines-jurgen-todenhofer-journalist-syria-iraq-my-journey-into-the-heart-of-terror; Jurgen Todenhofer, "Behind Enemy Lines: My Journey into the Heart of ISIS," *Telegraph*, April 8, 2016, http://s.telegraph.co.uk/graphics/projects/islamic-state-journey-into-isis/index.html.

31. For an interesting discussion of the politics behind nomenclature, see Asaf Siniver and Scott Lucas, "The Islamic State Lexical Battleground: US Foreign Policy and the Abstraction of Threat," *International Affairs* 92, 1 (2016), 63–79.

CHAPTER 2

1. Nabil al-Tikriti, "Was There an Iraq before There Was an Iraq?," *International Journal of Contemporary Iraqi Studies* 3, 2 (2009), 133–142; Reidar Visser, "Proto-political Conceptions of 'Iraq' in Late Ottoman Times," *International Journal of Contemporary Iraqi Studies* 3, 2 (2009), 143–154.

2. This entire chapter, which deals with the history of Iraq from ancient times to the period of Saddam Hussein, is a concise summary from my forthcoming book *God, Greed, and Guns: Iraqi State-Formation and Nation-Building*, Philadelphia: University of Pennsylvania Press, forthcoming. Even though I may not cite them much or at all throughout the chapter, it also draws heavily on the studies of Iraqi history and politics by well-known leading scholars who have spent their careers exploring that country: Hanna Batatu, Charles Tripp, Phebe Marr, Eric Davis, Toby Dodge, Amatzia Baram, Peter Sluglett, Adeed Dawisha, Ali Allawi, Joseph Sassoon, and Dina Khoury.

3. Jonathan Fine, *Political Violence in Judaism, Christianity and Islam: From Holy War to Modern Terror*, Lanham, MD: Rowman and Littlefield, 2015, 8.

4. Quoted in Mark Healy, *The Ancient Assyrians*, New York: Osprey, 1991, 5.

5. For this summary of the succession question I have relied on the highly readable account by Hugh Kennedy, *The Caliphate*, Milton Keynes, England: Pelican Books, 2016, 1–44.

6. See I. P. Petrushevsky, *Islam in Iran*, Albany: State University of New York Press, 1985, 22; Moojan Momen, *An Introduction to Shi'i Islam*, New Haven: Yale University Press, 1985, 11; Hamid Enayat, *Modern Islamic Political Thought*, Austin: University of Texas Press, 1982, 4.

7. Quoted in Enayat, *Modern Islamic Thought*, 4; see also Yann Richard, *L'Islam chi'ite: Croyances et ideologies*, Paris: Fayard, 1991, 30–31.

8. Petrushevsky, *Islam in Iran*, 30–31; Allamah S. Mohammad Hussein Tabataba'i, *Shi'ite Islam*, London: Allen and Unwin, 1973.

9. Richard, *L'Islam chi'ite*, 32–33.

10. Richard, *L'Islam chi'ite*, 44.

11. Rashid Wu Pai-nan, "The Fall of Baghdad and the Mongol Role in Al-Iraq, 1258–1335," Ph.D. diss., University of Utah, 1974.

12. Quoted in Suleiman Mourad and James E. Lindsay, *The Intensification and Reorientation of Sunni Jihad Ideology in the Crusader Period: Ibn 'Asakir of Damascus (1105–1176) and His Age, with an Edition and Translation of Ibn 'Asakir's "The Forty Hadith for Inciting Jihad,"* Leiden: Brill, 2013, 107.

13. Yvette Talhami, "The Fatwas and the Nusayri/Alawis of Syria," *Middle East Studies* 46, 2 (2010), 175–194.

14. Taqi al-Din Ahmed Ibn Taymiyya, *Kitab al-jihad*, quoted in Mourad and Lindsay, *Intensification and Reorientation of Sunni Jihad Ideology in the Crusader Period*, 107–108.

15. For brief summaries of Ottoman-Iranian geopolitical and religious contention over Mesopotamia, see al-Tikriti, "Was There an Iraq before There Was an Iraq?," 133–142; and Visser, "Proto-political Conceptions of 'Iraq' in Late Ottoman Times," 143–154.

16. Ann Lambton, *State and Government in Medieval Islam*, Oxford: Oxford University Press, 1981, 212–213.

17. Selim Deringil, "The Struggle against Shiism in Hamidian Iraq: A Study in Ottoman Counter-propaganda," *Die Welt des Islams*, new series, 40, 1–4 (1990), 45–62.

18. For more extensive details, see Khalil Osman, *Sectarianism in Iraq: The Making of State and Nation since 1920*, London: Routledge, 2015, 59–64.

19. Pierre-Jean Luizard, "La communauté chiite, premiere victime de l'implosion de la societe irakienne," *Herodote* 124, first quarter 2007, 118.

20. Faleh Jabar, "Le Leviathan et le sacré: Le Baas et les chiites," in Chris Kutschera, ed., *Le Livre Noir de Saddam Hussein*, Paris: Oh! Editions, 2005, 220–221.

21. Tom Nieuwenhuis, *Politics and Society in Early Modern Iraq: Mamluk Pashas, Tribal Shaykhs and Local Rule between 1802 and 1831*, The Hague: Martinus Nijhoff, 1981, 171.

22. Derived from my forthcoming book *God, Greed and Guns*; see also Michael Hechter and Nika Kabiri, "Attaining Social Order in Iraq," paper delivered at the Conference on Order, Conflict and Violence, Yale University, April 30–May 1, 2004, 8.

23. Charles Tripp, *A History of Iraq*, Cambridge: Cambridge University Press, 2007, 9.

24. Tom Nieuwenhuis, *Politics and Society in Early Modern Iraq*, vii.

25. Zoe Preston, *The Crystallization of the Iraqi State*, Oxford: Peter Lang, 87.

26. Ibid., 87; M. S. Hasan, "Growth and Structure of Iraq's Population, 1867–1947," in Charles Issawi, ed., *The Economic History of the Middle East, 1800–1914*, Chicago: University of Chicago Press, 1975, 155–162.

27. Rousseau, *Description*, 74–75, quoted and translated in Mohamad Ballan, "The Wahhabi Sack of Karbala (1802 A.D.)," *Ballandalus* (blog), August 2, 2014, https://ballandalus.wordpress.com/2014/08/02/the-wahhabi-sack-of-karbala-1802-a-d/.

28. For extensive details see Yitzhak Naqash, "The Conversion of Iraq's Tribes to Shiism," *International Journal of Middle East Studies* 26, 3 (August 1994), 443–463; Erhan Bektas, "The 'Tanzimat State' in the Ottoman Iraq: Tribes, Ideology/ Shiism and Taxation, 1830–1910," M.A. thesis, Bogazici University, 2015, 64–84.

29. Gertrude Bell, *Review of the Civil Administration, 1914–1920*, London: His Majesty's Stationery Office, 1920, 49.

30. On the Ottomans' relations with the Shia clerical establishment, see Pierre Martin (pseud.), "Le clergé chiite en Irak hier et aujourd'hui," *Maghreb-Machrek* 115 (January–February 1987), 29–53; Selim Deringil, "The Struggle against Shiism in Hamidian Iraq," *Die Welt des Islams* 30, 1 (1990), 45–62.

31. Gökhan Çetinsaya, "The Caliph and Mujtahids: Ottoman Policy towards the Shiite Community of Iraq in the Late Nineteenth Century," *Middle Eastern Studies* 41, 4 (July 2005), 561–574; see also Sami Zubaida, "The Fragments Imagine the Nation: The Case of Iraq," *International Journal of Middle East Studies* 34, 2 (May 2002), 205.

32. See Charles Tripp, *A History of Iraq*, Cambridge: Cambridge University Press, 2007, 8–29; Hala Mundhir Fattah, *The Politics of Regional Trade in Iraq, Arabia and the Gulf, 1745–1900*, Albany: State University of New York Press, 1997; Hashim, *God, Greed and Guns*.

33. Ebubekir Ceylan, "Carrot or Stick? Ottoman Tribal Policy in Baghdad, 1831–1876," *International Journal of Contemporary Iraqi Studies* 3, 3 (2009), 169–186.

34. John Frederick Williamson, "A Political History of the Shammar Jarba Tribe of Al-Jazirah, 1800–1958," Ph.D. diss., Indiana University, 1985.

35. Ibid., 45–46.

36. See Albertine Jwaideh, "Midhat Pasha and the Land System of Lower Iraq," in Albert Hourani, ed., *Middle Eastern Affairs*, Carbondale: Southern Illinois University Press, 1963, 103–136.

37. Pierre-Jean Luizard, *La Formation de l'Irak Contemporain*, Paris: CNRS Editions, 2002, 19.

38. Myriam Benraad, "Du phénomène arab sunnite irakien: Recompositions sociales, paradoxes identitaires et bouleversement geopolitiques sous occupation (2003–2008)," *Herodote* 130 (3rd quarter 2008), 59–75, https://www.cairn.info/revue-herodote-2008-3.htm.

39. Reeva Simon, "The Education of an Iraqi Ottoman Army Officer," in Rashid Khalidi, Lisa Anderson, Muhammad Muslih, and Reeva Simon, eds., *The Origins of Arab Nationalism*, New York: Columbia University Press, 1991, 151.

40. On Ottoman modernization practices in Iraq, see Abdul Wahab al-Qaysi, "The Impact of Modernization on Iraqi Society during the Ottoman Era: A Study of Intellectual Development in Iraq, 1969–1917," Ph.D. diss., University of Michigan, 1958, 1–114.

41. Gökhan Çetinsaya, "Ottoman-British Relations in Iraq and the Gulf, 1890–1908," *Turkish Review of the Middle East* 15 (2004), 137–175.

42. S. A. Cohen, "The Genesis of the British Campaign in Mesopotamia, 1914," *Middle Eastern Studies* 12, 2 (May 1976), 119–132.

43. Helmut Mejcher, "Oil and British Policy towards Mesopotamia, 1914–1918," *Middle Eastern Studies* 8, 3 (October 1972), 377–391.

44. Ravinder Kumar, "The Records of the Government of India on the Berlin-Baghdad Railway Question," *Historical Journal* 5, 1 (1962), 70–71.

45. V. H. Rothwell, "Mesopotamia in British War Aims, 1914–1918," *Historical Journal* 13, 2 (June 1970), 273–294.

46. Paul Knight, *The British Army in Mesopotamia, 1914–1918*, Jefferson, NC: McFarland, 2013, 6.

47. Quoted in Hew Strachan, *The First World War*, vol. 1, *To Arms*, New York: Oxford University Press, 2001, 660.

48. Rothwell, "Mesopotamia in British War Aims, 1914–1918," 273–294.

49. "Proclamation of Baghdad," March 11, 1917, https://archive.globalpolicy.org/component/content/article/169-history/48112-proclamation-of-baghdad.html.

50. For a recent extended analysis of Sykes-Picot see Walter Reid, *Empire of Sand: How Britain Made the Middle East*, Edinburgh: Birlinn, 2013, 97–108.

51. Eli Amarilyo, "History, Memory and Commemoration: The Iraqi Revolution of 1920 and the Process of Nation-Building in Iraq," *Middle Eastern Studies* 51, 1 (2015), 72–92.

52. Sir Aylmer Haldane, *The Insurrection in Mesopotamia*, Edinburgh: Blackwood, 1922, 35.

53. Kristian Coates Ulrichsen, "The British Occupation of Mesopotamia, 1914–1922," *Journal of Strategic Studies* 30, 2 (April 2007), 349.

54. Haldane, *Insurrection in Mesopotamia*, 64.

55. Ian Rutledge, *Enemy on the Euphrates: The Battle for Iraq, 1914–1921*, London: Saqi, 2015, xxiii.

56. Ghassan Attiyah, *Iraq, 1908–1921: A Socio-political Study*, Beirut: Arab Institute for Research and Publishing, 1973, 307.

57. Zubaida, "Fragments Imagine the Nation," 205–215.

58. Hanna Batatu, *The Old Social Classes and the Revolutionary Movements of Iraq*, Princeton: Princeton University Press, 1978, 23.

59. Abbas Kadhim, "Efforts at Cross-ethic [*sic*] Cooperation: The 1920 Revolution and Sectarian Identities in Iraq," *International Journal of Contemporary Iraqi Studies* 4, 3 (2010), 275–338.

60. See A. L. MacFie, "British Intelligence and the Causes of Unrest in Mesopotamia, 1919–21," *Middle Eastern Studies* 35, 1 (January 1999), 165–177.

61. Attiyah, *Iraq 1902–1921: A Socio-political Study*, 340.

62. Amarilyo, "History, Memory and Commemoration," 72–92.

63. Mark Jacobsen, "'Only by the Sword': British Counter-insurgency in Iraq, 1920," *Small Wars and Insurgencies* 2, 2 (August 1991), 323–363.

64. On Iraqi state-formation and nation-building from the time of the British onward, see Peter Sluglett, *Britain in Iraq, 1914–1032*, London: Ithaca Press, 1976; Phebe Marr, "The Development of Nationalist Ideology in Iraq, 1920–1941," *Muslim World* 75, 2 (April 1985), 85–101; Hanna Batatu, *The Old Social Classes and the Revolutionary Movements of Iraq*, Princeton: Princeton University Press, 1978; Adeed Dawisha, "The Unraveling of Iraq: Ethnosectarian Preferences and State Performance in Historical Perspective," *Middle East Journal* 62, 2 (Spring 2008), 219–230.

65. Ronen Zeidel, "A Harsh Readjustment: The Sunnis and the Political Process in Contemporary Iraq," *Middle East Review of International Affairs* 12, 1 (March 2008), http://www.rubincenter.org/2008/03/zeidel-2008-03-04/.

66. On early Anglo-Kurdish relations see Saad Eskander, "Britain's Policy in Southern Kurdistan: The Formation and Termination of the First Kurdish Government, 1918–1919," *British Journal of Middle Eastern Studies* 27, 2 (November 2000), 139–163.

67. On the formation of the Iraqi army, see Mark Heller, "Politics and the Military in Iraq and Jordan, 1920–1958," *Armed Forces and Society* 4, 1 (November 1977), 77–86; Faisal Al Samir, "The Role of the Army in the National, Social and Political Development of Iraq," in Claude Heller, ed., *The Military as an Agent of Social Change*, Mexico City: El Colegio de Mexico, 1981, 107–126.

68. See Nils Naastad, "Policing the British Empire from the Air," in Carsten F. Ronnfeldt and Per Erik Solli, eds., *Use of Air Power in Peace Operations*, Oslo: Norwegian Institution of International Affairs, 1997, 19–37; Alison Williams, "*Hukumat al Tayarrat:* The Role of Air Power in the Enforcement of Iraq's Boundaries," *Geopolitics* 12 (2007), 505–528.

69. Jaffna Cox, "A Splendid Training Ground: The Importance to the Royal Air Force of Its Role in Iraq, 1919–1922," *Journal of Imperial and Commonwealth History* 13, 2 (1985), 157–184.

70. Lawrence James, *Imperial Rearguard: Wars of Empire, 1919–1985*, London: Brassey's Defence, 1988, 77.

71. Troutbeck to Eden, Confidential, October 31, 1952, Foreign Office 371/98747, British National Archives, London.

72. Ibid.

73. Troutbeck to Eden, December 9, 1954, Foreign Office 371/110991, British National Archives, retrieved July 2009.

74. Pierre Martin, "Une grande figure de l'Islamisme en Irak," *Les Cahiers de l'Orient* 8–9 (4th quarter 1987 and 1st quarter 1988), 121–122.

75. Jabar, "Le Leviathan et le sacré," 224.

76. Faisal al-Samir, "The Role of the Army in the National, Social and Political Development of Iraq," in Heller, *Military as an Agent of Social Change*, 107–126; Hamid al-Shawi, "Le Ba'th et l'armée en Irak et en Syrie," *Maghreb-Machrek* 71 (January–February 1976), 66–72.

77. See John Devlin, "The Baath Party: Rise and Metamorphosis," *American Historical Review* 96, 5 (December 1991), 1396–1407.

78. May Chartouni-Dubarry, "The Development of Internal Politics in Iraq from 1958 to the Present Day," in Derek Hopwood, Habib Ishow, and Thomas Koszinowski, eds., *Iraq: Power and Society*, Reading: Ithaca Press, 1993, 19–36.

79. For an excellent analysis of the origins of the second Baathist regime, see Marion Farouk-Sluglett and Peter Sluglett, "From Gang to Elite: The Iraqi Ba'th Party's Consolidation of Power, 1968–1975," *Peuples Mediterraneens* 40 (July–September 1987), 89–113.

80. Amatzia Baram, "Qawmiyya and Wataniyya in Ba'thi Iraq: The Search for a New Balance," *Middle Eastern Studies* 19, 2 (April 1983), 188–200.

81. For an extensive analysis of the strengths and weaknesses of the Baathist state's political economy see Isam al-Khafaji, "In Search of Legitimacy: The Post-rentier Iraqi State," *Contemporary Conflicts*, March 26, 2004, http://conconflicts.ssrc .org/archives/iraq/khafaji/.

82. Charles Saint-Prot, *Saddam Hussein: Un Gaullisme Arabe?*, Paris: Albin Michel, 1987, 16.

83. Ahmed S. Hashim, "Military Power and State Formation in Modern Iraq," *Middle East Policy* 10, 4 (Winter 2003), 29–47.

84. Salar Bassireh, "Das politische System im Irak unter den Baath-Partei: Stabilisierungs-und Destabilisierungs faktoren der Baath-Herschaft," Ph.D. diss., Wuppertal University, 2003.

85. Ofra Bengio, "Shi'is and Politics in Ba'thi Iraq," *Middle Eastern Studies* 21, 1 (January 1985), 1–14.

86. The most extensive and best analyses of the "Shia problem" in Iraq in Western languages and on which I relied heavily are Ferhad Ibrahim, *Konfessionalismus und Politik in der arabischen Welt: Der Schiiten im Irak*, Muenster: Lit Verlag, 1997;

Faleh A. Mahmood, "The Social Origins and Ideology of the Shi'i Islamist Movements in Iraq 1958–1990," Ph.D. diss., Birkbeck College, University of London, 1999; Florian Bernhardt, "Die schiitisch-islamistische Bewegung im Irak: Hizb al-Da'wa al-Islamiya (1958–1992)," M.A. thesis, Freie Universität Berlin, November 2001.

87. Mahmood, "Social Origins and Ideology of the Shi'i Islamist Movements in Iraq, 1958–1990," 170–171.

88. On the 1977 episode, see Bengio, "Shi'is and Politics in Ba'thi Iraq," 1–14.

89. On Baathist Iraq's Shia problem, see ibid., 1–14.

90. For more on the rise of the radical Shia religious parties see Joyce Wiley, *The Islamic Movements of Iraqi Shias*, Boulder: Rienner, 1992; Amatzia Baram, "The Radical Shi'ite Opposition in Iraq," in Emanuel Sivan and Menachem Friedman, eds., *Religious Radicalism and Politics in the Middle East*, Albany: State University of New York Press, 1990.

91. Saddam Hussein, "A View of Religion and Heritage," in Saddam Hussein, *On History, Heritage and Religion*, Baghdad, 1981, 24.

92. Amatzia Baram, *From Militant Secularism to Islamism: The Irai Ba'th Regime 1968–2003*, Washington, DC: Woodrow Wilson Center, 2011.

93. Fred Halliday, "Ba'th Command: 'Initially We Were Happy to See the Downfall of the Shah,'" *MERIP Report*, June 1981, 19.

94. Chibli Mellat, "Religious Militancy in Contemporary Iraq: Muhammad Baqer as-Sadr and the Sunni-Shia Paradigm," *Third World Quarterly* 10, 2 (April 1988), 699–729; Marius Lazar, "Les Origines Ideologiques et Sociopolitiques de l'Islamisme Chiite Irakien: Muhammad Baqer Al-Sadr et Le Parti *Al-Da'wa*," *Cultura* 10 (2008), 1–24.

95. On the notion of "demonstration effect," see Elbaki Hermassi, "Towards a Comparative Study of Revolutions," *Comparative Studies in Society and History* 18 (1976), 211.

96. *British Broadcasting Corporation/Summary of World Broadcasts/Middle East*, April 11, 1980, 6392/A/2.

97. [Untitled Baghdad Radio broadcast], Foreign Broadcasting Information Service— Middle East and Africa (FBIS-MEA), June 25, 1980, E2. For more details, see Hashim, *God, Greed and Guns*.

98. T. M. Aziz, "The Role of Muhammad Baqir al-Sadr in Shii Political Activism in Iraq from 1958 to 1980," *International Journal of Middle East Studies* 25, 2 (May 1993), 207–222.

99. *Iraq, Economist* Intelligence Unit Quarterly Economic Review, nos. 3–4 (1979), and no. 1 (1980).

100. Karl-Heinrich Göbel, *Moderne Schitische Politik und Staatsidee nach Taufiq al-Fakaiki, Mohammad Gawad Mughniya, und Ruhollah Khomeini*, Opladen: Budrich, 1984, 236.

101. Mahmood, "Social Origins and Ideology of the Shi'i Islamist Movements in Iraq, 1958–1990," 189.

102. See "Voice of the Masses in Arabic," FBIS-MEA, 068, April 7, 1980, E4.

103. Richard Harmon, "Iran, Iraq on War Footing, Khomeini Urges Coup," *Washington Post*, April 9, 1980, A13.

104. See Michael Getter, "Iraq Gets Key Regional Role as Iran's Military Deteriorates," *Washington Post*, April 11, 1980, A14; Drew Middleton, "Iraqis Hold Military Edge in Confrontation with Iranians," *New York Times*, April 13, 1980, 14.

105. "Saddam and His Advisers Discussing Iraq's Decision to Go to War with Iran," Iraqi government document, September 16, 1980, SH-SHTP-A-000-835, Conflict Records Research Center, National Defense University, Washington, DC.

106. Baram, *From Militant Secularism to Islamism*, 6.

107. D. Gershon Lowenthal, "Saddam's 'Qadisiyyah': Religion and History in the Service of State Ideology in Ba'thi Iraq," *Middle Eastern Studies* 50, 6 (2014), 891–910.

108. See Jon Sigler, "The Iran-Iraq Conflict: The Tragedy of Limited Conventional War," *International Journal* 41 (1986), 424–456; Joseph Maila, "Irak-Iran: Conflit de civilizations et enejux strategiques," *Etudes* 365, 4 (October 1986), 293–306. For the best and most recent book-length analyses, see Rob Johnson, *The Iran-Iraq War*, New York: Palgrave, 2011; Williamson Murray and Kevin Woods, *The Iran-Iraq War: A Military and Strategic History*, Cambridge: Cambridge University Press, 2014; Pierre Razoux, *The Iran-Iraq War*, Cambridge, MA: Harvard University Press, 2015.

109. The Iran-Iraq War was, until recently, not very well analyzed. In recent years it has become the subject of a burgeoning literature of a high standard, which I referred to in the previous note.

110. "Saddam Husayn Speaks on Israel, War, Economy," FBIS-MEA, January 7, 1983, E1–E8.

111. Staff Major-General 'Abd ar-Rahim Taha al-Ahmad, "Why Is the Iraqi-Iranian War Continuing?," *Al-Jumhuriyah*, December 22, 1983, 3, in "General Calls for Striking Deep in Iran," FBIS-MEA, 83-249, December 27, 1983, E2–E3.

112. Nasir ad-Din an-Nashashibi, "Interview with President Saddam Husayn," *Al-Anba*, April 27, 1983, 12–15, translated as "Text of Saddam Husayn 27 April Al-Anba' Interview," FBIS-MEA, May 2, 1983, E2.

113. Lowenthal, "Saddam's 'Qaddisiyah.'"

114. See Kamran Ekbal, "Islam, Nationalismus und Identitätsfragen: Islamische, ideologische und soziale Dimensionen der Irakisch-Iranischen Krieges," *Peripherie*, nos. 18/19 (1985), 85–115.

115. See Dina Rizk Khoury, "The Security State and the Practice and Rhetoric of Sectarianism in Iraq," *International Journal of Contemporary Iraqi Studies* 4, 3 (2010), 325–338.

116. Klaus Reinhard and Adel Elias, "Jawohl, wir sind eindeutig die Sieger" [Yes, We Are Clearly the Winners], *Der Spiegel* 23 (1981), 136. This is my translation of the German, which runs as follows: "Wir regieren nicht im Namen der

Religion, weil wir der Meinung sind, dass das im Interesse des Volkes der arabischen Nation liegt. Die Welt wird in Chaos und Anarchie sturzen, wenn die Volker dieser Welt sich von Mullahs und Religionen beherrschen lassen. Wir glauben, dass das Regieren durch die Religion mehr Probleme schafft, als dass es Probleme löst."

117. Baram, *From Militant Secularism to Islamism*, 6.

118. See Arab Ba'th Socialist Party, Iraq, *The Central Report of the Ninth Regional Congress [sic] June 1982*, Baghdad, January 1983, 245–284.

119. Saddam Hussein, *The Arabs Are the Leading Role in the Message of Islam*, Baghdad: Dar al-Ma'mun, 1983, 12.

120. On the wartime situation in Iraq in the 1980s, see Marion Farouk-Sluglett, Peter Sluglett, and Joe Stork, "Not Quite Armageddon: Impact of the War on Iraq," *Middle East Report* 14 (September–October 1984), 22–30; Milton Viorst, "A Reporter at Large: The View from the Mustansiriyah—II," *New Yorker,* October 19, 1987, 76–97; Marion Farouk-Sluglett and Peter Sluglett, "Iraq since 1986: The Strengthening of Saddam," *Middle East Report* 167 (November–December 1990), 19–24.

121. Isam al-Khafaji, "Iraq's Seventh Year: Saddam's *Quart d'Heure?*," *Middle East Report* 51 (March–April 1988), 35–39.

122. Saddam Hussein, *Religious Political Movements and Those Disguised with Religion*, Baghdad: Dar al-Ma'mun, 1987, 8.

123. "Saddam Husayn on Arab Position toward Gulf War," Foreign Broadcast Information Service—Near East and South Asia (FBIS-NES), February 6, 1988, 19.

124. Ibid.

125. Alan Cowell, "Iraq's Dark Victory," *New York Times Magazine*, September 25, 1988, 34–48.

126. See Thierry Gongora, "The Impact of War and War Preparation on State Formation in the Third World: Four Case Studies from the Middle East," Ph.D. diss., Carleton University, Ottawa, 1995, 228–299.

127. See Farouk-Sluglett and Sluglett, "Iraq since 1986," 19–24.

128. Jill Smolowe, "Sword of the Arabs," *Time*, June 11, 1990, 32; Caryle Murphy, "Iraqi Leader Presses Drive for Regional Dominance," *Washington Post*, March 23, 1990, A16; Tony Walker and Victor Mallet, "Bombastic Iraq Brings Pride and Fear to Arabs," *Financial Times*, April 19, 1990; Lamis Andoni, "Arabs Welcome Iraq's Renewed Militancy toward the State of Israel," *Christian Science Monitor*, April 23, 1990, 1.

129. For an introduction to Iraqi strategic thinking between 1988 and 1990, see "Husayn, 'Aziz Address News Conference 3 May," FBIS-NES, 90-087, May 4, 1990, 16–17; Karen Elliot House, "Interview with Saddam Husayn," *Wall Street Journal*, June 26, 1990.

130. "Saddam Speaks on Peace with Iran," FBIS-NES, 89-215, November 8, 1989, E4.

131. Ibid.; my italics.

132. Elizabeth Picard, "Le régime irakien et la crise: Les resorts d'une politique," *Maghreb-Machrek* 130 (October–December 1990), 25–35; Rolf Schwarz, "From Rentier State to Failed State: War and the De-formation of the State in Iraq," *A Contrario* 5, 2 (2007), 102–113.

133. For analysis of the uprising, see Pierre Martin, "Les chiites d'Irak ou le retour de la question irakienne," *Peuples Méditerranéens* 58–59 (January–February 1992), 87–129.

134. Trudy Rubin, "The Shiite Rebels Paid Dearly for Resisting Saddam Hussein," *Philadelphia Inquirer*, May 9, 1991, A21.

135. For Saddam Hussein's scathing critique of the Baath Party's conduct during the insurrection in the south, see (FBIS-NES), Daily Report, May 3, 1991, and June 27, 1991, 13–14 and 14–17, respectively.

136. FBIS-NESA, Daily Report, September 18, 1991, 31.

137. Ahmed S. Hashim, "Baghdad Blues: Observations from Iraq," diary, vol. 1, Observations from Baghdad, November–December 2003. This diary's two volumes of observations were written while stationed primarily in the Republican Palace in the Green Zone of Baghdad. However, during that time I ventured into Sadr City on multiple occasions, met with former military officers in Mansur, visited Mosul, where I met with General David Petraeus and members of the Iraqi Islamic Party (the Muslim Brotherhood), and visited Tikrit, Ramadi, Fallujah, and Hilla.

138. Rajiv Chandrasekaran and Anthony Shadid, "Ethnic and Religious Fissures Deepen in Iraqi Society," *Washington Post*, September 29, 2003, A1.

139. Nicholas Pelham, "Iraq's Holy Warriors Draw Inspiration from Arab Puritan of Another Century," *Financial Times*, March 18, 2004.

140. Fanar Haddad, *Sectarianism in Iraq: Antagonistic Visions of Unity*, London: Hurst, 2011, 119.

141. Borzou Daraghi, "The Puzzle of Sunnis' Leadership Vacuum," *Los Angeles Times*, July 5, 2005, http://articles.latimes.com/2005/jul/05/world/fg-sunnis5.

142. Isam al-Khafaji, "A mi-chemin de la democratie: Les options de transition de l'Irak," in Hosham Dawod and Hamit Bozarslan, eds., *La société irakienne: communautés; pouvoirs et violences*, Paris: Karthala, 2003, 89.

143. Isam al-Khafaji, "Repression, Conformity, and Legitimacy: Prospects for an Iraqi Social Contract," in John Calabrese, ed., *The Future of Iraq*, Washington, D.C.: Middle East Institute, 1997, 21.

144. Tony Horwitz, "Casualties of War," *Wall Street Journal*, July 15, 1991, A1.

145. John Battersby, "Saddam Squeezes His People as World Squeezes Iraq," *Christian Science Monitor*, June 28, 1995, 10.

146. [Untitled Baghdad Radio broadcast], FBIS-NES, 92-008, January 13, 1992, 32–34.

147. Francoise Rigaud, "La societe et le politique en Irak au temps de l'embargo," *Mouvements* 15–16 (May–August 2001), 138–144; Schwartz, "From Rentier State

to Failed State"; David Baran, "Iraq: The Party in Power," *Le Monde Diplomatique*, December 2002, http://mondediplo.com/2002/12/05iraq. All dollar amounts mentioned in this book refer to U.S. dollars.

148. Faleh Jabbar, "Parti, clans et tribus, le fragile equilibre du regime irakien," *Le Monde Diplomatique*, October 2002, 4–5, http://www.monde-diplomatique .fr/2002/10/JABAR/9456.

149. See Amatzia Baram, "Neo-tribalism in Iraq: Saddam Hussein's Tribal Policies," *International Journal of Middle East Studies* 29, 1 (February 1997), 1–31; Faleh A. Jabar, "Shaykhs and Ideologues: Detribalization and Retribalization in Iraq, 1968–1998," *Middle East Report* 215 (Summer 2000), 28–48; Elizabeth Nathan and Kevin Woods, "Saddam and the Tribes: How Captured Documents Explain Regime Adaptation to Internal Challenges (1979–2003)," *Joint Center for Operational Analysis Journal* 12, 1 (Spring 2010), 12–31; Myriam Benraad, "Une lecture de la Sahwa ou le mille et un visages du tribalisme Irakien," *Etudes Rurales* 184 (July–December 2009), 95–106.

150. See Jabar, "Parti, clans et tribus, le fragile equilibre du regime irakien," *Le Monde Diplomatique*, October 2002, http://www.monde-diplomatique.fr/2002/10/ JABAR/9456; Nathan and Woods, "Saddam and the Tribes," 12.

151. Hugh Pope, "Iraq's Hussein Emphasizes Islamic Identity to Shore Up Legitimacy," *Wall Street Journal*, April 29, 2002, A14.

152. Jason Burke, "Saddam Wields Sword of Islam," *Observer*, December 19, 1999, https://www.theguardian.com/world/1999/dec/19/iraq.jasonburke.

153. Ibid.

154. Baram, *From Militant Secularism to Islamism*, 25.

155. Ofra Bengio, "How Does Saddam Hold On?," *Foreign Affairs* 79, 4 (July–August 2000), 90–103. See also Joanna McGeary, "Inside Saddam's World," *Time*, May 4, 2002, http://www.time.com/world/0,8816,2355385,00.html.

156. "Saddam's Regime Prospering and Confident According to Longtime Journalist," telegram, U.S. Embassy, Amman, May 16, 2002, http://wikileaks.org/plusd/ cables/02AMMAN2423_a.html.

157. Benjamin Claude Brower, "The Amir Abd al-Qadir and the 'Good War' in Algeria, 1832–1847," *Studia Islamica* 106 (2011), 170.

158. Charles Tripp, "The United States and State-Building in Iraq," *Review of International Studies* 30 (2004), 547.

159. For an excellent account of exogenous state-building efforts, see Toby Dodge, "Iraq: The Contradictions of Exogenous State Building in Historical Perspective," *Third World Quarterly* 27, 1 (2006), 187–200.

160. On the lack of qualifications of these individuals, apart from their ideological convictions, see Rajiv Chandrasekaran, "Ties to GOP Trumped Know-how among Staff Sent to Rebuild Iraq," *Washington Post*, September 17, 2006, A1; Michiko Kakutani, "From Planning to Warfare to Occupation, How Iraq Went Wrong," review of *Fiasco* by Thomas Ricks, *New York Times*, July 25, 2006, http://www.nytimes.com/2006/07/25/books/25kaku.html.

161. Michael R. Gordon and Bernard E. Trainor, *Cobra II: The Inside Story of the Invasion and Occupation of Iraq*, New York: Vintage Books, 2007, 479.

162. Oren Barak, "Dilemmas of Security in Iraq," *Security Dialogue* 38, 4 (2007), 460–462.

CHAPTER 3

1. Charles Clover and Roula Khalaf, "Shia Politicians Benefit from Being Sectarian, Kurds from Nationalism, Sunnis by Opposing the Occupation," *Wall Street Journal*, August 21, 2003, 15; Rod Nordland, "The Iraqi Intifada," *Newsweek*, April 10, 2004, http://www.newsweek.com/iraqi-intifada-125263.

2. See Ahmed S. Hashim, *Insurgency and Counterinsurgency in Iraq*, Ithaca: Cornell University Press, 2006; Geraint Hughes, "The Insurgencies in Iraq, 2003–2009: Origins, Developments and Prospects," *Defence Studies* 10, 1–2 (March–June 2010), 152–176.

3. Yaroslav Trofimov, "Gulf Grows between U.S. Forces and Iraq's Sunnis—Nation's Dominant Group Is Embittered by the Rise of Rival Shiites and Kurds," *Wall Street Journal*, April 30, 2003, A15.

4. Dan Murphy, "Radical Islam Grows among Iraq's Sunnis," *Christian Science Monitor*, July 28, 2004, https://www.csmonitor.com/2004/0728/p01s04-woiq.html.

5. Thomas Ricks and Anthony Shadid, "A Tale of Two Baghdads," *Washington Post*, June 2, 2003, 1; Anthony Shadid, "Frustration and Foreboding in Fallujah," *Washington Post*, June 19, 2003, A16.

6. See Hamza Hendawi, "Shiites March in Baghdad against U.S.," *Guardian*, May 19, 2003, 4.

7. Mohammad Bazzi, "A Challenge from Shiites," *Newsday*, March 31, 2003.

8. Yochi Dreazen, "Rebuilding in Iraq Fuels Sectarian Tension," *Wall Street Journal*, December 23, 2003, 4.

9. The literature on Zarqawi and his original organization is still quite sparse in comparison with the burgeoning literature on the successor state. See Myriam Benraad, "De la Tentation Hégémonique Au Declin De L'Organization D' Al-Qa'ida en Iraq: Miroir Des Metamorphoses D'une Insurrection (2004–2008)," *Maghreb-Machrek* 197 (Autumn 2008), 87–101.

10. "Iraq: Voice of the Mujahidin Reports Iraqi Officers' Protests in Baghdad," FBIS (Foreign Broadcasting Information Service)-GMP20030526000208, 16:00 GMT, May 26, 2003, https://imos.rccb.osis.gov/cgi-bin/cqcgi/@rware.env?CQ_CUR_DOCUMENT=1&CQ_US.

11. Medea Benjamin, "The Reluctant Warrior," August 11, 2003, https://www.countercurrents.org/iraq-benjamin110803.htm.

12. See Hazem al-Amin, "The Resistance in the Sunni Triangle," *al Hayat*, November 10, 2003, translated in *Dar al-Hayat*, November 13, 2003, http://english.daral-hayat.com/Spec/11-2003/Article-20031110-c6a45ce3-c0a8-01ed-007c.

13. Abd al-Latif al-Sa'dun, "Al-Fallujah, City of Mosques," *al-Hayat*, July 17, 2003, 15, in FBIS-GMP20030717000098, July 17, 2003, https://imos.rccb.osis.gov/sgi-bin/cqcqi@rware.env?CQ-CUR_DOCUMENT=1&CQ_US.

14. Anthony Shadid, "Frustration and Foreboding in Fallujah," *Washington Post*, June 19, 2003, 16, https://www.washingtonpost.com/archive/politics/2003/06/19/frustration-and-foreboding-in-fallujah/82012218-d959-4da3-aa39-db42adbcdf7d/?utm_term=.7b3914cd6567; Patrick Bishop, "Americans Are Object of Hatred in Falluja's Mosques," *Daily Telegraph*, September 15, 2003, http://www.telegraph.co.uk/news/worldnews/middleeast/iraq/1441521/Americans-are-objects-of-hatred-in-Fallujas-mosques.html.

15. Ghaith Abdul Ahad, "We Are Not Here to Liberate Iraq, We Are Here to Fight the Infidels," *Guardian*, November 9, 2004.

16. See Lee Gordon, "Foreign Fighters Gain Fallujah Foothold," *Age*, June 1, 2004; Dan Murphy, "Iraqi Rebels Dividing, Losing Support," *Christian Science Monitor*, July 12, 2004, 1.

17. Ahmed S. Hashim, interviews with Sunni Turkmen former military personnel in Tel Afar, August and September 2005, when deployed there as human terrain advisor to the Third Armored Cavalry Regiment.

18. Ahmed S. Hashim, specific diary of observations and interviews from Tel Afar, Jebel Sinjar, Abu Maria, and Rabiya border post, July–October 2005.

19. Cited in Susan Sachs, "Baathists, Once Reviled, Prove Difficult to Remove," *New York Times*, November 22, 2003.

20. See Didier Francois, "Mossoul sous la ferule des imams sunnites," *Liberation*, April 24, 2003, http://www.liberation.fr/planete/2003/04/24/mossoul-sous-la-ferule-des-imams-sunnites_462577; Michael Kennedy, "A 'Model City' Is Caught in Cross Hairs of Violence," *Los Angeles Times*, March 18, 2004, http://articles.latimes.com/2004/mar/18/world/fg-mosul18.

21. Daniel Williams, "In Sunni Triangle, Loss of Privilege Breeds Bitterness," *Washington Post*, January 13, 2004, 1.

22. Michael Slackman and John Daniszewski, "U.S. Policies Lead to Dire Straits for Some in Iraq," *Los Angeles Times*, June 10, 2003, 1.

23. Daniel Williams, "Violence in Iraq Overtakes an Oasis of Relative Calm," *Washington Post*, November 16, 2003, 24.

24. "Iraqi Officers' League Warns Arab Leaders of Iran's Plan to Control Gulf Area," Open Source Center-GMP20080429050001, April 26, 2008, https://www.opensource.gov/portal/server.pt/gateway/PTARGS_0_0_200_240_51_43/http.

25. "Spokesman of Iraqi Army General Command Interviewed on Issues, Objectives," Open Source Center-GMP20080223459003, February 19, 2008, https://www.opensource.gov/portal/server.pt/gateway/PTARGS_0_0_200_240_51_43/http.

26. Ibid.

27. Ibid.

28. See, for example, Steve Negus and Dhiya Rasan, "Tips on How to Beat US from Insurgents' Consultant," *Financial Times*, August 24, 2005, 6.

29. See "Saddam Hussein in an Exclusive Interview: 'The Americans Will Leave Iraq by the Small Door,'" *Al-Baath al-Iraqi* 53 (January 14, 2005).

30. "Ba'th Party Predicts Defeat of 'Paper Tiger' US through Guerrilla Warfare," Open Source Center-GMP2007062681003, March 20, 2007, https://www.open-source.gov/portal/server.pt/gateway/PTARGS_0_0_200_972_51_43/http.

31. Ibid.

32. Ibid.

33. Ibid.

34. Ibid.

35. "*Al-Jazirah* Interviews Party Spokesman on Post-Saddam Ba'th Party," Open Source Center-GMP20070318647001, March 18, 2007, https://www.opensource .gov/portal/server.pt/gateway/PTARGS_0_0_200_212_51_43/http.

36. Ibid.

37. "Naqshabandi Order Spokesman Discusses Group's Beliefs, Operational Goals: *Al-Barah Network* Posts an Interview with Dr. Salah al-Din al-Ayyubi, Official Spokesman of the Army of the Men of the Naqshabandi Order," Open Source Center-GMP20070607382001, June 6, 2007, https://www.opensource.gov/ portal/server.pt/gateway/PTARGS_0_0_200_212_51_43/http.

38. Ibid.

39. "Jayshuna" [Our Army], May 24, 2007, and "Hada huw aqidat jaysh rajal al-tariqa al-Nakshabandia" [This Is the Doctrine of the Army of the Naqshabandiya Order], al-nakshabandia-army.com (website is now banned and inaccessible).

40. "Supreme Command for Jihad and Liberation Spokesman Interviewed," Open Source Center-GMP20080307873003, March 2, 2008. https://www.opensource .gov/portal/server.pt/gateway/PTARGS_0_0_200_240_51_43/http.

41. Saddam Hussein, *The Khomeini Religion*, Baghdad: Dar al-Ma'mun, 1988, 16, 22.

42. Edward Wong, "Uprising Has Increased the Influence of Sunni Clerics," *New York Times*, May 31, 2004.

43. Ibid.

44. See Anthony Shadid, "Iraq's Rising Forces of Faith Create Fears for Future," *Washington Post*, March 15, 2003, A14.

45. Didier Francois, "Mossoul sous la ferule des imams Sunnites," *Liberation*, April 24, 2003.

46. Evan Osnos, "Sunnis Begin Pushing to Regain Influence," *Chicago Tribune*, January 2, 2004, http://articles.chicagotribune.com/2004-01-02/news/040102 0272_1_sunni-leaders-sunni-triangle-battles-mosque.

47. James Hider, "We Follow Usama, Not Saddam, Say Desert Guerrillas," *Times* (London), December 27, 2003.

48. Ibid.

49. Dan Murphy, "Radical Islam Grows among Iraq's Sunnis," *Christian Science Monitor*, July 28, 2004, https://www.csmonitor.com/2004/0728/p01s04-woiq .html.

50. Nicholas Blanford, "Insurgent Speaks Out on Anti-US Attacks in Fallujah," *Daily Star* (Beirut), February 14, 2004, 3.

51. Ibid.

52. Ahmed S. Hashim, interview with members of the Iraqi Islamic Party, Mosul, September 2005.

53. Ouma Website Interviews Resistance Fighters in Iraq, Views Situation on the Ground, *Open Source Center-EUP 20050119000413*, January 18, 2005, https://www.opensource.gov/portal/server.pt/gateway/PTARGGS_0_0_200_240_51_43/http.

54. Quoted in "Iraqi Al-Mujahidin Army Spokesman Explains Policies towards Shi'i, US," *BBC Monitoring—Middle East*, November 15, 2006.

55. Ibid.

56. Ibid.

57. Ibid.

58. "Hamas al-Iraq: Bayan bishaan fitna Samarra" [Hamas-Iraq: Statement Concerning the Samarra Strife], Muslm.net, June 13, 2007, July 19, 2007, http://muslm.net/vb/showthread.php?t=236850.

59. "Hasriat: Alaa safahat al-Multaqa, Liqa al-aadhaa min haraka Hamas al-Iraq," [Exclusive: In the Pages of al-Multaqa, a Meeting with Members of Hamas-Iraq], Ikhwan.net, July 10, July 23, 2007, http://www.ikhwan.net/vb/showthread.php?t=34940; "Hamas al-Iraq: Ijabat eudw al-maktab al-siyasi wa al-jawlat al-thaniyat min al-hiwar" [Hamas al-Iraq: Responses from a Member of the Political Bureau and the Second Round of Dialogue], Ikhwan.net, July 18, July 23, 2007, http://www.ikhwan.net/vb/showthread.php?t=35402.

60. "Front of Iraq Outlines Political Stance, Countenances Negotiations with US," Open Source Center-GMP20071230075003, December 23, 2007, https://www.opensource.gov/portal/server.pt/gateway/PTARGS_0_0_200_240_51_43/http.

61. I have relied heavily on the following to advance my understanding of Salafism: Behnam T. Said and Hazim Fouad, eds., *Salafismus: Auf Suche nach dem wahren Islam*, Freiburg: Herder Verlag, 2014, and Shiraz Maher, *Salafi-Jihadism: The History of an Idea*, London: Hurst, 2016.

62. Quintan Wiktorowicz, "Anatomy of the Salafi Movement," *Studies in Conflict and Terrorism* 29 (2006), 207.

63. Merlin Coverley, *Utopia*, Harpenden, England, Herts, 2010, 9.

64. Asma Afsaruddin, "The 'Islamic State': Genealogy, Facts, and Myths," *Journal of Church and State* 48, 1 (2006), 153–173.

65. See Robert Rabil, *Salafism in Lebanon: From Apoliticism to Transnational Jihadism*, Washington, DC: Georgetown University Press, 2014, 21–56.

66. Quoted in Rudolph Peters, *Jihad in Classical and Modern Islam*, Princeton: Markus Wiener, 1996, 47.

67. The literature on al-Qaeda and its evolution is now enormous. There is no point in citing all of it here. I have benefited from most of it, but the most helpful for

the writing of this book were Mustafa Hamid and Leah Farrall, *The Arabs at War in Afghanistan,* London: Hurst, 2015, and Flagg Miller, *The Audacious Ascetic: What the Bin Laden Tapes Reveal about Al-Qa'ida,* London: Hurst, 2015; Brian Fishman, *The Master Plan: ISIS, Al-Qaeda, and the Jihadi Strategy for Final Victory,* New Haven: Yale University Press, 2016.

68. "Jordanian Islamic Weekly Profiles Jihadist Groups Operating in Iraq," *BBC Monitoring—Middle East,* July 20, 2007, 1.

69. Remy Ourdan, "Al-Fallujah, l'emirate du mujahidin," *Le Monde,* July 1, 2004.

70. *"Ansar al-Sunnah* Army Publishes Its Creed on Website," Open Source Center-GMP20050308000210, *FBIS Report,* March 8, 2005, https://www.opensource.gov/portal/server.pt/PTARGS_0_0_6005_989_0_43/http.

71. "Islamic Army in Iraq Amir Promises Iran 'Great Losses,'" *Open Source Center-FEA 20070117074881,* January 5, 2007, https://www.opensource.gov/portal/server.pt/gateway/PTARGS_0_0_6006_989_0_43/http.

72. "Iraqi Islamic Army on Resistance Operations, Talks with Americans," *Without Borders,* presented by Ahmad Mansur, Al-Jazeera Satellite TV, April 11, 2007.

73. Ibid.

74. Ibid.

75. Ibid.

76. Ibid.

77. Ibid.

78. Ibid.

79. Ibid.

80. "*Al-Bayan* Magazine Interviews Islamic Army in Iraq Spokesman Ibrahim al-Shammari," Open Source Center-GMP20080403071001, March 31, 2008, https://www.opensource.gov/portal/server.pt/gateway/PTARGS_0_0_200_240_1019_43/htt.

81. Ibid.

82. Ibid.

83. Sheikh Yusuf Bin Salih al-Ayiri, "The Future of Iraq and the Arabian Peninsula after the Fall of Baghdad: Religious, Military, Political and Economic Prospects," in *The Crusader Campaign against Iraq,* n.p.: Center for Islamic Studies and Research, Jumada II, 1424 (c. August 2003), 3; mimeograph document was downloaded from the Internet.

84. Ibid.

85. Ibid.

86. See Thomas Hegghammer, "Global Jihadism after the Iraq War," *Middle East Journal* 60, 1 (Winter 2006), 17–18.

87. Qoqaz Website Publishes Interview with Jihad Leader Al-Zawahiri, FBIS-GMP 20021011000026, October 11, 2002.

88. Ibid.

89. Ibid.

90. Ibid.

91. My approach here of examining the trajectory of Zarqawi's life and the evolution of his ideology and execution of strategy is derived from Dirk Baehr, *Kontinuuitat und Wandel in der Ideologie des Jihadi-Salafismus: Eine ideentheoretische Analyse der Schriften von Abu Mus'ab al Suri, Abu Mohammad al-Maqdisi und Abu Bakr Naji*, Bonn: Bouvier Verlag, 2009.

92. Christoph Gunther, *Ein zweiter Staat im Zweistromland?: Genese und Ideologie des Islamischen Staats Irak*, Wurzburg: Ergan Verlag, 2014, 63.

93. Megan Stack, "Zarqawi Took Familiar Route into Terrorism," *Los Angeles Times*, July 2, 2004, http://www.latimes.com/news/la-fg-zarqawi2jul0204-story.html.

94. "Translation of Old Al-Zarqawi Interview, Says God's Law Must Rule 'Entire World,'" Open Source Center-GMP20061211281001, December 6, 2006, https://www.opensource.gov/portal/server.pt/gateway/PTARGS_0_0_762_303_0_43/http.

95. Brian Fishman, *Master Plan*, 5. For more on Abdul Rasul Sayyaf, see Hamid and Farrall, *Arabs at War in Afghanistan*, 62–63, 67–68, 73–77.

96. Fishman, *Master Plan*.

97. Mary Ann Weaver, "The Short, Violent Life of Abu Musab al-Zarqawi," *Atlantic*, July–August 2006, http://www.theatlantic.com/magazine/archive/2006/07/the-short-violent-life-of-abu-musab-al-zarqawi/304983/

98. Joas Wagemakers, "Invoking Zarqawi: Abu Mohammad al-Maqdisi's Jihad Deficit," *CTC Sentinel* 2, 6 (June 15, 2009), https://www.ctc.usma.edu/posts/invoking-zarqawi-abu-muhammad-.

99. Khattab, "Abu-Muhammad al-Maqdisi's Testimony of Al-Zarqawi," *Millat Facebook* (blog), December 22, 2010, http://mymfb.com/blog/15926/abu-muhammad-al-maqdis-039-s-te.

100. For a very readable and entertaining history of the incarceration of Maqdisi and Zarqawi in Jordan's prisons, see Joby Warrick, *Black Flags: The Rise of ISIS*, New York: Doubleday, 2015. Warrick claims that their last prison before being released in 1999 was al-Jafr Prison, which held only a handful of high-risk Islamist militants. Other sources claim that most of them were held in Sawaqa Prison.

101. Ibid.

102. Ibid.

103. Much of this section is based on the succinct survey of Maqdisi's relationship with Zarqawi in the definitive study of Maqdisi and his ideology by Joas Wagemakers, *A Quietist Jihadi: The Ideology and Influence of Abu Muhammad al-Maqdisi*, Cambridge: Cambridge University Press, 2012, 215–222.

104. I will refer to him by his full name, Abu Abdullah al-Muhajir, rather than al-Muhajir or just Muhajir, to avoid confusion with Abu Hamza al-Muhajir, one of the successors to Zarqawi as leader of the organization that Zarqawi was responsible for founding and establishing in Iraq.

105. Charlie Winter and Abdullah al-Saud, "The Obscure Theologian Who Shaped ISIS," *Atlantic*, December 4, 2016, https://www.theatlantic.com/international/archive/2016/12/isis-muhajir-syria/509399/.

106. Ibid.

107. The section also relies heavily on the extensive secondary literature on the jihadists' ideology and their actions in Iraq: Gilles Keppel, *Beyond Terror and Martyrdom: The Future of the Middle East*, Cambridge, MA: Belknap Press, 2008, 153–160, which addresses Zarqawi; Jason Burke, *The 9/11 Wars*, London: Allen Lane, 2011, 163–176. Here are the sources of the three statements from Zarqawi that are discussed in this section, which are introduced in the text as follows: "an audio message in early April 2004": "Text of Al-Zarqawi Message Threatening More Attacks," Open Source Center-FBIS, April 6, 2004 (hard copy), p. 1, speech originally posted on the "Jihadist Political Fortress Forum," www.qal3ah.net, by Ibn Abu Waqqas, a jihadist participant; "a well-known letter he wrote to bin Laden in February 2004": "Text of Al-Zarqawi's Letter to Bin Ladin on Future of Mujahidin in Iraq," Open Source Center-GMP20040615000107, June 15, 2004, https://www.opensource.gov/portal/server.pt/gateway/PTARGS_0_0_200_240_51_43/http; "On May 18, 2005, a jihadist… posted to the Ana al-Muslim forum several links to an audiotape by Zarqawi titled 'The Descendants of Ibn al-Alqami Are Back'": "Al-Zarqawi Justifies Killing of Innocent Muslims, Condemns the 'Betrayal' of Sunnis," FBIS-GMP20050518336602, May 18, 2005. It has been cited by Mohammed Hafez in *Terrorism and Political Violence*, Vol.19, 2007 and CTC's *Self-Inflicted Wounds*.

108. Camille Tawil, *Brothers in Arms: The Story of Al-Qa'ida and the Arab Jihadists*, London: Saqi Books, 2010, 190.

109. Khalil Ezzeledin, "Partners to Foes—Al-Qaeda-ISIL Split Worsens Civil Conflict in Syria," *Jane's Intelligence Review* 26, 6 (June 1, 2014).

110. "Al Zarqawi's Group Creed and Methodology Reiterates the Mandate of Jihad, Battling Infidels, Apostates, Shia," statement posted by the Legal Council of AQI on al-Anbar.net, Open Source Center-GMP20050324000125, March 24, 2005, https://www.opensource.gov/portal/server.pt/gateway/PTARGS_0_0_6005_989_0_43/http.

111. See Ahmed S. Hashim, *Iraq's Sunni Insurgency*, International Institute for Strategic Studies, Adelphi Paper No. 402, London: Routledge, 2009, 34–35.

112. Neil MacFarquhar, "Iraq's Anxious Sunnis Seek Security in the New Order," *New York Times*, August 10, 2003, comment by Sheikh Abdullah Dakhil al-Jibouri.

113. Thanassis Cambanis, "Shiites Quietly Emerge as Political Force," *Boston Globe*, April 27, 2003, 1.

114. The U.S. effort to reverse the tide of war has been analyzed in great detail in various books; among the best are Michael Gordon and Bernard Trainor, *The Endgame: The Inside Story of the Struggle for Iraq from George W. Bush to Barack*

Obama, New York: Pantheon Books, 2012, and Peter Mansoor, *The Surge: My Journey with General David Petraeus and the Remaking of the Iraq War*, New Haven: Yale University Press, 2013.

115. "Saudi Daily Profiles Abu Mohammad al-Maqdisi, Views His Ideology," Open Source Center-GMP20050705514006, July 5, 2005, https://www.opensource .gov/portal/server.pt/gateway/PTARGS_0_0_200_240_51_43/http.

116. "Al-Zarqawi Ex-mentor Al-Maqdisi Downplays Differences with Jihadists," *BBC Monitoring—Middle East*, July 7, 2005.

117. Khattab, "Abu Muhammad al-Maqdisi's Testimony of Al-Zarqawi," *Millat Facebook* (blog), December 22, 2010, http://mymfb.com/blog/15926/abu-muhammad-al-maqdis-039-s-te.

118. For details see Muhammad al-Najjar, "Al kati'a bayn al-Zarqawi wa al-Maqdisi: Al-khalafatun fi tafsir aw inqisam fi al-tayyar al-salafi?" [The Estrangement between Al-Zarqawi and Al-Maqdisi: Disputes in Interpretation or Splits in the Salafi Trend?], *Al Sabil*, July 19, 2005, 4.

119. "Zarqaawi's Reply to Sheikh Abu Muhammad al-Maqdisi," *Ansarukhilafah* (blog), April 4, 2015, https://ansaaar1.wordpress.com/2015/04/15/abu-musab-zarqawis-reply-to-sheikh-abu-muhammad-al-maqdisi/.

120. Ibid.

121. Ibid.

122. "Letter Exposes New Leader in Al-Qai'ida High Command," Center for Combatting Terrorism, September 26, 2006, West Point, https://ctc.usma.edu/posts/letter-exposes-new-leader-in-al-qaida-high-command.

123. Ibid.

124. Ibid.

125. Ibid.

126. Ibid.

127. Ibid.

128. Michael Ryan, "ISIS: The Terrorist Group That Would Be a State," *Center for Irregular Warfare and Armed Groups*, Newport: U.S. Naval War College, 2015, 12.

129. "Al Qa'ida, Other Armed Groups Set Up Mujahidin Shura Council in Iraq," Open Source Center-FEA20060115017424, January 18, 2006, https://www .opensource.gov/portal/server.pt/gateway/PTARGS_0_0_5769_972_0_43/http.

130. "New Amir of Al-Qa'ida in Iraq Issues Statement," Open Source Center-FEA20060613024147, June 13, 2006, https://www.opensource.gov/portal/ server.pt/gateway/PTARGS_0_0_877_303_0_43/http.

131. Ibid.

132. Quoted in Yaman Mukhaddab, "Al-Qa'ida between a Past Stage and One Announced by Al-Muhajir," Open Source Center-GMP20061115281002, November 15, 2006, https://www.opensource.gov/portal/server.pt/gateway/PTA RGS_0_0_10160_989_0_43/.

133. Ibid.

134. Ibid.

135. Ibid.

136. "MSC Announces Establishment of 'Islamic State of Iraq,'" Open Source Center-FEA20061015028735, October 15, 2006, https://www.opensource.gov/portal/server.pt/gateway/PTARGS_0_0_5769_972_0_43/http.

137. Ibid.

138. Summarized in "Forum Participant Posts Analysis, History, Objectives of Islamic State of Iraq," Open Source Center-GMP20070513138001, May 14, 2007, https://www.opensource.gov/portal/server.pt/gateway/PTARGS_0_0_200_24 0_1019_43/h.

139. See Bill Rogio, "Letters from al Qaeda Leaders Show Iraqi Effort in Disarray," *Long War Journal*, September 11, 2008, http://www.longwarjournal.org/archives/2008/09/letters_from_al_qaed.php.

140. For expanded discussions of Abu Hamza al-Muhajir's obsession with the apocalypse see the excellent analysis in Will F. McCants, *The ISIS Apocalypse*, New York: St. Martin's Press, 2016, 31–32, 40–41; Fishman, *Master Plan*, 112–116.

141. Ghaith Abdul-Ahad, "We Don't Need Al-Qa'ida," *Guardian*, October 27, 2005, https://www.theguardian.com/world/2005/oct/27/iraq.alqaida.

142. Ibid.

143. Ibid.

144. Ibid.

145. Benraad, "De la tentation hégémonique au declin de l'organisation d' Al-Qa'ida en Irak," 87–101.

146. Jesse Nunes, "Widening Schism in Iraq between Sunni Insurgents, Al Qaeda," *Christian Science Monitor*, March 27, 2007, http://www.csmonitor.com/2007/0327/p99s01-duts.html.

147. Maher al-Jasem, "Sunnis Face New Conflicts in Iraq War," *Aljazeera.net*, November 24, 2006.

148. Ned Parker, "Insurgents Report a Split with Al Qaeda in Iraq," *Los Angeles Times*, March 27, 2007, 1.

149. Ibid.

150. Ibid.

151. "Prominent Jihadist Says Situation in Iraq Has Deteriorated since Establishment of ISI," Open Source Center-GMP20070307376001, *Jihadist Website—Open Source Center Summary*, March 1, 2007.

152. "Iraq: 1920 Revolution Brigades Spokesman Discusses Differences with Al-Qa'ida," Open Source Center-GMP20070409641001, from Al-Arabiya TV, Dubai, April 9, 2007, https://www.opensource.gov/portal/server.pt/gateway/PTARGS_0_0_200_240_1019_43/h.

153. "Islamic Army in Iraq Accuses Al-Qa'ida in Iraq of 'Transgressing Islamic Law,'" Open Source Center-GMP20070411298002, April 5, 2007, https://www.opensource.gov/portal/server.pt/gateway/PTARGS_0_0_200_240_10 19_43/h.

154. Ibid.

155. Ibid.

156. Ibid.

157. Ibid.

158. "Islamic Army in Iraq Accuses Islamic State of Transgressing Islamic Law," Open Source Center-FEA20070415116748, https://www.opensource.gov/portal/server.pt/gateway/PTARGS_0_0_6411_989_0_43/http.

159. "Islamic Army of Iraq Leader Grants Interview on US, Al-Qa'ida, Awakening Councils, Iran," on jihadist website Ana al-Muslim, Open Source Center-GMP 20080303050021, February 25, 2008, https://www.opensource.gov/portal/server.pt/gateway/PTARGS_0_0_200_240_1019_43/htt; see also "Islamic Army in Iraq Spokesman Denounces US-Iran Alliance, Views Jihadist Rifts," on jihadist website Al-Buraq Media Establishment.

160. "Islamic Army of Iraq Leader Grants Interview on US, Al-Qa'ida, Awakening Councils, Iran."

161. Abu Azzam al-Tamimi should not be confused with Thamir al-Tamimi, who played a role in the Sahwa movement.

162. "Al-Arabiyah Interviews Former Leading Islamic Army Figure Abu Azzam al-Tamimi," Open Source Center-GMP20080118643004, January 18, 2008, https://www.opensource.gov/portal/server.pt/gateway/PTARGS_0_0_200_240_1019_43/htt.

163. Iyad al-Dulaimi, "HAMAS-Iraq Spokesman to Al-Arab: These Are Our Proofs That Al-Qa'ida Is Affiliated to Iran," *Al-Arab* (Doha), March 26–27, 2008.

164. Seumas Milne, "Out of the Shadows," *Guardian*, July 19, 2007.

165. "JAMI Military Spokesman Interviewed on Jihad, ISI, Militias, Other Issues," Open Source Center-GMP20080624050001, June 19, 2008, https://www.opensource.gov/portal/server.pt/gateway/PTARGS_0_0_200_212_51_43/http.

166. "Islamic Army Spokesman Says Conditions Not Yet Ripe for Islamic State in Iraq," *BBC Monitoring—Middle East*, November 3, 2006.

167. "Islamic Army in Iraq Spokesman Denounces US-Iran Alliance, Views Jihadist Rifts," Open Source Center-GMP20071224050001, December 9, 2007, https://www.opensource.gov/portal/server/pt/gateway/PTARGS_0_0_200_240_1019_43/h.

168. Ibid.

169. Ibid.

170. Sudarshan Raghavan, "Sunni Factions Split with Al-Qaeda Group," *Washington Post*, April 13, 2007.

171. Ibid.

172. Ibid.

173. The literature on Iraqi tribes' political roles and role in the rising up against AQI and then ISI is vast. I have relied on Amatzia Baram, "Neo-tribalism in Iraq: Saddam Hussein's Tribal Policies, 1991–1996," *International Journal of*

Middle Eastern Studies 29, 1 (1997), 1–31; Myriam Benraad, "Une lecture de la Sahwa ou les milles et un visages du tribalisme irakien," *Etudes Rurales* 184 (July–December 2009), 95–106; David Kilcullen, "Anatomy of a Tribal Revolt," *Small Wars Journal*, August 2007, http://smallwarsjournal.com/blog/anatomy-of-a-tribal-revolt/.

174. Matthew Penney, "The Anbar Awakening in Context ... and Why It Is So Hard to Replicate," *Military Review* 95, 2 (March–April 2015), 106–117.

175. Charles Levinson, "Sunni Tribes Turn against Jihadis," *Christian Science Monitor*, February 6, 2006, http://www.christiansciencemonitor.com/2006/0206/p01s01-woiq.htm.

176. Ibid.

177. Ibid.

178. Khalid al-Ansary and Ali Adeeb, "Most Tribes in Anbar Agree to Unite against Insurgents," *New York Times*, September 18, 2006, http://www.nytimes.com/2006/09/18/world/middleeast/18iraq.html.

179. "Al-Qaida: En Perte De Vitesse En Irak," Centre de Recherches sur le Terrorisme, January 2007, http://www.recherches-sur-le-terrorisme.com/Documentsterrorisme/qaida-irak-anbar.html.

180. John Burns, "Iraqi Tribal Leader Is Killed, and Mourners Are Attacked," *New York Times*, May 25, 2007, 6; John Ward Anderson, "Iraqi Tribes Strike Back at Insurgents," *Washington Post*, March 7, 2006, A12.

181. "Iraq's Sunni Armed Groups Reportedly Planning Alliance against Al-Qa'ida," Open Source Center-GMP20070411825007, from *Al-Hayah*, April 11, 2007, https://www.opensource.gov/portal/server.pt/gateway/PTARGS_0_0_200_2 40_1019_43/h.

182. "Report: Al-Jazirah TV Highlights Criticism of Al-Qa'ida-Affiliated Islamic State of Iraq," Open Source Center-FEA20070510141266, May 10, 2007, https://www .opensource.gov/portal/server.pt/gateway/PTARGS_0_0_5762)972_100578.

183. "Al-'Arabiyah's 'Death Industry' on Awakening Councils' Battle against Al-Qa'ida," Al-'Arabiyah TV, Dubai 19:10 GMT, March 28, 2008, Open Source Center-GMP20080328643004, https://www.opensource.gov/portal/server .pt/gateway/PTARGS_0_0_200_240_1019_43/h.

184. "Tribal Awakening against Al-Qaida in Iraq Grows; Part I: Salah Al-Din Province," *Global Issues Report* June 18, 2007, (Center for International Issues Research for U.S. Department of Defense), 1.

185 "Iraq's Sunni Arabs Confront the Islamic State of Iraq, Part II: Al Qa'ida Strikes Back," *Global Issues Report*, May 2, 2007.

186 "MSC and Al-Qaida in Iraq Denounce Anbar Tribal Leaders," *Global Issues Report*, October 3, 2006.

187. "Al-Qa'idah in Iraq Leader Urges Specific Groups to Join Islamic State," Open Source Center-GMP20061110950010, https://www.opensource.gov/portal/server.pt/gateway/PTARGS_0_0_200_240_1019_43/.

188. "Mujahideen Shura Council Fires Back at Critics," *Global Issues Report*, October 19, 2006, 1–3.

189. "Islamic State of Iraq Lashes Out at Its Enemies and Rivals," *Global Issues Report*, March 15, 2007.

190. "Say, for Me, I Work on a Clear Sign from the Lord," Open Source Center-FEA20070314102073, March 13, 2007, https://www.opensource.gov/portal/server.pt/gateway/PTARGS)_0_0_5766_972_0_43/http.

191. Ibid.

192. Ibid.

193. Ibid.

194. Ibid.

195. Ibid.

196. Ibid.

197. Ibid.

198. Ibid.

199. Ibid.

200. Ibid.

201. Ibid.

202. Ibid.

203. Ibid.

204. In "Al-Baghdadi Statement Views 'Dividends and Losses' after Four Years of 'Jihad,'" Open Source Center-FEA20070417118651, April 17, 2007, https://www.opensource.gov/portal/server.pt/gateway/PTARGS_0_0_449_240_0_43/http.

205. Ibid.

206. "The Islamic State of Iraq and Its Critics, Part I: Why We Fight," *Global Issues Report*, April 13, 2007, 1–5.

207. Ibid.

208. "Growing Rifts within the Insurgency in Iraq, part I: The Islamic State of Iraq vs. the Islamic Army in Iraq," *Global Issues Report* April 11, 2007, (Center for International Issues Research for U.S. Department of Defense), 1–3.

209. "Al Furqan taqadim: Qilmat Amir al-Mu'minin bi-anwan Wa Yamkarun wa Yamkar Allah" [Al-Furqan Media Presents: Statement of the Commander of the Faithful: They Plot but God Also Plots], Muslm.net, September 15, 2007, http://www.muslm.net/vb/showthread.php?t=252169.

210 "Bin Laden Belatedly Comments on Insurgent Problems in Iraq," *Global Issues Report* October 30, 2007, (Center for International Issues Research for U.S. Department of Defense), 1–5.

211. "Tabayun al-asad# Al-Sahab#taqadim# (al-sabil ala-habat al-mu'amarat—al-Sheikh Usama Bin Ladin)," [Exposition of the Lion#Al-Sahab# Presents the Path to Thwart Conspiracies—Sheikh Usama Bin Laden], Ekhlaas.org, http://www.ekhlaas.org/forum/showthread.php?t=110903.

212. Ibid.

213. Ibid.

214. "Quwat al-Sahwa tarud ala Bin Ladin: La Maqan lil-Qa'ida fi al-Iraq" [Awakening Forces Respond to Bin Ladin: Al Qa'ida Has No Place in Iraq], *Middle East Online*, December 31, 2007, http://www.middle-east-online.com/?id=56326.

215. Jonathan Steele, "Iraqi Insurgents Regrouping, Says Sunni Resistance Leader," *Guardian*, December 3, 2007, https://www.theguardian.com/world/2007/dec/03/usa.iraq.

216. "Al-Muqawama al-Iraqiya taalan tashkil awal majlis siyasi liha" [Iraqi Resistance Annnounces the Formation of Its First Political Council], *Middle East Online*, October 11, 2007, http://middle-east-online.com/?id=53455.

217. "Prominent Iraqi Insurgent Factions Form 'Political Council and Issue Pragmatic Platform'," *Global Issues Report* (Center for International Issues Research for U.S. Department of Defense), November 6, 2007, 3.

218. "Iraq's Tribal Counterinsurgency Fuels Internal Sunni Rivalries," *Global Issues Report*, December 7, 2007, 1–3.

219. Jack Fairweather, "Political Ambitions of Sunni Tribal Leader Worry Baghdad Elite," *Financial Times*, April 19, 2008, http://www.ft.com/cms/s/0/112332c8-0dad-11dd-b90a-0000779fd2ac.html?ft_site=falcon&desktop=true#axzz4my5UxZq6.

220. Edward Wong, "Some Insurgents Are Asking Iraq for Negotiations," *New York Times*, June 27, 2006, 1; "Iraq's Tribal Counterinsurgency Fuels Internal Sunni Rivalries."

221. Doug Smith and Saif Rasheed, "Sects Unite to Battle Al Qaeda in Iraq," *Los Angeles Times*, November 19, 2007, 1.

222. "Insurgent Groups Unite to Form 'Jihad and Reformation Front,'" Open Source Center-FEA20070504131508, *Open Source Feature—Jihadist Websites*, May 3, 2007, https://www.opensource.gov/portal/server.pt/gateway/PTARGS_0_0_6006_989_0_43/http.

223. "Jihad and Change Front Answers on Issues, Constants, Positions," statement posted on jihadist website Ana al-Muslim, in Open Source Center-GMP 200803160500I, March 11, 2008, https://www.opensource.gov/portal/server.pt/gateway/PTARGS_0_0_200_1010_51_43/http.

224. "Al-Bayan Raqm 21: Da'wa lil 'auda aly jadat al-sawaf" [Statement No. 21: Invitation to Return to the Just Path], Jhadfront.com, September 11, 2008, http://www.jhadfront.com/index/php?p=351.

225. Gadahn letter, n.d., Harmony Documents Collection, Counter Terrorism Center, West Point Military Academy, SOCOM-2012-0000004-HT. For more on Adam Gadahn, see Brian Dodwell, "The Abbottabad Documents: The Quiet Ascent of Adam Gadahn," *CTC Sentinel* 5, 5 (May 22, 2012), 19–21. He also figures in my further discussion below.

226. Paul Cruickshank, "New Direction—Ayman al-Zawahiri's Leadership of Al-Qaeda," *Jane's Intelligence Review* 24, 7 (July 1, 2012).

227. Vicken Cheterian, "ISIS and the Killing Fields of the Middle East," *Survival* 57, 2 (2015), 105–118.

228. "Interview with Syrian President Bashar al-Assad," *Wall Street Journal*, January 31, 2011, https://www.wsj.com/articles/SB10001424052748703833204576114712441122894.

229. Fabrice Balanche, "Insurrection et Contre-Insurrection en Syrie," *Geostrategic Maritime Review* 2 (Spring–Summer 2014), 40.

230. Thomas Pierret, "The Syrian Baath Party and Sunni Islam: Conflicts and Connivance," *Middle East Brief* (Crown Center for Middle East Studies, Brandeis University) 77 (February 2014), 1.

231. Mahmud Faksh, "The Alawi Community of Syria: A New Dominant Political Force," *Middle Eastern Studies* 20, 2 (April 1984), 135–136; Kais Firro, "The 'Alawis in Modern Syria: From Nusayriya to Islam via 'Alawiya," *Der Islam* 82 (2005), 1–31.

232. The French recruitment of Syria's minorities into colonial forces is discussed in N. E. Bou-Nacklie, "Les Troupes Speciales: Religious and Ethnic Recruitment, 1916–46," *International Journal of Middle Eastern Studies* 25, 4 (November 1993), 645–660.

233. Gitta Yaffe-Schatzmann, "Alawi Separatists and Unionists: The Events of 25 February 1936," *Middle Eastern Studies* 31, 1 (January 1995), 28–38.

234. Stephane Valter, "Islamist Forces in the Syrian Conflict: Doctrinal Deficit and Military Radicalization," *Singapore Middle East Papers* (National University of Singapore) 18 (March 7, 2016), 1–29; Raymond Hinnebusch, "Syria: From 'Authoritarian Upgrading' to Revolution?," *International Affairs* 88, 1 (2012), 96.

235. Sami Moubayed, "The History of Political and Militant Islam in Syria," Jamestown Foundation, *Terrorism Monitor* 3, 16 (August 11, 2005), https://jamestown.org/program/the-history-of-political-and-militant-islam-in-syria/.

236. For extensive details of the encounters between the Sunni radicals and the Baathist regime in Syria, see Raphael Lefevre, *Ashes of Hama: The Muslim Brotherhood in Syria*, London: Hurst, 2013; Umar Abd-Allah, *The Islamic Struggle in Syria*, Berkeley: Mizan Press, 1983; Line Khatib, "Islamic and Islamist Revivalism in Syria: The Rise and Fall of Secularism in Ba'thist Syria," Ph.D. diss., McGill University, 2010; and Creighton Mullins, "Syria and the Rise of Radical Islamist Groups," M.A. thesis, Naval Postgraduate School, Monterey, California, 2015.

237. Raymond Hinnebusch, *Syria: Revolution from Above*, London: Routledge, 2001, 147.

238. Ibid., 53–56.

239. Volker Perthes, *Syria under Bashar al-Asad: Modernization and the Limits of Change*, International Institute of Strategic Studies, Adelphi Papers, London: Oxford University Press, 2004; David Lesch, *The New Lion of Damascus: Bashar al-Asad and Modern Syria*, New Haven: Yale University Press, 2005.

240. See Caroline Donati, *L'Exception Syrienne: Entre Modernisation et Resistance*, Paris: La Decouverte, 2009, 271–310.

241. Anthony Shadid, "Syria's Unpredictable Force: The State-Sponsored Clergy," *Washington Post*, May 27, 2005.

242. Scott Wilson, "Religious Surge Alarms Secular Syrians," *Washington Post*, January 23, 2005.

243. Ethan Corbin, "Lessons from the Interior: Insurgency and Counter-insurgency in Syria," *al-Nakhlah*, Spring 2007, 1–10.

244. See Patrick Seale, *Asad: The Struggle for the Middle East*, Oakland: University of California Press, 1990.

245. For more details on the relationship between the Baath regime in Syria and the Islamists, see Thomas Pierret, "The Syrian Baath Party and Sunni Islam."

246. Nicholas Blanford, "Syrian Reformer Rankles Islamists," *Christian Science Monitor*, January 13, 2005, https://www.csmonitor.com/2005/0113/p06s01-wome.html; Nicholas Blanford, "In Secular Syria, an Islamic Revival; A State with a History of Quashing Rebellious Islamic Groups Is Seeing an Upswing in Religious Faith," *Christian Science Monitor*, October 3, 2006, 6.

247. Scott Wilson, "Religious Surge Alarms Secular Syrians," *Washington Post*, January 23, 2005, A21.

248. Blanford, "In Secular Syria, an Islamic Revival," 6.

249. Ibid.

250. For detailed analyses of the revival of Islam and the erosion of the seemingly secular state in Syria, see in particular, Khatib, "Islamic and Islamist Revivalism in Syria," especially 122–228; Philippe Droz-Vincent, "'State of Barbary' (Take Two): From the Arab Spring to the Return of Violence in Syria," *Middle East Journal* 68, 1 (Winter 2014), 33–54.

251. On JN and its formation see Christopher Anzalone, "The Multiple Faces of Jabhat al-Nusra/Jabhat Fath al-Sham in Syria's Civil War," *Insight Turkey* 18, 2 (Spring 2016), 41–50; Abdul Rahim Atoun (aka Abu Abdullah al-Shami), *Ta'asis jabhat al-Nusra wa ahdath al-Sham badayat al-khilaf ila 'alan al-dawla* [The Establishment of Jabhat al-Nusra and the Events of al-Sham from the Beginning of the Disagreement to the Announcement of the State (IS)], November 20, 2016, translated into English by Bilad al-Sham Media, November 27, 2016, *Pietervanostaeyen* (blog), November 27, 2016; https://pietervanostaeyen.com/page2/.

252. "The Al-Nusrah Front: A Perplexing Puzzle, Accused of Insubordination to the Al-Asad Regime and of Being a Creation of His Intelligence Service, It Later Became Popular Following Its Ferocious Battle Performance in Aleppo," *Al-Sharq al-Awsat*, February 27, 2013, in *BBC Monitoring—Middle East*, March 10, 2013.

253. "Pan Arab Daily Profiles Syrian Al-Nusrah Front Leader," *BBC Monitoring—Middle East*, November 5, 2013.

254. Taysir Alluni, "Interview with Abu Muhammad al-Jawlani," *Today's Encounter Program*, Al-Jazeera TV, December 19, 2013, in *BBC Monitoring—Middle East*, December 22, 2013.

255. Ibid.

256. Ibid.

257. Ibid.

258. Ibid.

259. Ibid.

260. "JTIC Brief: The Pen and the Sword—Al-Qaeda Attempts to Mediate Jihadist Dispute," *Jane's Terrorism and Security Monitor* 13, 7 (July 1, 2013).

261. "Al-Jazeera's Treatment of Al-Zawahiri's Audio Message Dissolving ISIL," *BBC Monitoring—Middle East* (November 9, 2013).

262. "Al-Qaeda Loses Authority over Affiliates in Iraq and Syria," *Jane's Intelligence Weekly* 5, 26 (June 19, 2013).

263. "JTIC Brief: The Pen and the Sword."

264. Shiv Malik and Spencer Akerman, "How ISIS Crippled Al-Qaida," *Guardian*, June 10, 2015; see also J. M. Berger, "The Islamic State vs. al Qaeda," *Foreign Policy*, September 2, 2014, http://www.foreignpolicy.com/articles/2014/09/02/islamic_state_v; Aaron Zelin, "The War between ISIS and al-Qaeda for Supremacy of the Global Jihadist Movement," Research Notes 20, Washington, DC: Washington Institute for Near East Policy, June 2014, http://www.washingtoninstitute.org/uploads/Documents/pubs/ResearchNote_20_Zelin.pdf.

265. Malik and Akerman, "How ISIS Crippled Al-Qaida."

266. Cole Bunzel, "The Caliphate's Scholar-in-Arms," *Jihadica* (blog), July 9, 2014, http://www.jihadica.com/the-caliphate's-scholar-in-arms/.

267. Ibid.

268. Ibid.

269. Maria Abi-Habib, "Al Qaeda Emissary in Syria Killed by Rival Islamist Rebels; Violent Power Struggles between Groups Deepen," *Wall Street Journal*, February 23, 2014.

270. "Ma kan hadha Manhajuna wa lan yakun," *Pietervanostaeyen* (blog), April 18, 2014, https://pietervanostaeyen.wordpress.com/2014/04/18/message-by-.

271. For Zawahiri's interview, titled "Reality between Pain and Hope," see Aaron Zellin, "Gust Post: Ayman al-Zawahiri on Jihadist Infighting and the Islamic State of Iraq and al-Sham," *Jihadology* (blog), April 21, 2014, http://jihadology.net/2014/04/21/guest-post-ayman-al-zawahiri-on-.

272. "New Audio Message by ISIS Shaykh Abu Muhammad al-'Adnani as-Shami—Apologies, Amir al-Qa'ida," *Pietervanostaeyen* (blog), April 12, 2014, https://pietervanostaeyen.wordpress.com/2014/05/12/new-audio-m.

273. Abu Qatada, "Message to the People of Jihad and Those Who Love Jihad," *Pietervanostaeyen* (blog), April 19, 2014, https://pietervanostaeyen.wordpress.com/2014/04/page/2/.

274. Abu Mohammad al-Maqdisi, "The Case of ISIS and the Position of Duty towards It," *Jihadology*, May 26, 2014; http://jihadology.net/2014/05/26/minbar-al-ta-wḥid-wa-l-jihad-presents-a-new-release-from-abu-muḥammad-al-maqdisi-the-case-of-the-islamic-state-of-iraq-and-al-sham-and-the-position-of-the-duty-toward-it/. "Deviant Organization: Influential Jihadist Ideologue Criticizes ISIL," *Jane's Islamic Affairs Analyst* 14, 5 (July 1, 2014).

275. See Thomas Joscelyn, "Jailed Jihadist Ideologue Says the ISIS Is a 'Deviant Organization,'" *Long War Journal*, May 28, 2014, http://www.longwarjournal .org/archives/2014/05/jailed_jihadist_ideo.php; and Zellin, "War between ISIS and al-Qaeda for Supremacy of the Global Jihadist Movement."

276. Daniel Nisman and Ron Gilran, "Jihadist versus Jihadist; Young Islamists see al Qaeda as a Spent Force. They Admire ISIS for Its Brutality," *Wall Street Journal*, June 24, 2014.

277. Malik and Akerman, "How ISIS Crippled Al-Qaida."

278. Ibid.

279. See Ludovico Carlino, "How Al-Qaeda and Islamic State Differ in Pursuit of Common Goal," *Jane's Intelligence Review* 27, 4 (April 1, 2015).

280. "A Call to Hijrah," *Dabiq*, iss. 3, Shawwal 1435 (August 2014), https://clarion-project.org/docs/isis-isil-islamic-state-magazine-Issue-3-the-call-to-hijrah.pdf.

281. Carlino, "How Al-Qaeda and Islamic State Differ in Pursuit of Common Goal."

282. For an informative minibiography of Adam Gadahn (aka Adam Pearlman) but which only goes up to 2007, see Raffi Khatchadourian, "Azzam the American," *New Yorker*, January 22, 2007, http://www.newyorker.com/magazine/2007/01/22/azzam-the-american.

283. "An Exclusive Interview with Adam Yahiye Gadahn," *Resurgence*, special issue (Summer 2015), 31.

284. Ibid., 37–38.

285. Ibid., 39.

286. Ibid., 46–49.

287. Malik and Akerman, "How ISIS Crippled Al-Qaida."

288. For Maqdisi's letter, see "Sheikh Abu Muhammad al-Maqdisi's Efforts to Arrange Prisoner Exchange Deal to Free Jordanian Pilot," Special Dispatch no. 5969, Middle East Media Research Institute (MEMRI), February 19, 2015, https://www.memri.org/reports/sheikh-abu-muhammad-al-maqdisis-efforts-arrange-prisoner-exchange-deal-free-jordanian-pilot.

289. Kasasbeh was probably murdered in this horrific manner before IS entered into duplicitous negotiations over the "release" of al-Rishawi. The video of the execution was released, however, in February 2015.

290. Joby Warrick in *The Black Flags* has brilliantly and extensively narrated the story of this episode.

291. "Jihadi-Salafi Spiritual Leader Abu Muhammad Al-Maqdisi Slams ISIS over Immolation of Jordanian Pilot," *Middle East Media Research Institute TV*

Monitor Project (MEMRI TV), Transcript Clip no. 4767, February 2015, https://www.memri.org/tv/jihadi-salafi-spiritual-leader-abu-muhammad-al-maqdisi-slams-isis-over-immolation-jordanian-pilot.

CHAPTER 4

1. "Translation of Old Al-Zarqawi Interview, Says God's Law Must Rule 'Entire World,'" Open Source Center-GMP20061211281001, December 6, 2006, https://www.opensource.gov/portal/server.pt/gateway/PTARGS_0_0_762_303_0_43/http.
2. Ibid.
3. Ibid.
4. Ibid.
5. Ibid.
6. Ibid.
7. *The Rise of ISIS* (ebook), New York: New York Times Books, 2015, http://graphics8.nytimes.com/packages/other/times-premier/The_Rise_Of_Isis_NYTimes_062315.pdf.
8. See "Profile: Abu Musab al-Zarqawi," *BBC News*, November 10, 2005, http://news.bbc.co.uk/2/hi/middle_east/3483089.stm; Joby Warrick, *The Black Flags: The Rise of Isis,* New York: Doubleday, 2015.
9. Joas Wagemakers, "A Terrorist Organization That Never Was: The Jordanian 'Bay'at al-Imam' Group," *Middle East Journal* 68, 1 (Winter 2014), 59–75.
10. Ari Weisfuse, "Negotiating Oblivion, Say al-'Adl: Al-Qaeda's Top Operative," B.A. thesis, Brandeis University, 2014, 17.
11. Ibid.
12. "Detained Al-Qa'ida Leader Sayf al-Adl Chronicles Al-Zarqawi's Rise in Organization," Open Source Center-GMP20050606371001, May 21, 2005, https://www.opensource.gov/portal/server.pt/gateway/PTARGS_0_0_200_203-121123.
13. Ibid.
14. Ibid.
15. Ibid.
16. Ibid.
17. Ibid.
18. Mustafa Setmarian Nassar, a Syrian, is one of the best-known jihadist practitioners and strategic thinkers. He wrote *The Global Islamic Resistance Call,* a manual for Islamist guerrilla warfare in trying times. He has been the subject of an outstanding biography by one of the world's leading academics on the jihadists, Brynjar Lia, *The Architect of Global Jihad.* The best analyses of his complicated and difficult relations with al-Qaeda are by Brian Fishman, *The Master Plan: ISIS, Al-Qaeda, and Jihadi Strategy for Final Victory,* New Haven: Yale University Press, 2016, 13–17, 166–167.

19. Hazim al-Amin, "Al-Zarqawi's Followers in Jordan Visit Their Shaykhs in Jail and Wait for the Chance to Join Abu-Mus'ab in Iraq," *al-Hayat*, December 14, 2004, 15, in Open Source Center-GMP20041214000069, https://www.open-source.gov/portal/server.pt/gateway/PTARGS_0_0_200_240_51_43/http.

20. Ibid.

21. Ibid.

22. "Afghan Militant Azzam Discusses Al-Zarqawi's Strife with Bin-Ladin," *BBC Monitoring—Middle East*, April 25, 2006, 1.

23. Ibid.

24. Subsequently, the name Jund or Junud al-Sham was adopted by other groups, particularly after the Syrian civil war erupted.

25. "Detained Al-Qa'ida Leader Sayf al-Adl Chronicles Al-Zarqawi's Rise in Organization."

26. Ibid.

27. Ibid.

28. Ibid.

29. Ibid.

30. Scott Peterson, "Rumbles of Radicalism in Kurdistan; Al Qaeda's Presence Stunned Iraq's Moderate North," *Christian Science Monitor*, November 3, 2005, 4.

31. "Detained Al-Qa'ida Leader Sayf al-Adl Chronicles Al-Zarqawi's Rise in Organization."

32. Anthony Cordesman, *Zarqawi's Death: Temporary "Victory" or Lasting Impact?*, Washington, DC: Center for Strategic and International Studies, 2006, 4.

33. Fuad Hussein, "Al-Zarqawi: Al-jil al-thani min tanzim al-Qaida" ["Al-Zarqawi: The Second Generation of Al-Qaida], serialized in *Al-Quds al-Arabi*, May 26, 2005, 17. Statement by "Raad" to *al-Hayat* quoted in "Report Profiles Armed Groups in Iraq, Al-Qa'ida Presence (1)," OSC-GMP20060225700005, February 25, 2006, https://www.opensource.gov/portal/server.pt/gateway/PTARGS_0_0 _200_240_1019_43/h.

34. Quoted in Nimrod Raphaeli, "The Sheikh of the Slaughterers: Abu Mus'ab al-Zarqawi and the Al-Qaeda Connection," *Middle East Media Research Institute* (MEMRI), Inquiry and Analysis Report 231, June 30, 2005, https://www.memri .org/reports/%E2%80%98-sheikh-slaughterers%E2%80%99-abu-musab-al-zarqawi-and-al-qaeda-connection. Statements by "S.S." to *al-Hayat* quoted in "Report Profiles Armed Groups in Iraq, Al-Qa'ida Presence (1)," OSC-GMP20060225700005, February 25, 2006, https://www.opensource.gov/portal /server.pt/gateway/PTARGS_0_0_200_240_1019_43/h. Article by Hazem al-Amin for *al-Hayat* quoted in "Iraq: Paper Outlines Background of Abu Mus'ab al-Zarqawi's Followers (1)," OSC-GMP20041214000069, December 14, 2004, https://www.opensource.gov/portal/server.pt/gateway/PTARGS_0_0_200_ 240_51_43/http.

35. Ahmed S. Hashim, "Baghdad Blues: Observations from Iraq," diary, vols. 1–5, 2003–2005; Urs Gehriger and Marwan Shehadeh, "Abu Musab al-Zarqawi: In the Network of the Phantom," *Signandsight*, October 11, 2005, http://www .signandsight.com/features/451.html. Statements by IAI commander quoted in "Report Profiles Armed Groups in Iraq, Al-Qa'ida Presence (1)."

36. "Jordan Security Say Al-Zarqawi Expanding outside Iraq," *BBC Monitoring— Middle East*, July 17, 2005, 1.

37. "Death Industry Program," presented by Rima Salihah, Al-Arabiya TV, Dubai, 19:09 GMT, January 1, 2010.

38. This MSC is not to be confused with the Mujahidin Shura Council, which was set up in Falluja in 2004 to coordinate the strategies of the jihadist and local fighters in the urban battles with U.S. forces.

39. "Statement of Mujahidin Shura Council on Establishment of 'Islamic State of Iraq,'" Open Source Center-GMP20061015684004, https://www.open-source.gov/portal/server.pt/gateway/PTARGS_0_0_691_212_0_43/http; "MSC Announces Establishment of 'Islamic State of Iraq,'" Open Source Center-FEA20061015028735, https://www.opensource.gov/portal/server.pt/gateway/PTARGS_0-0_5769_972_0_43/http.

40. From Barah Mikhaïl, "Al-Qaida en Mesopotamie: Emergence d'une nouvelle generation au sein de l'organisation?," no. 31, Institut de Relations Internationales et Strategiques, 2006, 34–35; http://www.iris-france.org/wp-content/uploads/2014/11/2007_alqaida.pdf.

41. The seminal account of Islamization in Iraq under Saddam Hussein is Amatzia Baram, *Saddam Husayn and Islam, 1968–2003: Baathi Iraq from Secularism to Faith*, Wasington, DC: Woodrow Wilson Press, 2014. Statement by ISI on May 16, 2010, announcing Abu Bakr al-Baghdadi as emir: "New Al-Qa'idah Iraq 'War Minister' Moroccan with Syrian Nationality," *BBC Monitoring—Middle East*, May 17, 2010.

42. Martin Chulov, "Isis: The Inside Story," *Guardian*, December 11, 2014, https://www.theguardian.com/world/2014/dec/11/-sp-isis-the-inside-story.

43. Ibid.

44. Ibid.

45. Ibid.

46. Ibid.

47. Ibid.

48. Ali Hashem, "The Many Names of Abu Bakr al-Baghdadi," *Al-Monitor*, March 23, 2015, http://www.al-monitor.com/pulse/ru/contents/articles/originals/2015/03/isis-baghdadi-islamic-state-caliph-many-names-al-qaeda.html; Terence McCoy, "How ISIS Leader Abu Bakr al-Baghdadi Became the World's Most Powerful Jihadist Leader," *Washington Post*, June 11, 2014, http://www.washingtonpost .com/news/morning-mix/wp/201.

49. Ibid.

50. Chulov, "Isis: The Inside Story." Quotation from the jihadist Abu Ahmed: "the mujahideen all came through Syria…" is from ibid.

51. Samuel Helfont and Michael Brill, "Saddam's ISIS?: The Terrorist Group's Real Origin Story," *Foreign Affairs*, January 12, 2016, https://www.foreignaffairs.com/articles/iraq/2016-01-12/saddams-isis.

52. Ibid.

53. Ahmed S. Hashim, "Baghdad Blues: Observations from Iraq," diary, vols. 2 and 3, November 2003–April 2004.

54. Shiv Malik, Mustafa Khalil, Spencer Ackerman, and Ali Younis, "How ISIS Crippled al-Qaida," *Guardian*, June 10, 2015, https://www.theguardian.com/world/2015/jun/10/how-isis-crippled-al-qaida.

55. Ibid.

56. See for a fuller description of what we *know* (or think we know) about Haji Bakr, see Kyle Orton, "The Riddle of Haji Bakr," *The Syrian Intifada*, November 10, 2015; https://kyleorton1991.wordpress.com/2015/11/10/the-riddle-of-haji-bakr/

57. The following paragraphs rely heavily on Christoph Reuter, "Secret Files Reveal the Structure of Islamic State," *Der Spiegel Online*, April 18, 2015, http://www.spiegel.de/international/world/islamic-state-files-show-structure-of-islamist-terror-group-a-1029274.html.

58. Ibid.

59. Ibid.

60. Ibid.

61. See also Richard Barrett, "The Islamic State," Soufan Group, October 28, 2014, 18–20.

62. Sunni Arabs and Sunni Turkmen expressed these sentiments to me in 2003–2004, 2006, and 2007. The sentiments got more dire and shrill as time went by; i.e., in parallel with growing Shia power and triumphalism. Not only Islamists expressed these sentiments but also Baathists, ranging from former officers to officials, tribal sheikhs, and even children. I remember distinctly, while I was standing on the rooftop of a house in Tel Afar surveying that "charming" little town, a Sunni Turkmen child of eleven, whose house this was, pointing literally across the street to a Shia neighborhood and saying: "hadha ard al-fasad" (that there is the land of corruption). *Fasad* is a form of moral corruption, degradation, and mayhem spread within Muslim territories by apostates.

63. Helene Sallon, "Comment l'État islamique a organisé son 'caliphat,'" *Le Monde*, November 12, 2015, http://www.lemonde.fr/proche-orient/article/2015/12/11/comment-l-etat-islamique-a-organise-son-califat_4830138_3218.html.

64. Nick Thompson and Atika Shubert, "The Anatomy of ISIS: How the 'Islamic State' Is Run, from Oil to Beheadings," *CNN*, September 22, 2014, 20:34 GMT, http://edition.cnn.com/2014/09/18/world/meast/isis-syria-iraq-hierarchy/index.html.

65. Ruth Sherlock, "Inside the Leadership of Islamic State: How the New 'Caliphate' Is Run," *Telegraph*, July 9, 2014, http://www.telegraph.co.uk/news/worldnews/middleeast/iraq/10956280/Inside-the-leadership-of-Islamic-State-how-the-new-caliphate-is-run.html.

66. This discussion on the shura council is derived from various newspaper reports and from Barrett, "Islamic State," 29–30; Hassan Abu Haniyeh, "Daesh's Organisational Structure," *Al Jazeera Center for Studies*, December 4, 2014, http://studies.aljazeera.net/en/dossiers/decipheringdaeshoriginsimpactandfuture/2014/12/201412395930929444.html; Helene Lavoix, "Understanding the Islamic State's System—Means of Violence," *Red (Team) Analysis*, June 15, 2015, https://www.redanalysis.org/2015/06/15/understanding-the-islamic-states-system-means-of-violence/; Cameron Glenn, *Al Qaeda v ISIS: Leaders and Structure*, Washington, DC: Woodrow Wilson Center, September 28, 2015, https://www.wilsoncenter.org/article/al-qaeda-v-isis-leaders-structure.

67. This discussion on the sharia council is derived from various newspaper reports, such as Gianluca Mezzofiore, "Isis Leadership: Who's Who in 'Fluid' Islamic State Structure of Power," *IBTimes*, July 2, 2015, http://www.ibtimes.co.uk/isis-leadership-whos-who-fluid-islamic-state-structure-power-1509014; longer and more substantive sources from which I derived my data include Barrett, "Islamic State," 30–31; Haniyeh, "Daesh's Organizational Structure"; Lavoix, "Understanding the Islamic State's System," Ali Hashem, "Who Holds the Real Power in IS?," *Al-Monitor*, February 19, 2015, http://www.al-monitor.com/pulse/originals/2015/02/islamic-state-sharia-council-power.html; "The Islamic State's Organizational Structure One Year In," *Al-Monitor*, July 2, 2015, http://www.al-monitor.com/pulse/security/2015/07/islamic-state-caliphate-ministries-armies-syria-iraq.html.

68. Terence McCoy, "ISIS, Beheadings and the Success of Horrifying Violence," *Washington Post*, June 13, 2014, http://www.washingtonpost.com/news/morning-mix/wp/2014/06/13; James Farwell, "How ISIS Uses Social Media," *IISS Blog*, October 2, 2014, http://www.iiss.org/en/politics%20and%20strategy/blogsections/2014-d2de/october-931b/isis-media-9d28.

69. Caroline Piquet, "Comment Daech attire de jeunes médecins et ingénieurs," *Le Figaro*, February 16, 2016, http://www.lefigaro.fr/international/2016/02/16/01003-20160216ARTFIG00035-comment-daech-attire-de-jeunes-medecins-et-ingenieurs.php.

70. Faisal Irshaid, "How ISIS Is Spreading Its Message Online," *BBC News—Middle East*, June 19, 2014, http://www.bbc.com/news/world-middle-east-27912569; Greg Miller and Souad Mekhennet, "Inside the Surreal World of the Islamic State's Propaganda Machine," *Washington Post*, November 20, 2015, https://www.washingtonpost.com/world/national-security/inside-the-islamic-states-propaganda-machine/2015/11/20/051e997a-8ce6-11e5-acff-673ae92ddd2b_story.html?utm_term=.2ee387830224.

71. Rita Katz, "Follow ISIS on Twitter: A Special Report on the Use of Social Media by Jihadists," *Site Intelligence Group* (blog), June 26, 2014, http://news.siteintel-group.com/blog/index.php/entry/192-follow-isis-on-twitter-a-special-report-on-the-use-of-social-media-by-jihadists.

72. Harriet Alexander and Alistair Beach, "How Isil Is Funded, Trained and Operating in Iraq and Syria," *Telegraph*, August 23, 2014, http://www.telegraph .co.uk/news/worldnews/middleeast/iraq/11052919/How-Isil-is-funded-trained-and-operating-in-Iraq-and-Syria.html.

73. Helima Croft and Christopher Louney, "ISIS and Oil: Off the Radar but On Our Minds," Commodity Strategy Research, *RBC Capital Markets*, September 29, 2015, 2.

74. Erika Solomon, "Isis Proves Vulnerable to Its Own 'Ghost Armies,'" *Financial Times*, December 21, 2015, https://www.ft.com/content/fb86019e-a240-11e5-bc70-7ff6d4fd203a; Mirren Gidda, "ISIS Is Facing a Cash Crunch in the Caliphate," *Newsweek*, September 23, 2015, http://europe.newsweek.com/isis-are-facing-cash-crunch-caliphate-333422; Yusuf al-Dini, "Internal Sedition inside DA'ISH... Warns of Disappearance of Organization, Civil War, Divisions, Confrontation between Muhajirin, Locals over Strategy, Leadership," *Al-Sharq al-Awsat*, March 16, 2015, in *BBC Monitoring—Middle East*, March 22, 2015.

CHAPTER 5

1. See Basil H. Liddell Hart, *The British Way in Warfare*, London: Faber, 1932.

2. For a cogent discussion and review of the debate as it stood in the 1980s, see Hew Strachan, "The British Way in Warfare Revisited," *Historical Journal* 26, 2 (June 1983), 447–461. For a more recent review see Brian Holden Reid, "The British Way in Warfare," *Royal United Services Institute Journal* 156, 6 (2011), 70–76.

3. See Russell Weigley, *The American Way: A History of United States Military Strategy and Policy*, Bloomington: Indiana University Press, 1977; Richard Harrison, *The Russian Way of War: Operational Art, 1904–1940*, Lexington: University of Kansas Press, 2001. Since the revival of the Russian military under its leader Vladimir Putin, there has been a massive increase in the literature seeking to understand the new Russian way of warfare in the twenty-first century. On Germany, see Robert M. Citino, *The German Way of War: From the Thirty Years War to the Third Reich*, Lexington: University of Kansas Press, 2005.

4. Ehud Eilam, *Israel's Way of War: A Strategic and Operational Analysis, 1948–2014*, Jefferson, NC: McFarland, 2016; Christine Fair, *Fighting to the End: The Pakistan Army's Way of War*, Oxford: Oxford University Press, 2014.

5. "Translation of Old Al-Zarqawi Interview, Says God's Law Must Rule Entire World," Open Source Center-GMP20061211281001, December 6, 2006, https:// www.opensource.goc/portal/server.pt/gateway/PTARGS)_0_0_762_363_0_43/ http.

6. In seeking a way or method of war against the Japanese occupiers of his country, Luis Taruc stated: "We wanted to fight, but the question of how to go about it was at first obscure. The Chinese guerrilla movement, we knew, had been enormously successful, but in China the country was better adapted to guerrilla warfare. China had vast distance to hide an army and to provide space for maneuvering... in our case we had a tiny area, easily reached by overwhelming Japanese reinforcements. In China, there was an established base, from which the guerrillas radiated; we did not even have a base. It was obvious that our tactics would have to be different"; Luis Taruc, *Born of the People*, New York: International, 1953, 61–62, cited in Robert McColl, "The Insurgent State: Territorial Bases of Revolution," *Annals of the Association of American Geographers* 59, 4 (1969), 613–631.

7. Carlo Kopp, "Defeating Improvised Explosive Devices," *Defence Today*, September 2009, http://www.ausairpower.net/SP/DT-IED-Defeat-Sept-2009.pdf.

8. James Capobianco, "IEDs: Enemy Steps Up Attacks Using Explosive Devices," *Infantry* 92, 2 (Winter 2003), 30.

9. Ibid.

10. Jared Jalbert, "Defending Fallujah," *Marine Corps Gazette* 93, 9 (September 2009), 47; Greg Grant "Insurgent's IEDs Stay a Step Ahead: Enemy Adapts Faster Than U.S. Can Find Fixes," *Marine Corps Times*, July 18, 2005, 22; Greg Grant, "No 'Silver Bullet' to Counter IEDs as Attacks Increase, Researchers Focus on Intelligence as Well as Technology," *Marine Corps Times*, September 18, 2006, 12.

11. Ahmed S. Hashim, "Baghdad Blues: Observations from Iraq," diary, vol. 6, March 2004.

12. Greg Grant, "Inside Iraqi Insurgent Cells Captured Terrorist Intel May Help Defeat IEDs," *Defense News*, August 1, 2005, 1.

13. Brad Knickerbocker, "Relentless Toll to US Troops of Roadside Bombs: The IED Has Caused over a Third of the 3,000 American GI Deaths in Iraq," *Christian Science Monitor*, January 2, 2007, 1; see also John Bokel, "IEDs in Asymmetric Warfare," *Military Technology* 31, 10 (October 2007), 34.

14. For the discussion of VBIEDs and SVBIEDs, I relied extensively on the exhaustively detailed and valuable "The History and Adaptability of the Islamic State Car Bomb," *Zaytunarjuwani blog*, https://zaytunarjuwani.wordpress.com/2017/02/14/the-history-and.

15. Ibid.

16. Ron Nordland and Babak Dehghanpisheh, "Surge of Suicide Bombers: The Iraq War Has Turned into a Veritable 'Martyr' Factory, Unlike Any Seen in Previous Conflicts," *Newsweek*, August 13, 2007, 13.

17. Katherine R. Seifert and Clark McCauley, "Suicide Bombers in Iraq, 2003–2010: Disaggregating Targets Can Reveal Insurgent Motives and Priorities," *Terrorism and Political Violence* 26, 5 (2014), 803–820.

18. "Al-jaysh al-islami fi al-Iraq: Qasf tajmi' l-jaysh al-dajjal al-murtadd bi al-sawarikh fi madinat al-Sadr" [The Islamic Army of Iraq: The Missile Bombardment of a Meeting of the Apostate Army of the Devil (Mahdi Army) in Sadr City], Mohajroon .com, November 26, 2006.

19. "Dawlat al-iraq al-islamiyya: Hawla al-tasaaiyid al-Safawiya al-akhira dhid ahl al-Sunna fi Baghdad" [Islamic State of Iraq: On the Latest Safawi Escalation against the Sunnis of Baghdad], Tajdeed.org.uk, November 28, 2006.

20. Khatta al-defa' aan Baghdad, "Dawlat al-Iraq al-islamiya: Lilnashr al-sari" [The Baghdad Defense Plan, Islamic State of Iraq: Quick Distribution], Al faloja.com, January 7, 2007.

21. "Iraqi Sunnis Say Zarqawi, Ba'thists, Political Opponents Target Their Families," *BBC Monitoring—Middle East*, April 28, 2006.

22. Ahmed S. Hashim, "Baghdad Blues: Observations from Iraq," diary, vol. 8 (Tel Afar), September 2005.

23. "Jihadist Website Publishes 'Instructions' for Jihadists Leaving for Iraq," Open Source Center-GMP20070426342005, April 25, 2007, https://www.opensource .gov/portal/server.pt/gateway/PTARGS_0_0_4707_860_1639_43/.

24. Ibid.

25. Ibid.

26. Major W. Jack Dees, "Iraqi Military Effectiveness in the War with Iran," Research Paper, Operations Department, Naval War College, Newport, RI (February 11, 1990).

27. This section is based on a variety of vignettes from Iraq in 2003–2004, 2005–2006, and 2007, when I was fortunate enough to see the Iraqis in action and in training as advisor to United States Central Command (CENTCOM), to the Third Armored Cavalry Regiment, visits to MiTT (Military Transition Teams) units in Iraqi bases, and then as part of a team that looked at the paramilitary, police, and army training. I have also benefited immensely from reading the works of Norvelle DeAtkine, Kenneth Pollack, Risa Brooks, and Caitlin Talmadge on Arab and Global South militaries concerning their effectiveness. The theoretical literature on military effectiveness by Williamson Murray, Andrew Millett, Stephen Biddle, and Risa Brooks has also been immensely helpful. Most of the discussion of military effectiveness, however, deal with it at the macro level, or the level at which regime structure and political culture affects a nation's military effectiveness.

28. For more details on this issue, see Brynjar Lia, "Doctrines for Jihadist Terrorist Training," *Terrorism and Political Violence* 20, 4 (2008), 518–542.

29. Ahmed S. Hashim, "Baghdad Blues: Observations from Iraq," diary, vol. 1, 2003–2004.

30. Alexandra Zavis, "Militants Stake Claim on Diyala River Valley," *Los Angeles Times*, February 5, 2008, http://www.latimes.com/world/la-fg-militants5feb05-story.html.

31. For extensive details on Diyala as a jihadist sanctuary, see "How Terrorism Started, Spread in the Stricken Towns of Diyala Governorate," *Al-Bayyinah*, April 2, 2007, 5, in "Iraqi Paper Discusses History of Terrorism in Diyala Governorate, Those Responsible," Open Source Center-GMP20070407628002, https://www.opensource.gov/portal/server.pt/gateway/PTARGS_0_0_200_972_100578_4.

32. John Sattler and Daniel Wilson, "Operation AL FAJR: The Battle of Fallujah—Part II," *Marine Corps Gazette*, July 2005, 12.

33. F. J. "Bing" West, "The Fall of Fallujah," *Marine Corps Gazette*, July 2005, 52–58; Sattler and Wilson, "Operation AL FAJR," 14.

34. Scott Peterson, "Rebels Return to Cleared Areas; In Fallujah, US Forces Are Going Through 50,000 Houses One by One. But Iraq Insurgents Are Coming Back," *Christian Science Monitor*, December 3, 2004, 6.

35. Thomas Ricks and Karen DeYoung, "Al-Qaeda in Iraq Reportedly Crippled," *Washington Post*, October 15, 2007, http://www.washingtonpost.com/wp-dyn/content/article/2007/10/14/AR2007101401245.html.

36. Melinda Liu, "The Tribes of Iraq: America's New Allies," *Newsweek*, June 4, 2007, http://www.newsweek.com/tribes-iraq-americas-new-allies-101825.

37. Sudarsan Raghavan, "Diary of an Insurgent in Retreat," *Washington Post*, February 10, 2008, http://www.washingtonpost.com/wpdyn/content/article/2008/02/0.

38. Ibid.

39. Ibid.

40. Amit Paley, "Shift in Tactics Aims to Revive Struggling Insurgency," *Washington Post*, February 8, 2008, http://www.washingtonpost.com/wpdyn/content/article/2008/02/0.

41. Ibid.

42. Ibid.

43. Kyle Orton, "The Islamic State Was Winning When We Thought It Was Losing," *The Syrian Intifada* (blog), January 28, 2017, https://kyleorton1991.wordpress.com/2017/01/28/the-islamic-state-was-winning-when-we-thought-it-was-losing/.

44. Cited in Jonathan Baker, "Harbingers of the Caliphate: Islamic State Revolutionary Actions 2011–2014," M.A. thesis, Naval Postgraduate School, Monterey, 2016, 1.

45. Jane Arraf, "Wave of Iraq Suicide Bombings Target Police," *Christian Science Monitor*, August 25, 2010, 4; Sam Dagher, "Violence Jolts Iraq—Day of Bombings Kills Dozens, Stokes Sectarian Divisions," *Wall Street Journal*, December 23, 2011, A1.

46. J. T. Nguyen, "Study: Suicide Bombings Inflicted Massive Deaths in Iraq, 2003–2010," *McClatchy-Tribune Business News*, September 2, 2011. For more details see the article itself, Madalyn Hsiao-Rei Ricks et al., "Casualties in Civilians and Coalition Soldiers from Suicide Bombings in Iraq, 2003–2010: A Descriptive Study," *Lancet* 378 (September 3, 2011), 906–914.

47. The best and most detailed analyses of these military campaigns are by Jessica Lewis, "Al-Qaeda in Iraq Resurgent: The Breaking the Walls Campaign, Part

I" and "Al-Qaeda Resurgent, Part II," Washington, DC: Institute for the Study of War, September and October 2013, respectively.

48. Sam Jones, "Iraq Crisis: Sophisticated Tactics Key to ISIS Strength," *Financial Times*, June 26, 2014.

49. Matt Bradley and Ali Nabhan, "Wave of Car Bombings Targets Shiites in Iraq," *Wall Street Journal*, May 20, 2013, 1.

50. Charles Lister, "OSINT Summary: Prison Assault Indicates Escalation of Deadly Violence in Iraq," *Jane's Terrorism and Security Monitor* 13, 8 (September 1, 2013).

51. Tom Peter, "Where Iraq's Maliki Pins the Blame for Baghdad's Bombings," *Christian Science Monitor*, August 28, 2013, 5.

52. "Attack on Iraqi Transport Ministry Shows Sustained Insurgent Capability Despite Month-Long Military Campaign in al-Anbar," *Jane's Intelligence Weekly* 6, 7 (June 29, 2014).

53. Matt Bradley, "Fledgling Iraqi Military Is Outmatched on Battlefield: On the Eve of Elections, Demoralized Army Is Losing Fight against Islamist Militants," *Wall Street Journal*, April 27, 2014.

54. Ibid.

55. Ibid.

56. On the ISIS assault see Bryan Price, Dan Milton, and Muhammad al-'Ubaydi, "Al-Baghdadi's Blitzkrieg, ISIL's Psychological Warfare, and What It Means for Syria and Iraq," *CTC Perspectives*, June 12, 2014, https://www.ctc.usma.edu/posts/ctc-perspectives-al-baghdadis-blitzk; "Inside Mosul: How Did Extremists Take Over One of Iraq's Biggest Cities in Just Five Days?," *Niqash*, June 10, 2014, http://www.niqash.org/en/articles/security/3455/how-did-extremist; "JTIC Brief: Gaining Ground—ISIL Seizes Key Territory in Offensive across Northern Iraq," *Jane's Terrorism and Insurgency Monitor* 14, 7 (July 1, 2014).

57. Lister, "OSINT Summary: Prison Assault Indicates Escalation of Deadly Violence in Iraq."

58. Shaun Walker, "Isis War Minister Targeted in Airstrike Had Been in Georgia Army," *Guardian*, March 9, 2016, http://www.theguardian.com/world/2016/mar/09/isis-war-minister-targeted-in-syria-had-been-in-georgian-army.

59. For this and the following sections, I have relied heavily on watching combat footage on YouTube videos, on newspaper articles, and especially on Laurent Touchard, "Organisation tactique et methodes de combat de l'État Islamique," *CONOPS*, May 21, 2015, http://conops-mil.blogspot.sg/2015/05/revue-de-details-organisation-tactique.html; Michael Knights, "The Cult of the Offensive: The Islamic State on Defense," *CTC Sentinel*, April 30, 2015, https://www.ctc.usma.edu/posts/the-cult-of-the-offensive-the-islami; Barak Barfi, "The Military Doctrine of the Islamic State and the Limits of Ba'athist Influence," *CTC Sentinel*, February 19, 2016, https://www.ctc.usma.edu/posts/the-military-doctrine-of-the-islamic; and Jessica Lewis McFate, "The ISIS Defense in Iraq and Syria: Countering an Adaptive Enemy," Middle East Security Report No. 27, Washington, DC: Institute

for the Study of War, May 2015; Craig Whiteside, Trulls Tonnesson, and Daveed Gartenstein-Ross, "The Islamic State's Anbar Offensive and Abu Umar al-Shishani," *War on the Rocks*, October 9, 2014, http://warontherocks.com/2014/10/the-islamic-states-anbar-offensi.

60. This notion was initially developed by Craig Whiteside, "New Masters of Revolutionary Warfare: The Islamic State Movement (2002–2016)," *Perspectives on Terrorism* 10, 4 (August 2016), and Jonathan Baker, "Harbingers of the Caliphate."

61. See Aymenn Jawad al-Tamimi, "Comprehensive Reference Guide to Sunni Militant Groups in Iraq," *Aymennjawad.org*, January 23, 2014, http://www.aymennjawad.org/14350/comprehensive-reference-guide-to-sunni-militant; see also Ruth Sherlock and Carol Malouf, "Islamic Army of Iraq Founder: ISIS and Sunni Islamists Will March on Baghdad," *Daily Telegraph*, June 20, 2014.

62. Zarqawi's original approach can be compared to a jihadist version of the left-wing concept of *foco* guerrilla warfare, which was the hallmark of the Cuban Revolution, while that of ISIS and IS can be compared more usefully to the mainstream Marxist-Leninist and national liberation approaches of preparing or shaping the ground beforehand for eventual military operations.

63. For this section I have relied heavily on *Oryx Blog,* by two extremely well-informed Dutch bloggers, and on Touchard, "Organisation tactique et methods de combat de l'Etat Islamique," and Laurent Touchard, "Etat Islamique, naissance d'un monster de guerre 1 & 2," *Blog defense de Jeune Afrique*, September 24 and 26, 2014, http://www.jeuneafrique.com/43643/politique/tat-islamique-naissance -d-un-monstre-de-guerre-1/ and http://www.jeuneafrique.com/43556/politique /tat-islamique-naissance-d-un-monstre-de-guerre-2/.

64. Very little information is available on the Inghimasiyun unit. A video, "Preparation for an ISIS Attack—Damascus," http://www.liveleak.com/view?i=c6f_1457636895, shows a group of fit young men preparing for an attack on a Syrian position. They seem to be wearing military load-bearing equipment and what looks like body armor, although it could have been explosives. Also noticeable was that an IS artillery unit was softening the target in preparation for the assault. See also Ala Walid, "The Inghimasiyyun and the Dhabbihah and the Terror of the Islamic State," *Al-Quds al-Arabi*, August 12, 2014; Absi Sumairen, "Inghimasiyun, force de frappe pour les jihadistes," *Al-Araby*, December 22, 2104, http://www.alaraby .co.uk/politics/G0a97eac-95da-4177-9960-74ff503952ea.

65. See Michael Knights, "ISIL's Political-Military Power in Iraq," *CTC Sentinel* 7, 8 (August 2014), 1–7.

66. See Barak Barfi, "The Military Doctrine of the Islamic State and the Limits of Ba'athist Influence," *CTC Sentinel* 9, 211 (February 19, 2016).

67. For more on the arms of IS, see "Taking Stock: The Arming of Islamic State," *Amnesty International*, December 2015, https://www.amnesty.org/en/documents/mde14/2812/2015/en/.

68. See Zaytunarjuwani, "The Devastating Islamic State Suicide Strategy," *TSG Intel Brief,* Soufan Group, May 29, 2015, http://www.soufangroup.com/tsg-intelbrief-the-devastating-islamic-state-suicide-strategy/; "Islamic State Development and Employment of SVBIEDs," (2016) Armament Research Services, http://armament research.com/islamic-state-development-employment-of-svbieds/.

69. Missy Ryan and Mustafa Salim, "Islamic State Has Unleashed over 600 Car Bombs in Mosul Battle," *San Francisco Chronicle*, December 1, 2016, http://www .sfgate.com/news/article/Islamic-State-has-unleashed-over-600-car-bombs-in-10657152.php.

70. For more extensive details on the development of IS drone warfare, see Susannah George and Lori Hinnant, "Islamic State Turns to Drones to Direct Suicide Car Bombers," *Seattle Times*, February 1, 2017, http://www.seattletimes.com/nation-world/is-using-drones-other-innovating-tactics-with-deadly-effect/. "Islamic State's Weaponized Drones," Frontline Perspective, Conflictarm.com, October 2016; Eric Schmitt, "Papers Offer a Peek at ISIS' Drones, Lethal and Largely Off-the-Shelf," *New York Times*, January 31, 2017, https://www.nytimes.com/2017/01/31/ world/middleeast/isis-drone; Scott Stewart, "Beyond the Buzz: Assessing the Terrorist Drone Threat," *Security Weekly*, Stratfor, February 9, 2017, https:// worldview.stratfor.com/weekly/beyond-buzz-assessing-terrorist-drone-threat; Ben Sullivan, "The Islamic State Conducted Hundreds of Drone Strikes in Less Than a Month," *Motherboard*, February 22, 2017.

71. This term was used by Basil Liddell Hart to examine how the German generals saw World War II from their perspective. It has since come to mean addressing the "other side's" perspectives, intentions, capabilities, and military strategy.

72. See Bernhard Zand, "The Legacy of the Jundis," *Der Spiegel*, September 10, 2007, http://www.spiegel.de/international/world/iraq-s-military-the-legacy-of-the-jundis-a-504893.html.

73. Philip Shishkin, "Politics and Economics: Iraqi Troops Bedeviled by a Range of Problems: Supply Shortfalls, Sectarian Tensions Limit Effectiveness," *Wall Street Journal*, January 19, 2007, A4.

74. For summaries of the efforts to rebuild the Iraqi army, see Major Timothy Davis, U.A. Army, *Building the Iraqi Army: Teaching a Nation to Fish*, Research Paper, Quantico, VA: U.S. Marine Corps, Command and Staff College, Marine Corps University, 2005; Colonel Frederick Kienle, "Creating the Iraqi Army from Scratch: Lessons for the Future," American Enterprise Institute, May 25, 2007, http://www .aei.org/publication/creating-an-iraqi-army-from-scratch/; Solomon Moore, "In Mosul, New Test of Iraqi Army," *New York Times*, March 20, 2008, http://www .nytimes.com/2008/03/20/world/middleeast/20mosul.html?_r=2&hp=&oref=sl.

75. Matt Bradley, "Some Iraqi Troops Moonlight with Militias; Soldiers Say They Fight Islamic State Better on Their Days Off as Part of Militias, Some of Which Once Fought U.S. Troops," *Wall Street Journal*, April 12, 2015.

76. Jane Arraf, "Iraqi Army: Almost One-Quarter Lacks Minimum Qualifications," *Christian Science Monitor*, May 22, 2009, 5.

77. "Islamic State Ascendant—Iraq Struggles to Tackle the Proto-caliphate," *Jane's Terrorism and Security Monitor* 14, 8 (September 1, 2014).

78. Ibid.

79. Matt Bradley and Ali Nabhan, "Almost Helpless: In Iraq, Fledgling Army Is Outmatched on Battlefield," *Wall Street Journal*, April 28, 2014, A1.

80. Ibid.

81. Loveday Morris, "Islamic State Seizes Third Iraqi Army Base in Anbar after Military Retreat," *Washington Post*, October 13, 2014, http://www.washingtonpost.com/world/islamic-state-seizes-third-ir; Ruth Sherlock and Carol Malouf, "Iraq Crisis: Generals in Army 'Handed Over' Entire City to al-Qaeda Inspired ISIS Forces," *Daily Telegraph*, June 13, 2014, http://www.telegraph.o.uk/news/world-news/middleeast/iraq/108.

82. Dominique Soguel, "With Islamic State Threatening Region, Can Iraq's Peshmerga Turn the Tide?," *Christian Science Monitor*, August 18, 2014, 5.

83. "Turkish Paper Views Reasons for Peshmerga Retreat in Iraq," *BBC Monitoring—Europe*, August 10, 2014, translated from Nihat Ali Ozcan, "The Peshmerga's Retreat," *Milliyet*, August 8, 2014.

84. Hetav Rojan, "Why the Kurdish Peshmerga Have Many Troubles in Stopping the Islamic State," *Vice*, August 13, 2014, https://news.vice.com/article/why-the-kurdish-peshmerga-have-many-troubles-in-stopping-the-islamic-state.

85. For an incisive analysis of Peshmerga weaknesses, see Kenneth Pollack, "Iraq: Understanding the ISIS Offensive against the Kurds," *Brookings*, August 11, 2014, https://www.brookings.edu/blog/markaz/2014/08/11/iraq-understanding-the-isis-offensive-against-the-kurds/; see also the very detailed historical study of the Peshmerga by Michael Lortz, "Willing to Face Death: A History of Kurdish Military Forces—the Peshmerga—from the Ottoman Empire to Present-Day Iraq," M.A. thesis, Florida State University, 2005.

86. Jamie Ingram, "Factional Rivalry in Iraq's Kurdistan Region Affects Distribution of Foreign Military Aid and Inhibits Peshmerga Military Effectiveness," *Jane's Intelligence Weekly* 7, 44 (October 7, 2015).

87. Andrew Slater, "The Paper Tiger of the Tigris: How ISIS Took Tikrit without a Fight," *Daily Beast*, June 29, 2014, http://www.thedailybeast.com/the-paper-tiger-of-the-tigris-how-isis-took-tikrit-without-a-fight.

88. Marcus Wesigerber, "ISIS Is Using Tunnel Bombs in Iraq," *Defense One*, June 8, 2015, http://www.defenseone.com/threats/2015/06/isis-using-tunnel-bombs-iraq/114730/.

89. Nicolas Pelham, "ISIS and the Shia Revival in Iraq," *New York Review of Books*, June 4, 2015, http://www.nybooks.com.

90. This section relies heavily on Andrew Slater, "Paper Tiger of the Tigris."

91. Tamer El-Ghobashy, "Iraqi Forces, Shiite Militias Form Uneasy Alliance: Each Group Claims Precedence as They Move Together to Regain Tikrit from Islamic State," *Wall Street Journal*, March 5, 2015.

92. Matt Bradley and Ghassan Adnan, "Fighting Islamic State: Militias Win Bloody Battles for Iraq," *Wall Street Journal*, December 6, 2014, A1.

93. For an extensive discussion of the origins of the militia phenomenon in Iraq, see Andrew Hubbard, "Plague and Paradox: Militias in Iraq," *Small Wars and Insurgencies* 18, 3 (2007), 345–362.

94. For a discussion of the current structure of the Shia militias see Jonathan Spyer, "Rise of Shia Militias Shapes the Future of Iraq," *Jane's Intelligence Review* 27, 8 (August 1, 2015).

95. Patrick Cockburn, "Isis in Iraq: Thousands of Shia Militiamen to Join Decisive Battle to Take Back Fallujah—But Lack of Experience Risks Heavy Casualties," *Independent*, July 14, 2015, http://www.independent.co.uk/news/world/middle-east/isis-in-iraq-thousands-of-shia-militiamen-to-join-decisive-battle-to-take-back-fallujah-but-lack-of-10386501.html.

96. Anne Mulrine, "Worse Than Islamic State? Concerns Rise about Iraq's Shiite Militias," *Christian Science Monitor*, December 23, 2014, 10.

97. Ibid.

98. Mustafa Habib, "Better Pay, Better Weapons: Are Shiite Militias Growing More Powerful Than Iraqi Army?," *Niqash*, January 29, 2015, http://www.niqash.org/en/articles/security/3614/Are-Shiite-Militia.

99. Mustafa Habib, "Guardians and Guerrillas in an Era of 'Small Armies': Iraqis See Their Military in a New Light," *Niqash*, January 8, 2015, http://www.niqash.org/en/articles/security/3606/In-An-Era-of-'Sma.

100. Ibid.

101. Ibid.

102. Mustafa Habib, "Divided Loyalties: Iraq's Controversial Shiite Militias Fight among Themselves," *Niqash*, June 18, 2015, http://www.niqash.org/en/articles/politics/5033/Iraq's-Controversi.

103. This section relies on Paul Blake, "Ramadi Assault: How a Small Change in Tactics Helped Iraqi Forces," *BBC News*, December 22, 2015, http://www.bbc.com/news/world-us-canada-34902757; Ibrahim al-Marashi, "How Iraq Recaptured Ramadi and Why It Matters," *Al-Jazeera*, January 3, 2016, http://www.aljazeera.com/indepth/opinion/2016/01/iraq-recaptured-ramadi-matters-160103061219164.html.

104. For some discussion of the slow transformation of the Iraqi forces, see Loveday Morris, "The Force Leading the Iraq Army's Fight against Isis Went from 'Dirty Division' to Golden Boys," *Washington Post*, July 26, 2016, https://www.washingtonpost.com/world/middle_east/the-force-leading-the-iraqi-militarys-fight-against-isis-went-from-dirty-division-to-golden-boys/2016/07/25/

8e6b0164-389e-11e6-af02-1df55f0c77ff_story.html?utm_term=.ae416bfb4cf6; Ben Kesling and Matt Bradley, "Victory Marks Turnaround for Iraq Army—Recapture of Ramadi Represents Military's First Success as Mostly Independent Force," *Wall Street Journal*, December 29, 2015, A7.

105. Jane Arraf, "How Iraqi Forces Drove ISIS from Ramadi," *Newsweek*, March 4, 2016.

106. "Reclaiming the Ruins from Islamic State, January 2, 2016, http://www .economist.com/news/middle-east-and-africa/21684689-retaking-ramadi-iraqs-security-forces-have-won-morale-boosting.

107. Nancy Youssef and Shane Harris, "How ISIS Actually Lost Ramadi," *Daily Beast*, December 30, 2015, http://www.thedailybeast.com/how-isis-actually-lost-ramadi.

108. Tamer El-Ghobashy, "Fallujah's Importance to Islamic State Helped Iraqi Forces Retake It," *Wall Street Journal*, June 29, 2016.

109. This section relies heavily on Mustafa Habib, "The Fight for Fallujah: Why Can't the Iraqi Army Win in Anbar's Extremist Capital," *Niqash*, March 8, 2016, http://www.niqash.org/en/articles/security/5210/Why-Can't-The-Ira.

110. For more on the transformation of the Peshmerga, see Campbell MacDiarmid, "Foreign Troops Training Kurdish Peshmerga Fighters Encounter Language Barriers, Lack of Basic Skills," *National Post*, March 20, 2015, http://www .nationalpost.com/m/news/blog.html?b=news.nationalpost.com/2015/03/20/anti-isis-coalition-training-kurdish-peshmerga-fighters; Jim Garamone, "Peshmerga Training Effort Moves into High Gear," *Defense Department News*, December 15, 2015, https://www.defense.gov/News/Article/Article/637381/peshmerga-training-effort-moves-into-high-gear/; Thomas Gibbons-Neff, "Inside the Kurdish Fighting Forces: The U.S.'s Proxy Ground Troops in the War against ISIS," *Washington Post*, February 2, 2016, https://www.washingtonpost.com/ news/checkpoint/wp/2016/02/02/inside-the-kurdish-fighting-forces-the-u-s-s-proxy-ground-troops-in-the-war-against-isis/?utm_term=.7fad68bc3618.

111. I completed the substantive analysis for this book in the third week of June 2017; hence the discussion of the battle for Mosul (as indeed everything else within the book) ends on June 25, 2017.

112. Morris, "Forces Leading the Iraq Army's Fight against Isis Went from 'Dirty Division' to Golden Boys."

113. Hamza Hendawi and Qassim Abdul Zahra, "In Drawn-Out Battle of Mosul, Limits of Iraqi Military Show," *Associated Press*, November 28, 2016, https:// apnews.com/53c41d7639e547d9885991c53b8898a0/drawn-out-battle-mosul-limits-iraqi-military-show.

114. Jean-Bernard Pinatel, "Analyse de la situation politique et militaire en Irak mi-septembre 2016," *Géopolitique-Géostratégie: Analyses et debats*, September 18, 2016,http://www.geopolitique-geostrategie.fr/analyse-de-la-situation-politique-et-militaire-en-irak-mi-septembre-2016-2016.

115. For an excellent analysis of the Iraqi forces' efforts to shape the battlefield in preparation for the offensive to recover Mosul, see Derek Henry Flood, Jeremy Binnie, and Columb Strack, "Forces Prepare for Iraq's Most Complex Battle," *Jane's Intelligence Review* 28, 10 (October 1, 2016).

116. Ian Merritt and Kenneth Pollack, "Racing to the Finish Line, Ignoring the Cliff: The Challenges after Mosul," *Brookings*, September 19, 2016, https://www .brookings.edu/blog/markaz/2016/09/19/racing-to-the; Jack Watling, "Future Looks Bleak for Iraq Post–Mosul Assault," *Jane's Intelligence Review* 28, 12 (December 1, 2016).

117. Jamie Dettmer, "Sectarian Disputes Plague Planning for Long-Awaited Battle of Mosul," *Voice of America*, October 9, 2016, https://www.voanews.com/a/sectarian-disputes-plague-planning-for-long-awaited-battle-of-mosul/3543140.html.

118. See, for example, the derisive comments of a Peshmerga officer in Martin Chulov, "Battle for Mosul: This Is Going to Take a Long Time—ISIS Won't Give Up," *Guardian*, October 18, 2016, https://www.theguardian.com/world/2016/oct/18/battle-for-mosul-day-two-isis-iraqi-kurdish.

119. Zaineb al-Assam, "Political Struggle between Iraqi PM and Hashd Al-Shaabi Intensifies, Increasing Government Instability and Undermining Campaign against Islamic State," *Jane's Intelligence Weekly*, September 9, 2015.

120. Ron Nordland, "Iraqi Forces Attack Mosul, a Beleaguered Stronghold for ISIS," New York Times, October 16, 2016, https://www.nytimes.com/2016/10/17/world/middleeast/in-isis-held-mosul-beheadings-and-hints-of-resistance-as-battle-nears.html; Kareem Fahim and Loveday Morris, "Evidence of a 'Difficult Fight' Ahead as Forces Move toward ISIS-Held Mosul," *Washington Post*, October 18, 2016, https://www.washingtonpost.com/world/tough-resistance-from-islamic-state-slows-iraqi-advance-on-mosul/2016/10/18/09ad029c-9505-11e6-bb29-bf2701dbe0a3_story.html?utm_term=.48eb0a54c883.

121. Tim Arango and Falih Hassan, "Iraqi Forces Breach Mosul City Limits, Heralding Complex Phase in Campaign," *New York Times*, November 1, 2016, https://www .nytimes.com/2016/11/02/world/middleeast/iraq-mosul-isis.html; Muthana al-Obeidi, "The Battle for Mosul: Challenges to Liberating the Last Bastions of ISIS in Iraq," Future for Advanced Research and Studies, Abu Dhabi, United Arab Emirates: August 20, 2016; https://futureuae.com/en/Mainpage/Item/220/the-battle-for-mosul-challenges-to-liberating-the-last-bastions-of-isis-in-iraq.

122. Alexandre Mello and Michael Knights, "The Cult of the Offensive: The Islamic State on Defense," *CTC Sentinel* 8, 43 (April 30, 2015), https://www.ctc.usma .edu/posts/the-cult-of-the-offensive-the-islami.

123. Kenneth Pollack, "Part I: The Military Campaign against ISIS," *Iraq Situation Report*, March 28, 2016; Stijn Mitzer and Joost Oliemans, "The Islamic State Going DIY, the Telskuf Offensive," *Oryx Blog*, May 9, 2016, http://spioenkop .blogspot.sg/search/label/The-Islamic-State; James Brandon, "Airstrikes, Ground Offensives Put Islamic State on the Backfoot," *Terrorism Monitor*

(Jamestown Foundation) 12, 23 (December 5, 2014), https://jamestown.org/brief/briefs-31/.

124. Bill Powell, "As ISIS's Caliphate Crumbles, Jihadist Tactics Are Evolving," *Newsweek,* October 21, 2016.

125. Ryan and Salim, "Islamic State Has Unleashed over 600 Car Bombs in Mosul Battle."

126. Mustafa Habib, "Urban Warfare: In Mosul, Where Every Street Corner Is the Front Line," *Niqash,* November 23, 2016, http://www.niqash.org/en/articles/security/5413/

127. See Hendawi, "In Drawn-Out Battle of Mosul, Limits of Iraqi Military Show"; see also Habib, "Urban Warfare."

128. Dominic Evans and Ahmed Rasheed, "'Crashing Waves' of Jihadists Fray Soldiers' Nerves in Mosul Battle," *Reuters,* November 10, 2016, http://www.reuters.com/article/us-mideast-crisis-iraq-battle-idUSKBN1350GB.

129. See Florian Neuhof, "Battle for Mosul: How IS Is Making Life Tough for Iraq's Elite Forces," *Middleeasteye,* November 30, 2016, http://www.middleeasteye.net/news/battle-mosul-how-islamic-state-has-made-life-tough-iraq-s-eli.

130. Tim Arango, Eric Schmitt, and Rukimini Callimachi, "Hungry, Thirsty and Bloodied in Battle to Retake Mosul from ISIS," *New York Times,* December 18, 2016, https://www.nytimes.com/2016/12/18/world/middleeast/iraq-mosul-islamic-state.html; Patrick Cockburn, "Iraqi Forces Begin Bitter Battle for Mosul," *Independent,* February 20, 2017.

131. Gareth Browne, "Attack on Mosul: World's Biggest Military Operation Runs into Trouble," *Middleeasteye,* January 2, 2017, http://www.middleeasteye.net/columns/manpower-shortage-plagues-mosul-offensive-2023724912.

132. See Loveday Morris and Mustafa Salim, "Signs of Panic and Rebellion in the Heart of Islamic State's Self-Proclaimed Caliphate," *Washington Post,* September 21, 2016, https://www.washingtonpost.com/world/middle_east/signs-of-panic-and-rebellion-in-the-heart-of-islamic-states-so-called-caliphate/2016/09/20/55421e4a-7520-11e6-9781-49e591781754_story.html?utm_term=.86de0335add4; Fazel Hawramy, Emma Graham-Harrison, and Kareem Shaheen, "ISI Seize and Kill Dozens in Strongholds around Mosul to Quell Uprising," *Guardian,* October 25, 2016, https://www.theguardian.com/world/2016/oct/25/islamic-state-atrocities-reported-around-mosul-says-un.

133. "The Battle for Mosul," *Economist,* October 8, 2016, https://www.economist.com/news/middle-east-and-africa/21708246-imminent-offensive-hopes-end-jihadists-reign-terror-iraqs-second.

134. Mustafa Habib, "Payback Time: Militias Betrayed by Mosul's Extremists Say They Too Will Have Revenge," *Niqash,* November 1, 2016, http://www.niqash.org/en/articles/security/5345/militias-betrayed.

135. "Iraqi Forces Face Their Toughest Test in Mosul," *Economist,* February 23, 2017, http://www.economist.com/news/middle-east-and-africa/2171738; see also the

excellent report by Ronen Zeidel, "The Battle for Mosul: A Situation Report," *Tel Aviv Notes* 10, 20 (Moshe Dayan Center, Tel Aviv University), December 29, 2016, http://dayan.org/content/battle-mosul-situation-report.

136. Tamer el-Ghobashy and Ali Nabbhan, "Local ISIS Fighters Deserting Foreign Jihadis in Battle for Mosul," *Wall Street Journal*, March 18, 2017, http://www.theaustralian.com.au/business/wall-street-journal/local-isis-fighters-deserting-foreign-jihadis-in-battle-for-mosul/news-story/2105f99b2536830f53fe57c6d86b70d4.

137. Salar Salim and Maamoun Youssef, "Islamic State Struggles to Retain Grip as It Loses Ground in Iraq," *Denver Post*, August 24, 2016, http://www.denverpost.com/2016/08/24/islamic-state-struggles-to-retain-grip-iraq/; Maria Abi-Habib, "Islamic State Shifts Tactics—As Foes Cut into Group's Pseudo-state, Its Militants Turn More to Suicide Bombings," *Wall Street Journal*, May 14, 2016, A1.

138. Fatima Bhojani, "How ISIS Makes IEDs: The Supply Chain of Terrorism," *Foreign Affairs*, March 2, 2016, https://www.foreignaffairs.com/articles/2016-03-02/how-isis-makes-ieds.

139. "Attacks in Baghdad and Diyala, Iraq, Indicate Islamic State Increasingly Resorting to Guerrilla Warfare in Government-Controlled Territory," *Jane's Country Risk Daily Report*, January 12, 2016. This report, which details a number of suicide attacks at the beginning of 2016, is erroneous in referring to them as guerrilla attacks; they were nothing more than purely terrorist attacks, largely on innocent civilians.

140. Otso Iho, "OSINT Summary: Islamic State Bombings Aim to Exacerbate Sectarian Divisions in Iraq," *Jane's Terrorism and Insurgency Monitor* 16, 4 (April 1, 2016).

141. Maria Abi-Habib, "Islamic State Shifts Tactics, from War-Fighting to Suicide Bombing," *Wall Street Journal*, May 14, 2016, https://www.wsj.com/articles/islamic-state-shifts-tactics-from-war-fighting-to-suicide-bombing-1463181100.

142. Raja Abdulrahim and Tamer El-Ghobashy, "ISIS's Claim Shows How Group Is Expanding Targets; Members of Islamic State Taking Cues to Strike Soft Civilian Targets Far beyond Its Bases in Syria, Iraq," *Wall Street Journal*, November 14, 2015.

143. Eric Schmitt, "As ISIS Loses Land, It Gains Ground in Overseas Terror," *New York Times*, July 3, 2016, https://www.nytimes.com/2016/07/04/world/middleeast/isis-terrorism.html.

144. Rafaello Pantucci, "Foreign Fighters—Battle-Hardened Europeans Return from Syria," *Jane's Intelligence Review* 26, 2 (February 1, 2014).

145. This section relies very much on my reconstruction of the data on terrorist attacks in Europe and elsewhere and on the following: "Paris Attack Marks Breakthrough in Islamic State's Ongoing Strategic Shift," *Jane's Intelligence Weekly* 7, 50 (November 18, 2015); Rukmini Callimachi, Katrin Bennhold, and

Laure Fourquet, "How the Paris Attackers Honed Their Assault through Trial and Error," *New York Times*, November 30, 2014, https://www.nytimes.com/2015/12/01/world/europe/how-the-paris-attackers-honed-their-assault-through-trial-and-error.html; "Inside ISIS's Covert Ops," *Intelligence Online* (November 18, 2015); Mathieu Suc, "Les réseaux terroristes de l'état islamique: La chaine de commandement qui conduit aux attentats," *Mediapart* (March 23, 2016); various issues of *Oryx Blog*, http://www.spioenkop.blogspot.sg/search/label; Shaul Shay, "The Islamic State (ISIS) and the Subterranean Warfare," Institute for Policy and Strategy, December 2015; Jean-Charles Brisard and Kevin Jackson, "The Islamic State's External Operations and the French-Belgian Nexus," *CTC Sentinel* 9, 11 (November 10, 2016).

146. "Paris Attack Marks Breakthrough in Islamic State's Ongoing Strategic Shift."

147. See Luis de la Calle and Ignacio Sanchez-Cuenca, "How Armed Groups Fight: Territorial Control and Violent Tactics," *Studies in Conflict and Terrorism* 38 (2015), 795–813; Lorenzo Bosi, "Safe Territories and Violent Political Organizations," *Nationalism and Ethnic Politics* 19, 1 (2013), 80–101.

148. I am working on developing these ideas further elsewhere, as they cannot be fully accommodated here. However, I have relied on a large body of works, both theoretical and case studies, for developing my ideas on "patterns," or ways of warfare, both among states and nonstate actors. I am particularly interested in the jihadist way of warfare and developing this idea for a paper. The following works were useful for this short discussion: Suzanne Martin and Leonard Weinberg, "Terrorism in an Era of Conventional Warfare," *Terrorism and Political Violence* 28, 2 (2016), 236–253; Lawrence Freedman, "Terrorism as a Strategy," *Government and Opposition* 42, 3 (Summer 2007), 314–339; Uri Joseph Fisher, "Military Entrepreneurship and War Duration," Ph.D. diss., Department of Political Science, University of Colorado, 2007; Truls Hallberg Tønnessen, "Training on a Battlefield: Iraq as a Training Ground for Global Jihadis," *Terrorism and Political Violence* 20, 4 (2008), 543–562; Abdulkader Sinno, *Organizations at War in Afghanistan and Beyond*, Ithaca: Cornell University Press, 2008; C. J. Chivers, "Where the Islamic State Gets Its Weapons," *New York Times Magazine*, April 27, 2015, https://www.nytimes.com/2015/04/27/magazine/where-the-islamic-state-gets-its-weapons.html; Jorge Le Blanc, "The Urban Environment and Its Influences on Insurgent Campaigns," *Terrorism and Political Violence* 25, 5 (2013); Isabelle Duyvesteyn and Mario Fumerton, "Insurgency and Terrorism: What's the Difference?," in C. Holmqvist-Joncaster and Christophr Coker, eds., *The Character of War in the Early 21st Century*, London: Routledge, 2009.

149. The developments of my ideas concerning territorial control rely heavily on Robert McColl, "The Insurgent State: Territorial Bases of Revolution"; Robert McColl, "A Political Geography of Revolution: China, Viet Nam, and Thailand," *Journal of Conflict Resolution* 2 (1967), 153–167; Eric Jardine, "Controlling Territory and Population during Counterinsurgency: State Security Capacity and the Costs

of Power Projection," *Civil Wars* 14, 2 (2012); 228–253; Albert Harris, "Insurgency Defensive Postures under Extreme Duress," *Global Change, Peace and Security* 27, 2 (2015), 153–172; and Truls Tønnessen, "Destroying the Islamic State Hydra: Lessons Learned from the Fall of Its Predecessor," *CTC Sentinel* 19, 8 August 2016), https://ctc.usma.edu/posts/destroying-the-islamic-state-hydra-lessons-learned-from-the-fall-of-its-predecessor.

150. For similar assessments, see also Reed Wood, "Rebel Capability and Strategic Violence against Civilians," *Journal of Peace Research* 47, 5 (2010), 601–614; Tonnesson, "Destroying the Islamic State Hydra."

151. Unfortunately, little has been written about subterranean or tunnel warfare. Among the latest short pieces that specifically address Syria and Iraq are Shaul Shay, "The Islamic State (ISIS) and the Subterranean Warfare," Institute for Policy and Strategy, Lauder School of Government, Diplomacy and Strategy, IDC Herzeliya, December 2015, http://www.herzliyaconference.org/eng/?Cat egoryID=448&ArticleID=2704; Benjamin Runkle, "Preparing for Warfare's Subterranean Future," *War on the Rocks*, April 16, 2015, https://warontherocks .com/2015/04/preparing-for-warfares-subterranean-future/.

152. Martin Chulov, "Losing Ground, Fighters and Morale—Is It All Over for Isis?," *Guardian*, September 7, 2016, https://www.theguardian.com/world/2016/ sep/07/losing-ground-fighter-morale-is-it-all-over-for-isis-syria-turkey.

153. Liz Sly, "In Syria and Iraq, the Islamic State Is in Retreat on Multiple Fronts," *Washington Post*, March 24, 2016, https://www.washingtonpost.com/world/ middle_east/in-syria-and-iraq-the-islamic-state-is-in-retreat-on-multiple-fronts/2016/03/24/a0e33774-f101-11e5-a2a3-d4e9697917d1_story .html?utm_term=.81e2273250ac.

154. Dion Nissenbaum, "U.S. Says Airstrikes Put Islamic State on Defensive; Campaign in Iraq, Syria Hits More Than 3,000 Targets; Group's Financing Activities Struck," *Wall Street Journal*, January 27, 2015, A1.

155. Isabel Coles, "As ISIS Fighters Begin to Blend In, Defeating Them No Easy Matter," *Al-Arabiya News*, August 31, 2014, http://english.alarabiya.net/en/ perspective/2014/31/As-ISIS-figh.

156. Raheem Salman and Yara Bayoumy, "Wary of Air Strikes, ISIS Militants Change Tactics," *Al-Arabiya English*, September 27, 2014, http://english .alarabiya.net/en/perspective/analysis/2014/09/27/Wary-of-air-strikes-ISIS-militants-change-tactics.html.

157. Nour Malas, Dion Nissenbaum, and Maria Abi-Habib, "Islamic State Proves Resilient—U.S.-Led Airstrikes Disrupt Extremist Group, but Don't Loosen Grip on Territory," *Wall Street Journal*, October 6, 2014, A1.

CHAPTER 6

1. Will McCants, *ISIS Apocalypse*, New York: St. Martin's Press, 2015.

2. "Caliphate Claim Divides Jihadis," *Oxford Analytica Daily Brief*, July 10, 2014; "Rare Interview with Experienced Al Qaeda Commander Shows How Group

Using ISIL to Make Itself Look 'Moderate,'" *Asia News Monitor*, October 30, 2015.

3. Eli Berman and Jacob Shapiro, "Why ISIL Will Fail On Its Own," *Politico*, November 29, 2015, http://www.politico.com/magazine/story/2015/11/why-isil-will-fail-on-its-own-213401.

4. For an excellent analysis of the structural inability of IS's "primitive" economic base to sustain warmaking and state-formation, see Jamie Hansen-Lewis and Jacob Shapiro, "Understanding the Daesh Economy," *Perspectives on Terrorism* 9, 4 (August 2015), 142–155.

5. See Charles Tilly, ed., *The Formation of National States in Western Europe*, Princeton: Princeton University Press, 1975; Charles Tilly, *Coercion, Capital, and European States, AD 990–1992*, Cambridge, MA: Blackwell, 1992; Bruce Porter, *War and the Rise of the State: The Military Foundations of Modern Politics*, New York: Free Press, 1994.

6. For a similar discussion see Will McCants and Quinn Mecham, "Experts Weigh In (part 5): Is ISIS Good at Governing?," *Brookings*, March 7, 2016, https://www.brookings.edu/blog/markaz/2016/03/07/experts-weigh.

7. Though the tide had turned against the jihadists by 2007, the consensus was that Iraq continued to face profound problems; see Joost Hiltermann, "Iraq on the Edge," *New York Review of Books* 56, 18 (November 19, 2009).

8. Quoted in Matthieu Aikins, "Baghdad on the Brink," *Rolling Stone*, March 26, 2015, 49.

9. Apart from the wide-ranging journalistic coverage, I have relied on the following for the discussion of Nuri al-Maliki's time in power: Toby Dodge, "Iraq: The Contradictions of Exogenous State Building in Historical Perspective," *Third World Quarterly* 27, 1 (2006), 187–200; Myriam Benraad, "L'Impossible Réconciliation Nationale Irakienne?," *Revue International et Strategique* 81 (2011), 44–53; Toby Dodge, "Iraq's Road Back to Dictatorship," *Survival* 54, 3 (2012), 147–168; Hosham Dawood, "Construction et déconstruction du pouvoir politique en Irak: Le cas de Nouri al-Maliki," *Les cahiers de l'IFPO*, October 5, 2012, http://ifpo.hypotheses.org/4302; Marisa Sullivan, "Maliki's Authoritarian Regime," Middle East Security Report No. 10, Institute for the Study of War, April 2013; Dexter Filkins, "What We Left Behind," *New Yorker*, April 28, 2014; Ali Khedery, "Iraqi in Pieces: Breaking Up to Stay Together," *Foreign Affairs* 94, 6 (November–December 2015), 33–43; Florence Gaub, "An Unhappy Marriage: Civil-Military Relations in Post-Saddam Iraq," Carnegie Middle East Center, January 13, 2016, http://carnegieendowment.org/2016/01/13/unhappy-marriage-civil-military-relations-in-post-saddam-iraq-pub-61955; Ahmed S. Hashim, *God, Greed and Guns*, Philadelphia: University of Pennsylvania Press, forthcoming.

10. For an excellent biographical sketch of Nuri al-Maliki, see Ned Parker and Raheem Salman, "Notes from the Underground: The Rise of Nouri al-Maliki," *World Policy Journal*, Spring 2013, http://www.worldpolicy.org/journal/spring2013/

maliki; Jason Burke, "Iraq: How Much Is the Divisive Approach of Maliki Responsible for the Turmoil?," *Guardian*, June 15, 2014, https://www.theguardian .com/commentisfree/2014/jun/15/nouri-al-maliki-is-he-the-man-to-blame-in-iraq.

11. Edward Wong, "Doubts Rise on Iraqi Premier's Strength," *New York Times*, September 20, 2006, http://www.nytimes.com/2006/09/20/world/middleeast/ 20maliki.html?_r=1&oref=slogin&.

12. Ghaith Abdul-Ahad, "Six Years after Saddam Hussein, Nouri al-Maliki Tightens His Grip on Iraq," *Guardian*, April 30, 2009, https://www.theguardian.com/ world/2009/apr/30/iraqi-prime-minister-maliki; Toby Dodge, "The Resistible Rise of Nuri al-Maliki," *Open Democracy*, March 22, 2012, https://www.open democracy.net/toby-dodge/resistible-rise-of-nuri-al-maliki.

13. See Ed Blanche, "Maliki Takes Control," *Middle East*, January 2010, 12–15; "Iraqi Prime Minister Reportedly Tightens Grip on Armed Forces," *BBC Monitoring— Middle East*, June 28, 2010; "Iraq's Jihadi Jack-in-the-Box," Policy Briefing No. 38, International Crisis Group, June 20, 2014, https://www.crisisgroup.org/middle-east-north-africa/gulf-and-arabian-peninsula/iraq/iraq-s-jihadi-jack-box; Bobby Ghosh, "ISIS: A Short History," *Atlantic*, August 14, 2014, https://www.theatlantic .com/international/archive/2014/08/isis-a-short-history/376030/.

14. On the Kurds see Janine Di Giovanni, "The Move on Mosul," *Newsweek*, March 6, 2015, 12–16; Robin Wright, "The 194th State: The Kurds' Bid for Nationhood," *New Yorker*, July 17, 2014, http://www.newyorker.com/news/news-desk/the-194th-state-the-kurds-bid-for-nationhood; Dexter Filkins, "The Fight of Their Lives," *New Yorker*, September 29, 2014, http://www.newyorker.com/magazine/2014/09/ 29/fight-lives; Wladimir von Wilgenburg, "Breaking from Baghdad: Kurdish Autonomy vs. Maliki's Manipulation," *World Affairs Journal*, November/December 2012, http://www.worldaffairsjournal.org/article/breaking-baghdad-kurdish-autonomy-vs-maliki%E2%80%99s-manipulation; Christian Caryl, "The World's Next Country," *Foreign Policy*, January 21, 2015, http://foreignpolicy.com/2015/ 01/21/the-worlds-next-country-kurdi.

15. See Luke Harding, "Kurds on Iraq's New Faultline Feel Destiny Beckoning," *Guardian*, July 12, 2014, https://www.theguardian.com/world/2014/jul/11/kurds-isis-frontier-destiny-beckons; Martin Chulov and Fazel Hawramy, "Iraq Crisis: Islamic State Savagery Exposes Limits to Kurdish Authority," *Guardian*, August 25, 2014, https://www.theguardian.com/world/2014/aug/25/iraq-crisis-islamic-state-limits-kurdish-peshmerga; Loveday Morris, "As Their Power Grows, Iraq's Kurds Are Fighting among Themselves," *Washington Post*, October 12, 2015, https://www.washingtonpost.com/world/middle_east/as-their-power-grows-iraqs-kurds-are-fighting-among-themselves/2015/10/12/2f86ef74-70d4-11e5-ba14-318f8e87a2fc_story.html?utm_term=.47fc78e006d3.

16. Chulov and Hawramy, "Iraq Crisis"; Ben Kesling, "Iraqi Kurds Seize Islamic State-Held Land, Bolstering Leverage for Future," *Wall Street Journal*, September

14, 2016, https://www.wsj.com/articles/iraqi-kurds-seize-islamic-state-held-land-bolstering-leverage-for-future-1473903162.

17. For excellent analyses of the Sunni community's political turbulence in the late 2000s, see Michael Knights, "Struggle for Control: The Uncertain Future of Iraq's Sunni Arabs," *Jane's Intelligence Review*, 19, 1 (January 2007), 18–23; Nir Rosen, "The Big Sleep," *National*, April 24, 2009, http://www.thenational.ae/article/20090424/REVIEW/704239996/1008.

18. Dylan O' Driscoll, "Autonomy Impaired: Centralisation, Authoritarianism and the Failing Iraqi State," *Ethnopolitics*, September 18, 2015, 6–10, https://www.academia.edu/15919831/O_Driscoll_Dylan._Sep_2015_._Autonomy_Impaired_Centralisation_Authoritarianism_and_the_Failing_Iraqi_State._Ethnopolitics_tbc_tbc_pp._1-18._Doi_10.1080_17449057.2015.1086126.

19. Megan Greenwell and Saad al-Izzi, "Maliki Aide Lashes Out over Sunni Demands," *Washington Post*, July 28, 2007, 12; Richard Oppel, "Iraq Takes Aim at U.S.-Tied Sunni Groups' Leaders," *New York Times*, August 22, 2008, http://www.nytimes.com/2008/08/22/world/middleeast/22sunni.html?ref=awakening_mov.

20. Oppel, "Iraq Takes Aim at U.S.-Tied Sunni Groups' Leaders."

21. Ibid.

22. Marina Ottaway and Danial Kaysi, *The State of Iraq*, Washington, DC: Carnegie Papers, February 2012, 14–15.

23. See Rafid Jaboori, "Iraqi Sunnis' Long Struggle since Saddam," *BBC News—Middle East*, December 31, 2013, http://www.bbc.com/news/world-middle-east-25559872; "Sunni Grievances Drive Spike in Iraq Unrest," *Al-Arabiya News*, May 26, 2013, http://english.alarabiya.net/en/perspective/features/2013/05/26/Sun; "Al-Jazeera Views Iraqi Military Campaign in Al-Anbar, Sunni Grievances," *BBC Monitoring—Middle East*, February 23, 2014.

24. "Sunni Protests Gather Momentum in Iraq," *Jane's Intelligence Weekly* 5, 2 (January 2, 2013); Jane Arraf, "A New Anbar Awakening," *Foreign Policy*, August 2014, http://foreignpolicy.com/2014/01/08/a-new-anbar-awakening/.

25. See Stephen Wicken, "Iraq's Sunnis in Crisis," Middle East Security Report No. 11, *Institute for the Study of War*, May 2013.

26. "Al-Jazeera Views Iraqi Military Campaign in Al-Anbar, Sunni Grievances."

27. See Cameron Barr, "Outside a Mosque, Sunnis Critique the New Iraq; Under Saddam, the Sunni Minority Enjoyed Favored Status. Now They Find Themselves Outnumbered on the Governing Council," *Christian Science Monitor*, August 29, 2003, 3; Howard LaFranchi, "Iraq's Sunni-Shiite Tension Rising; The Killing of Two Sunni Clerics Earlier This Week Could Be Part of a Slide toward Sectarian Civil War, Analysts Say," *Christian Science Monitor*, September 22, 2004, 6; Ghaith Abdul-Ahad, "Iraqi Sunnis Await a Baghdad Spring," *Guardian*, March 13, 2013, https://www.theguardian.com/world/2013/mar/13/iraq-sunnis-unite-oust-shia-government; Abigail Hauslohner, "In Baghdad, Middle-Class Sunnis

Say They Prefer Militants to Maliki," *Washington Post*, July 12, 2014, http://www .washingtonpost.com/world/middle_east/in-baghdad-mi; Yaroslav Trofimov, "After Minority Rule, Iraq's Sunnis Refuse Minority Role," *Wall Street Journal*, April 9, 2015, https://www.wsj.com/articles/iraqs-sunnis-dont-accept-minority-role-1428571127. Both articles highlight the power of the residual Sunni sense of entitlement. It is not surprising that it engenders such Shia paranoia in reaction.

28. Serena Chaudhry, "Feeling Marginalized, Some Iraq Sunnis Eye Autonomy," *Reuters*, January 1, 2012, http://www.reuters.com/article/us-iraq-politics-sunnis-idUSTRE80005620120101.

29. Ronen Zeidel, "Between Aqalliya and Mukawin: Understanding Sunni Political Attitudes in Post-Saddam Iraq," in Benjamin Isakhan, ed., *From the 2003 War to the "Islamic State*," Edinburgh: Edinburgh University Press, 2015, 97–109.

30. For Sunni perceptions of reempowerment after the outbreak of anti-Maliki protests in Sunni regions, see the revealing article by Ghaith Abdul-Ahad, "Iraqi Sunnis Await a Baghdad Spring."

31. Ghaith Abdul-Ahad, "Baghdad's Sunni Fighters: We Are Ready for Zero Hour," *Guardian*, June 20, 2014, https://www.theguardian.com/world/2014/jun/20/ baghdad-sunni-fighters-we-are-ready-for-zero-hour.

32. Abdel Qadir Saadi, "Special Assignment," Al-Arabiya TV, Dubai, 18:34 GMT, November 27, 2008.

33. See Sudarsan Raghavan, "A New Breed Grabs Reins in Anbar," *Washington Post*, October 21, 2008, A1.

34. Sam Dagher, "In Anbar Province, New Leadership, but Old Problems Persist," *New York Times*, September 13, 2009, http://www.nytimes.com/2009/09/13/ world/middleeast/13anbar.html.

35. See "Al-Arabiyah Program Discusses Iraqi Awakening Councils Political Ambitions," Al-Arabiya TV, Dubai, 18:34 GMT, November 27, 2008, Open Source Center-GMP20081127647005, https://www.opensource.gov/portal/ server.pt/gateway/PTARGS_0_0_200_240_51_43/http.

36. Ibid.

37. On the rampant corruption in Anbar during the twilight years of the American presence, see Dagher, "In Anbar Province, New Leadership, but Old Problems Persist."

38. Matt Bradley and Bill Spindle, "Unlikely Allies Aid Militants in Iraq," *Wall Street Journal*, June 17, 2014, A1.

39. This section is based on Abu Bakr al-Naji, *The Management of Savagery* (translated by Will McCants), Cambridge, MA: John Olin Institute for Strategic Studies, Harvard University, 2006; Jim Lacey, ed., *The Canons of Jihad: Terrorists' Strategy for Defeating America*, Annapolis: Naval Institute Press, 2008, 48–87; Michael Ryan, *Decoding Al-Qaeda's Strategy: The Deep Battle against America*, New York: Columbia University Press, 2013, 147–192; Etienne Dubuis, "Les theoriciens de l'Etat islamique," *Le Temps*, September 1, 2014, https://www

.letemps.ch/monde/2014/09/01/theoriciens-islamique; Abdel Bari Atwan, *Islamic State*, London: Saqi Books, 2015, 153–164; Michael Weiss and Hassan Hassan, *ISIS: Inside the Army of Terror*, New York: Regan Arts, 2015, 40–47.

40. Michael Ryan, *Decoding Al-Qaeda's Strategy*, 150.

41. Citing Naji's book accurately is difficult, as Will McCants's translation does not include pagination. The summary of Naji's ideas that I present in this chapter comes from various places in his book, which presents another problem, as the book is not very well organized.

42. Hassan Hassan, "Isis Has Reached New Depths of Depravity. But There Is a Brutal Logic behind It," *Guardian*, February 8, 2015, http://www.theguardian.com/world/2015/feb/08/isis-islamic-state-ideology-sharia-syria-iraq-jordan-pilot.

43. "The Return of the Khilafah," *Dabiq*, iss. 1, Ramadan 1435 (June 2014).

44. Ibid.

45. "Fatal Attraction—Islamic State Ramps Up Foreign Recruitment after Proclamation of Caliphate," *Jane's Islamic Affairs Analyst* 14, 9 (October 1, 2014).

46. This is based on the excellent summary by Murad Batal al-Shishani, "The Islamic State's Strategic and Tactical Plan for Iraq," *Terrorism Monitor* 12, 16 (August 2014), http://www.jamestown.org/single/?tx_ttnews%5Btt_news%5D=42728&no_cache=1#.VzMAGumD5-U.

47. "Iraq: Is It Really Coming Right?," *Economist*, November 27–December 3, 2008.

48. Daveed Gartenstein-Ross and Sterling Jensen, "The Role of Iraqi Tribes after the Islamic State's Ascendance," *Military Review* 95, 4 (July–August 2015), 102–110.

49. Hasan Abu Hanieh and Mohammad Abu Rumman, *The "Islamic State" Organization: The Sunni Crisis and the Struggle of Global Jihadism*, Amman: Friedrich Ebert Stiftung, 2015.

50. One of the best contemporary analyses of what the caliphate entails was written by Andrew Mack and Mara Revkin, "The Caliphate of Law," *Foreign Affairs*, April 15, 2015, https://www.foreignaffairs.com/articles/syria/2015-04-15/caliphate-law. I have relied heavily on this incomparable piece for helping me understand IS's notion of the caliphate. Will McCants's book *ISIS Apocalypse* was also extremely helpful in this respect.

51. Ibid.

52. Aymenn Jawad al-Tamimi, "The Evolution in Islamic State Administration: The Documentary Evidence," *Pundicity Blog*, August 5, 2015, http://www.aymennjawad.org/17687/the-evolution-in-islamic-state-administration.

53. See Mack and Mara, "Caliphate of Law."

54. Ludovico Carlino, "How Al-Qaeda and Islamic State Differ in Pursuit of Common Goal," *Jane's Intelligence Review* 27, 4 (April 1, 2015).

55. Megan Stewart, "What's So New about the Islamic State's Governance?," *Washington Post*, October 7, 2014, https://www.washingtonpost.com/blogs/monkey-cage/wp/2014/10/.

56. "The Return of the Khilafah," *Dabiq*, iss. 1 (2014), 25.

57. For an excellent analysis of IS nation-building, see Adam Bazcko, Gilles Dorronsoro, Arthur Quesnay, and Maai Youssef, "The Rationality of an Eschatological Movement: The Islamist State in Iraq and Syria," Working Paper No. 7, Gothenburg: Program on Governance and Local Development, University of Gothenburg, 2016, http://gld.gu.se/media/1122/gld-wp7.pdf.

58. See Sara Mahmoud, "The Women of ISIS: Gendered Roles and Agency under the Caliphate," M.A. thesis, Rajaratnam School of International Relations, Nanyang Technological University, Singapore, 2016.

59. *The Cubs of the Caliphate: How the Islamic State Attracts, Coerces and Indoctrinates Children to Its Cause*, Baghdad: Al-Bayan Center for Planning and Studies, 2016; Noman Benotman and Nikita Malik, *The Children of Islamic State*, London: Quilliam Foundation, March 2016.

60. Mona Alami, "ISIS's Governance Crisis (Part II): Social Services," *Atlantic Council*, December 24, 2014, http://www.atlanticcouncil.org/blogs/menasource/isis-s-governance-crisis-part-ii-social-services; Ben Hubbard, "Offering Services, ISIS Digs in Deeper in Seized Territories," *International New York Times*, June 16, 2015, https://www.nytimes.com/2015/06/17/world/middleeast/offering-services-isis-ensconces-itself-in-seized-territories.html.

61. See "Syria: With Its Caliphate Faltering, Islamic State Rushes to Indoctrinate Children," *Asia News Monitor*, June 22, 2016; Hassan Hassan, "The Secret World of Isis Training Camps—Ruled by Sacred Texts and the Sword," *Guardian*, January 25, 2015, https://www.theguardian.com/world/2015/jan/25/inside-isis-training-camps; Mark Townsend, "How Islamic State Is Training Child Killers in Doctrine of Hate," *Guardian*, March 5, 2016, https://www.the-guardian.com/world/2016/mar/05/islamic-state-trains-purer-child-killers-in-doctrine-of-hate.

62. See Mohammed Salih and Akhten Asaad, "New Evidence Reveals How ISIL Controls Its Territories," *McClatchy-Tribune Business News*, August 5, 2015; Margaret Coker, "In a Shift, Islamic State Tries to Show It Can Govern," *Wall Street Journal*, October 14, 2015, A1.

63. Svante Cornell, "Narcotics and Armed Conflict: Interaction and Implications," *Studies in Conflict and Terrorism* 30, 3 (2007), 207–227.

64. Jeremy Weinstein, *Inside Rebellion: The Politics of Insurgent Violence*, New York: Cambridge University Press, 2007.

65. Hannah Allam, "Records Show How Iraqi Extremists Withstood U.S. Anti-terror Efforts," *McClatchy*, June 23, 2014, http://www.mcclatchydc.com/news/nation-world/world/article24769573.html.

66. Haytham Mouzahem, "How Islamic State Gets Its Cash," *Middleeasteye*, March 19, 2015, http://www.middleeasteye.net/columns/how-isis-gets-cash-39592257; Michael Joannes, "The Role of Taxation in Insurgent Movements," M.A. thesis, Elliott School of International Affairs, George Washington University, 2016.

67. Berman and Shapiro, "Why ISIL Will Fail on Its Own"; "Degraded, Not Yet Destroyed: Islamic State's Finances," *Economist*, December 12, 2015, 48.

68. Ruth Sherlock, "Why Business Is Booming under Islamic State One Year On," *Daily Telegraph*, June 8, 2015, http://www.telegraph.co.uk/news/worldnews/islamic-state/11657918/Why-business-is-booming-under-Islamic-State-one-year-on.html.

69. Jamie Hansen-Lewis and Jacob Shapiro, "Understanding the Daesh Economy," *Perspectives on Terrorism* 9, 4 (August 2015), 142–155.

70. Howard Schatz and Erin-Elizabeth Johnson, "The Islamic State We Knew," RAND Corporation, 2015, http://www.rand.org/content/dam/rand/pubs/research_reports/RR1200/RR1267/RAND_RR1267.pdf, 2.

71. "Where Islamic State Gets Its Money," *Economist*, January 4, 2015, https://www.economist.com/blogs/economist-explains/2015/01/economist-explains; Mathilde Damge, "Esclavage, rancons, petrole, pillage... Comment l'Etat islamique se finance," *Le Monde*, November 19, 2015, http://www.lemonde.fr/les-decodeurs/article/2015/11/19/esclavage-rancons-petrole-pillage-comment-se-finance-l-etat-islamique_4812961_4355770.html; Mona Alami, "ISIS's Governance Crisis (Part I): Economic Governance," *Atlantic Council* (blog), December 19, 2014, http://www.atlanticcouncil.org/blogs/menasource/isis-s-governance.

72. Mohammad Zaid Mastou and Carl Guensberg, "VOA Special Report: IS Militants Draw Millions from Vast Sources," *Voice of America*, September 14, 2014, https://www.voanews.com/a/islamic-state-militants-draw-millions-from-vast-funding-sources/2451897.html.

73. "Islamic State Can Survive Oil Losses," Oxford Analytica Daily Brief Service, January 13, 2016.

74. "Iraq: Islamic State Financing Caliphate by Smuggling Oil [1]," *Asia News Monitor*, July 25, 2014.

75. Luay al-Khatteeb and Eline Gordts, "How ISIS Uses Oil to Fund Terror," *Brookings*, September 27, 2014, https://www.brookings.edu/on-the-record/how-isis-uses-oil-to-fund-terror/.

76. See "Comment Daech se finance," *Le Figaro*, March 23, 2016, http://www.lefigaro.fr/economie/le-scan-eco/decryptage/2016/03/23/29002-20160323ART-FIG00236-le-nebuleux-financement-de-daech.php.

77. Benoit Faucon and Ayla Albayrak, "Complex Network Smuggles Militants' Oil—West Pushes for Crackdown on Major Funding Source for Islamic State; Moving into Turkey via Pipeline, Truck and Mule," *Wall Street Journal*, September 16, 2014, A10.

78. Julian Barnes and Sam Dagher, "Strikes Expand to Hit Militants' Oil Assets—U.S. and Arab Allies Target Mobile Refineries Controlled by Islamic State, Aiming to Choke Off Group's Financial Lifelines," *Wall Street Journal*, September 25, 2014, A8.

79. Benoit Faucon and Margaret Coker, "The Rise and Deadly Fall of Islamic State's Oil Tycoon," *Wall Street Journal*, April 24, 2016, https://www.wsj.com/articles/the-rise-and-deadly-fall-of-islamic-states-oil-tycoon-1461522313.

80. Jacob Shapiro, "A Predictable Failure: The Political Economy of the Decline of the Islamic State," *CTC Sentinel* 9, 9 (September 7, 2016), https://www.ctc.usma.edu/posts/a-predictable-failure-the-political-; "The Truth of the Islamic State's Governance," *Atlantic Council* (blog), July 28, 2016, http://www.atlantic-council.org/blogs/syriasource/the-truth-of-the-islamic-state-s-governance.

81. Michael Jonsson, "Funding the Islamic State: Sources of Revenue, Financing Requirements and Long-Term Vulnerabilities to Counter-measures," Swedish Defense Research Agency, FOI Memo No. 5525, Asian Security Briefing, December 2015.

82. "Islamic State Monthly Revenue Drops to $56 Million, IHS Says," *Business Wire*, April 18, 2016.

83. "Removing the Islamic State from Local Economies," *TSG IntelBrief*, Soufan Group, October 27, 2014, http://www.soufangroup.com/tsg-intelbrief-removing-the-islamic-state-from-local-economies/.

84. Raja Abdulrahman, "In Syria's Mangled Economy, Truckers Stitch Together Warring Regions; Trade between Islamic State, the Assad Regime and Others Continues Despite War; Leaving It to Drivers to Crisscross Dangerous Front Lines," *Wall Street Journal*, May 24, 2016.

85. Jean-Charles Brisard and Damien Martinez, *Islamic State: The Economy-Based Terrorist Funding*, Accelus, Thomson Reuters, October 2014, 5.

86. Matthew Rosenberg, Nicholas Kulish, and Steve Lee Myers, "Predatory Islamic State Wrings Money from Those It Rules," *New York Times*, November 29, 2015, https://www.nytimes.com/2015/11/30/world/middleeast/predatory-islamic-state-wrings-money-from-those-it-rules.html.

87. Hugh Naylor, "Islamic State's Moneymaking Streams Take a Hit as It Loses Territory," *Washington Post*, December 4, 2015, https://www.washingtonpost.com/world/middle_east/islamic-states-money-makers-take-a-hit-as-it-loses-territory/2015/12/03/b08910aa-91f6-11e5-befa-99ceebcbb272_story.html?utm_term=.2e408c979dfc; Patrick Johnston, "The Islamic State's Money Problems," *Rand Commentary*, March 5, 2016, http://www.rand.org/blog/2016/03/the-islamic-states-money-probl; Lizzie Dearden, "Isis' 'Business Model' Failing as Group Haemorrhages Millions While Losing Territory across Syria and Iraq," *Independent*, February 18, 2017, http://www.independent.co.uk/news/world/middle-east/isis-islamic-state-daesh-funding-iraq-syria-territory-losses-oil-air-strikes-icsr-report-antiquities-a7586936.html.

88. "So They Kill and Are Killed—Audio Statement by Abu Muhammad al-Adnani," *Pietervanostaeyen* (blog), March 12, 2015, https://www.pietervanostaeyen.com/2015/03/13/so-they-kill-and-are-kill.

89. Erika Solomon, "The Isis Economy: Meet the New Boss," *Financial Times*, January 5, 2015, https://www.ft.com/content/b2c6b5ca-9427-11e4-82c7-00144feabdc0.

90. For a detailed analysis of IS governance failures, see Tomas Kavalek, "Running the Islamic State Part 3: Limits of Governance," *Sekuritaci* 25, 4 (2015), http://www.sekuritaci.cz/running-the-islamic-state-part-3-limits-of.

91. Dominique Soguel, "Heard at Syria's Border: Life in the Islamic State Is Orderly, but Brutal," *Christian Science Monitor*, September 21, 2014.

92. Fazel Hawramy, Shalaw Mohammad, and Kareem Shaheen, "Life under Isis in Raqqa and Mosul: 'We're Living in a Giant Prison,'" *Guardian*, December 9, 2015.

93. Mara Revkin and Will McCants, "Experts Weigh In: Is ISIS Good at Governing?," *Markaz Blog, Brookings*, November 20, 2015, https://www.brookings.edu/blog/markaz/2015/11/20/experts-weigh.

94. Aymenn al-Tamimi and Will McCants, "Experts Weigh In (part 2): Is ISIS Good at Governing?," *Markaz Blog, Brookings*, February 3, 2016, https://www.brookings.edu/blog/markaz/2016/02/03/experts-weigh.

95. Liz Sly, "Islam's Dysfunctional State: In ISIS-controlled Syria and Iraq Everyday Life Is Falling Apart," *Independent*, December 26, 2014, http://www.independent.co.uk/news/world/middle-east/islams-dysfunctional-state-in-isiscontrolled-syria-and-iraq-everyday-life-is-falling-apart-9945774.html.

96. See Robert Worth, "The Reluctant Jihadi; How One Recruit Lost Faith in Isis," *Guardian*, April 12, 2016, https://www.theguardian.com/news/2016/apr/12/reluctant-jihadi-recruit-lost-faith-in-isis.

97. Mona Alami, "ISIS's Governance Crisis (Part I): Economic Governance," *Atlantic Council* (blog), December 19, 2014, http://www.atlanticcouncil.org/blogs/menasource/isis-s-governance.

98. Mona Alami, "ISIS Recruitment Tactics Stumble," *Atlantic Council* (blog), February 26, 2015, http://www.atlanticcouncil.org/blogs/menasource/dispatch-isis-recruitment-tactics-stumble.

99. Richard Engel, Ben Plesser, and Amar Cheikh Omar, "Leaked ISIS Personnel Files Paint Picture of Group's Recruits," *NBC News*, March 10, 2016, http://www.nbcnews.com/storyline/isis-uncovered/leaked-isis-personnel-files-paint-picture-group-s-recruits-n535676.

100. See Michael Weiss, "How I Escaped from ISIS," *Daily Beast*, November 18, 2015, http://www.thedailybeast.com/how-i-escaped-from-isis.

101. Mark Jonathan Wegner, "Islamic Government: The Medieval Sunni Islamic Theory of the Caliphate and the Debate over the Revival of the Caliphate in Egypt, 1924–1926," Ph.D. diss., University of Chicago, 2001, 66–67.

102. Quoted in Mirren Gidda, "ISIS Is Facing a Cash Crunch," *Newsweek*, September 28, 2015, http://europe.newsweek.com/isis-are-facing-cash-crunch-caliphate-333422.

103. Ibid.; see also Abu Ibrahim al-Raqqawi, "Inside the Islamic State 'Capital': No End in Sight to Its Grim Rule," *Guardian*, February 21, 2015, https://www .theguardian.com/world/2015/feb/21/islamic-state-capital-raqqa-syria-isis.

104. Kevin Sullivan, "Spoils for the Rulers, Terror for the Ruled," *Washington Post*, October 1, 2015, http://www.washingtonpost.com/sf/life-in-the-islamic-state/ 2015/1.

105. Mohammad Moslawi, Fazel Hawramy, and Luke Harding, "Citizens of Mosul Endure Economic Collapse and Repression under Isis Rule," *Guardian*, October 27, 2014, https://www.theguardian.com/world/2014/oct/27/citizens-mosul-iraq-economic-collapse-repression-isis-islamic-state; Ben Hubbard, "ISIS Promise of Statehood Falling Far Short, Ex-residents Say," *New York Times*, December 1, 2015, https://www.nytimes.com/2015/12/02/world/middle east/isis-promise-of-statehood-falling-far-short-ex-residents-say.html.

106. On conditions within the Caliphate, specifically in Raqqa, see Abu Ibrahim al-Raqqawi, "Inside the Islamic State's 'Capital,'" *Guardian,* February 21, 2015, https://www.theguardian.com/world/2015/feb/21/islamic-state-capital-raqqa-syria-isis; Uwe Buse and Katrin Kuntz, "The Everyday Horrors of the Islamic State," *Der Spiegel*, January 7, 2015, http://www.spiegel.de/international/world/ reports-of-everyday-life-under-the-islamic-state-a-1041317.html.

107. Maria Abi-Habib, "As Islamic State Grows, Internal Rifts Spread—Defectors Describe Discord Fueled by Pay Disparities, Ideological Rifts and Low Morale," *Wall Street Journal*, March 10, 2015, A7.

108. Mona Alami, "ISIS Recruitment Tactics Stumble."

109. Matt Bradley and Mohammad Nour Alakraa, "Islamic State Scrambles to Stem Exodus of Skilled Workers; Militants Step Up Propaganda to Try to Woo Doctors, Teachers and Others Who Are Increasingly Fleeing to Europe," *Wall Street Journal*, October 6, 2015.

110. For a good overview of IS terror as instrument, see Hassan, "Isis Has Reached New Depths of Depravity," *Guardian*, February 8, 2015, https://www.theguardian .com/world/2015/feb/08/isis-islamic-state-ideology-sharia-syria-iraq-jordan-pilot.

111. Martin Reardon, "ISIL and the Management of Savagery," *Al-Jazeera*, July 6, 2015, http://www.aljazeera.com/indepth/opinion/2015/07/isil-management-savagery-150705060914471.html.

112. See Erika Solomon, "Isis Tightens Grip with Mix of Soft Power and Terror: Governance," *Financial Times*, July 28, 2014, 8; Tim Arango, "ISIS Transforming into Functioning State That Uses Terror as Tool," *International New York Times*, July 21, 2015, https://www.nytimes.com/2015/07/22/world/middleeast/isis-transforming-into-functioning-state-that-uses-terror-as-tool.html?mtrref=www .google.com.sg&assetType=nyt_now&mtrref=www.nytimes.com&gwh=8739E2 EE1F60B978991A1928ACF6C820&gwt=pay&assetType=nyt_now.

113. "Islamic State Struggles to Maintain Economic Viability," *NewArab*, December 15, 2014, https://www.alaraby.co.uk/english/news/2014/12/15/islamic-state-struggles-to-maintain-economic-viability.

114. Erika Solomon, "Fines, Sell-offs and Subsidy Cuts: Life under Cash-Squeezed Isis," *Financial Times*, February 27, 2015, http://ft.com/intl/cms/s/015b493ca-bdbb-11e4-9d09-00144f.

115. Sam Jones and Erika Solomon, "Isis Inc: Jihadis Fund War Machine but Squeeze 'Citizens,'" *Financial Times*, December 15, 2015, https://www.ft.com/content/2ef519a6-a23d-11e5-bc70-7ff6d4fd203a?mhq5j=e2.

116. Ibid.

117. "A Raqqa Student: 'Daily Life Is Good' under ISIS," *Syria Direct*, April 27, 2014, http://www.syriadirect.org/news/a-raqqa-student-'daily-life-is-good'-und.

118. Lauren Williams, "'This Is Not Islam': Refugees Describe Life under ISIL in Raqqa, Syria," *Al-Jazeera*, August 1, 2015, http://america.aljazeera.com/articles/2015/8/1/this-is-not-islam-refugees-describing-life-under-isil-in-raqqa-syria.html.

119. Michael Weiss, "Leaked ISIS Documents Show Internal Chaos," *Daily Beast*, August 30, 2016, http://www.thedailybeast.com/leaked-isis-documents-show-internal-chaos.

120. Maria Abi Habib, "Splits in Islamic State Emerge as Its Ranks Expand," *Wall Street Journal*, March 9, 2015, https://www.wsj.com/articles/islamic-state-feels-growing-pains-1425903933.

121. Liz Sly, "Syria Tribal Revolt against Islamic State Ignored, Fueling Resentment," *Washington Post*, October 20, 2014, https://www.washingtonpost.com/world/syria-tribal-revolt-against-islamic-state-ignored-fueling-resentment/2014/10/20/25401beb-8de8-49f2-8e64-c1cfbee45232_story.html?utm_term=.fffa95b9d899.

122. Ibid.

123. Sam Dagher, "Control of Syrian Oil Fuels War between Kurds and Islamic State," *Wall Street Journal*, November 23, 2014, https://www.wsj.com/articles/control-of-syrian-oil-fuels-war-between-kurds-and-islamic-state-1416799982.

124. Ibid.

125. See Roger Beaumont, "Al-Qaida's Brutal Effort to Build a Caliphate Prompts Growing Fury," *Guardian*, January 11, 2014, https://www.theguardian.com/world/2014/jan/11/al-qaida-repeats-mistakes-falluja-tragedy.

126. Matt Bradley and Ali Nabhan, "Tribes Once Loyal to Baghdad Give Fealty to Militants; Some Tribal Leaders Who Once Fought for Iraq's Government Succumb to Rule by Sunni Insurgents," *Wall Street Journal*, June 24, 2014.

127. Scott Peterson, "In Iraq, Sunni Tribes Pay Heavy Toll for Joining Fight against Islamic State," *Christian Science Monitor*, December 14, 2014, https://m

.csmonitor.com/index.php/World/Middle-East/2014/1214/In-Iraq-Sunni-tribes-pay-heavy-toll-for-joining-fight-against-Islamic-State.

128. See Cécile Hennion, "Ces alliances heteroclites qui renforcent l' EIIL en Irak," *Le Monde*, June 20, 2014, http://www.lemonde.fr/proche-orient/article/2014/06/20/ces-alliances-hétéroclites-qui-renforcent-l-eiil-en-irak_4441067_3218.html.

129. See Richard Spencer, "Assassinations, Unrest and Military Defeat—Has the Tide Turned against Islamic State?," *Daily Telegraph*, March 7, 2016, http://www.telegraph.co.uk/news/worldnews/islamic-state/12186766/Assassinations-unrest-and-military-defeat-has-the-tide-turned-against-Islamic-State.html.

130. "Guerrilla Group Hunt Down Islamic State in Syria," *Reuters*, October 13, 2014, http://www.reuters.com/article/uk-mideast-crisis-syria-shrouds-idUSKCN0I21JW20141013.

131. Erika Solomon, "Sunni Tribes in Bitter Rift over ISIS's Iraq Gains," *Financial Times*, May 27, 2015, http://www.ft.com/cms/s/a39fb628-044d-11e5-a5c3-00144feabd.

132. Ibid.

133. "Iraq's Abadi Struggles to Gain Sunni Tribal Support," *MailOnline*, October 30, 2014, http://www.dailymail.co.uk/wires/reuters/article-2813717/Iraqs-A.

134. On Haider al-Abadi's problems see "Abadi Agonists," *Economist*, April 16, 2016, http://www.economist.com/news/middle-east-and-africa/21696954-two-new-governments-month-abadi-agonistes; John Hudson, Dan De Luce, and Paul McLeary, "Is Iraq's Most Important Battle in Baghdad?," *Foreign Policy*, May 2, 2016, http://foreignpolicy.com/2016/05/02/is-iraqs-most-important-battle-in-baghdad/.

135. Scott Peterson, "Islamic State: Iraqi Leaders Created the Problem... and Can End It, Say Sunnis," *Christian Science Monitor*, September 16, 2014, 6; see also Maria Abi-Habib, "Insurgents Give Boost to Region's Sunni Sect; Sunnis Believe the Extremist Group Is Checking Shiite Power," *Wall Street Journal*, June 20, 2014, 4.

136. Matt Bradley, "Iraq Sects Find Some Common Cause in War—Successful Sunni, Shiite Coordination against Islamic State Encourages Alliances," *Wall Street Journal*, April 14, 2015, A11; Yaroslav Trofimov, "Middle East Crossroads: Iraqi Sunnis Reject Minority Role, Hindering Political Solution," *Wall Street Journal*, April 10, 2015, A6; "Islamic State's Reported Gains in Iraq's Ramadi Reflect Government's Failure to Arm Anbar's Sunnis," *Jane's Intelligence Weekly* 7, 2 (April 22, 2015); "Iraqi Sunnis Ready to Fight ISIS but Lack Support, Says Tribal Leader," *Al-Arabiya*, October 10, 2015, http://english.alarabiya.net/en/perspective/analysis/2015/10/27/Ira.

137. "Reliance on Militias Complicates Iraqi Government's Plan to Retake Islamic State–Controlled Cities in Al-Anbar before Mosul Operation," *Jane's Intelligence*

Weekly 7, 18 (April 8, 2015); see also "Islamic State's Reported Gains in Iraq's Ramadi Reflect Government's Failure to Arm Anbar's Sunnis"; Mitchell Prothero, "Training for Iraq's Sunni Tribes to Fight Islamic State Off to Slow Start," *McClatchy*, May 12, 2015, http://www.mcclatchydc.com/news/nation-world/world/article24784438.html.

138. Tamer al-Ghobashy, "An Uneasy Alliance Moves on Tikrit—Iraqi Forces and Shiite Militia Share the Goal of Pushing Out Islamic State, but They Differ on Who Is Out in Front in the Fighting," *Wall Street Journal*, March 6, 2015, A9.

139. Scott Peterson, "In Northeast Iraq, Flashes of Resistance against Islamic State's Militants," *Christian Science Monitor*, December 17, 2014, 4.

140. Bradley, "Iraq Sects Find Some Common Cause in War."

141. Nour Malas and Ghassan Adnan, "Sunnis Divided in Iraq Battle—Addition of Shiite Militias to Beat Back Islamic State's Gains Complicates Loyalties," *Wall Street Journal*, May 22, 2015, A1.

142. Ibid.

143. See Harith Hasan, "Iraq's Sunni Divide May Be Too Great," *Al-Monitor*, June 13, 2014, http://www.al-monitor.com/pulse/originals/2014/06/iraq-sunni-divide-too-great-isis-isil-mosul.html.

144. Prothero, "Training for Iraq's Sunni Tribes to Fight Islamic State Off to Slow Start"; Angelique Ferat, "Irak: Les tribus Sunnite d'al-Anbar se dissent aban-donnees face a l'EI," *RFI*, November 7, 2014, http://www.rfi.fr/moyen-orient/20141107-irak-ei-tribus-al-anbar-albounimer-terrorisme-chiites.

145. Loveday Morris, "Iraq's Victory over Militants in Sunni Towns Underlines Challenges Government Faces," *Washington Post*, October 29, 2014, http://www.washingtonpost.com/world/middle_east/iraqs-victory.

146. W. G. Dunlop, "Iraq Victory in Jurf al-Sakhr Marred by Destruction, Anger," *Daily Star* (Beirut), November 10, 2014, http://www.dailystar.com.lb/News/Middle-East/2014/Nov-10/277041-iraq-victory-in-jurf-al-sakhr-marred-by-destruction-anger.ashx.

147. Richard Spencer, "Between the Hammer and the Anvil—How ISIL Spelt Doom for the Sunnis," *Telegraph*, June 7, 2015, http://www.telegraph.co.uk/news/11657113/islamic-state-spells-doom-for-iraqs-sunni-muslims.html.

148. Ibid.

149. See Cathy Otten, "Isis in Iraq: Why Tikrit Remains a Ghost Town Two Months after Its Liberation from Militant Fighters," *Independent*, June 9, 2015, http://www.independent.co.uk/news/world/middle-east/isis-in-iraq-why-tikrit-remains-a-ghost-town-two-months-after-its-liberation-from-militant-fighters-10308521.html.

150. See "Four Iraqi Armed Organizations Declare War on Jihadist Group," *BBC Monitoring—Middle East*, June 3, 2014; Aymmen Jawad al-Tamimi, "Sunni Opposition to the Islamic State," *Middle East Review of International Affairs* 18, 3 (Fall 2014), 5.

151. Vivian Salama and Qasim Abdul–Zahra, "Sunni Tribes, Abandoned by Iraq, Key to Islamic State Fight," *Wall Street Journal*, June 21, 2015, http://www .salon.com/2015/06/20/sunni_tribes_abandoned_by_ir.

152. Ian Johnston, "Isis Executioner Killed by Assassins in Occupied Iraqi City of Mosul," *International Business Times*, March 27, 2016, http://www.ibtimes .co.uk/isis-executioner-killed-by-assassins-occupied-iraqi-city-mosul-1551756.

153. Matt Bradley, "Fight against Islamic State Deepens Divides within Iraq's Sunni Minority; Government Supporters Threaten Those Loyal to Insurgents," *Wall Street Journal*, December 9, 2014.

154. Ibid.

155. Ibid.

156. Ibid.

157. Spencer, "Between the Hammer and the Anvil."

158. In Frederick Wehrey and Ala Alrababah, "An Elusive Courtship: The Struggle for Iraq's Sunni Arab Tribes," *Syria Deeply* (Carnegie Endowment for International Peace, Washington, DC), November 7, 2014; Dafna Rand and Nicholas Heras, "Iraq's Sunni Reawakening: How to Defeat ISIS and Save the Country," *Foreign Affairs*, March 16, 2015, https://www.foreignaffairs.com/articles/ iraq/2015-03-16/iraqs-sunni-reawakening.

159. Borzou Daraghi, "Isis Brutality in Iraq Reawakens Sunni Resistance," *Financial Times*, February 25, 2015.

160. "Islamic State's Reported Gains in Iraq's Ramadi Reflect Government's Failure to Arm Anbar's Sunnis."

161. Loveday Morris and Mustafa Salim, "Islamic State Faces New Trouble in Fallujah as Sunni Tribesmen Revolt," *Washington Post*, February 19, 2016, https://www.washingtonpost.com/world/middle_east/sunni-tribesmen-clash- with-islamic-state-in-fallujah-as-resentment-boils/2016/02/19/2a21ce95-e7c0 -4a3c-89e8-f02005d9400b_story.html?tid=a_inl.

162. Richard Spencer, "Assassinations, Unrest and Military Defeat—Has the Tide Turned against Islamic State?," *Telegraph*, March 7, 2016, http://www.telegraph .co.uk/news/worldnews/islamic-state/12186766/Assassinations-unrest-and- military-defeat-has-the-tide-turned-against-Islamic-State.html.

163. Mustafa Habib, "Low Supplies, Political Disputes in Anbar: Not Long Now before Extremists Take Over," *Niqash*, December 18, 2014, http://www.niqash .org/en/articles/politics/3597/Not-Long-Now-Be.

164. Khales Joumah, "Whose Side Are They On? Iraq's Arab Tribes Decide between Kurdish [*sic*] and Extremists," *Niqash*, April 16, 2015, http://www.niqash.org/ en/articles/politics/3637/Whose-Side-Are.

165. Ibid.

166. Ibid.

167. "Lack of Trust Hinders Second Sunni Awakening," *TSG IntelBrief*, Soufan Group, October 22, 2014, http://www.soufangroup.com/tsg-intelbrief-lack-of- trust-hinders-second-sunni-awakening/.

168. Jim Muir, "Iraq Crisis; Sunni Rebels Ready to Turn on Islamic State," *BBC News*, August 29, 2014, https://www.bbc.com/news/world-middle-east-28978941.

169. Ibid.

170. Ibid.

171. On government negotiations with Sunni groups, see Judit Neurink, "War on Isis: Iraq Seeks Sunnis Militia Support for Fight against Islamic State," *Independent*, October 6, 2015, http://www.independent.co.uk/news/world/middle-east/war-on-isis-iraq-seeks-sunni-militia-support-for-fight-against-islamic-state-a6680926.html.

172. See "Iraq: Militias Escalate Abuses, Possibly War Crimes," *Human Rights Watch*, February 15, 2015, https://www.hrw.org/news/2015/02/15/iraq-militias-escalate-abuses-possibly-war-crimes. Malas Nour, "Restrictions on Sunnis Fleeing Violence Deepen Iraq's Sectarian Divide; Officials Intermittently Closed Bridge to Baghdad, Saying They Feared Islamic State Supporters Might Try to Cross," *Wall Street Journal*, June 4, 2015.

173. Adnan Aby Zeed, "Sunnis Eye Their Piece of Iraq Pie," *Al-Monitor*, August 18, 2016, http://www.al-monitor.com/pulse/originals/2016/08/iraq-sunni-region-after-is-sectarianism.html.

174. See Caryl, "The World's Next Country"; Jack Moore, "Kurdish Land-Grab Stuns Baghdad," *Newsweek*, January 27, 2015, http://www.newsweek.com/2015/02/06/kurdish-land-grab-stuns-baghdad-302303.html; Honar Hama Rasheed, "Borders Not Drawn in Blood: Iraqi Kurdish Say They're Willing to Negotiate Disputed Territories," *Niqash*, May 21, 2015, http://www.niqash.org/en/articles/politics/5012/Iraqi-Kurdish-Say; Rebecca Collard, "The Big Question in the Battle for Mosul Is What Comes After," *Time*, October 18, 2016, http://time.com/4535273/isis-mosul-iraq-kurdish-peshmerga-fallout/; Jared Malsin, "The Next War for Iraq," *Time*, June 22, 2016, http://time.com/isis-mosul/.

CONCLUSION

1. The most extensive and best analysis of IS's millenarian and apocalyptic thinking remains Will McCants, *ISIS Apocalypse*. See also Scott Philip Segrest, "ISIS's Will to Apocalypse," *Politics, Religion and Ideology* 17, 4 (2016), 1–18. The best general treatments of Islamic apocalyptic thinking are by David Cook and Pierre Filiu.

2. See Tareq Ismail and Max Fuller, "The Disintegration of Iraq: The Manufacturing and Politicization of Sectarianism," *International Journal of Contemporary Iraqi Studies* 2, 3 (2008), 443–473.

3. Andrew Philips, "How al Qaeda Lost Iraq," *Australian Journal of International Affairs* 63, 1 (2009), 64–84.

4. Wladimir von Wilgenburg, "Breaking with Baghdad: Kurdish Autonomy vs. Maliki's Manipulation," *World Affairs* (November–December 2012), 47–53.

5. See Loveday Morris, "As Their Power Grows, Iraq's Kurds Are Fighting among Themselves," *Washington Post*, October 12, 2015, http://www.washingtonpost .com/world/middle_east/as-their-power.

6. See the recent essay by a former British ambassador to Iraq who witnessed the decline of Iraq firsthand: John Jenkins, "The Islamist Zero Hour: How Should the West Respond to the Barbarism of ISIS?," *New Statesman* (August 28– September 3, 2015), 26–33.

7. "Worse and Worse; Strife in Iraq," *Economist*, May 25, 2013, 49–50.

8. Ben Hubbard and Eric Schmitt, "Military Skill and Terrorist Technique Fuel Success of ISIS," *New York Times*, August 27, 2014, https://www.nytimes.com/2014/08/28/ world/middleeast/army-know-how-seen-as-factor-in-isis-successes.html.

9. Yezid Sayigh, "ISIS: Global Islamic Caliphate or Islamic Mini-state in Iraq?," *al-Hayat*, July 24, 2014, http://www.carnegie-mec.org/2014/07/24/isis-global-islamic-caliph.

10. Faisal Itani, "The Limits of Islamic State Expansion," *Foreign Policy Essay*, June 14, 2015, http://www.lawfareblog.com/limits-islamic-state-expansion.

11. On this see Kathy Gilsinan, "The Many Ways to Map the Islamic 'State,'" *Atlantic*, August 27, 2014, https://www.theatlantic.com/international/archive/ 2014/08/the-many-ways-to-map-the-islamic-state/379196/.

12. See Patrick Cockburn, "The Killing of Abu Mohammed al-Adnani Is a Major Blow for Isis, but the Terror Group Was Already Badly Battered," *Independent*, September 1, 2016, http://www.independent.co.uk/voices/abu-mohammed-al-adnani-dead-isis-major-blow-jihadist-group-already-badly-battered-a7218976. html; Robin Wright, "Abu Muhammad al-Adnani, the Voice of ISIS, Is Dead," *New Yorker*, August 30, 2016, http://www.newyorker.com/news/news-desk/ abu-muhammad-al-adnani-the-voice-of-isis-is-dead.

13. Joby Warrick and Souad Mekhennet, "Inside ISIS: Quietly Preparing for the Loss of the Caliphate," *Washington Post*, July 12, 2016, https://www.washington-post.com/world/national-security/inside-isis-quietly-preparing-for-the-loss-of-the-caliphate/2016/07/12/9a1a8a02-454b-11e6-8856-f26de2537a9d_story .html?utm_term=.d7e33054f139.

14. Carol Morello and Joby Warrick, "Islamic State's ambitions and allure grow as territory shrinks," *Washington Post*, July 4, 2016, https://www.washingtonpost .com/politics/islamic-states-ambitions-and-allure-grow-as-territory-shrinks/ 2016/07/03/b465c502-414a-11e6-88d0-6adee48be8bc_story.html?utm_ term=.2f05a0eba84a.

15. See Firas Abi Ali, "Political and Military Obstacles to Defeating the Islamic St\ ate," *Jane's Intelligence Weekly* 8, 31 (June 29, 2016).

16. "Islamic State Is Losing Its Caliphate, but It Remains Deadly: Islamic Stateless?," *Economist*, July 6, 2016.

17. See Shiraz Maher, "Burning the Earth," *New Statesman*, November 13–19, 2015, 23–26.

18. Daniel Davis, "How Mosul's Liberation Could Lead to Another Iraqi Civil War," *Politico*, September 17, 2016, http://www.politico.com/magazine/story/2016/09/mosul-liberation-iraq-civil-war-214256.

19. For an excellent analysis of potential post-Mosul scenarios written before the fall of the city, see Talha Abdulrazaq and Gareth Stansfield, "The Day After: What to Expect in Post–Islamic State Mosul," *Royal United Services Institute* 161, 3 (2016); 14–20.

20. Paul Moss, "Kurdish Fears of Land Fight after Mosul Battle," *BBC World News*, November 10, 2016, http://www.bbc.com/news/world-middle-east-37907801.

Index